Regional Economic Voting

This study demonstrates that in a time of massive change characterized by the emergence of entirely new political systems and a fundamental reorganization of economic life, systematic patterns of economic conditions affecting election results at the aggregate level can in fact be identified during the first decade of postcommunist elections in five postcommunist countries: Russia, Poland, Hungary, Slovakia, and the Czech Republic. Intriguingly, incumbency status is not the best predictor of these effects. Instead, parties that are primarily identified with the "Old Regime" that predated the transition enjoy more electoral success in regions with more economic losers, while the "New Regime" parties that are most closely identified with the movement away from communism consistently enjoy more electoral support in regions with more economic winners. A variety of theoretical arguments concerning the conditions in which these effects are more or less likely to be present are also proposed and tested. Analysis is conducted using an original data set of regional-level economic, demographic, and electoral indicators and features both broadly based comparative assessments of the findings as well as more focused case study analyses of pairs of individual elections.

Joshua A. Tucker is an Assistant Professor of Politics and International Affairs at Princeton University and currently holds Princeton's Ralph O. Glendinning University Preceptorship. His work has appeared in a variety of academic journals, including the *American Journal of Political Science*, the *Annual Review of Political Science*, *Demokratizatsiya: The Journal of Post-Soviet Democratization*, *Electoral Studies*, *Political Analysis*, *Perspectives on Politics*, and *Post-Soviet Affairs*. His research has been supported by grants from the National Academy of Sciences, the National Council for Eurasian and East European Research, and the Princeton Institute for International and Regional Studies. He was the recipient of Harvard University's 2001 Edward M. Chase Dissertation Prize and the Mid-West Political Science Association's 1999 Westview Press Award.

Cambridge Studies in Comparative Politics

General Editor
Margaret Levi   *University of Washington, Seattle*

Assistant General Editor
Stephen Hanson   *University of Washington, Seattle*

Associate Editors
Robert H. Bates   *Harvard University*
Peter Hall   *Harvard University*
Peter Lange   *Duke University*
Helen Milner   *Princeton University*
Frances Rosenbluth   *Yale University*
Susan Stokes   *University of Chicago*
Sidney Tarrow   *Cornell University*

Other Books in the Series
Lisa Baldez, *Why Women Protest: Women's Movements in Chile*
Stefano Bartolini, *The Political Mobilization of the European Left,
     1860–1980: The Class Cleavage*
Mark Beissinger, *Nationalist Mobilization and the Collapse of the Soviet State*
Nancy Bermeo, ed., *Unemployment in the New Europe*
Carles Boix, *Democracy and Redistribution*
Carles Boix, *Political Parties, Growth, and Equality: Conservative and Social
     Democratic Economic Strategies in the World Economy*
Catherine Boone, *Merchant Capital and the Roots of State Power in Senegal,
     1930–1985*
Catherine Boone, *Political Topographies of the African State: Territorial
     Authority and Institutional Change*
Michael Bratton and Nicolas van de Walle, *Democratic Experiments in
     Africa: Regime Transitions in Comparative Perspective*
Michael Bratton, Robert Mattes, and E. Gyimah-Boadi, *Public Opinion,
     Democracy, and Market Reform in Africa*

Series list continues following the Index.

Regional Economic Voting

RUSSIA, POLAND, HUNGARY, SLOVAKIA, AND THE CZECH REPUBLIC, 1990–1999

JOSHUA A. TUCKER

Princeton University

CAMBRIDGE
UNIVERSITY PRESS

CAMBRIDGE UNIVERSITY PRESS
Cambridge, New York, Melbourne, Madrid, Cape Town, Singapore, São Paulo

Cambridge University Press
40 West 20th Street, New York, NY 10011-4211, USA

www.cambridge.org
Information on this title: www.cambridge.org/9780521856607

First published 2006

Printed in the United States of America

A catalog record for this publication is available from the British Library.

Library of Congress Cataloging in Publication Data

Tucker, Joshua A. (Joshua Aaron), 1971–
Regional economic voting : Russia, Poland, Hungary, Slovakia and the
Czech Republic, 1990–1999 / Joshua A. Tucker.
   p.   cm. – (Cambridge studies in comparative politics)
Includes bibliographical references and index.
ISBN 0-521-85660-4 (hardcover) – ISBN 0-521-67255-4 (pbk.)
1. Europe, Eastern – Economic conditions – 1989– . 2. Europe,
Central – Economic conditions – 1989– . 3. Europe, Eastern – Politics and
government – 1989– . 4. Europe, Central – Politics and government – 1989– .
5. Elections – Economic aspects – Europe, Eastern. 6. Elections – Economic
aspects – Europe, Central. I. Title. II. Series.
HC240.25.E852T83   2006
324.437'05 – dc22   2005028768

ISBN-13 978-0-521-85660-7 hardback
ISBN-10 0-521-85660-4 hardback

ISBN-13 978-0-521-67255-9 paperback
ISBN-10 0-521-67255-4 paperback

For my parents, Linda and Robert

Contents

Tables

Tables

Acknowledgments

In writing a book about twenty elections in five different countries, one is by necessity forced to turn to many different sources for advice, suggestions, and information. I want to begin therefore by thanking the many people in Russia, Poland, Hungary, Slovakia, and the Czech Republic who took the time to meet with me during my various visits to these countries. While conducting my fieldwork, I benefited from the presence of a number of excellent academic and research institutions, including the Polish Academy of Science's Institute for the Study of Politics, the Institute for Sociology of the Czech Academy of Sciences, the Central European University in Hungary, the Institute for Public Affairs in Slovakia, and the Carnegie Moscow Center. Although the list of people from these countries to whom I owe a debt of gratitude is too large to cover adequately, I would in particular like to thank Radek Markowski, Bogdan Cichomski, Krzysztof Jasiewicz, Gabor Toka, Petr Matějů, Jiří Večerník, Klára Vlachová, Olga Gyárfášová, Grigorij Mesežnikov, Vladimír Krivý, Yevgenya Albats, Ekaterina Zhuravskaya, Nikoloai Petrov, Andrey Ryabov, Alexsei Titkov, Ekaterina Egorova, Boris Makarenko, and Polina Kozyreva, all of whom provided helpful advice at various stages of the project. In addition, none of what follows would have been possible without the expert and patient support provided by people working at the various state statistical and election offices and libraries in all five countries; this list includes but is by no means limited to Henryk Bielski, Barbara Lech-Zakrzewska, Andrzej Florczyk, Kálmán Szász, Ádám Hébenstreit, Jana Bondyová, Dana Švejnarová, Pavel Hortig, František Burdan, Peter Heidinger, and Milan Zirko.

Debts of gratitude are also owed to many on the other side of the Atlantic Ocean. I am extremely grateful to Tim Frye, Steve Hanson, Jeffrey

Herbst, D. Roderik Kiewiet, Alex Pacek, Thomas Remington, and William Zimmerman, all of whom read the manuscript in its entirety and provided invaluable suggestions for revisions; Atul Kohli and Grigore Pop-Eleches also provided very helpful feedback regarding particular parts of the manuscript. I also would like to thank Steve Hanson, Margaret Levi, and Lewis Batemen at Cambridge University Press for their support and encouragement throughout the publication process, as well as Laura Lawrie and Erica Shein for copyediting the manuscript and Becky Hornyak for preparing the index. At the other end of the project, Timothy Colton was an exemplary dissertation chair. Tim has been both a mentor and an inspiration throughout my academic career and it is impossible for me to imagine how this project would have developed without Tim's guidance and support; moreover, as will become obvious from the large number of citations to his work, I have greatly benefited from Tim's voluminous research on voting and elections in Russia. I am also extremely indebted to the other members of my dissertation committee, Robert Bates and Gary King, who have provided expert advice and feedback throughout the project. Since arriving at Princeton, I have been fortunate to have had a number of excellent research assistants assist me in various phases of the project, including Andrew DeMello, Mary Beth Ehrhardt, Scott Golenbock, Shana Kushner, Karen Long, Andrew Owen, Ellie Powell, and especially David Yang. I would also like to thank Georgette Harrison, Edna Lloyd, and Timothy Waldron for administrative assistance.

The number of other individuals who have had a positive impact on the content of the manuscript is of course far too long to list. However, I would like to thank in particular Chris Achen, John Aldrich, Larry Bartels, Gary Bass, Ken Benoit, Adam Berinsky, Nancy Bermeo, Ted Brader, Nancy Burns, Jeffrey Carlson, Kanchan Chandra, Joshua Clinton, Grzegorz Ekiert, Mo Fiorina, Anna Grzymała-Busse, Joel Hellman, Yoshiko Herrera, John Jackson, Henry Hale, Shigeo Hirano, Ray Kennedy, Donald Kinder, Ken Kollman, Evan Lieberman, John Londregan, Pauline Jones-Luong, Bonnie Meguid, Nolan McCarty, Michael McFaul, Rory MacFarquar, Adam Meirowitz, Bing Powell, Robert Rittner, Graeme Robertson, Phillip Roeder, Tom Romer, Howard Rosenthal, Andrew Rudalevige, Anne Sartori, Ken Scheve, Regina Smyth, Kathryn Stoner-Weiss, Oxana Shevel, Susan Stokes, Mike Tomz, Robert Van Houweling, Guy Whitten, Jason Wittenberg, and Deborah Yashar.

I am also grateful for the repeated opportunities I received to present the materials from this project at various seminars, conferences, and workshops.

Acknowledgments

In particular, I received invaluable feedback from a series of talks I gave in the spring of 2004 at the University of Michigan's National Election Studies Workshop, New York University's Department of Political Science, and Princeton University's Center for the Study of Democratic Politics. The manuscript would not have been the same without the feedback I received during and after these presentations, so I am very appreciative of everyone who attended.

As with most projects, this one would not have been possible without financial support from a wide variety of sources. I would therefore like to publicly acknowledge the support of the American Council for Learned Societies, Harvard University's Center for European Studies, Harvard University's Center for International Affairs, Harvard University's Davis Center for Russian and Eurasian Studies, the Institute for the Study of World Politics, the International Foundation for Electoral Systems, the Krupp Foundation, the Mellon Foundation, the National Council for East European and Eurasian Research, Princeton University's Center for the Study of Democratic Politics, the Princeton University Committee on Research in the Humanities and Social Sciences, the Princeton Institute for International and Regional Studies, the Sawyer Foundation, and the United States Department of Education. In addition, I am extremely appreciative of the opportunity that I received to serve as a visiting National Election Studies Scholar at the University of Michigan's Center for Political Studies while writing this manuscript.

In closing, I would like to thank my friends and family, who have alternately encouraged and tolerated me throughout the process of working on this project. I am particularly grateful to my grandparents, Manuel and Virginia Schechet, for all they have done to provide so many opportunities for all of us, and to my sister Rebecca for all her support over the years. This book is dedicated to my parents, Robert and Linda Tucker, for the unfailing love they have always had for their children, as well as many, many years of last-minute editing. Finally, I thank my wife Ellie and my daughter Sasha for making home such a wonderful place to return to when the work is done. I love you both more than I can ever say.

Party Acronyms and Candidate Abbreviations

Table P1. *Party Acronyms and Candidate Abbreviations: English Translation of Party Names*

Abbreviation	Party/Candidate Name	Country
AWS	Solidarity Electoral Action	Poland
Bakatin	Vadim Bakatin	Russia
Cimoszewicz	Wlodzimierz Cimoszewicz	Poland
CPSU	Communist Party of the Soviet Union	Russia
CSSD	Czech Social Democratic Party	Czech Republic
DS	Democratic Party	Slovakia
DU	Democratic Union of Slovakia	Slovakia
DVR	Russia's Democratic Choice	Russia
FIDESZ	League of Young Democrats	Hungary
Fidesz-MPP	Fidesz-Hungarian People's Party	Hungary
FKgP	Independent Smallholders Party	Hungary
Gronkiewicz-Waltz	Hanna Gronkiewicz-Waltz	Poland
HZDS	Movement for a Democratic Slovakia	Slovakia
KDH	Christian Democratic Movement	Slovakia
KDNP	Christian Democratic People's Party	Hungary
KDU	Christian Democratic Union	Czech Republic
KKW	Catholic Electoral Committee "Fatherland"	Poland
KLD	Congress of Liberal Democrats	Poland
KPN	Confederation for an Independent Poland	Poland
KPRF	Communist Party of the Russian Federation	Russia
KRO	Congress of Russian Communities	Russia
KSČ	Communist Party of Czechoslovakia	Czech Republic
KSČM	Communist Party of Bohemia and Moravia	Czech Republic

(continued)

Table P1 (*continued*)

Abbreviation	Party/Candidate Name	Country
KSS	Communist Party of Slovakia	Slovakia
KTR-SS	Communist Workers of Russia for the Soviet Union	Russia
Kuroń	Jacek Kuroń	Poland
Kwaśniewski	Aleksander Kwaśniewski	Poland
LB	Left Bloc	Czech Republic
LDPR	Liberal Democratic Party of Russia	Russia
Mazowiecki	Tadeusz Mazowiecki	Poland
Meciar	Vladimír Meciar	Slovakia
MDF	Hungarian Democratic Forum	Hungary
MP	Workers Party	Hungary
MSzMP	Hungarian Socialist Workers Party	Hungary
MSzP	Hungarian Socialist Party	Hungary
NDR	Our Home Is Russia	Russia
ODA	Civic Democratic Alliance	Czech Republic
ODS	Civic Democratic Party	Czech Republic
ODU	Civic Democratic Union	Slovakia
OH	Civic Movement	Czech Republic
OVR	Fatherland – All Russia	Russia
PC	Center Alliance	Poland
PL	Agrarian Alliance	Poland
PRES	Party of Russian Unity and Concord	Russia
PSL	Polish Peasant Party	Poland
ROP	Movement for the Reconstruction of Poland	Poland
Ryzhkov	Nikolai Ryzhkov	Russia
Schuster	Rudolf Schuster	Slovakia
SDK	Slovak Democratic Coalition	Slovakia
SDL'	Party of the Democratic Left	Slovakia
SdRP	Social Democracy of the Republic of Poland	Poland
SLD	Democratic Left Alliance	Poland
SNS	Slovak National Party	Slovakia
SPS	Union of Right Forces	Russia
SV	Common Choice Coalition	Slovakia
SzDSz	Alliance of Free Democrats	Hungary
UD	Democratic Union	Poland
Unity	Inter-Regional Movement Unity	Russia
US	Freedom Union	Czech Republic
UW	Freedom Union	Poland
VPN	Public Against Violence	Slovakia
VR	Russia's Choice	Russia
WAK	Catholic Electoral Action	Poland
Wałęsa	Lech Wałęsa	Poland

Party Acronyms and Candidate Abbreviations

Yabloko	Yavlinskii/Boldyrev/Lukin Bloc (Yabloko)	Russia
Yavlinskii	Grigorii Yavlinskii	Russia
Yeltsin	Boris Yeltsin	Russia
ZRS	Association of Workers of Slovakia	Slovakia
Zyuganov	Gennadii Zyuganov	Russia

Table P2. *Party Acronyms and Candidate Abbreviations: Party Names in Original Language*

Abbreviation	Party Name	Country
AWS	Akcja Wyborcza Solidarność	Poland
Bakatin	Vadim Bakatin	Russia
Cimoszewicz	Wlodzimierz Cimoszewicz	Poland
CSSD	Česká Strana Sociálně Demokratická	Czech Republic
CPSU	Kommunisticheskaia Partiia Sovetskogo Soiuza	Russia
DS	Demokratická Strana	Slovakia
DU	Demokratická Únia Slovenska	Slovakia
DVR	Demokraticheskii Vybor Rossii	Russia
FIDESZ	Fiatal Demokraták Szővetsége	Hungary
Fidesz-MPP	Fidesz-Magyar Polgári Párt	Hungary
FKgP	Független Kigazdapárt	Hungary
Gronkiewicz-Waltz	Hanna Gronkiewicz-Waltz	Poland
HZDS	Hnutie za Demokratické Slovensko	Slovakia
KDH	Krest'anskodemokratické Hnutie	Slovakia
KDNP	Kereszténzdemokrata Néppárt	Hungary
KDU	Krestanská a Demokratická Unie	Czech Republic
KKW	Katolicki Komitet Wyborczy "Ojczyna"	Poland
KLD	Kongres Liberalno-Demokratyczny	Poland
KPN	Konfederacja Polski Niepodleglej	Poland
KPRF	Kommunisticheskaia Partiia Rossiiskoi Federatsii	Russia
KRO	Kongress Russkikh Obshchin	Russia
KSČ	Komunistická Strana Československa	Czech Republic
KSČM	Komunistická Strana Čech a Moravy	Czech Republic
KSS	Komunistická Strana Slovenska	Slovakia
KTR-SS	Kommunisty Trudovoi Rossii: za Sovetskii Soiuz	Russia
Kuroń	Jacek Kuroń	Poland
Kwaśniewski	Aleksander Kwaśniewski	Poland
LB	Levý Bloc	Czech Republic

(continued)

Table P2 (*continued*)

Abbreviation	Party Name	Country
LDPR	Liberal'no-Demokraticheskaia Partiia Rossii	Russia
Mazowiecki	Tadeusz Mazowiecki	Poland
Meciar	Vladimír Meciar	Slovakia
MDF	Magyar Demokrata Fórum	Hungary
MP	Munkáspárt	Hungary
MSzMP	Magyar Szocialista Munkáspárt	Hungary
MSzP	Magyar Szocialista Párt	Hungary
NDR	Nash Dom – Rossiia	Russia
ODA	Občanská Demoktraická Aliance	Czech Republic
ODS	Občanská Demoktraická Stran	Czech Republic
ODU	Občanska Demokratická Únia	Slovakia
OH	Občanská Hnutí	Czech Republic
OVR	Otechestvo – Vsia Rossiia	Russia
PC	Porozumienie Centrum	Poland
PL	Porozumienie Ludowe	Poland
PRES	Partiia Rossiiskogo Edinstva i Soglasiia	Russia
PSL	Polskie Stronnistwo Ludowe	Poland
ROP	Ruch Odubowy Polski	Poland
Ryzhkov	Nikolai Ryzhkov	Russia
Schuster	Rudolf Schuster	Slovakia
SDK	Slovenská Demokratická Koalícia	Slovakia
SDL'	Strana Demokratickej L'avici	Slovakia
SdRP	Socjaldemokracja Rzeczpospolitej Polskiej	Poland
SLD	Sojusz Lewicy Demokratycznej	Poland
SNS	Slovenská Národná Strana	Slovakia
SPS	Soiuz Pravykh Sil	Russia
SV	Spoločna Volba	Slovakia
SzDSz	Szabad Demokraták Szővetsége	Hungary
UD	Unia Demokratyczna	Poland
Unity	Mezhregional'noe Dvizhenie "Edinstvo"	Russia
US	Unie Svobody	Czech Republic
UW	Unia Wolności	Poland
VPN	Verejnost Proti Násiliu	Slovakia
VR	Vybor Rossii	Russia
WAK	Wyborcza Akeja Katolicka	Poland
Wałęsa	Lech Wałęsa	Poland
Yabloko	Yavlinskii/Boldyrev/Lukin Bloc (Yabloko)	Russia
Yavlinskii	Grigorii Yavlinskii	Russia
Yeltsin	Boris Yeltsin	Russia
ZRS	Združenie Robotníkov Slovenska	Slovakia
Zyuganov	Gennadii Zyuganov	Russia

1

Introduction

The story of postcommunism is, to a large extent, the story of simultaneous transitions. The speed at which so many countries fundamentally and simultaneously reorganized both their political and economic systems may be unprecedented in human history. To understand the postcommunist experience, therefore, one must understand the interaction between these two different and yet interconnected processes. A great deal of academic energy has been expended in an effort to understand how political factors have affected economic developments in the postcommunist world.[1] Less attention, however, has been paid to systematic studies of the manner in which economic conditions have reverberated back into the political process.

One fundamental way in which economic developments affect political developments is through elections and voting. Political science has a rich literature on the topic of economic voting in established democracies but has only begun to scratch the surface of the topic in newer democracies.[2] The politics of economic reform literature in particular often seems

---

[1] See, for example, Przeworski 1991; Sachs 1993; Lavigne 1994; Aslund 1995; Lavigne 1995; Goldman 1997; Gustafson 1999; Woodruff 1999; Frye 2000; Hancock and Logue 2000; Orenstein 2001; Reddaway and Glinski 2001. The larger literature on the politics of economic reform of course extends beyond the postcommunist context; for reviews, see Haggard and Webb 1993; Bunce 2001.

[2] Elections and voting generally in postcommunist countries have attracted a good deal of attention from the scholarly community. But the vast majority of this work has focused on providing comprehensive explanations for voting behavior in particular elections or particular countries. Much less effort has been expended attempting to test general hypotheses concerning factors affecting election results across multiple countries and multiple elections; for a review of this literature noting this pattern, see Tucker 2002. One exception has been the small number of articles that have appeared in recent years examining economic voting;

to sidestep the topic entirely, relying on conclusions generated from the economic voting literature in established democracies to assume that voters will turn against incumbent parties when faced with the economic pain that is an inevitable by-product of a transition to a more market oriented economy.[3] The uncertainty paradigm, also applied in discussions of postcommunist transitions, takes this one step further by highlighting the many factors working against the likelihood of identifying any systematic effects on political behavior in the wake of the transition's complete and utter upheaval of citizens' political and economic worlds.[4]

The study that follows demonstrates that in a time of massive change characterized by the emergence of entirely new political systems and a fundamental reorganization of economic life, systematic patterns of cross-regional variation in economic conditions affecting cross-regional variation in election results at the aggregate level can in fact be identified during the first decade (1990–99) of postcommunist elections in five postcommunist countries: Russia, Poland, Hungary, Slovakia, and the Czech Republic. And although these patterns strengthened as time passed, they were present even in the earliest part of the decade. Even more surprisingly, these patterns do

---

see in particular the sources cited in note 25. Studies of economic voting in new democracies outside the postcommunist world are, if anything, even less frequent. In Latin America, see Remmer 1991, 1993; Roberts and Wibbels 1999; in Africa, see Posner and Simon 2002. For studies spanning multiple regions that include new democracies, see Wilkin, Haller, and Norpoth 1997; Aguilar and Pacek 2000.

[3] See, for example, Haggard and Kaufman 1989; Waterbury 1989; Offe 1991; Nelson 1994; Haggard and Kaufman 1995a; Naim 1995; Plattner and Diamond 1995. And when elections are considered, it is usually only in passing to note that they provide a means for reformists to be voted out of office (e.g., Nelson 1994, 9; Roland 1994, 32; Haggard and Kaufman 1995b, 157) or to open the door for antidemocratic parties to be returned to office; see, for example, Offe 1991; Haggard and Kaufman 1992; Pereira, Maravall, and Przeworski 1993; Maravall 1995. Such views also were common in the Western press following the second round of postcommunist elections in the early to mid-1990s. For example, the Montreal *Gazette*'s editorial page following the 1993 Polish elections contained the headline "Polish Voters Want Less Pain," and the text read, "Viewed from the receiving end, Poland's economic "shock therapy" has not been such a roaring success ... [and] voters used Sunday's legislative elections to register their disappointment" (Editorial 1993, B2). Writing about the same election, Thomas Eagleton of the *St. Louis Post-Dispatch* led off his article with the headline "Road to Capitalism Proves Bumpy" and noted that voters "did express their abiding displeasure with the pervasive hardships that accompany an instantaneous conversion to free enterprise" (Eagleton 1993, 3B).

[4] In an often-cited essay on the topic, Bunce and Csanadi 1993 claimed early in the 1990s that "the structure of post-communism is the absence of much structure" (241). See as well Colton 2000b, 5–16, for an informative discussion of uncertainty in the postcommunist context.

not merely take the simplest form envisioned by the politics of economic reform literature with areas more heavily populated by economic losers attempting to "throw the bums out" by turning against incumbent parties in greater numbers than those living in areas of the country with more economic winners. Instead, I find that the presence of economic losers in a region leads more consistently to more votes for particular types of political parties, regardless of who is currently in power. The same is true of economic winners, although the presence of more economic winners of course helps different types of political parties. I identify these types of parties by taking the transition seriously, although not as an event that renders rational political behavior impossible, but, rather, as a focal point that allows voters to make sense of the often chaotic political environment emerging around them by focusing on the "Transitional Identity" of political parties. Thus, it is parties identified primarily with the "Old Regime" that predated the transition that enjoy more electoral success in regions with more economic losers, whereas the "New Regime" parties that are most closely identified with the movement away from communism consistently enjoy more electoral support in regions with more economic winners. So although postcommunist voters may in part have been motivated by economic conditions to throw the bums out, ultimately economic winners and losers acted in the aggregate as if they were more interested in the type of party they were trying to throw in.

In an effort to provide a systematic test of these claims, I employ a broadly comparative framework in this study that takes two forms. First, the study examines elections results from twenty separate presidential and parliamentary elections that took place over a ten-year period in five different countries. Thus, none of the patterns identified can be said to be a product of a particular set of circumstances peculiar to a given country at a given time, or even in a given country over time. Second, the study looks for concentrations of economic winners and losers and their effects on election results not at the national level – which would have yielded but one observation of economic conditions and election results per election – but, rather, at the regional level. In this manner, I am able to examine on a party-by-party basis whether or not individual parties in each of the twenty elections performed better in areas of the country where economic conditions were better or where economic condition were worse. At the same time, I employ a method of analysis that allows for comparison of these party by party results with one another, allowing me to search for patterns of support for hypotheses across the entire set of cases contained

3

in the study. Thus, the use of regional level data facilitates both election-by-election case study analysis and broadly based comparative analysis across all twenty elections. These two types of analyses complement one another: for the case study analyses, the broader analysis presents an opportunity to see how the results fit in a larger comparative format; for the overall comparative analysis, the case studies provide an opportunity to explore the context in which larger patterns do or do not hold. Taken together, the two forms of analyses offer a window into the question of how regional patterns of political support for postcommunist parties and party systems have developed and the role that economic conditions have played in that process.

Overall, this book takes advantage of the fact that enough time has now passed since the onset of the postcommunist transitional experience to begin to explore in a detailed, comparative, and systematic manner this important aspect of the relationship between the two distinguishing facets of that transition: the inception of massive economic change combined with the adaptation of competitive multiparty elections (at least for the time period and countries included in this particular study). Unlike previous work that has considered the effect of economic conditions on election results as one of a handful of factors to explain the results of a particular election or series of elections, the study places this crucial intersection between the postcommunist world's simultaneous political and economic transitions at the center of its analysis. In doing so, findings are generated that can shed light on multiple facets of both postcommunist politics specifically and mass political behavior more generally.

Economic Voting

Beyond the postcommunist context, the book also offers important contributions to the study of economic voting more generally. Political scientists have long been fascinated by the question of how economic conditions affect election results.[5] Yet despite the wide range of questions one can ask on this topic, most analyses have focused on one particular type of relationship between economic conditions and election results – the effect of

---

[5] Indeed, one can find an article on the topic in the *American Political Science Review* from more than sixty years ago on the effect of economic conditions on the vote for Franklin Roosevelt; see Ogburn and Coombs 1940.

Table 1.1. *Questions Asked by Economic Voting Studies*

	Party Affected by State of the Economy	
	Governing Status	Party "Type"
Standard Economic Voting Hypotheses	Do incumbent parties perform better if the economy is better?	Do certain "types" of parties perform better if the economy is better/worse?
Conditional Economic Voting Hypotheses	Under what conditions do we find more support for the claim that incumbent parties perform better if the economy is better?	Under what conditions do we find more support for the claim that "types" of parties perform better if the economy is better/worse?

economic conditions on the vote for incumbent parties and candidates – based largely on findings from one country – the United States[6] – and attempts to replicate these findings in other established democracies.[7] Put another way, the vast majority of the literature has attempted to answer some variation of the question found in the upper left-hand corner of Table 1.1.

In addition to shifting the location of the study of economic voting to the more turbulent electoral environment of postcommunist Russia, Poland, Hungary, Slovakia, and the Czech Republic in the 1990s, this study also differs from most that have preceded it by addressing questions found in all four quandrants of Table 1.1. At the most basic level, there are two ways to conceive of economic conditions having a systematic impact on election results. The first is for economic conditions to affect the vote for the parties that comprise the government at the time of the election.[8] This question

[6] See, for example, Kramer 1971; Tufte 1975; Kinder and Kiewiet 1979, 1981; Erikson 1989, 1990; and MacKuen, Erikson, and Stimson 1992.

[7] Although it should be noted that recent innovations in terms of applying what I will call conditional economic voting hypotheses – and in particular the proposition that economic conditions will be more important when governments are more likely to be held responsible for the state of the economy – have largely emanated from cross-national studies of advanced industrialized democracies. See, for example, the sources cited in note 15.

[8] This continued focus on the relationship between economic conditions and the vote for incumbent parties has long been justified in terms of what it can reveal about the political accountability of governments to their citizens. However, as is discussed in more detail in Chapter 9, Manin, Przeworski, and Stokes (1999b) argue that political representation is as much dependent on beliefs about what parties will do in office in the future as it is on sanctioning the current government for past behavior. Thus, understanding how economic

is almost always phrased in terms of whether or not incumbent parties or candidates (hereafter I use the term *parties* to refer to both for simplicity) are helped by better economic conditions. As noted earlier, this question has dominated the study of economic voting in established democracies. But there is a second way to think about the systematic effect of economic conditions on election results, which is by focusing on a party's "type." In practice, this has involved examining whether or not the economy has different effects on the vote for right-wing or left-wing parties, but, as I will note momentarily (and address in much greater detail in the following chapter), there is no reason why partisan orientation along a traditional left–right spectrum is the only "type" that can be considered.[9]

Moving our analyses beyond the effect of the economy on the vote for just incumbent parties becomes increasingly important as political systems move farther from the ideal type of a two-party system best exemplified by the United States. Within the confines of a stable two-party system, knowing how the economy affects the vote for *the* incumbent party tells us almost all we need to know about the effect of the economy on election results; if the incumbent party performs better under certain economic conditions, then the opposition party must perform worse almost by definition when facing these same conditions.[10] As we move our analyses to more of a multiparty context, however, the simple dichotomy of an incumbent versus nonincumbent approach disappears as multiple parties can be found both in and out of government (with some parties even moving in and out during a single electoral period). Analyses of the effect of the economy on the vote for parties on the basis of something inherent in the party itself – what I am loosely calling here the party's type or identity – have the potential to expand the range of our understanding of how the economy can affect election results, both in terms of the parties most likely to benefit from better economic conditions but also, perhaps even more crucially, in terms of the parties that are more likely to benefit when economic conditions are worse.

conditions affect the vote for parties beyond incumbent parties can also play an important role in assessing the representative character of democracies. I return to this point in Chapter 9.

[9] See, for example, Rosa and Amson 1976; Lewis-Beck and Bellucci 1982; Kiewiet 1983; Bellucci 1984; Host and Paldam 1990; Powell and Whitten 1993; and Palmer and Whitten 2000.

[10] Of course, issues such as turnout and protest votes make this a slightly more complicated picture, but the basic point holds, especially in comparison to a genuine multiparty political system.

Introduction

As opposed to most work on the topic that examines only one of these two questions (and, in almost all cases, this is the incumbency question), my study is framed as an explicit comparison between hypotheses drawn from both of these two approaches. Each of the two quadrants in the top row of Table 1.1, therefore, yields a different model. The Referendum Model, based on the upper left-hand quadrant of Table 1.1, predicts simply that incumbent parties ought to perform better in areas of the country where economic conditions are stronger. In contrast, the Transitional Identity Model, based on the upper right-hand quadrant of Table 1.1, categorizes parties in terms of their relationship to the transition itself. On the basis of this classification, one type of party – the aforementioned New Regime parties – is predicted to receive more electoral support in areas of the country where economic conditions are better, whereas another type of party – the Old Regime parties – is predicted to receive more electoral support in areas of the country where economic conditions are worse.[11]

It is possible to compare the empirical support for each of these models with one another because they make predictions about the effects of economic condition on the electoral fortunes of different parties. Across the twenty elections, there are forty-nine parties coded as incumbent parties, forty parties coded as New Regime parties, and twenty-nine parties coded as Old Regime parties.[12] As will be explained in much greater detail later in this book, the method of analysis I employ generates an estimate of our confidence that each particular party provides support for the relevant hypothesis, thus allowing comparisons of the number and proportion of parties that generate support for each of the three primary hypotheses across all twenty elections. The result of this comparative analysis is remarkably clear: across a wide variety of empirical tests, there is consistently stronger empirical support for the predictions of the Transitional Identity Model than for the predictions of the Referendum Model. Furthermore, there are

---

[11] These categories are mutually exclusive but they are not exhaustive; there are parties that are not coded as either a New Regime or an Old Regime party. The first half of Chapter 2 is dedicated to a thorough explication of both models, and detailed coding rules for New Regime and Old Regime parties can be found in Chapters 6 and 7, respectively.

[12] Although there is some overlap between these groups – there are twenty-one parties coded as New Regime parties and incumbent parties and nine parties coded as Old Regime parties and incumbent parties – there are also nineteen New Regime and twenty Old Regime parties that are not coded as incumbent parties and nineteen incumbent parties that are neither Old Regime nor New Regime parties. This variation is leveraged to provide an additional robustness test of the overall finding of greater empirical support for the Transitional Identity Model than the Referendum Model in Chapter 8; see Table 8.11.

individual elections in which the two models generate competing hypotheses for the same parties. Strikingly, these head-to-head comparisons also yield the same conclusions as the more general analysis: stronger empirical support for the Transitional Identity Model than the Referendum Model.[13]

As the empirical tests are conducted at a relatively unexplored level of analysis – the regional level – and the models are based on microlevel arguments developed with the postcommunist political context in mind, these results are not intended in any way to serve as a refutation of existing beliefs about the relationship between economic conditions and election results that have been generated from studies in established democracies. Nevertheless, they do demonstrate clear evidence of a relationship between economic conditions and election results that has a more consistent effect on parties based on their "type" (here, the parties' Transitional Identity) than on whether or not the party is currently an incumbent, thus providing support for the claim that there are other illuminating ways to examine the effect of the economy on election results besides focusing solely on the vote for incumbent parties.

The second important contribution of the study to the economic voting literature is to focus attention on the possibilities for analyses that move beyond the first row of Table 1.1 into questions raised in the second row. In doing so, I am building off of a small strand of recent work on the effect of economic conditions on election results in OECD[14] countries that focuses on what has come to be called the "clarity of responsibility" argument.[15] The basic idea of the argument is that economic conditions are more likely to have the predicted effect on the vote for incumbent parties in countries that feature institutional arrangements that could lead voters to believe that the government has more control over economic policy than in countries

---

[13] One of the paired case studies – the 1997 Polish and 1998 Hungarian parliamentary elections – highlights exactly this type of head-to-head comparison.

[14] OECD stands for the Organisation of Economic Co-operation and Development (http://www.oecd.org/home/). Technically, the term "OECD countries" is used to refer to members of the organization, although conventionally it is used as a shorthand for the advanced industrialized democracies of Western Europe plus the United States, Canada, Japan, South Korea, Australia, and New Zealand; it is in this latter format that I employ the term in this book.

[15] The "clarity of responsibility" argument was introduced by Powell and Whitten 1993, and provided the impetus for a variety of work that has attempted to either refine or refute it; see, for example, Whitten and Palmer 1999; Anderson 2000; Chappell and Veiga 2000; Royed, Leyden, and Borrelli 2000; and Nadeau, Niemi, and Yoshinaka 2002 in the OECD context, as well as Tucker 2001 in the postcommunist context.

with institutional arrangements that could lead voters to believe that the government has less control over these policies.[16] In the terms of this book, such a hypothesis fits squarely in the lower left-hand corner of Table 1.1, as it predicts the context (high responsibility institutional arrangements) in which there ought to be more support for the claim that better economic conditions help incumbent parties.

I expand this insight in three important directions. First, I adapt and augment the clarity of responsibility argument for testing in the postcommunist context. Second, I move the clarity of responsibility argument out of just the lower left-hand corner of Table 1.1 and show how responsibility-based arguments can also be applied in the lower right-hand corner as well. In doing so, I test whether the effect of economic conditions on election results for New Regime and Old Regime parties are also more consistent when the parties are more likely to be able to affect policy outcomes than when they are less likely to be able to do so. Third, and perhaps most importantly, I move beyond the framework of the clarity of responsibility argument and provide a whole set of new theoretical approaches for generating hypotheses that belong in the second row of Table 1.1, or, put another way, new arguments about the conditions under which there should be more empirical support for predictions about the effect of economic conditions on election results. These "conditional economic voting" hypotheses are presented in detail in the second half of Chapter 2, but they include a supply-side approach (does the economy matter more when other factors matter less?), a time-based approach (does the effect of the economy change as time passes?), and a partisan orientation approach (do different types of political orientations lead to more or less consistent effects for the economy within the New Regime and Old Regime categories?). Moreover, the emphasis on exploring questions in the second row of Table 1.1 also allows me to focus on results disaggregated to intuitively interesting levels of analysis, such as whether there are differences in the findings across parliamentary and presidential elections, while at the same time placing such analyses within a coherent theoretical framework.

The findings based on these types of questions are too numerous to address in detail here, but it is worth noting that they offer interesting observations for both those interested in the general topic of economic voting and those concerned more specifically with the development of political

---

[16] For details on which institutions are important in this regard, see the discussion of the institutional responsibility hypothesis in Chapter 2.

behavior in the postcommunist context. In terms of making a contribution to the general economic voting literature, evidence from a variety of tests points toward at least limited support for the "clarity of responsibility" approach, even in the turbulent environment of postcommunist elections. At the same time, analysis of these approaches leads to more focused findings such as the fact that there is little difference between the effect of regional variation in economic conditions on regional variation in the vote for reformed communist successor parties and their unreformed counterparts – and that this relationship changes little over time – a point likely to be of interest to those concerned with postcommunist political behavior.

Examining these conditional economic voting hypotheses also provides an opportunity for retesting the primary conclusion of the study – that there is more empirical support for the Transitional Identity Model than the Referendum Model – across alternative subsets of cases. For example, does this conclusion hold up for elections that took place early in the decade? Or only for political parties that received a particularly large percentage of the overall vote? Each subset of cases therefore provides another opportunity for assessing the comparative empirical support for the Referendum and Transitional Identity Models, but identifying theoretically relevant categories for these subsets of cases requires the types of questions found in the second row of Table 1.1.

Beyond providing additional insight into the effect of economic conditions on the vote in the elections included in this study, the conditional economic voting hypotheses I present here can also hopefully provide a blueprint for a wider incorporation of these types of hypotheses into the general economic voting literature. Most specifically, this book offers a host of new hypotheses – detailed in the following chapter – about the conditions under which there ought to be a more consistent effect for economic conditions on election results. At a more general level, I present a number of new categories of these types of approaches that move beyond the responsibility-based approach. Others who might not want to test the specific hypotheses presented here could still use the basic approaches (e.g., supply-side, time-based) to generate their own (and perhaps more country specific) hypotheses. And at the most general level, the whole idea of generating frameworks for thinking about the context in which economic conditions affect election results hopefully will spur others to identify new theoretical approaches beyond those offered in either this book or in the existing work on the clarity of responsibility argument.

A final contribution to the economic voting literature concerns the level of analysis at which the study is conducted. The first modern wave of work on the effect of economic conditions on election results focused almost entirely on time-series analysis of American election results, or, in some cases, presidential approval ratings.[17] This work spawned two different types of attempts to replicate its findings in different contexts. Within the field of American politics, numerous scholars turned to survey data to see if they could identify the microlevel links between attitudes toward the economy and voting behavior, leading to debates concerning whether voters were more prospective or retrospective and whether voters cared more about personal economic circumstances (pocketbook voting) or national economic conditions (sociotropic voting).[18] At the same time, other scholars attempted to replicate the findings in a comparative context. These studies included cross-national analyses of national election results,[19] cross-national time-series analyses,[20] survey data in single countries,[21] and survey data from multiple countries.[22]

Left almost completely unexplored in all of this economic voting scholarship has been the relationship between regional variation in economic conditions and regional variation in the distribution of votes.[23] Why this has been the case remains an interesting question, as the relationship between regional economic conditions and regional election results is an equally valid way to test for effects of the economy on aggregate election results.[24] After all, if we think that when greater numbers of people are dissatisfied

[17] See, for example, Kramer 1971; Tufte 1975, 1978; Chappell and Keech 1985; Erikson 1989, 1990; and MacKuen, Erikson, and Stimson 1992.

[18] See, for example, Kinder and Kiewiet 1979; Fiorina 1981; Kinder and Kiewiet 1981; Lockerbie 1991; Lanoue 1994, as well as the discussion of these topics in Chapter 2.

[19] See, for example, Wilkin, Haller, and Norpoth 1997.

[20] See, for example, Powell and Whitten 1993; Remmer 1993; Palmer and Whitten 1999; Roberts and Wibbels 1999; Whitten and Palmer 1999; Chappell and Veiga 2000; and Palmer and Whitten 2000.

[21] See, for example, Blount 1999; Lewis-Beck and Nadeau 2000; Paldam and Nannestad 2000; and Sanders 2003.

[22] See, for example, Wlezien, Franklin, and Twiggs 1997; Anderson 2000; and Nadeau, Niemi, and Yoshinaka 2002.

[23] Although see Rattinger 1991 and Posner and Simon 2002 for work of this type on Germany and Zambia, respectively.

[24] Interestingly, the earliest work I have found on the topic of economic voting in the American politics literature also uses cross-regional data; see Ogburn and Coombs 1940. Moreover, cross-regional analysis of election results generally in the American context also can be found as early as 1928 in a text on using quantitative methods in the study of politics; see Rice 1928.

with the state of the economy, they are likely to vote for (or against) a particular party, then we should be able to observe the effects of variation in greater numbers of dissatisfied people across different geographic areas at the same time in much the same way that we observe variation in the same geographic area over time. Moreover, it is well known that substantial variation in economic conditions can occur within a country, and yet all analyses that compare national indicators of the state of the economy ignore this variation.

With these observations in mind, this book joins a small number of recent studies in using cross-regional analysis to study the relationship between economic conditions and election results in postcommunist countries.[25]

---

[25] One of the first examples of this is Pacek 1994, which uses regional level data to compare the relationship between economic conditions and election results in four elections from Bulgaria, Czechoslovakia, and Poland. His study was followed later in the decade by a number of other articles that also presented comparative studies of economic voting in postcommunist countries using cross-regional data, including Bell 1997; Fidrmuc 2000a, 2000c; Tucker 2001; Jackson, Klich, and Poznańska 2003a, 2003b; and Zielinski, Slomczynski, and Shabad 2004. (The two articles by Fidrmuc warrant particular mention, as they are the only other studies of regional economic voting – other than my own work – of which I am aware that attempt to compare results across more than four elections from multiple countries and because a number of the countries in this book overlap with the countries in his articles. In addition, I am pleased to note that despite the fact that we use different cases, variables, categories, and methods of comparison, we both share the central conclusion that hypotheses focused on incumbency have less empirical support than hypotheses focused on a party's "type.") See as well Tworzecki 2003, one of the few book-length comparative studies of voting behavior generally in postcommunist countries, which includes a chapter utilizing cross-regional economic data as one of a number of variables to analyze election results (Chapter 8), and Jackson, Klich, and Poznańska 2005, which devotes two chapters to cross-regional analyses of Polish election results. Interestingly, all of these except my own work follow Pacek's lead in including exclusively East-Central European countries and excluding Russia. In addition, a number of recent methodological articles on modeling election results from multiparty elections have all used regional data from the 1993 Polish parliamentary election. See, for example, Honaker, Katz, and King 2002; Jackson 2002; Mikhailov, Niemi, and Weimer 2002; Tomz, Tucker, and Wittenberg 2002; and Mebane and Sekhon 2004. Two of these replicate data originally presented in Gibson and Cielecka 1995. For work on Russia that utilizes regional level data to trace relationships between demographic conditions and election results, see the pioneering studies of Ralph Clem and Peter Craumer (e.g., Clem and Craumer 1995b, 1995a, 1995c, 1997, 2001, 2002). Strikingly, I am aware of only a single published cross-national time-series analysis of economic voting in the postcommunist context relying on national level data (Fidrmuc 2000b) – and even here the primary focus of the working paper is on explaining economic as opposed to political outcomes – although there have been a number of articles on economic voting in postcommunist countries that have analyzed survey data; see, for example, Colton 1996a and Mason and Sidorenko-Stephenson 1997 on Russia, Powers and Cox 1997 on Poland, Duch 2000 on Poland and Hungary, and Harper 2000 on Lithuania, Bulgaria, and Hungary.

Introduction

I chose to focus the analysis at the regional level primarily because it facilitated the type of blended case study and general comparative analysis
discussed earlier, but equally important was the fact that it presented an
appropriate manner to conduct comparative research on the topic of economic voting in the postcommunist context. In particular, by restricting my
pooling of data to regional data from within individual elections, I am able
to insulate the analysis against the threats of systematic bias in my results
caused by the inevitable presence of measurement error in these types of
data, a point to which I will return in much greater detail later in this book.
Taken together, the use of regional level analysis allows me to conduct a
rich comparative study of a relatively unexplored substantive area of interest
while doing so in a manner that is most appropriate for the available data.
The study also highlights the fact that for a phenomenon in which there
has been a great deal of scholarly interest in the political science literature –
the relationship among the economy, voting, and elections – there exists an
entire dimension of this relationship – that which occurs at the aggregate
subnational level – about which very little is currently known.

Case Selection

Any study of postcommunist political developments begins with a potential
universe of twenty-seven or so countries. In an effort to focus the study
primarily on competitive elections, I eliminated from consideration countries that did not hold meaningful elections throughout the 1990s, countries
where elections were dominated by fraud, and countries that had undergone
serious violent conflict at some point during the decade. After taking these
factors into account, one is still left with approximately a dozen countries
that could be included in a study. And although it would have been desirable
to include all of these countries in the study, consideration of resources – in
particular, the time and money needed to collect, code, and translate into
both English and electronic format all of the data – necessitated relying on
a sample of these remaining countries.

In selecting cases for analysis, an often recommended strategy is to max-
imize variation in the independent variables in which one is most interested. In this particular instance, however, this rule provides little guidance
in selecting which countries and elections to include in the study, as the
variation in the independent variables of interest – measures of macroeconomic conditions at the regional level – are found within each election (e.g.,
the variation in unemployment across Polish regions in 1997) as opposed

to across the different elections. Thus in choosing which countries and elections to include in the study, I was guided by a desire to select cases with some important underlying similarities – thus, the limiting of the study to postcommunist countries undergoing political and economic transitions in the first decade of these transitions – but that also varied along theoretically interesting political and economic dimensions in an effort to enhance the generalizability of the findings.

As a guide to selecting countries with important underlying similarities and differences, I chose to rely on a two-pronged strategy of mixing precedent with innovation. Of all the postcommunist countries of Eastern Europe and the former Soviet Union, Russia has received by far the most academic attention. For example, in a survey I conducted of just over one hundred articles written on elections and voting in postcommunist countries in sixteen English language journals between 1990 and 2000, over half of the articles were written on Russia, and the vast majority of these were on Russia alone. Only one other country – Poland – came close to appearing in even a quarter of the articles; most countries appeared in far fewer.[26] Within Eastern Europe, however, there has been a tradition of including certain countries together in comparative studies. Although there are certainly exceptions, one often sees studies comparing the Visegrad Four of Poland, Hungary, the Czech Republic and Slovakia, the three Baltic States of Estonia, Latvia, and Lithuania, and, perhaps less frequently, some combination of Bulgaria, Romania, and Moldova.[27] There are many reasons why scholars choose to group countries for comparison in this manner – including important similarities in both the pre- and postcommunist eras – but for the purpose of this discussion it is sufficient to note that the precedent exists for comparison within each set of countries. Of these three groups of countries, there has clearly been the most Western interest in the Visegrad Four; to return to the literature survey, Poland, Hungary, and the Czech Republic were the second, third, and fourth most popular countries chosen for

[26] See Tucker 2002, Figure 2.

[27] The term "Visegrad Four" stems from the Visegrad group, which was created in 1991 to coordinate foreign policy among Hungary, Poland, and Czechoslovakia, which then became the Czech Republic and Slovakia in 1993. (Pehe 1998, 40). The five Central Asian states are also often grouped together, but these were excluded from consideration because of the lack of meaningful elections in a number of these states, especially as the decade progressed. Likewise, studies comparing the countries of the former Yugoslavia also can be found in the literature, but again I excluded these states from consideration as a result of the Balkan conflicts of the 1990s.

analysis.[28] This group of countries also had the advantage of providing more cases for analysis than the other two groups. So the precedent component of my case study selection involved selecting a group of countries that had often been compared with one another in scholarly work and in which interest had run high.

The innovative component of the case study selection involved including Russia as a fifth case. Although studying voting behavior in the Russian context is hardly novel, there seems to be an almost unwritten rule in the discipline against including Russia in comparative analyses with Eastern European cases; indeed, of the 101 articles included in the literature review noted earlier, only three featured comparative analysis including both Russian and Eastern European elections.[29] And yet, as this study will demonstrate, there is no reason not to compare electoral patterns in Russia with those in Eastern Europe, and there is actually much to be learned from doing so.[30] So by including Russia along with the Visegrad Four, the study is able to present findings regarding the countries that have generated the most interest in the scholarly literature but in a manner that has rarely been employed in the past.

In addition to following a precedent for comparison and reflecting scholarly interest, these five countries enhance the generalizability of the study's findings by providing useful variation in terms of patterns of both macroeconomic and political development during 1990s. As the data in Table 1.2 demonstrate, all three countries followed the familiar pattern of countries undergoing economic reform: initial declines in gross domestic product as the transition got under way (what Przeworski has labeled the J-Curve), a rise in inflation as prices adapt to market conditions, and the emergence of unemployment.[31] However, the manner in which this overall pattern played out differs significantly across the countries. Although all five suffered serious declines in GDP in the early 1990s, Poland was already enjoying economic growth by 1992, whereas Russia suffered declines in GDP every

---

[28] Slovakia was tied for eighth. See Tucker 2002, Figure 2.

[29] See Moser 1995; Ishiyama 1997; and Moraski and Loewenberg 1999.

[30] In recognition of the fact that studies including both Russia and Eastern European cases are relatively rare in the postcommunist elections and voting literature, results used to assess the standard economic voting hypotheses (e.g., the first row of Table 1.1) are all also reported on a country by country basis so readers can see for themselves exactly how the Russian results do or do not differ from the results from the other four countries; see Chapter 2 for details.

[31] See Przeworski 1991.

Table 1.2. *Percentage Unemployment, Percentage GDP Growth, and Percentage Inflation by Country and Year*

	1990	1991	1992	1993	1994	1995	1996	1997	1998	1999
Unemployment										
Czech Republic	0.7	4.1	2.6	4.3	4.3	4.0	3.9	4.8	6.5	8.7
Hungary	1.7	8.5	9.9	12.1	10.8	10.2	9.9	8.7	7.8	7.0
Poland	6.5	11.8	13.3	14.0	14.4	13.3	12.4	11.2	10.7	12.5
Russia	0.0	0.1	5.2	5.9	8.1	9.5	9.7	11.8	13.3	12.6
Slovakia	n/a	6.6	11.4	12.9	13.7	13.1	11.3	11.9	12.6	16.4
GDP Growth										
Czech Republic	-1.2	-11.61	-0.52	-0.41	2.70	5.94	4.29	-0.77	-1.04	0.47
Hungary	-3.50	-11.89	-3.06	-0.58	2.95	1.49	1.34	4.58	4.85	4.16
Poland	-11.6	-7.00	2.60	3.80	5.20	7.00	6.00	6.80	4.80	4.10
Russia	-3.00	-5.05	-14.53	-8.67	-12.57	-4.14	-3.60	1.40	-5.30	6.40
Slovakia	-2.67	-14.57	-6.72	-3.70	5.18	6.47	5.84	5.64	3.96	1.32
Inflation										
Czech Republic	10.8	56.6	11.1	20.8	9.96	9.17	8.80	8.55	10.63	2.14
Hungary	28.97	34.23	22.95	22.45	18.87	28.30	23.60	18.28	14.23	10.00
Poland	555.38	76.71	45.33	36.87	33.25	28.07	19.82	15.08	11.73	7.31
Russia	5.6	93	1526	874.62	307.63	197.47	47.73	14.74	27.67	85.68
Slovakia	10.8	61.2	10.1	23.2	13.41	9.89	5.81	6.11	6.70	10.57

Source: World Bank (http://devdata.worldbank.org/dataonline/) for all data except inflation from 1990–92 and unemployment in 1990 for the Russian Federation, inflation from 1990–93 in the Czech and Slovak Republics, and GDP growth in 1990 for Poland and the Czech Republic, which are all taken from the European Bank for Recovery and Development's 1997 Transition Report.

year through 1996, and then again in 1998. Similarly, all five countries did in fact see an increase in unemployment, but the magnitude of this rise varies across countries. Unemployment in the Czech Republic managed to stay below 5 percent for most of the decade, whereas Poland and Slovakia both were mired in double-digit unemployment rates by the early part of the decade that proved difficult to reverse. It is also worth noting that although unemployment began to decline in the middle of the decade in Poland, Hungary, and Slovakia, only in Hungary did this decline continue through the end of decade; Poland and Slovakia (along with the Czech Republic) saw increasing unemployment rates as the decade came to a close. The countries also had different experiences with inflation. Russia and Poland pursued the now well-known "shock therapy" approach to prices, and consequently had very high inflation rates early in the decade that decreased – albeit more quickly in Poland – as time passed. By contrast, Slovakia and the Czech Republic both had only one year (1991) in which inflation was over 50 percent, and both managed to keep inflation in the single digits for most of the second half of the decade. Hungary lies somewhere in between these two experiences, with inflation never exploding as it did in Russia and Poland but at the same time averaging close to 25 percent a year through 1997.

Likewise, these particular five countries provide important variation in patterns of political development. This is especially so with regard to the movement of New Regime and Old Regime parties in and out of government, which facilitates useful comparisons between the predictions of the Transition and Referendum Models. In the Czech Republic and Russia, for example, once voted out of office, Old Regime parties never returned to power. In Poland and Hungary, however, Old Regime parties were elected to office in 1993 and 1994, and consequently ran for reelection as incumbent parties in 1997 and 1998, respectively. Poland, Hungary, and Russia all featured Old Regime parties that were the primary opposition party when they were not in power, whereas the Old Regime parties in Slovakia and the Czech Republic played less important roles. Additionally, Slovakia provides a case in which New Regime parties were marginalized for much of the decade; Slovakia is also the only case where a nationalist party controlled the government for much of the decade. Overall, the five cases provide many different coding arrangements, including Old Regime parties that were also incumbents, New Regime parties that were also incumbents, and incumbent parties that were neither Old Regime nor New Regime parties.

In addition to patterns of political and economic developments, an analysis of elections from Russia, Poland, Hungary, Slovakia, and the Czech Republic provides a wealth of other useful variation. In particular, these five countries feature variation in terms of the types of elections held (presidential and parliamentary), the timing of elections (all held elections throughout the decade), the types of governing systems employed (presidential, parliamentary, and mixed systems), macrohistorical backgrounds (leaders of empires, subjects of single empires, and subject of multiple empires), most popular religions (Eastern Orthodox, Catholic, and atheist), presence of ethnic minorities, and patterns of political and economic development before the start of the transition. While all of these factors are useful for enhancing the generalizability of the study's findings, many of them have theoretical value as well, in sofaras they facilitate the testing of the types of conditional economic voting hypotheses identified in the second row of Table 1.1; I address this point in much greater detail in the next chapter.

Taken together, these factors all help to ensure that the findings of the study are not dependent on the unique set of political or economic realities in a particular country or at a particular point in time. Although the question of generalizing findings from one set of cases – here, Russia, Poland, Hungary, Slovakia, and the Czech Republic – to a larger set of cases – here, the postcommunist world more generally – is always tricky, the fact that these five countries contain variation on all of these dimensions hopefully makes the task easier. At the very least, it makes it more difficult to claim that the findings are only peculiar to countries undergoing shock therapy, or only to countries where Old Regime parties played an important political role in the 1990s, or only to countries with parliamentary systems of government, or only to Eastern Orthodox cultures, and so on.

A final, and not trivial, consideration in selecting these particular cases is that all five countries reported their economic and electoral data at the same level of regional disaggregation, thus facilitating cross-regional statistical analysis using primary source data.[32]

---

[32] The one major exception is the 1991 Polish parliamentary elections, which required reliance on a recoding of the election results by a Polish scholar to match the commensurate unit of economic disaggregation; this point is discussed in more detail in Chapter 8 and is explicitly reflected in one of the robustness tests of the overall findings. Additionally, in a very few instances (some economic statistics for Bratislava in Slovakia, election results in Warsaw and Katowice in Poland), results have been aggregated up a level by the author to match the commensurate unit of analysis. But with these very few exceptions, the remaining data included in the analysis are the exact data reported by the relevant statistical agency,

Table 1.3. *Elections Included in Study*

Country	Date*	Type
Czech Republic	June 5–6, 1992	Legislative
Czech Republic	May 31–June 1, 1996	Legislative
Czech Republic	June 19–20, 1998	Legislative
Hungary	April 8, 1990	Legislative
Hungary	May 8, 1994	Legislative
Hungary	May 10, 1998	Legislative
Poland	November 25, 1990	Presidential
Poland	October 27, 1991	Legislative
Poland	September 19, 1993	Legislative
Poland	November 5, 1995	Presidential
Poland	September 21, 1997	Legislative
Russia	June 12, 1991	Presidential
Russia	December 12, 1993	Legislative
Russia	December 17, 1995	Legislative
Russia	June 16, 1996	Presidential
Russia	December 19, 1999	Legislative
Slovakia	June 5–6, 1992	Legislative
Slovakia	September 30–October 1, 1994	Legislative
Slovakia	September 25–26, 1998	Legislative
Slovakia	May 15, 1999	Presidential

* For two-round elections, date refers to first round

Moving from the choice of countries to the choice of actual elections, all elections for national office – parliamentary and presidential – that took place in each of these countries between 1990 and 1999 are included in the study (see Table 1.3). This excludes initial parliamentary elections that were contested largely between two forces, the communists and a broad anticommunist umbrella coalition; these elections also often included restrictions on participation and competition for certain seats.[33] Thus, the study begins

national bank, non-governmental organization, or electoral commission. Moreover, in all cases, variation in both the independent variables and dependent variables can be found across all observations; in no cases are economic data from a higher level of aggregation (e.g., U.S. states) used to predict variation in election results in a lower level of aggregation (e.g., U.S. counties).

[33] In practice, this excludes the 1989 Polish parliamentary election and the 1990 Supreme Soviet election in Russia. For the Czech and Slovak Republics, I use the 1992 republic level elections that took place when both were still part of Czechoslovakia as the "first" election because the parliaments selected in these elections would become the parliament of each independent republic following the dissolution of Czechoslovakia at the end of 1992, and

with the first true multiparty parliamentary elections that occur in each of the countries, in addition to all directly contested presidential elections. For two-round presidential elections, results from the first round are analyzed; for mixed legislative electoral systems (Hungary and Russia), results from the party list proportional representation vote are analyzed.[34]

Terms

Several terms employed in this book warrant additional attention to ensure precision in their interpretation. First and foremost, the use of the term *transition* in this book refers to the simultaneous transitions away from the single-party political systems and command economies employed under communist rule in the former Soviet Union and Eastern Europe.[35] It is intended to be unrelated to the current debate over whether the use of such a term implies an inevitably successful transition to a democracy or a market economy or anything else for that matter; I use the term here only to identify the circumstances faced by these countries in the wake of the collapse of communist rule.[36] Similarly, I use the term *postcommunist countries* solely to refer to the collection of countries that emerged from the breakup of the Soviet Union, Czechoslovakia, and Yugoslavia, as well as

because the 1990 elections featured prominent anticommunist umbrella movements. See the case study discussion of these two elections in Chapter 4 for more details.

[34] Had the data permitted, it also would have been interesting to examine the vote for individuals in parliamentary elections by examining the vote in the single member district component of the Hungarian and Russian parliamentary elections. Unfortunately, economic data disaggregated to the single member district boundaries were not available in either case. Moreover, this allows me to only have one observation per party to compare in the comparative analysis, thus eliminating what would be an otherwise complex question on how to compare results when some elections generated two sets of results per party and others only one set of results. The same logic holds for only including the first round of presidential elections as opposed to both rounds of presidential elections.

[35] For a thorough survey of the relationship between the postcommunist politics literature and both the term and concept of transitions, see Gans-Morse 2004.

[36] Of late, the question of whether the postcommunist experience can best be explained as a transition toward capitalist democracy (clearly inappropriate in some of the former Soviet Republics) or just away from Soviet-style central planning and dictatorship and toward a wide variety of different formats has become an important topic of discussion; see, for example, Carothers 2002; Levitsky and Way 2002; and Way 2004. Although interesting, a resolution to this debate is not necessary for any of the points in this book to hold. Regardless of whether the transitional experience is best understood as heading toward a particular outcome or just away from a certain type of rule, the fact remains that competitive multiparty elections held in this context do differ in important ways from those held in established democracies.

the other former satellite states of Soviet Union in Eastern Europe; there is no hidden claim here that there is any peculiar postcommunist form of political or economic organization common to all of these countries.[37] I use the term *East European* countries to refer to all of the non-former Soviet postcommunist countries, and *East-Central European* countries to refer more specifically to the four Eastern European countries included in this study. This is not meant to imply that any other East European countries cannot legitimately be considered part of East-Central Europe; it is simply employed as a shorthand term to refer to the non-Russian countries in this book.

The *Transitional Identity* of a party refers simply to whether a party is coded as a *New Regime* party, an *Old Regime* party, or neither for the purpose of testing the predictions of the Transitional Identity Model. Coding rules for these categories are discussed in the next chapter and reiterated in Chapters 6 and 7. Similarly, the use of the term *incumbent* party refers to parties that are coded as incumbent parties for the purpose of this study according to the rules presented in the next chapter and Chapter 5.

The term *region* refers to a subnational unit at which the country in question has chosen to report disaggregated election results and measures of macroeconomic conditions and demographic variables. There is no implication in the use of this term of any form of subnational government or administration, although regional administration is usually organized along the same lines to at least some degree.

To differentiate between models and hypotheses that attempt to answer the questions in the first and second rows of Table 1.1, the terms *standard economic voting hypotheses* (or *standard hypotheses* for short) and *conditional economic voting hypotheses* (or *conditional hypotheses* for short) are employed. As illustrated in Table 1.1, standard economic voting hypotheses are hypotheses that make predictions about the type of party (e.g., incumbent, New Regime, or Old Regime) affected by economic conditions and the direction (e.g., better economic conditions help the party) in which the economy pushes the vote for that type of party. In contrast, a conditional economic voting hypothesis is one that predicts the conditions in which we expect to find more or less empirical support for a standard economic voting hypothesis, or, put more generally, the context in which we expect economic conditions to have more or less of an effect on election results.

---

[37] For an informative discussion of the different terms used by scholars to refer to what I have called "postcommunist," see Roberts 2004.

I also employ the terms *economic winners* and *economic losers* throughout the book. These terms are simply used as a shorthand for people whose economic situations are either better or worse than their fellow citizens (and not necessarily than their own personal situations before the initiation of the transition, although in many cases the two do overlap). By definition, the terms are not intended to be precise; as explained in the next chapter, the only assumption at work here is that there will be a larger proportion of economic winners in areas of the country where the economy is performing better than where it is performing worse, and similarly a larger proportion of economic losers in areas of the country where economic conditions are worse than in areas where the economy is performing well.

The final term worth noting is the phrase at the center of the academic literature to which this book contributes, which is *economic voting*. Over the years, there have been a number of different research topics floating under the rubric of the term "economic voting." Originally, the term was applied to the idea that voters would select the party with the closest positions to their own on important policy issues.[38] The theory was "economic" insofar as it was dependent on voters' making cost-benefit analyses of the utility they would receive from different parties being in power. Economic issues could be considered by voters, but they were by no means the only issues voters would consider. Indeed, in Fiorina's pioneering study of retrospective voting, economic concerns were only one of three major issue areas assessed in the study.[39] In time, however, the term economic voting also has come to be applied much more generally to encompass both studies that attempt to identify a relationship between economic conditions and election results and studies looking for the influence of economic factors on individual voting behavior. It is in this looser sense that the term is applied in this book, referring to any form of study that looks for links between the state of the economy and aggregate election results or individual voting behavior.

The more detailed term *regional economic voting*, however, is used to refer specifically to analyses of the relationship between variation in macroeconomic conditions and election results at the regional level within a given election, or, put another way, the focus of the empirical analysis contained in this book. I use this new term for two reasons. First, it serves as a convenient shorthand for the more lengthy description contained in the previous sentence. But perhaps more importantly, it reflects the fact that the study

---

[38] See Downs 1957.

[39] The other two were war/peace and civil rights (Fiorina 1981, Chapter 2).

of the variation in economic conditions and election results at the regional level is indeed an important component of understanding the way in which the economy affects electoral outcomes, albeit one that has received much less attention in the general economic voting literature to date than either microlevel or cross-national studies. Thus, the very newness of the term can hopefully highlight the opportunities afforded by this level of analysis in the future.

Finally, I employ the following procedure regarding party names and acronyms. The first time a party is mentioned in any chapter, the party's name will be given along with the acronym in parentheses. When the party is mentioned again in the chapter, the acronym is usually although not always employed instead of the party name. The acronyms employed are based on the name of the party in the language of its country (e.g., the acronym for the Hungarian Socialist Party is the MSzP as opposed to the HSP) because this is the convention in much of the literature, although occasional exceptions are made for very commonly used acronyms (e.g., CPSU for the Communist Party of the Soviet Union). In the text, however, I almost always refer to parties by their English names. Tables reporting results of the case study analyses (Tables 5.2, 6.2, and 7.2) use parties' full names, but the remaining tables use party acronyms; in the case of presidential candidates, their last names are included in the tables. To assist readers unfamiliar with these acronyms, an alphabatized list of acronyms and full party names (both in English and the original language) can be found at the front of the book (see Tables P1 and P2).

Research Design and Organization of the Book

As has been noted throughout this chapter, the hypotheses assessed in this book are tested using regional level data from the twenty elections listed in Table 1.3. More specifically, a separate dataset is constructed for each election consisting of regional level observations of election results, macroeconomic conditions, and demographic characteristics of the population.[40] These election-specific datasets are then used to estimate the effect of regional variation in economic conditions on the regional distribution

---

[40] As explained in the following chapters, demographic characteristics of the regions are included in the analysis as control variables. It is also important to note that although regional level electoral data are used in the analysis – for example, the amount of the vote received by Party A in Region 1 – these are all results from *national* elections disaggregated to the regional level.

of votes for every party identified by one of the standard economic voting hypotheses. In other words, the effect of the economy is estimated for every incumbent, New Regime, and Old Regime party that contested one of the twenty elections. The estimates, in turn, are used to assess the degree of empirical support for the different standard and conditional economic voting hypotheses. The specifics of this process are discussed in great detail in Chapter 3.

The results of these analyses are presented in two different formats. The primary method of presenting results involves a comparative assessment of the degree of support for the different hypotheses across the entire sample of elections; the details of how this is done can be found in Chapter 3. These analyses lie at the heart of the overall empirical conclusions of the study, as they draw on all the evidence from the different parties, elections, and countries.

However, a drawback of comparative analysis of this nature is that it tells us little about the specifics of how economic conditions affected the vote for any one individual party or in one particular election.[41] For this reason, the broad-based comparative analysis across all of the elections is supplemented by an in-depth examination of the results across four "paired" election case studies (although one "pair" actually contains three elections). For each of the nine elections included in these case studies, I present a more in-depth description of the analysis, including background information on the election, discussion of the specific coding decisions for parties contesting that election, and a party-by-party presentation of the degree to which the empirical evidence for that individual party supports the relevant hypotheses. As described earlier, it is the cross-regional nature of the analysis that permits this dual-level approach of examining results both on an election-by-election basis and across the entire set of elections.

Even in the case studies, however, I maintain the comparative nature of the analysis by including two or three elections in each case study. The elections included in the case studies were chosen with two goals in mind. First, I wanted to include examples of as many different types of elections in the case studies as possible. Second, I sought to group the elections in intuitively interesting "pairs" that shared important similarities. Thus, the four case

---

[41] Indeed, as is addressed in Chapter 3, this is one of the principal drawbacks of studies that compare only national election results, and, conversely, one of the benefits of the cross-regional approach is that it does not sacrifice party-specific findings in an effort to produce comparative findings as well.

studies are the 1992 Czech and Slovak parliamentary elections; the 1995 Polish and 1996 Russian presidential elections; the 1993, 1995, and 1999 Russian parliamentary elections; and the 1997 Polish and 1998 Hungarian parliamentarian elections. This final case study is particularly important because it features Old Regime parties that are running for reelection as incumbent parties, and thus there are contradictory predictions across the two models. The Transitional Identity Model predicts that as Old Regime parties these parties should perform better in areas of the country where economic conditions are worse, whereas the Referendum Model predicts that as incumbent parties they should perform better in areas of the country where the economic is performing better. Similarly to the larger comparative analysis, there is significantly stronger empirical support in the 1997 Polish-1998 Hungarian parliamentary elections paired case study for the Transitional Identity Model than for the Referendum Model.

In addition, it should be noted that the regional level data analyzed in the study are all part of an original database constructed almost entirely from primary source materials obtained by the author at the national statistical offices, national banks, or election headquarters of the five countries included in the study.[42] In conjunction with the publication of this book, the entire database I constructed for the project will be made publically available over the Internet.[43]

In the next two chapters, I flesh out this research design in much greater detail. In Chapter 2, I present both the standard and conditional economic voting hypotheses that will be tested in the remainder of this book, as well as the theoretical arguments underlining these hypotheses. In Chapter 3, I present the method by which I conduct my empirical analysis, including the variables in the datasets, the statistical model used to analyze the data, and the method of comparing results across different elections and countries.

---

[42] In a limited number instances, data were obtained from publications of official government statistics by non-governmental organizations; documentation of the sources for all data used in the statistical analyses can be found in Appendix II.

[43] The database now contains over sixty-four thousand regional level observations in electronic format with documentation in English; readers interested in using these data for their own research should check my home page (currently http://www.wws.princeton. edu/jtucker) as well as the home page associated with this book on the Cambridge University Press Web site for information on searching the database and downloading desired data. In addition to repeated trips to the region to collect these data, I also was present for at least one election campaign in each of the five countries. During these periods of fieldwork, I conducted numerous interviews with party officials, candidates, political consultants, academics, and journalists, which were invaluable in shaping both my understanding of postcommunist elections and the theoretical approaches of this book.

Chapter 3 concludes with a section that addresses in great detail the advantages and disadvantages of the method of analysis employed in the book. In Chapter 4, I provide background information on each of the nine elections included in the paired case studies.

As the goal of this book is to test the empirical support for the hypotheses laid out earlier in this chapter (and elaborated upon in Chapter 2) as opposed to providing a narrative of the twenty elections included in this study, the empirical component of the book is not divided into chapters by country or case studies but, rather, by the different standard economic voting hypotheses, resulting in four chapters. Chapter 5 is devoted to testing the empirical support for the Referendum Model. Chapters 6 and 7 test the empirical support for the Transitional Identity Model, with the former focusing on New Regime parties and the latter on the Old Regime parties. Each chapter begins with a brief summary of the overall support for the hypothesis across all twenty elections. The coding rule for the relevant category of parties is then reiterated and is followed by an explanation in the text of the coding decisions in the nine elections included in the paired case studies. I then present the party-by-party results for each of the paired case studies. This includes an assessment of the degree to which that case study provides empirical support for the relevant standard economic voting hypothesis as well as any variation in empirical support across the cases that might suggest support for one of the conditional hypotheses. The remainder of each chapter is then devoted to assessing the degree to which the different conditional hypotheses can explain the variation in support for the standard economic voting hypothesis featured in that chapter across the entire set of twenty elections. (For example, is there more support for the New Regime hypothesis earlier in the decade than later in the decade? Does the incumbency hypothesis have more support in "high responsibility" than "low responsibility" elections?) In Chapter 8, these findings are combined and supplemented with a variety of robustness tests that further demonstrate the stronger empirical support for the Transitional Identity Model as compared to the Referendum Model. Chapter 8 also assesses the overall support for the different conditional economic voting hypotheses. The book concludes with a final chapter that discusses the implications of the findings presented in Chapters 5–8 for our understanding of both the postcommunist political experience and economic voting more generally.

2

Economic Conditions and Election Results

In Chapter 1, I introduced the concept of standard and conditional economic voting hypotheses. The purpose of this chapter is to lay out the specific standard and conditional hypotheses tested in the book and to present the theoretical arguments underlying each of them. The chapter is divided into three sections. In the first section, I briefly address some of the characteristics that differentiate elections in post-communist countries from elections in more established democracies. In the second section, I introduce the standard economic voting models and their associated hypotheses: the Referendum Model, which produces the Incumbency hypothesis; and the Transitional Identity Model, which yields the New Regime and Old Regime hypotheses. This section also includes a discussion of how these hypotheses relate to some of the larger themes in the existing economic voting literature. The final section of the chapter introduces a number of different frameworks for thinking about conditional economic voting hypotheses, as well as the specific conditional economic voting hypotheses associated with each of these frameworks.

Distinguishing Characteristics of Elections in Transition Countries

Before turning to models of regional economic voting in transition countries, it is important to consider the ways in which elections in these countries differ from elections in advanced industrialized democracies. Considering the differences between elections in established democracies and transition countries can help inform the manner in which we ought to build off of – but also depart from – the existing economic voting literature in designing a study appropriate for the postcommunist context. Although the potential list of differences is endless, three of the most important factors are the number of political parties competing in elections, the familiarity that voters have with political parties, and the fact that elections in transition countries occur against a backdrop of fundamental economic changes.

The first of these is a relatively simple concept: elections in transition countries tend to be contested by a greater number of parties than in more established democracies, especially early in the transition. A quick glance at Appendix I reveals a larger number of parties contesting, and receiving significant numbers of votes in, the twenty elections analyzed here than one is accustomed to seeing in established democracies. Indeed, elections with at least ten to twenty parties competing were the norm for this period of time, with individual elections exceeding forty or even one hundred parties (Russia in 1995 and Poland in 1991, respectively). The difference in the number of political parties is particularly striking in comparison with the two-party system of the United States, but it is also true in comparison to most stable established democracies.

More fundamentally, voters in transitional elections are less familiar with the parties competing in elections than their counterparts are in more established democracies. In particular, voters have significantly less experience on which to base their expectations about how parties will perform as part of a government formed following a competitive election. In elections in established democracies, voters usually have already had an opportunity to see most of the major parties – and indeed many of their smaller coalition partners – perform as governing parties. In fact, in many cases voters will have had multiple opportunities to watch the parties move in and out of government. Indeed, the assumption that voters are familiar enough with parties to have developed either attachment to or identification with a party is a fundamental component of most voting models in established democracies, even if the strength of these attachments remains a source of debate.

The same cannot be said for voters in transition countries. Especially in the earliest elections, voters will be confronted with a wide array of political parties that have never been represented in the parliament, let alone formed a democratic government. As time passes, voters will have the opportunity to watch some of these parties participate in government, but even this learning process is hampered by the fluidity of postcommunist party systems, in which parties split, merge, appear and disappear between electoral cycles.[1] This is not to suggests that voters are not capable of developing

---

[1] See, for example, Millard 1994c; Kostelecky 1995; Mesežnikov 1997; Rose, Munro, and White 2001; Marsh 2002; and especially Zielinski, Slomczynski, and Shabad 2004.

nascent attachments to political parties in this time period; indeed, this has been a subject of scholarly inquiry in the literature.[2] But no matter how one conceptualizes this developing attachment, the prerequisite conditions for full-scale partisan identification were unlikely to be present in the first elections in postcommunist countries.[3] Although there is no reason to assume that partisan identification will not develop in the future, it clearly was not present in the beginning of the transition period in the same form as is found in advanced democracies.

In addition to the fact that there is generally less information about political parties in transitional countries than in established democracies, there is also significant variation in the amount of information that voters possess about different parties. In the United States, for example, it is usually safe to assume that voters will possess roughly similar amounts of information about both political parties. In postcommunist countries, by contrast, voters can confront an election in which some parties are completely new, some have clear ties to the nondemocratic regime that ruled for forty or more years, and others have participated in a government that ushered in dramatic political and economic changes. While this logic suggests that as time passes these disparities should decrease, even elections held later in the decade were contested by parties that had never participated in the government, never had representatives in parliament, and, in some cases, had never even contested a previous election.

A final factor that distinguishes transition countries from established industrialized democracies is the presence of fundamental changes in the nature of the economy that occur concurrently with the development of

---

See as well the background information on the paired case studies presented in Chapter 4.

[2] See, for example, Rose 1998; Whitefield and Evans 1999; Colton 2000a; Miller and Klobucar 2000; Brader and Tucker 2001.

[3] To greatly simplify a large literature, there are two broad ways to think about partisan identification. The classic conception of partisan identification, put forth in *The American Voter*, characterizes partisan identification as a stable inclination toward one particular party that is transmitted through a socialization process (Campbell, Converse et al. 1960). Following in the footsteps of V. O. Key, recent rational choice analysts have thought of partisan identification as more of a running tally of one's opinions about political parties that is constantly being updated based on one's own experiences (Key 1966; Fiorina 1981; Lohmann, Brady, and Rivers 1997). As most political parties in postcommunist transition countries did not exist before the postcommunist era, neither the opportunity to be socialized into supporting a particular party nor the chance to build up a reservoir of experiences about that party was present, especially in the earlier part of the transition; the notable exception to this rule of communist successor parties is discussed in greater detail later in this chapter.

competitive elections. On the one hand, voters are presented with exciting new economic opportunities. They have the opportunity to earn higher salaries and to buy goods with those salaries without waiting on long lines. Businesses gain access to foreign trade and foreign investment, and consumers are able to purchase foreign goods. Entrepreneurs can start their own businesses. On the other hand, transitions can also bring all sorts of new economic problems that can provide a sharp contrast to economic conditions before the transition. Unemployment becomes a reality and often skyrockets to high levels early in the transition. Inflation, also often nonexistent in planned economies with price controls, is almost always present from the inception of the transition. Poverty can spread dramatically in short periods of time. Another problem is that wages and pensions are sometimes not paid, as was the case in many of the states of the former Soviet Union. Such problems are especially compelling in postcommunist societies where the prior regime staked its most basic claim to legitimacy on the mantle of not only classifying certain economic benefits as the rights of all citizens (e.g., a job, pension, housing subsidies, free education, and health care, etc.), but even – at least in theory – on the idea that these benefits ought to be distributed relatively equally. As economic benefits were equated with fundamental rights, an economic crisis in these societies has the potential to become a crisis in values as well as just material wealth.

Taken together, voters in postcommunist transition countries faced an electoral environment with large numbers of parties about which they would have known little – although with a subset of parties about which they likely knew a great deal more – competing for office against a backdrop of a serious, fundamental reorganization of economic life.

Standard Economic Voting Hypotheses

The primary empirical goal of this book is to test the relative support for the two regional economic voting models introduced in Chapter 1: the Referendum Model and the Transitional Identity Model. Both models take into account the defining features of the postcommunist electoral environment described in the previous section by building off of the inherent uncertainty of transitions. While both models reflect the overall lack of familiarity that voters have with parties, they weight this information differently, with the Referendum Model placing a stronger emphasis on the uncertainty of the transitional environment and the Transitional Identity Model placing a higher premium on the nature of the information that voters are likely to possess about parties. And while the models are firmly grounded in the logic of explaining cross-regional variation in election results within a given election, the hypotheses produced by these models are in fact similar to those found in the wider economic voting literature.

In the following sections, I detail the theoretical arguments underlying both the Referendum and the Transitional Identity Models. In doing so, I follow a familiar pattern from the economic voting literature in attempting to underlie aggregate level hypotheses with plausible assumptions about individual level behavior. This relies on what is essentially a three-step process. The first step involves assumptions about the types of parties that are likely to be preferred by individuals with certain opinions about the economy (e.g., people who are upset with the state of the economy are less likely to vote for incumbent parties). The second step involves assumptions about the likelihood of finding fewer or more voters with these types of opinions about the economy in certain geographic areas at certain times (e.g., there will be more voters dissatisfied with the state of the economy in a country during elections when the economy is performing worse than when it performing better, or, in the case of this study, within a given election, there will be more dissatisfied voters in parts of the country where economic conditions are worse than where they are better). The final step is then to produce aggregate level hypotheses based on the first two assumptions (e.g., incumbent parties will enjoy more electoral support where (or when) economic conditions are stronger). Providing plausible microlevel foundations for aggregate level hypotheses greatly enhances the internal consistency of one's theoretical arguments, but, as will be emphasized throughout this book, it does *not* mean that the aggregate level hypothesis can function as a test of the microlevel propositions. Thus, the empirical analysis in the following chapters tests the aggregate level implications of these microlevel assumptions about individual behavior presented in the following section, but not the individual level behavior itself.[4]

---

[4] This is not to say, however, that the findings are any less "real" for this reason. Even if evidence is found to falsify some of the microlevel assumptions about individual level behavior, it does not make the aggregate level findings any less significant. It would, however, provide an impetus for additional theorizing about the type of individual-level behavior underlying the aggregate hypotheses.

A Referendum Model

The Referendum Model produces a single hypothesis, the Incumbency hypothesis, which predicts that incumbent parties should receive more electoral support in areas of the country where economic conditions are better and less electoral support in areas of the country where economic conditions are worse. In this section, I present the theoretical arguments underlying this hypothesis. As discussed in the preceding paragraph, it is important to note that although these arguments rely on microlevel assumptions about individual level behavior, this is a not a study of individual behavior and as such does not attempt to directly test any of these microlevel propositions.

Setting aside the peculiarities of the postcommunist world for a moment, consider an electoral environment in which voters possessed no information about how parties were likely to behave vis-à-vis the economy once elected to office. Although such a claim may seem far-fetched, there are numerous reasons why voters could have no information in this regard: the election could be contested by parties that had never held office before, either because the election is taking place in a new democracy or following a major shake-up of the party system in a more established democracy; voters could lack the will or the ability to make judgments about the relationship between a victory for certain parties and the likely effect on economic conditions; or there could be so much uncertainty about the current economic situation that even the most informed citizens would be hard-pressed to predict future economic developments.[5]

Even in such a low information environment, however, we would expect voters to be aware of the parties that make up the government.[6] And in the absence of information about differences between the political parties contesting the election, the only way we could expect the economy to have an effect on election results would be through the vote for or against incumbent parties. To generate this prediction, we need to make two additional assumptions, neither of which ought to be particularly controversial. First, we assume that people concerned with the state of the economy are more

---

[5] See Aidt (2000) for a theoretical argument concerning the question of whether we ought to expect citizens even in established democracies to expend effort to acquire enough information about the state of the economy to judge the competence of the government.

[6] The distinction between the lead party in the government and other coalition members is discussed later in this chapter in the responsibility subsection of the conditional hypotheses section.

likely to want to vote the government out of office than people who think the economy is performing well. Note that this assumption is different from a retrospective evaluation of government performance or competence based on evaluating the impact of the current government on economic conditions during its tenure in office (a point that I return to in more detail later in this section). Instead, it simply proposes that the more dissatisfied an individual is with the state of the economy, the more likely he or she will be to choose to cast a vote for a party that is not currently in power. Similarly, the more satisfied an individual is with the state of the economy, the more likely he or she will be to cast a vote in favor of an incumbent party as opposed to an unknown "other" option.

The second assumption is that the worse economic conditions are in a particular area of the country, the more likely we should be to find more people dissatisfied with the state of the economy in that area. This effect can work both directly and indirectly. Consider unemployment as an example. If I have lost my job and cannot find work, then I am likely to think that the economy is performing poorly. The higher the unemployment rate, the more people there are who are likely to be unemployed and share these beliefs. Thus, the higher the unemployment rate, the more people there are who are likely to be dissatisfied with the state of the economy because they are out of work. However, the effect also works indirectly. Even if I am not unemployed, higher unemployment rates may mean that more people I know are unemployed. Indeed, Paldam and Nannestad (2000) argue that for every person who is unemployed, an estimated one hundred to three hundred people will know that person and "will notice and be concerned" (373). I also may see more unemployed people loitering on the streets, and I may be more afraid that I will become unemployed. All of these factors could lead me to the same conclusion as someone who is unemployed: the economy is not performing well. Now it is doubtful that everyone who is employed will feel this way, and perhaps it is just a small minority that will come to this conclusion. Nevertheless, the higher the unemployment rate, the more people we are likely to find sharing this belief.[7]

---

[7] It is important to note that this argument sets aside the debate about whether citizens actually perceive economic conditions correctly. A number of scholars have noted variation in the perception of similar economic circumstances across different voters – see, for example, Goidel and Langley 1994; Holbrook and Garand 1996; Duch 2000 – although in the Danish (Paldam and Nannestad 2000) and British cases (Sanders 2000), authors have found that perceptions of the economy at the micro level actually match well to conditions at the macro

With these assumptions in hand, the following aggregate level prediction falls out nicely. In areas of the country where economic conditions are stronger, incumbent parties should enjoy more electoral success than in areas of the country where economic conditions are weaker. This holds because we expect worse economic conditions to lead to a greater concentration of voters dissatisfied with the state of the economy and consequently fewer voters inclined to support incumbent parties than in areas of the country where economic conditions are better. Where the economy is better, we expect to find more voters who are likely to be satisfied with the state of the economy and, thus, more voters likely to support the incumbent parties.

It is important to note that this is *not* a relative deprivation argument. Voters are not posited to be voting against the government because they perceive that their region is being treated poorly in comparison to other regions. Nor is it dependent on any form of regional identity *per se*. (e.g., see Herrera 2005). Instead, the logic is simply that in the absence of information about different parties, voters who are more concerned about the state of the economy will be more likely to want to see a change in the government than voters who are less concerned about the state of the economy, and, on the aggregate-level, there should be more voters concerned about the state of the economy in areas of the country where economic conditions are worse.

Moreover, the same aggregate level hypothesis emerges even if the assumption that voters have no information about political parties is relaxed. Consider instead an environment in which voters do have some information about political parties, but which is also characterized by great uncertainty on the part of voters. This uncertainty could take many forms, including uncertainty about the future economic plans of parties, the likelihood that parties will actually try to carry through on these plans if elected, the chance that parties will actually prove successful in implementing these

---

level. In some ways, however, the cross-regional approach insulates the analysis from these kinds of concerns. Even if there are systematic misperceptions by voters of the state of the economy, as long as these misperceptions are randomly distributed across geographic regions the analysis should not be affected even if, as Hetherington (1996) found in the United States, perceptions are more important in affecting vote choice than actual macroeconomic conditions. We should still expect more voters to have a negative perception of the state of the economy in areas of the country where actual economic conditions are worse than in areas of the country where economic conditions are better even if the assessment of the economy does not map perfectly from actual conditions to perceptions.

plans even if they attempt to do so, and the question of whether the plans, even if implemented, would have the intended effect on economic conditions. Regardless of the source of the uncertainty, if the level of uncertainty is high enough and voters cannot trust their evaluations of the political parties, then the logic is essentially the same as in the no-information-about-political-parties world. Voters may have a sense of what parties stand for, but they are too uncertain about this information to use it in guiding their voting behavior. As these voters still know who the parties are in the government, we can make the same general arguments as were made above to arrive at the prediction that incumbent parties should perform better in areas of the country where economic conditions are stronger.

Furthermore, the same aggregate level hypothesis also can be arrived at if it is believed that voters use a two-step process in making their vote choice whereby they first decide whether or not to support an incumbent party and only then make the decision of which opposition party to support (if the decision is not to support an incumbent party). If this is the case, then regardless of the level of information voters possess about political parties, voters who are more satisfied with the state of the economy should still be more likely to support incumbent parties than voters who are dissatisfied with the state of the economy, and, consequently, based on the same assumptions described earlier, incumbent parties should perform better in areas of the country where economic conditions are stronger than in areas where economic conditions are weaker. Moreover, such an approach does look somewhat similar to the traditional "angry at the incumbent" approach to voting during periods of economic reform, whereby all that voters who are angry about the state of the economy are presumed to care about is venting their frustration at the party currently in power. This interpretation also presumes that voters will focus first and foremost on whether to punish or reward the incumbent party for the current state of the economy irrespective of their level of information or beliefs about alternative vote choices. And even if their preference for some alternatives are stronger than others, there should still be a pattern of more support for incumbent parties in areas of the country where economic conditions are better and less support where they are worse.

While this particular formulation of the voting choice process stands in marked contrast to traditional spatial models of voting,[8] the logic is not

---

[8] See, in particular, Downs 1957.

that far off from the theories underlying most cross-national models of the effect of economic conditions on national election results, which inevitably focus on the vote for incumbent parties independent of the options presented by other parties.[9] Moreover, the idea of voters first making up their minds about whether or not to vote for incumbent parties is attractive in the transitional context because it emphasizes the only concrete information voters have: the knowledge of which parties are currently incumbents. If voters have beliefs about what other parties are likely to do when they are in office but are at all uncertain about these beliefs, one could imagine that voters who are pleased with the state of the economy might not want to take the risk of being wrong about the economic consequences of electing a different party to office. Conversely, voters who are unhappy about the state of the economy might be much more willing to risk replacing the current governing parties with other parties, even if they run the risk of being wrong about their assessment of these other parties. While such a calculus is not necessarily peculiar to transition countries, the levels of uncertainty that force voters to fall back on a yes/no assessment of the incumbent parties are probably more likely to be found in transitional countries than in established democracies.

Thus, we have three different variants of what is largely the same theoretical question – how economic conditions might affect the distribution of votes in an electoral environment characterized by a lack of information about political parties – that result in the same aggregate level hypothesis, which I have labeled the Incumbency hypothesis. The Incumbency hypothesis predicts that incumbent parties should perform better in areas of the country where economic conditions are stronger and worse in areas of the country where economic conditions are weaker. To reiterate, the goal of the empirical analysis that follows is to ascertain the degree of support for this aggregate level hypothesis and not to attempt to distinguish between the different microlevel foundations presented in the previous paragraphs. To do the latter would at the very least require microlevel data, and in a larger sense would not even be a particularly interesting enterprise, as the three explanations are to a large extent all variants on the same argument: how uncertainty elevates the importance of incumbency in determining the manner in which cross-regional variation in economic conditions affects election results.

---

[9] Although see Anderson (2000) for an example of a cross-national study that considers the availability of alternative options.

Before turning to an alternate set of hypotheses, I want to emphasize that although the hypothesis looks very similar to standard economic voting hypotheses insofar as it predicts that better economic conditions will lead to more votes for incumbent parties, the argument is theoretically distinct from the standard retrospective economic voting models discussed later in this chapter. The argument presented here is *not* one in which voters use changes in the economy since the previous government took office as a way to measure the competence of the existing government, but, rather, one in which uncertainty about parties and policy-making leads economically satisfied citizens to be more likely than economically dissatisfied citizens to want the current government to remain in office. Thus, the prediction is that incumbent parties ought to enjoy greater electoral success in areas of the country where the economy is stronger, as opposed to hypotheses that focus on either change in vote totals or changes in economic conditions since the previous election. While the distinction may be subtle, it has important connotations for how the empirical analysis is structured, which will be discussed in the next chapter. Moreover, it also helps emphasize the point that a lack of empirical support for the Referendum Model in this study should not be interpreted as conflicting with evidence that has been found in support of incumbency-based hypotheses in established democracies by studies that do not employ a cross-regional framework.

At the same time, it is also useful to be aware of the similarities between the Incumbency hypothesis proposed in this chapter and arguments common to the economic voting literature. Although the focus here is not on using economic conditions to assess the competence of the current government, both approaches do rely on the basic argument that dissatisfaction with economic conditions can lead voters to be more likely to want to "throw the bums out." At the end of the day, both approaches suggest that the worse economic conditions are, the less likely incumbent parties are to be favored by voters. Furthermore, in some ways such an approach is a direct descendent of what Fiorina (1981) calls the "pure" retrospective approach of V. O. Key, based on "retrospective voters – unaffected by party ties, ideologies, and future issue expectations – who regard elections as referenda on the state of the country" (p. 36). If ever there was an opportunity to locate such pure retrospective voters, it would seem to be in the uncertain environment of postcommunist elections.

As the Incumbency hypothesis suggests that economic conditions affect election results solely by increasing or decreasing the likelihood that voters will support incumbent parties, the model has the feel of a referendum on the current government. For this reason, I have labeled this approach the Referendum Model. The obvious shortcoming of the Referendum Model is that it offers analysts no leverage over the question of where voters who are dissatisfied with incumbent parties are likely to turn in casting their vote. This is not a large concern in the context of a two-party system, where a vote against the incumbent by definition means a vote for the opposition party. As the number of parties contesting an election increases, however, models that make predictions solely based on incumbency status are likely to suffer from an increasingly narrow scope and an inability to comment on the relationship between economic conditions and the vote for large numbers of parties. So the next question to consider is how to motivate a model of the effect of economic conditions on election results that can move beyond this limitation.

A Transitional Identity Model

The simplest way to create a model with a wider degree of predictive power is to relax our assumptions about the magnitude of uncertainty in transitional elections and allow voters to have some beliefs about the political parties competing for office. The standard way in which to do so would be to introduce the idea of partisanship, which, as will be explained momentarily, does have some precedence in the existing economic voting literature. I argue in this section, however, that simply transporting a left-right based model to the post-communist context is problematic, and that instead we should think about voters' knowledge of parties in terms of parties' "Transitional Identities," as either Old Regime parties, New Regime parties, or neither. Old Regime parties are those that are clearly linked to the ruling party from the pretransition communist era, whereas New Regime parties are those whose primary identity lies with the political and economic transformations undertaken since the start of the transition era; both categories are defined in much greater detail below. Allowing voters to possess some information about these types of parties leads to hypotheses that predict that New Regime parties should enjoy greater electoral success in areas of the country where the economy is performing better, whereas Old Regime parties should perform better in parts of the country where the economy is performing worse.[10] In the

---

[10] Because of the lack of a specific prediction about the effect of economic conditions on the vote for non-New Regime or non-Old Regime parties, I do not systematically assess

rest of this section, I draw out the theoretical arguments to support these propositions.

The Partisan Approach to Economic Voting in Established Democracies

Although almost all studies of economic voting in established democracies tend to concentrate on how economic conditions affect the vote for incumbent parties, a much smaller and secondary strand of the literature either conditions these effects on partisan orientation or makes explicit predictions about the effect of economic conditions on the vote for parties based on their partisan alignment. The basic thrust of the argument is that certain economic conditions – generally unemployment – are likely to have a particular effect on left-wing parties, whereas other economic conditions – generally inflation – are likely to have a distinct effect on right-wing parties. The logic underlying the argument is that voters are concerned with specific economic problems and have a belief about which parties would be better suited to solving those particular problems (or ought to be held particularly responsible for failing to solve these problems).[11] In the context of advanced industrialized democracies, it is generally assumed that right-wing parties are more likely to favor control of inflation at the expense of rising unemployment, while left-wing parties are more likely to take the opposite approach. Thus, an electorate faced with high inflation might be more likely to turn to right-wing parties, while an electorate scarred by unemployment might turn toward left-wing parties. For example, Kiewiet (1983) examines whether American voters that were concerned with unemployment were more likely to vote for the Democratic Party and, conversely, if voters that were concerned with inflation were more likely to vote for the Republican Party. Although Kiewiet refers to this as a "policy-oriented" economic

---

the effect of the economy on these "other" parties while testing the Transitional Identity Model. However, as part of this study the effects of the economy on fifty-six of these "other" parties were estimated. (These estimates were generated either as part of the process of testing the Referendum Model or during robustness tests of both models; see Chapter 8 for details.) Had these estimates been used to test a hypothetical "Other Transitional Identity" hypothesis, the findings would have been very supportive of the prediction that there should be no systematic evidence of a link between regional variation in economic conditions and election results for these "other" parties; see note 11 in Chapter 9 for details.

[11] For examples of work claiming greater likelihood of punishment, see Powell and Whitten 1993; Palmer and Whitten 2000. For examples or work testing whether higher levels of a particular economic ill lead to greater support for the appropriate type of party, see Rosa and Amson 1976; Lewis-Beck and Bellucci 1982; Bellucci 1984; Host and Paldam 1990. For microlevel research in the American context, see Kiewiet 1983.

voting hypothesis, the basic idea – that there is relationship between particular economic conditions and the vote for particular types of parties irrespective of governing status – is the same as what I have labeled here as a partisan approach to economic voting.

There are numerous concerns with directly employing this kind of a partisan-based approach in transition countries. First, it is very difficult to apply a simple left-right classification to parties in transition countries.[12] Alignments along political spectra can be difficult to classify, as it is often unclear where new parties stand on the relevant issues.[13] Moreover, even if parties declare themselves to stand on one end of the political spectrum, voters lack the years of experience with the parties necessary to build up confidence that the parties will behave in the manner they promise. Additionally, new parties have an opportunity to shift their political alignment during the early years of the transition. An interesting example of such a shift is the heague of Young Democrats (FIDESZ) in Hungary. In the 1990 parliamentary election, it presented itself as a liberal party led by radical young students. By the 1998 parliamentary election, it was not only portraying itself as a right-of-center political party but also claiming that it was the only legitimate center-right party in Hungarian politics.[14] Such experiences highlight the question of what exactly words such as right, left, liberal, or conservative mean in a transitional context, and especially whether such concepts mean the same thing across different countries or time periods.

The second problem with simply importing partisan models to transition countries is that it is doubtful that voters will be able to associate parties of a certain partisan persuasion with specific policies as closely as voters can in established democracies. When voters in an established democracy turn to the left out of a concern over rising unemployment, they believe that left-wing parties will actively fight unemployment not only because they claim they will but often in part because these parties have actually pursued similar policies in the past. Thus, the claims these parties make of being on the left are reinforced by voters' memories of how these parties behaved

---

[12] See, for example, Kitschelt, Manfeldova et al. 1999; Pettai and Kreuzer 1999; Pop-Eleches 2004.

[13] See, for example, Kitschelt 1992; Fish 1995a; White, Rose, and McAllister 1997; Colton 1998a.

[14] Interview by the author with FIDESZ International Secretary Andras Kiraly in Budapest, Hungary on May 5, 1998.

when last in power.[15] Additionally, voters can assess the competency of the left in carrying out these programs in the past. If the leftist parties did, in fact, pursue policies that successfully lowered unemployment rates in the past, then voters would have another assurance that their decision to turn to these parties in the face of rising unemployment was justified. In transition countries, such conditions are not present. Especially in the case of elections that take place early in the transition, voters are not likely to have enough experience in observing the behavior of parties to be confident that left-wing parties will pursue policies to reduce unemployment once in office, as well as whether left-wing parties will actually prove competent at reducing unemployment even if they do choose to pursue it as a goal.

Third, because of the enormity of the economic transition from a centrally planned economy to a market economy, it is unlikely that voters would be motivated by concerns over specific economic conditions as opposed to the state of the overall economy. Voters in advanced industrialized democracies are more likely to have the confidence to believe that the system works but that specific macroeconomic concerns need to be addressed. In transition countries, one would not expect this level of specification of concern to be present. Voters lack the experience with capitalism to understand which particular economic conditions they can afford to see worsen and which ones need to be improved. They are likely to be more concerned with assessing whether the new system works at all and if it is possible to survive and eventually prosper in view of all these new changes. With so many economic changes occurring at once, it is doubtful that voters would focus on one particular economic ill as the source of all their problems and instead are more likely to be motivated by a general concern to see the economy do "better" and avoid having it do "worse."

Finally, as scholars we are also faced with a lack of clearly defined categories for political parties. Certainly, most studies of elections in transition countries attempt to put political parties into different categories or camps as a way of addressing the vast number of political parties. But these categories tend to vary from article to article, depending on the inclination of the researcher.[16] This is not so much of a problem for single case studies, but it does make comparison inherently more difficult; it also points to the

---

[15] This idea of voters building up a set of expectations regarding the likely behavior of parties in office through past experience plays a fundamental role in Fiorina's conception of the retrospective voter; see Fiorina 1981, especially Chapter 4.

[16] For an illustration of this phenomenon, see Tucker 2002, 294.

41

importance of getting some consistency in the field. The problem becomes especially acute when one attempts to compare categories across countries.

Despite these problems, the partisan approach – defined loosely as thinking about the effect of economic conditions on election results based on what a party stands for as opposed to whether or not it is in the government – is attractive because it offers an alternative to the incumbency approach in two important ways. First, the incumbency approach is limited in the number of parties about which it can make predictions, as it only predicts the effect of economic conditions on incumbent parties and makes no useful predictions for the remaining parties. Second, the incumbency approach assumes that the only information voters have to help them assess economic prospects for the country under the leadership of different parties is whether or not they are incumbents, as was posited in the previous section. Given all of the problems with a partisan approach discussed earlier, it still seems likely that voters would have a different conception of the economic prospects for the country under the leadership of a party that is led by young Western-trained reformers as opposed to one that is composed of *nomenklatura* bureaucrats from the previous regime. Clearly, voters do possess some information about parties, even if it is not of the specific nature found in advanced industrialized democracies. And if voters do possess some information, then there is no reason not to use the knowledge of this information to gain leverage over our understanding of the relationship between economic conditions and election results in transition countries.

Applying the Partisan Approach to Transition Countries   In the previous discussion of the Referendum Model, I began from the assumption that voters possessed little relevant information about political parties generally – and in particular about the likely impact of their electoral success on economic developments – or chose to ignore or downgrade in importance whatever information in this regard they might possess. Here, I relax this assumption, and allow voters to have more developed beliefs about political parties. As the information required to motivate a full-fledged partisan based model of the type discussed earlier seems unlikely, I instead assume merely that voters have information regarding a party's "core identity."[17] Core

---

[17] Numerous other studies have taken a similar approach by focusing analyses of either voting or attitudes toward political parties not on the party itself but, rather, on the general "party family" to which the party belongs. See, for example, Lewis 1994; Clem and Craumer 1995a; Belin and Orttung 1997; Clem and Craumer 1997; Shabad and Slomczynski 1999; Colton

party identity can be thought of as the fundamental idea on which the party is based, or, alternatively, as the simplest category into which voters would be likely to put parties. No matter how chaotic the initial transition period, the assumption here is that voters will still have some understanding of parties' core identities.

Another way of thinking about the distinction between a partisan approach and a core identity approach is that the partisan approach assumes that the different parties can be organized in an ordinal manner: there is a clear spectrum on which all of the parties can be placed. A core identity approach instead argues that the relationship is categorical; parties can be organized into categories, but there is no clear linear relationship among the categories. There are different reasons why this linear relationship may not exist: parties themselves may not be clear where they stand in relation to one another; voters may not know where the parties stand in relation to one another; and outside analysts may not be able to consistently place parties on a single left–right dimension. In the case of transition countries, all three types of uncertainty are often present, as was described in the previous section.

A partisan-inspired model for transition countries could thus proceed by substituting the core identities of parties for the partisan (right–left) position of parties in the model. Instead of predicting how economic conditions are likely to affect the vote for right-wing and left-wing parties, this transition-appropriate model would predict how economic conditions are likely to affect the vote for parties based on their core identities.

Not all core party identities, however, can be used to generate viable regional economic voting predictions. Parties that are characterized by agrarian, religious, or ethnic core party identities are examples of such parties. In these cases, there is no clear theoretical reason why these types of parties should be expected to perform either better or worse in areas of the country where economic conditions are better or worse, as their primary appeal to voters is independent of an economic identity.

However, it is possible to predict a relationship between the state of the economy and the vote for political parties whose primary identities in the mind of voters are likely to be directly linked to the transition itself. These parties can be broken down into two categories: the parties most closely associated with the prior, single-party and non-capitalist regime, which I

2000b. For a Herculean effort to classify all parties in twenty postcommunist countries into party families, see Bugajski 2002.

label Old Regime parties; and the parties most closely linked to the newly emerging post-transition multi-party and capitalist world, which I label New Regime parties.

Old Regime parties are defined as those parties that are most clearly linked to the ruling party from the previous nondemocratic regime. This description is deliberately intended to be as general as possible in an effort to provide a framework for moving the analysis outside of the postcommunist context.[18] That being said, it is possible to provide a more focused definition of Old Regime parties within the postcommunist context of this particular book. More specifically, there are two sets of parties that are coded as Old Regime parties. The first are the official successors to the old ruling Communist parties.[19] The second group includes all alternative/spin-off communist successor parties that were established during the postcommunist period in an effort to remain closer to the old communist ideology; in the language of the field, these parties profess to be more orthodox than the official successor parties. In some cases, these parties are never a part of the legal successor, refusing to join it and immediately seeking a more orthodox alternative; in other cases they emerge as splinter parties that split from the legal successor party after some period of time. The key to the definition is that an Old Regime party is visibly linked to the previous regime, either through the people that make up the party, the ideology it continues to publicly embrace, or its legal obligations.

By contrast, New Regime parties are those that are most likely to appeal to voters primarily through their connection to, association with, and

---

[18] For example, in the case of nondemocratic regimes that are not ruled by a political party – such as a military regime – the definition of an Old Regime party could be defined so as to include the party or parties that clearly have the support of the military.

[19] Not surprisingly, scholars have been intrigued by the evolution of these postcommunist parties, and a small literature has sprung up around the topic. Five recommended books in this regard are Grzymala-Busse 2002, which compares the evolution of communist successor parties in Poland, Hungary, Slovakia, and the Czech Republic, Urban and Solovei 1997, which explores the development of Russia's communist successor parties, and Ishiyama 1999, Bozóki and Ishiyama 2002, and Curry and Urban 2003, three edited volumes that include both single-case study chapters and comparative analyses. Article-length comparative assessments of communist successor parties include Mahr and Nagle 1995; Ishiyama 1997; Grzymala-Busse 1998; and Orenstein 1998. Significant attention as well is often paid to communist successor parties in studies of emerging cleavages in postcommunist countries; see, for example, Evans and Whitefield 1998; Miller and White 1998; Kitschelt, Manfeldova et al. 1999; Lawson, Römmele, and Karasimeonov 1999; Bauer 2002; Whitefield 2002. Finally, Bugajski 2002 is an invaluable resource for charting the evolution of communist successor parties in all East European countries. See as well the discussion of this topic in Chapter 9.

general support for the transition itself. I employ a two-step process to code these parties. The first step is to trace out the descendents of the people or movements that initiated the transition away from communism in each of the countries. In practice, this usually means identifying the descendents of either round table negotiations or initial umbrella movements that formed to oppose the old communist regime; how this plays out on a country-by-country basis is addressed in Chapter 6. The second step is to then eliminate any parties that attempt to appeal to voters on grounds that are separate and distinct from the transition. In practice, this primarily means excluding parties that attempt to appeal to voters on the basis of their identity or profession, which excludes religious, ethnic, nationalist, agrarian, or trade union parties from the category of New Regime parties. This is not to say that any of these other types of parties would not share some identification in the minds of voters with either the struggle against communism or the new system that emerged to replace it, but only that their primary attraction to voters would likely be on another basis. The purpose of excluding these parties is therefore to make the category as "pure" as possible by limiting it to parties whose primary association in the mind of voters is likely to be to the transition away from the communist political and economic systems.

This approach maintains a low threshold of required knowledge about political parties, as all that is required of voters by this model is knowledge of whether a party is an Old Regime party, New Regime party, or neither. Voters are not required to have knowledge of the specifics of parties' economic platforms, the likelihood of the parties keeping promises regarding these platforms, or the ability of parties to implement such policies if elected. They are only required to be able to identify the parties most closely connected to the transition. For this reason, I label the model a Transitional Identity Model, as it is based on the idea that a voter is aware of a party's Transitional Identity and can use that identity to help inform his or her vote choice. The model yields two hypotheses. The New Regime hypothesis predicts that New Regime parties will perform better in parts of the country where economic conditions are better than where economic conditions are worse. Conversely, the Old Regime hypothesis predicts that Old Regime parties will enjoy more electoral success in parts of the country where economic conditions are worse than where economic conditions are better.

Both predictions stem from a conception of the transition as representing a sharp break from the past, complete with new opportunities and dangers. The New Regime hypothesis is based on a fairly straightforward logic. Following the massive economic upheaval associated with the transition, voters who have suffered the most from this transition are likely to want to avoid putting parties into power whose primary identity is with the transition. Based on a similar logic, voters who are enjoying more benefits from economic reforms and have avoided more of the pain from economic reforms are likely to prefer to have precisely these types of parties in power. If we continue to assume that there are more people satisfied with the state of the economy in areas of the country where economic conditions are better and more people dissatisfied with the state of the economy in parts of the country where economic conditions are worse, we arrive at the prediction of the New Regime hypothesis, which is that New Regime parties ought to enjoy more electoral success in areas of the country where economic conditions are better than in areas of the country where economic conditions are worse.

If a voter is dissatisfied with the state of the economy, we expect that she will be unlikely to cast a vote for a New Regime party. But in a multiparty system, this still leaves her with many choices. Although she may not posses much information about the likely effects on the economy of having most of these parties in power, she does know something about the Old Regime parties. When their predecessors were in power, the economic landscape looked very different from the present one. Thus, if the voter is particularly concerned about the current state of the economy, then she knows at least one type of party that in the past – at least on the surface – ruled in a period of time without the current economic difficulties. Even if a return to the past is not explicitly desired, the voter may still be more likely to have confidence in Old Regime parties to address the current economic ills than any of the other parties, with which she has no such association of a different type of economic circumstances. And the worse economic conditions are, the more likely she is to act on these concerns when she casts her ballot. As was described earlier, these effects can be both direct (e.g., actually being unemployed) and indirect (e.g., seeing others unemployed, more fear of becoming unemployed in the future). By no means should we expect everyone to vote for Old Regime parties if they are unhappy with the current path of reforms, but from a probabilistic sense we could expect voters dissatisfied with the state of the economy to be more likely to vote for an Old Regime party than any other particular option. If we maintain the assumption from the previous section that there are likely to be more people dissatisfied with the state of the economy in areas of the country where economic conditions are worse, then at the aggregate level we should expect to see more support for Old Regime parties in areas of the country where economic conditions are worse, and less support for Old Regime parties in areas of the country where economic conditions are better.

Although the flavor of the Transitional Identity Model is similar to a partisan model, it is important to note that it is not the same thing. There are Old Regime parties in the sample that clearly moved to the center in embracing market oriented principles during the 1990s (e.g., the Democratic Left Alliance [SLD] in Poland and the Hungarian Socialist Party [MSzP] in Hungary), social democratic parties that had no connection to the previous ruling regime and thus are not classified as Old Regime parties (e.g., the Czech Social Democratic Party [CSSD] in the Czech Republic), and New Regime parties with increasingly dubious liberal reformist credentials (e.g., Our Home is Russia [NDR] in Russia and Solidarity Electoral Action [AWS] in Poland). This highlights the point that the basic motivation for the Transitional Identity Model is voters' knowledge about a party's relationship to the transition itself, as opposed to nuances about the types of policies the party may currently be advocating.

Summary of and Observations on Standard Economic Voting Models and Hypotheses

To summarize, the preceding theoretical discussion focuses on two standard economic voting models, the Referendum Model and the Transitional Identity Model. Based on a low information and high uncertainty framework, the Referendum Model yields one hypothesis, the Incumbency hypothesis, which predicts that incumbent parties should receive more electoral support in parts of the country where economic conditions are better than in parts of the country where economic conditions are worse. The Transitional Identity Model, which assumes slightly lower levels of uncertainty and modest levels of information about political parties, and in particular the relationship of parties to the transition itself, generates two hypotheses. The New Regime hypothesis predicts that New Regime parties ought to perform better in areas of the country where economic conditions are stronger, whereas the Old Regime hypothesis predicts that Old Regime parties ought to perform better in areas of the country where economic conditions are worse. Thus, the primary empirical question of this book is to ascertain whether there is stronger empirical support for one of these models than the other. And as was noted in Chapter 1 and will be made clear in Chapters 5 through 8, there is indeed a clear answer to this question: there is consistently stronger empirical support for the Transitional Identity Model than there is for the Referendum Model.

It is also important to note that neither the Referendum Model nor the Transitional Identity Model offer predictions for the effect of economic conditions on all parties that contest elections. As will become clear in the later chapters, the Transitional Identity Model makes predictions for a larger number of parties than the Referendum Model, and as such enjoys greater scope in the postcommunist context. But there are certainly parties for which the Transitional Identity Model can not account as well. In some ways, this can be seen as a shortcoming of the model, as it is always desirable for models to have larger scope. At the same time, it may be the case that there are certain types of parties for which we should not expect variation in economic conditions to have a significant explanatory effect on election results, or at the very least not nearly as consistently as the effect of economic conditions on election results for New Regime and Old Regime parties. But in the interest of parsimony, I leave the topic of the systematic effect of economic conditions on the vote for parties outside of the incumbent, New Regime, and Old Regime classifications for future research.[20]

Before moving on to the topic of conditional economic voting hypotheses in the final section of this chapter, I pause briefly to consider the relationship between the standard economic voting models and hypotheses presented above and some of the overarching questions facing the economic voting literature. Specifically, I address the pocketbook versus sociotropic and prospective versus retrospective voting debates, both of which have figured prominently in the academic literature. In doing so, it is important to note that these are both essentially microlevel arguments about motivation for individual level behavior, whereas the models presented in this chapter yield aggregate level hypotheses about the relationship between election results and macroeconomic conditions. Thus, any link between the standard economic voting models presented in this book and these microlevel debates is going to be of a more speculative nature than anything else.

The pocketbook versus sociotropic debate concerns the question of whether or not voters are more likely to respond to their own personal

---

[20] The only exceptions here are nationalist parties, which I address briefly in Chapter 7 and in greater detail elsewhere (Tucker 2004), and the short description of the findings regarding the fifty-six non-New Regime and non-Old Regime parties (mentioned earlier in note 10 of this chapter) presented in note 11 of Chapter 9.

economic situation or to their perception of the overall economic health of society.[21] The models discussed in the preceding section are not dependent on having a position on this debate, as they are consistent with both pocketbook and sociotropic approaches. If the pocketbook approach is correct, then both models can rest on the belief that in areas of the country where economic conditions are worse, there are likely to be more people that are disenchanted with their own particular economic situation. This is especially apparent with a variable such as unemployment, which almost directly measures the percentage of people in a given region that we might expect to be most concerned with their personal economic situation. Likewise, if voters have more sociotropic concerns, then both models are consistent with the idea that voters living in areas of the country where economic conditions are worse are likely to have a worse impression of the state of the economy than voters living in areas where economic conditions are better. In a sense, this is just another reflection of the direct and indirect effects of economic conditions argument that I made earlier in this chapter. Given that the hypotheses are consistent with both sociotropic and pocketbook voting arguments, we can not hope to distinguish between them from the statistical tests employed in this book; indeed, to do so would require extensive use of microlevel data. Conversely, though, those who are convinced that either (or both) effects are important in understanding the effect of economics conditions on election results should be reassured that neither is inconsistent with the hypotheses tested here.

The other large standing debate in the literature concerns questions regarding whether voters are more likely to vote retrospectively, in relation to what has happened with the economy before the election, or prospectively, in terms of expectations about economic developments in the future.[22] Overall, the study in this book has little to say about this debate as well because the emphasis in the hypotheses is on cross-regional variation in economic conditions at the time of the election. Consequently, as will

---

[21] For advocates of the sociotropic approach, see Kinder and Kiewiet 1979; MacKuen, Erikson, and Stimson 1992; Lanoue 1994; Mughan and Lacy 2002. Empirical evidence of the pocketbook approach can be found in Palmer and Whitten 1999, which examines the effect of the economy on election results in twelve OECD countries, and Paldam 1986, which looks at Danish voters. For a related approach, see the argument regarding conditional pocketbook voting in Gomez 2001.

[22] For studies of retrospective effects, see Key 1966; Fiorina 1981; Lanoue 1994; Krause 1997; Nickelsburg and Norpoth 2000; Johnson and Pattie 2001. For more prospective arguments, see Downs 1957; Lockerbie 1991; MacKuen, Erikson, and Stimson 1992; and Erikson, MacKuen, and Stimson 2000.

be discussed in the next chapter, the variables used to test the hypotheses described in this chapter are intended to measure variation in macroeconomic conditions at the time of the election, and thus do not fall squarely in either the retrospective or prospective camp.[23] That being said, empirical support for the Transitional Identity Model is at the very least consistent with the idea that voters can be forward-looking, as voters are posited to be choosing parties based on how they will approach the economy (or whose economic interests they will represent) in the period of time after the election. Of course, this is not inconsistent with some of the more nuanced versions of retrospective voting (see especially Fiorina 1981) that view the voting calculus as an attempt to predict future behavior when in office based on a running tally of past performance. But overall, readers should be quite cautious about extrapolating any significant contribution to the retrospective versus prospective debate from this or any other study that employs exclusively aggregate level data from the period of time leading up to the election in question.

One final observation about the relationship between traditional models of retrospective voting and the models I have put forth in this section is in order. In an important sense, my approach takes account of a concern with all retrospective economic voting models, which is why citizens might ever expect a political party to have an effect on economic conditions, especially in an increasingly globalized world in which macroeconomic developments are more and more beyond the control of national governments. The models I have put forward in this chapter do so by stripping the retrospective blame/reward component out of the theoretical calculus by focusing on the state of the economy at the time of the election – in an effort to identify where there are greater concentrations of voters who are satisfied or dissatisfied with economic conditions generally – as opposed to changes in the state of the economy since the previous election. In the Referendum Model, voters are not holding the government accountable (or rewarding it) for changes in the economy since the government took office but, rather, are merely reflecting the fact that the worse one thinks current economic conditions are, the more likely one might be to want to see someone else in power. Thus, there is no threshold beyond which the government either performed well or poorly but, instead, the simple assumption that those

---

[23] Moreover, it questionable whether aggregate level analysis that does not take into account public opinion could ever hope to sort out prospective versus retrospective questions in the manner that a study employing survey data could (Kramer 1983; Markus 1988).

who are worse off are more likely to prefer change than those who are better off. Similarly, voters are not rewarding or punishing parties in the Transitional Identity Model but, rather, acting on the idea that a particular type of party is more likely to look out for the interest of economic winners (New Regime parties) or economic losers (Old Regime parties). This is not to argue that voters never try to reward or punish incumbent parties for changes in the state of the economy since the previous election, but, rather, that we can develop hypotheses about aggregate level relationships between economic conditions and election results that are not dependent on voters believing in the efficacy of a reward or punishment strategy.

This leads to another important topic, which is the question of the relationship between the microlevel arguments I have made above and the macrolevel hypotheses I test in the remainder of this book. To reiterate, the empirical component of this book tests the relationship between regional aggregate level economic conditions and election results. In the preceding section of this chapter, I have attempted to generate these aggregate level hypotheses through plausible microlevel arguments about how citizens might behave during transitional elections in postcommunist countries. But we cannot test microlevel hypotheses about motivations for individual level behavior using aggregate level data, nor do I claim to do so.[24] So although it is possible to say, for example, that evidence in support of the Transitional Identity Model is consistent with the idea that voters may be forward-looking, it should not in any way be interpreted as an empirical test of a prospective model of voting.

Similarly, the fact that I have put forward a set of microlevel arguments to justify the choice of aggregate level hypotheses I test in the following chapters should not in any way detract from the importance of testing aggregate level hypotheses as a research strategy. Political scientists have a clear interest in explaining macrolevel phenomena. Certainly we should be concerned with understanding how people vote, but we also want to know why parties receive the vote totals that they do. Indeed, if one of our main reasons for being interested in elections in the first place is the fact that they determine who makes up the government and the legislature, then the argument can be made that understanding why parties receive the votes that they do is just as important as understanding why any one individual

---

[24] The exception here is ecological inference analysis, but even these types of analyses only allow us to estimate relationships at the micro level for which we have data at the aggregate level. For more, see King 1997.

voted the way she did. Aggregate-level phenomena are real phenomena that demand our understanding just as microlevel phenomena do.

This study is an aggregate-level study insofar as it attempts to understand the link between regional variation in macroeconomic conditions and variation in election results for particular categories of political parties. It is not the only way one could hope to study the relationship between economic conditions and election results, but it is a valid way to do so, and, as will be explained in the next chapter, one that is particularly appropriate for comparative analysis given the nature of the available data. Moreover, in focusing this aggregate-level analysis at the regional level, the study highlights a relationship between economic conditions and election results that has been left largely unexplored by the existing literature on economic voting in established democracies.

Conditional Economic Voting Hypotheses

As described in Chapter 1, I distinguish between hypotheses that attempt to answer the questions in the first and second rows of Table 1.1 by using the terms standard and conditional economic voting hypotheses. To reiterate, standard economic voting hypotheses make predictions about the type of party affected by economic conditions and the direction in which the effect pushes the vote for that type of party. Conditional economic voting hypotheses, on the other hand, predict the conditions in which there should be more or less empirical support for a standard hypothesis, or, more generally, the context in which economic conditions should have a more or less consistent effect on election results. The best-known conditional hypothesis from the literature on economic voting in established democracies can be found in G. Bingham Powell and Guy Whitten's 1993 *American Journal of Political Science* article "A Cross-National Analysis of Economic Voting: Taking Account of the Political Context".[25] The authors were primarily concerned with testing a standard economic voting hypothesis: whether or not incumbent parties performed better when economic conditions were better across a cross-national time-series of OECD elections. However, one of their hypotheses was that they expected to find more support for this incumbency hypothesis when the "clarity of responsibility" of the government for policy was stronger than when it was weaker. To test this

---

[25] Note that Powell and Whitten did not use the terminology of standard and conditional hypotheses, which are original to this book.

hypothesis, they split their sample into two groups – high responsibility countries and low responsibility countries – and then ran their analysis separately on each subgroup. According to my terminology, this is a perfect example of a conditional economic voting hypothesis. It predicts the conditions (high responsibility elections) under which we ought to find more empirical support for a standard hypothesis (that incumbents [type] benefit from better [direction] economic conditions). Powell and Whitten did indeed find support for their conditional clarity of responsibility hypothesis, and, in doing so, provided the impetus for a variety of work that has attempted to either refine or refute the clarity of responsibility argument.[26]

While Powell and Whitten introduced one useful conditional hypothesis, the universe of conditional hypotheses can expand well beyond the clarity of responsibility argument. In the remainder of this section, I introduce a range of conditional hypotheses, a number of which build off of the clarity of responsibility argument. Others, however, build off different theoretical arguments that I present later in this section. It is important to note that although most of the conditional hypotheses I discuss can be applied to any standard hypothesis (e.g., we might expect to find more support for the Incumbency, New Regime, and Old Regime hypotheses in high responsibility elections), some will apply to only particular standard hypotheses; I will note specifically when this is the case.

There are two important reasons for including conditional hypotheses in the study. First and foremost, the conditional hypotheses present theoretically defined (or intuitively interesting) alternative subsets of data for retesting the standard hypotheses. As has been repeatedly noted, the overall conclusion of this book is that there is more empirical support for the Transitional Identity Model than for the Referendum Model. One way to conceptualize the conditional economic voting hypotheses, therefore, is as a series of robustness tests that allow us to examine whether this empirical conclusion continues to hold when we introduce a second layer of theory to predict contexts in which economic conditions ought to be more or less important. For example, is there still more support for the Transitional Identity Model than the Referendum Model in high responsibility elections? Or if we consider only elections in which the personality of candidates is particularly important?

---

[26] See, for example, Whitten and Palmer 1999; Anderson 2000; Chappell and Veiga 2000; Royed, Leyden, and Borrelli 2000; Tucker 2000b, 2001; and Nadeau, Niemi, and Yoshinaka 2002.

But the other reason for examining conditional hypotheses is because they are interesting unto themselves. In some ways, these types of arguments represent the cutting edge of research in the economic voting literature generally, especially if we are to judge by the flurry of recent activity that attempts to test the clarity of responsibility argument. In this vein, my work offers three new contributions. First, I present a number of ways of testing the clarity of responsibility argument in the context of new democracies. Second, I offer a set of other theoretical justifications for conditional hypotheses that move beyond responsibility-based arguments. Finally, I present some preliminary assessment of these hypotheses from the post-communist case studies I examine in the book.[27]

In the rest of this chapter, I present a number of conditional economic voting hypotheses. They are broken down into two general categories: theoretically motivated hypotheses and intuitively interesting hypotheses; I explain the distinction between the two in the following section. The theoretically based hypotheses are then grouped together around a number of common themes; for example, the hypotheses that build off of the clarity of responsibility concept are presented together. I turn first to the intuitive conditional economic voting hypotheses.

Intuitive Conditional Hypotheses

Most of the conditional hypotheses tested in the study are generated from theoretical arguments. However, in the years that I have been presenting this research, I have always been asked about the effect of including both parliamentary and presidential elections and both East-Central European and Russian elections in the same study. Although not based on any particular theoretical argument, many people seem to be at least curious as to whether the results are consistent across these divides. I also have been asked

---

[27] It is important to stress the preliminary nature of these conclusions. My research design is focused on providing as thorough a testing as possible of the three standard hypotheses presented in the previous section, and as such is not explicitly designed to test the conditional hypotheses. That being said, the manner in which I test the conditional hypotheses – by splitting my sample into the different categories proposed by the hypotheses and comparing the degree of support for the relevant standard hypothesis within each category – is fairly similar to the approach used by Powell and Whitten. But ultimately all I can really do is look for patterns across these cases, and not definitively reject or prove any of the hypotheses. But there are a number of interesting patterns to report, and as such the study can provide directions for future research that are more directly focused on tests of the more promising conditional hypotheses.

on numerous occasions for country-by-country breakdowns of the results. For this reason, I include these three "intuitive" conditional hypotheses in the analysis: presidential versus parliamentary elections; East-Central European versus Russian elections; and a country-by-country breakdown of results. It is almost a stretch to call these hypotheses, as there is no real prediction of the category in which we should expect to see more support for the relevant standard economic voting hypothesis. This is an informative point, because it distinguishes the intuitive conditional hypotheses from the theoretical conditional hypotheses that follow in the next section; the theoretical conditional hypotheses produce a prediction about the category in which there is expected to be greater support for standard hypotheses (e.g., Powell and Whitten expected to find more support for their incumbency hypothesis in the high responsibility category than in the low responsibility category), whereas for the intuitive conditional hypotheses, there is no particular expectation for (or no good reason to expect) more support in one case than the other, just the belief that they may be different. Another way of putting this is that the null for the intuitive hypotheses is that there is no difference across categories, while the null for the theoretical hypotheses is that there is either no difference across the categories or that there is a difference in the wrong direction (e.g., more support in the low responsibility than in the high responsibility category).

The categories for these intuitive conditional hypotheses require little explanation, other than to note that they are not equally balanced. There are five Russian elections in the study, as compared to a total of fifteen elections from the four East-Central European cases. Similarly, there are five presidential elections and fifteen parliamentary elections in the sample, because in both Hungary and the Czech Republic the president is selected by the parliament; the Slovak parliament also elected the president until 1999, when the first direct elections for Slovak president were held. The country-by-country analysis is more evenly distributed with five Polish and Russian elections, four Slovak elections, and three Czech and Hungarian elections; this includes three parliamentary elections for each country plus the applicable presidential elections.

Theoretically Based Conditional Economic Voting Hypotheses

In this book, I consider five different types of theoretically based conditional hypotheses: *Responsibility* based conditional hypotheses that build directly off of the Powell and Whitten (1993) approach to predict more support for standard economic voting hypotheses in contexts in which we expect parties to have more responsibility for government policy; *Supply-side* conditional hypotheses that predict more support for standard economic voting hypotheses when non-economic factors matter less; *Party orientation* conditional hypotheses that predict different effects for subsets of the New Regime and Old Regime parties; *Time-based* conditional hypotheses that predict changing support for standard hypotheses as time progresses; and, finally, *Interactive* conditional hypotheses that are generated by examining the interaction of the standard hypotheses (e.g., the effect of the economy on incumbent-New Regime parties vs. opposition-New Regime parties). In the rest of this section, I draw out the specific hypotheses in each of these categories.

Responsibility Hypotheses As has been mentioned earlier, responsibility-based conditional hypotheses are the one form of conditional hypotheses that have already taken hold in the literature thanks to a number of articles cited earlier that have attempted to test Powell and Whitten's original clarity of responsibility hypothesis. Simply put, the argument proposed that the relative importance of economic conditions in determining election results (or the extent to which we ought to find empirical support for standard economic voting hypotheses) is dependent on how *responsible* those being elected are perceived to be for government policy. The more responsible they are, the more economic conditions should matter.[28]

Although this is clearly a macrolevel theory insofar as it pertains to the relationship between economic conditions and election results, it is grounded in plausible microlevel foundations. In its most general form, it is based on the simple idea that, before voters decide to look to the economy to influence their vote choice, they first consider how much control over government policy the people for whom they are voting actually have. The more control those being elected have, the more voters are likely to factor macroeconomic conditions into their voting behavior. The less control, the less economic conditions should matter.

---

[28] Although not focused on the topic of voting, Javeline's recent work on whether Russian citizens responded in the 1990s to unpaid wages by protesting focuses heavily on the degree to which Russians can attribute blame for wage arrears to specific actors. She finds empirical support on the micro level for this variant of a clarity of responsibility hypothesis, as Russians who did attribute blame to specific actors were in fact more likely to participate in protest activities. See Javeline 2003a, 2003b.

Powell and Whitten operationalize the level of responsibility for policy by looking at a variety of institutional factors that speak to how likely the ruling party should be to be able to implement its preferred policies at will. Specifically, these factors are voting cohesion on the part of the governing party or parties, the nature of the committee system in the parliament, the presence of bicameral opposition, and whether the government was a minority or coalition government.[29]

Replicating the components of this index in postcommunist countries presents a theoretical problem. In constructing an index, the authors assume these factors are both known and relevant to voters. Although it seems plausible that many voters would be aware of whether parties were participating in a coalition government or not, it becomes more of a stretch to suggest that voters are aware of how committee chairmanships are assigned in the parliament, even in a well-established democracy. When we consider the case of new democracies where voters are constantly confronted with new and changing institutions everywhere they turn, these types of assumptions become even more difficult to sustain.

To replicate the spirit of this hypothesis in the postcommunist context, I rely on a more blunt measure of responsibility, something of which more voters are likely to be aware. At this point, the rich institutional variation found in postcommunist countries becomes useful. Looking across the postcommunist political landscape, one finds presidential systems, parliamentary systems, and variants of mixed systems of government.[30] Moreover, there are both presidential and parliamentary elections that take place in these systems. On the basis of this simple interaction between the type of election and the type of governing system, we can create an alternative index of responsibility that requires voters to have a much lower threshold of understanding about the political system than the Powell and Whitten index. Indeed, all such a responsibility hypothesis requires is that voters be aware of the office for which the parties/candidates are competing (president or parliament) and whether the country primarily has a parliamentary, presidential, or mixed system of government.[31]

---

[29] See Powell and Whitten 1993, 399–402.

[30] See, for example, Remington 1994; Hellman, Tucker, and Frye 1996; Taras 1997; and Fish 2000.

[31] Note that this does not assume that voters know the classical textbook definitions of presidentialism versus parliamentarism, but rather that more generally they understand whether the president or the prime minister is the functional head of the executive. As this is perhaps the most basic of information to possess about one's government, it is not unrealistic to

The hypothesis is based on the following simple assumption. If a country has both a parliament and a president, then voters should attach more responsibility for government policy to the "dominant" body (e.g., the presidency in a presidential system and the parliament in a parliamentary system). This assumption seems relatively uncontroversial, although it does lead to the question of how one classifies countries as presidential, parliamentary, or mixed systems. Fortunately, there is a wide range of literature that addresses exactly this topic.[32] There also exists a gray area between parliamentary and presidential systems, which has led scholars to come up with different hybrid categories such as premier-presidential and president-parliamentary,[33] moderate presidentialism,[34] or semipresidentialism.[35] For the sake of simplicity, I refer to cases that are not clearly presidential or parliamentary systems as "mixed" systems. Because a mixed system by definition does not have a dominant president or parliament, the level of responsibility for government policy for either type of election in a mixed system will be less than the level of responsibility for a dominant institution and clearly more responsible than the "dominated" institution (e.g., the parliament in a presidential system or president in a parliamentary system).

The classification of the five countries used in this study as either presidential, parliamentary, or mixed systems is especially straightforward. There is little doubt in the literature that Russia is a presidential system or that Hungary, Slovakia, and the Czech Republic are parliamentary systems.[36] Poland, by contrast, falls nicely into the category of a mixed system. Although the Polish law on the presidency has changed throughout the 1990s, the governing system has always been characterized by the fact that both the parliament and the president play a role in selecting the government and dismissing the government, both bodies are elected by the people, and both the president and prime minister have veto power over legislation.

suggest postcommunist voters will know this. For example, in an article written between the 1995 Russian Parliamentary elections and the 1996 Russian Presidential election, Colton notes that no matter what Russian voters had done in the 1995 parliamentary elections, "Boris Yeltsin was still going to be in the Kremlin after the votes were tallied and the parliamentary benches filled." However, the impending presidential election was not going to be for "legislators who can make fiery speeches about this or that, but the next thing to an elected monarch." This is a clear illustration of the fact that Colton expected voters to realize they were living in a presidential system (Colton 1996b, both quotes from p. 373).

[32] For good reviews, see Lijphart 1992; Shugart and Carey 1992.

[33] Shugart and Carey 1992.

[34] Fish 2000.

[35] Linz 1994; Sartori 1994; Bernhard 1997.

[36] See, for example, Shugart 1993; Holmes 1994; Lucky 1994; and Remington 1994.

While the government is headed by the prime minister, the president has always enjoyed a great deal of influence.[37]

Because the predicted variation in support for standard economic voting hypotheses in this regard is dependent on institutional characteristics of elections and governing systems, I label this the *institutional responsibility hypothesis*. To reiterate, it predicts that we should find the most support for the three standard hypotheses in elections for dominant institutions (presidential elections in Russia, parliamentary elections in Hungary, Slovakia, and the Czech Republic), the least support in elections for dominated institutions (parliamentary elections in Russia and presidential elections in Slovakia), and an intermediary level of support for either parliamentary or presidential elections in mixed systems (all Polish elections).

The original Powell and Whitten hypothesis applied only to the vote for incumbent parties, but the logic holds equally well for the predictions made by the Transitional Identity Model regarding New Regime and Old Regime parties. Recall that both of these hypotheses were based on the idea that certain economic conditions would prompt voters to be more or less likely to want either New Regime or Old Regime parties in power because of what they might do vis-à-vis the economy once in power. Similar to the original Powell and Whitten logic, it should be the case that if voters are less likely to believe that the contested institution has control over the state of the economy, they will also be less likely to care whether the institution is controlled by a New Regime or Old Regime party. Consequently, we should find less support for both the New Regime and Old Regime hypotheses in elections for low responsibility institutions as well.

The responsibility-based approach also can be used to generate hypotheses about other sources for variation in support for standard economic voting hypotheses that move beyond institutional environments. Perhaps the simplest measure to consider is the size of the political party. If voters suspect that smaller parties are less likely to be able to affect government policy, then it seems reasonable to at least test to see if there is more support for standard economic voting hypotheses amongst parties that receive a larger percentage of the overall vote. Therefore, the *size of vote hypothesis* predicts specifically that we ought to find more support for the standard economic voting hypotheses among parties that received larger percentages of the overall national vote; such a hypothesis fits nicely with the more general

---

[37] In comparative studies of presidentialism versus parliamentarism in postcommunist countries, Poland is almost always given one of the hybrid classification labels; see, for example, Remington 1994; Fish 2000.

proposition that the role of economic conditions in influencing the vote for political parties ought to increase as parties are considered to be more relevant to the political process. Of course, voters must decide for which party to cast their vote before they know what percentage of the overall vote these parties have received in the election. So this hypothesis rests on the assumption that voters have some rudimentary understanding about the popularity of different parties before the election date. While it seems a stretch to assume that voters could accurately predict vote totals for parties before the election – especially earlier in the decade – the assumption that voters would be able to differentiate between parties likely to receive a larger percentage of the vote (greater than 20%) and a relatively small percentage of the vote (less than 5%) seems more reasonable. In the actual empirical tests of the models, I will explicitly compare parties in these two categories, but I also will examine other intermediary thresholds as well.[38]

One other direction in which to push the responsibility-based approach is to consider the distinction between the lead member of a coalition and its junior partners.[39] If economic conditions have more of an effect on a party's electoral fortune the more responsible the party is for the economy, then we would expect the vote for the primary coalition partner to be more affected by the economy than supplementary or minor coalition partners. The logic here is based on the assumption that voters will be more likely to ascribe responsibility for government policy to the lead party of the coalition. Such a *coalition hypothesis* only can be applied to incumbent parties in parliamentary elections; it makes no sense to speak of distinctions within a coalition when discussing a unitary presidential candidate.[40] Additionally, an analysis of the support for the Transitional Identity Model would make

---

[38] For a similar idea, see the discussion of governing party target size in Anderson (2000).

[39] See Wilkin, Haller, and Norpoth 1997 and Tucker 2001 for direct applications of this type of hypothesis. The idea is also tangentially related to studies that examine whether there is more of an effect for economic conditions on the vote for single-party or coalition governments; see, for example, Lewis-Beck and Stegmaier 2000; and Royed, Leyden, and Borrelli 2000.

[40] It is possible, however, to think of primary and junior presidential candidates in a presidential election in a parliamentary system, if the different coalition members nominated different candidates for president. As there is only one such election in this study – the 1999 Slovak presidential election – and there was one clear candidate representing the coalition government – Rudolf Schuster – I have elected not to muddy the conceptual waters by including this specific scenario in the theoretical discussion. However, future research using this hypothesis may require addressing this possibility more explicitly.

Table 2.1. *Responsibility-Based Conditional Hypotheses*

Predicted Support for Standard Hypotheses	Type of Variation	Coding	Applicability
Panel 1: Institutional Responsibility Hypothesis			
More	Dominant Elections (Presidential election in Presidential system, Parliamentary election in Parliamentary system)	Russian Presidential, Czech Parliamentary, Slovak Parliamentary, Hungarian Parliamentary elections	
↓	Parliamentary or Presidential elections in Mixed system	Polish Presidential and Parliamentary elections	New Regime, Old Regime, and Incumbency Hypotheses
Less	Dominated Elections (Presidential election in Parliamentary system, Parliamentary election in Presidential system)	Russian Parliamentary and Slovak Presidential elections	
Panel 2: Size of Vote Hypothesis			
More	Higher National Vote Total		New Regime, Old Regime, and Incumbency Hypotheses
↓	↓	By individual party vote totals	
Less	Lower National Vote Total		
Panel 3: Coalition Hypothesis			
More	Primary Coalition Member		Incumbency Hypothesis in Parliamentary elections
Less	Other Coalition Member	See Table 5.7	

no sense in this context, so the hypothesis can only be tested in conjunction with the Referendum Model. Nevertheless, there are still forty-three parties in the sample that are classified as incumbent parties (see Chapter 5) that competed in parliamentary elections. As the specific criteria used to code incumbent parties are discussed in Chapter 5, I will hold off the discussion of the coding rules for primary incumbent parties until that chapter as well.

Thus, the responsibility-based approach yields three empirically testable conditional economic voting hypotheses: the institutional responsibility hypothesis, the size of vote hypothesis, and the coalition hypothesis.

Table 2.1 concisely summarizes their predictions and the standard hypotheses on which they will be tested in the following chapters.

Supply-Side Hypotheses In recent years, it has become fashionable in political science to turn to market metaphors as a way of organizing one's thinking about political phenomena. Terms such as exit and voice, collective action problems, and transaction costs have become commonplace in the literature.[41] In this spirit, consider the voting decision as creating a market place for information. Voters demand reasons to make a voting decision with which they feel comfortable. One potential source of a voter's choice is the state of the economy. But of course macroeconomic conditions are not the only factors that voters take into account in making their vote choices. In this sense, the state of the economy must "compete" with other factors to supply the voter with her reason for casting her vote in the manner she does.

One way to conceptualize this marketplace is to assume that in the absence of any other compelling reason to make a vote choice, voters will base their decisions on economic conditions in the manner suggested by a standard economic voting model such as the Transitional Identity Model or the Referendum Model. However, when other noneconomic factors are important, voters may be less likely to base their voting decisions purely on economic conditions. And the more important the noneconomic factors are, the less important economic conditions will be in determining election results. As this type of theory is based on the competition between different factors to supply a voter's demand for a reason to vote for a political party, I label it a supply-side approach.

As has been noted throughout this book, the last forty years have resulted in a rich literature on the subject of economic effects on electoral outcomes. Although it is difficult to give credit to any one person in particular for starting the debate, almost all scholars point at least somewhat to Gerald Kramer's 1971 *American Political Science Review* article "Short-Term Fluctuations in U.S. Voting Behavior."[42] In this article, Kramer mentions the fact that the model of the effect of economic conditions on elections

---

[41] See, for example, Hirshman 1970; Olson 1971; Williamson 1987.

[42] Indeed, Kiewet and Udell refer to this article as "one of the most influential empirical studies in the history of political science" (Kiewiet and Udell 1998, 219).

that he has proposed is based on a system "in which a voter must decide only between two candidates, who are running primarily as anonymous members of opposing party 'teams'" (Kramer 1971, 135). Kramer goes on to suggest that if the United States deviated too far from this pattern, the economic voting model would probably not work. However, he concludes this should not be a problem because "Congressional candidates appear to most voters simply as Democrats or Republicans, and not as clearly defined personalities" (Kramer 1971, 135).

In the parlance of this book, however, what Kramer was proposing was a conditional economic voting hypothesis, with candidate personality taking the role of the "noneconomic" factor that competes with economic conditions to supply a reason for a voter to cast her vote. Simply put, Kramer has suggested that the more important a role personality plays in affecting the voting decision, the less important economic conditions ought to be in affecting the outcome. Conversely, we can assume that the less important candidate personality is, or the more anonymous the candidate, the more important economic conditions ought to be in affecting election results.

Kramer leaves unstated how one would operationalize the importance of candidate personality, but he points us in the direction of electoral institutions, as he implicitly compares the anonymity of U.S. congressional candidates against candidates from a "quasi-parliamentary electoral system" (Kramer 1971, 135). Electoral institutions in turn can be used to create a personality index, spanning from electoral rules that create the most anonymous candidates (and therefore allow the smallest impact for candidate personality) to the least anonymous candidates (largest impact for candidate personality). Moreover, an index based on electoral institutions is particularly attractive in the context of postcommunist countries, as it fits the criteria of being a blunt measure of the information available to voters.

Again, the rich institutional variation in the postcommunist context helps in examining support for this hypothesis. Clearly, presidential candidates are the least anonymous, and presidential elections are when we would most expect candidate personality to play a role in voters' decision-making processes.[43] Next would be single member districts (SMD), where voters

---

[43] See, for example, the discussion of Lech Wałęsa's run for reelection in the 1995 Polish presidential election in Jasiewicz (1997).

are also voting for a single person to represent them, although one that they are likely to know less about than a presidential candidate. At the other end of the spectrum is closed-list proportional representation (PR), where voters are most clearly voting for a party. In between is the category of open-list proportional representation. Here voters have the opportunity to cast their ballots for an individual on a party list, and while seats are allocated to parties based on the the total number of votes received by all individuals on their list combined, the actual individuals that receive the seats can be determined by preferences of voters from that district.[44]

Therefore, the *personality hypothesis* predicts that we ought to find the most support for standard economic voting hypotheses in closed-list PR elections, followed by open-list PR, single member districts, and, finally presidential elections. Unfortunately, although there are examples of all four types of elections in this study (see Table 2.2), I did not include analyses of the SMD voting in Hungary or Russia as part of my study because of my inability to locate commensurate economic data. Therefore, the actual empirical tests of this hypothesis focus on variation in the three remaining categories. Table 2.2 lists the electoral rules for the twenty elections included in the study.

Of course, candidate personality is not the only factor that could compete with the economy to supply a reason for people to vote for a particular candidate or party. For example, there may be elections that occur under political circumstances that are so important in the eyes of the voter that they could crowd out economic considerations entirely. Given the large body of existing evidence on the importance of economic conditions on election results, we should probably expect the threshold for conditions at which political crises completely crowd out economic conditions to be quite high. One type of issue likely to meet this threshold would be "regime future" considerations, where the very essence of the country's political future is at stake in the election. Although such circumstances are unlikely

---

[44] One could make the argument that regardless of voting rules in a parliamentary election, parties are always associated with their leader and, thus, the whole question of distinguishing the role of personality by electoral laws is pointless. If one finds this argument convincing, then consider it as a null hypothesis that predicts that there should be no relationship between the importance of economic conditions in determining election results and the proposed role of personality under different electoral institutions.

Economic Conditions and Election Results

Table 2.2. *Electoral Rules by Election*

Country	Year	Election	Electoral Rules
Czech Republic	1992	Parliament	Regional PR* (8 regions). Party List + 4 preferential votes for individual candidates. 5% threshold (7% and 10% for coalitions).
Czech Republic	1996	Parliament	Regional PR (8 regions). Party List + 4 preferential votes for individual candidates. 5% threshold (7% and 11% for coalitions).
Czech Republic	1998	Parliament	Regional PR (8 Regions). Party List + 4 preferential votes for individual candidates. 5% Threshold (7% and 11% for coalitions).
Hungary	1990	Parliament	176 SMD*, two rounds. 152 Regional PR (20 regions), 5% threshold. 58 "compensation" list. Closed list.
Hungary	1994	Parliament	176 SMD, two rounds. 152 Regional PR (20 regions), 5% threshold. 58 "compensation" list. Closed list.
Hungary	1998	Parliament	176 SMD, two rounds. 152 Regional PR (20 regions), 5% threshold. 58 "compensation" list. Closed list.
Poland	1990	President	2 Round Majoritarian.
Poland	1991	Parliament	69 National PR, 391 Regional PR (37 regions). No thresholds for regional lists, 5% threshold (or winning seats in 5 regions) for national list. Open list voting regional lists.
Poland	1993	Parliament	69 National PR, 391 Regional PR (52 regions), 5% threshold for regional lists (8% for coalitions), 7% threshold for national lists. Open list voting regional lists.
Poland	1995	President	2 Round Majoritarian.
Poland	1997	Parliament	69 National PR, 391 Regional PR (52 regions), 5% threshold for regional lists (8% for coalitions), 7% threshold for national lists. Open list voting regional lists.
Russia	1991	President	2 Round Majoritarian (Only 1 round conducted).
Russia	1993	Parliament	225 SMD, simple majority. 225 National PR (closed), 5% threshold.
Russia	1995	Parliament	225 SMD, simple majority. 225 National PR (closed), 5% threshold.

(*continued*)

Table 2.2 (*continued*)

Country	Year	Election	Electoral Rules
Russia	1996	President	2 Round Majoritarian.
Russia	1999	Parliament	225 SMD, simple majority. 225 National PR (closed), 5% threshold.
Slovakia	1992	Parliament	Regional PR (4 regions). Party list + 4 preferential votes for individual candidates. 5% Threshold (7% and 10% for coalitions).
Slovakia	1994	Parliament	Regional PR (4 regions). Party list + 4 preferential votes for individual candidates. 5% Threshold (7% and 10% for coalitions).
Slovakia	1998	Parliament	National PR. Party list + 4 preferential votes for individual candidates. 5% Threshold for all parties.
Slovakia	1999	President	2 Round Majoritarian.

* PR = Proportional Representation, SMD = Single Member District.
Source: International Parliamentary Union (Chronicle of Parliamentary Elections, Vol. 24–34); Central Election Commission of the Russian Federation; Polish Central Election Commission; Hungarian Ministry of Interior National Election Office; Czechoslovakia Federal Statistical Office; Czech Republic Statistical Office; Slovak Republic Statistical Office.

in established democracies, they do occur with some degree of frequency in transition countries, making this potentially an empirically testable proposition.

However, only two elections in the entire dataset – the 1991 Russian presidential election and the 1992 Slovak parliamentary election – meet the criteria for being considered serious regime future elections.[45] So with

[45] The 1991 Russian presidential election can be considered a regime future election because it featured a direct confrontation between communist and anticommunist/pro-democracy candidates with the future of both communist rule and the USSR at stake. Fish writes that the referendum establishing the directly elected presidency "amounted to a vote against the Communist Party system of domination" (Fish 2000, 179). The election itself featured "the unique personality associated with reform and opposition to the existing regime [Boris Yeltsin and]...Nikolay Ryzhkov, the former USSR prime minister, who...was widely viewed as a representative of the status quo" (Myagkov, Ordeshook, and Sobyanin 1997b, 139). The success of Yeltsin in this election undoubtedly "contributed to the breakup of the USSR itself" (White, Rose, and McAllister 1997, 39). Recall as well that this election took place before the coup attempt of August 1991, and it is conceivable that a defeat for Yeltsin could have drastically altered the pace of democratization; in fact, Colton argues that "without these elections, Yeltsin could not have stared

eighteen elections in one category and two elections in the other category, the dataset does not really present a suitable opportunity for testing this *regime future hypothesis*. For this reason, I omit the discussion of the limited evidence that can be brought to bear on the hypothesis in Chapters 5–7, but I will return to it briefly in Chapter 8 to assess the overall evidence from across the entire study.

down the reactionary putsch of August 1991" (Colton 1998b). The 1992 Slovak election is included as one of the paired case studies, and as such is discussed in great detail in the next chapter.

Two elections excluded from the category warrant further discussion. At first glance, the decision not to consider the 1990 Hungarian parliamentary election – the first Hungarian election of the postcommunist era – as a regime future election might appear strange, as first elections in democratic transitions normally are contested between pro- and antidemocratization forces. However, this election was not contested by an umbrella anticommunist movement, but, rather, by a number of competing pro-democracy parties, including the Hungarian Democratic Forum (MDF), the Alliance of Free Democrats (SzDSz), the Christian Democratic People's Party (KDNP), and the League of Young Democrats (FIDESZ) (Schopflin 1991; Körösényi 1993; Tokes 1996). The communist successor party had already also split into separate hard line (the Hungarian Socialist Workers Party [MSzMP]) and moderate (the Hungarian Socialist Party [MSzP]) parties. Moreover, the election followed a period of roundtable discussions that had already provided a blueprint for the shape of the postelection democratic institutions. And unlike the Polish roundtable negotiations of the previous year, the Hungarian roundtable negotiations provided for free elections (Osiatynski 1996; Sajo 1996; Tokes 1996; Benoit and Schiemann 2001). Overall, the election was far from a competition between pro- and antidemocracy forces; instead, it was a competition between different varieties of pro-democracy and postcommunist forces that had already assumed the form of competing political parties. Thus, the same characteristics that led me to include the 1990 Hungarian Parliamentary elections in the study in the first place (while excluding the 1989 Czech, Slovak, and Polish elections) reflect the fact that it more closely resembles a normal transition election than it does a regime future election. And although it is possible that a victory by the hardline MSzMP would have had a significant outcome on the future of the regime, it was well known before the election that this would not happened (see especially Benoit and Schiemann 2001), and the party ultimately received only 3.7 percent of the vote in the election.

Furthermore, if the 1992 Slovak parliamentary election is a Regime Future election, then the obvious next question is why the 1992 Czech election is not in this category. After all, the two elections took place simultaneously, and both countries ended up going their separate ways following the breakup of the Czechoslovakian federation. The answer is that although Slovak autonomy played a large role in the Slovak half of the elections (see Chapter 4 for details), the Czech election was not fought over the future of Slovakia's relation to the rest of the country. Instead, this was clearly an election where the future of economic reform and the path of the transition was at the forefront; if this included continued commitment to a strong federation, that was because such an arrangement was necessary for economic reform (see, for example, Obrman 1992a; Bugge 1994; Innes 1997; Leff 1997). As this election is also included in one of the paired case studies, I refer interested readers to the discussion of this election in Chapter 4 for more information.

Table 2.3. *Supply-Side-Based Conditional Hypotheses*

Predicted Support for Standard Hypotheses	Type of Variation	Coding	Applicability
Panel 1: Personality Hypothesis			
More	Closed List Proportional Representation in Parliamentary elections	1993, 1995, 1999 Russian and 1990, 1994, 1998 Hungary Parliamentary elections	
↓	Open List Proportional Representation in Parliamentary elections	1992, 1996, 1998 Czech, 1991, 1993, 1997 Polish and 1992, 1994, 1998 Slovak Parliamentary elections	New Regime, Old Regime, and Incumbency Hypotheses
	Single Member Districts in Parliamentary elections	* * *	
Less	Presidential Elections	1991 and 1995 Russian, 1990 and 1995 Polish and 1999 Slovak Presidential elections	
Panel 2: Regime Future Hypothesis			
More	Normal Transition elections	All elections other than those listed below	New Regime, Old Regime, and Incumbency Hypotheses
Less	Regime Future elections	1991 Russian Presidential and 1992 Slovak Parliamentary elections	

*** The Russian and Hungarian parliamentary elections both had single member district components of the election as part of mixed electoral systems but are excluded from this study because of the lack of commensurate economic data.

Thus, the supply-side approach produces two hypotheses, the personality hypothesis and the regime future hypothesis, although only the former can be seriously assessed with the data at hand. Both predict variation in support for all three standard hypotheses to be a function of election by election (as opposed to party by party) characteristics; Table 2.3 concisely summarizes the predictions of both hypotheses.

Economic Conditions and Election Results

Party Orientation Hypotheses In a previous section of this chapter, I defined Old Regime parties in terms of their relationship to the regime that ruled before the transition. I deliberately avoided any reference to whether or not these parties had attempted to reinvent themselves in a social-democratic framework or whether they had continued to identify themselves as communist, or even hard-line communist, parties. However, as will be discussed in Chapter 7, some Old Regime parties clearly did try to reestablish themselves as social democratic parties in more of a West European mold, whereas other Old Regime parties stayed much closer to their communist roots. In the literature, these parties are often called reformed and unreformed (or unrepentant), respectively. If we think that the decision of some Old Regime parties to attempt to reinvent themselves as more modern social democratic parties might somehow "taint" their Old Regime status, then an *Old Regime orientation hypothesis* would predict less support for the Old Regime hypothesis among these reformed Old Regime parties and, conversely, more consistent empirical support for the Old Regime hypothesis among unreformed Old Regime parties.[46] This type of prediction fits the typology of a conditional economic voting hypothesis, as it predicts the circumstances in which we would expect to find more support for a standard hypothesis. It is important to note, however, that similarly to the coalition hypothesis, the Old Regime orientation hypothesis only predicts variation in support for one particular standard economic voting hypothesis, which is the Old Regime hypothesis.

It is also possible to present a similar hypothesis for two types of New Regime parties. Here the most relevant contrast appears to be between New Regime parties that stayed closer to their original pro-reform and pro-democracy roots, and those that strayed from this path to embrace more populist rhetoric or policies. While the distinction between the two types of New Regime parties is clearly not as sharp (nor as commonly discussed in the literature) as it is for the two types of Old Regime parties, it is at least theoretically possible to come up with predictions for the type of variation we might expect to find in the degree of empirical support for

---

[46] These two categories are very common in the literature on communist successor parties, although different scholars use different terminology (e.g., pragmatic, social democratic, unrepentant, orthodox). It is also of course possible to come up with more nuanced categories- see, for example, the three by three table in Bozóki and Ishiyama (2002, 8) – but the dichotomous categorization is quite common and ensures enough examples of both cases to test the hypothesis.

Table 2.4. *Party Orientation Conditional Hypotheses*

Predicted Support for Standard Hypotheses	Type of Variation	Coding	Applicability
Panel 1: Old Regime Orientation Hypothesis			
More	Unreformed Old Regime Parties		
		See Table 7.A1	Old Regime Hypothesis
Less	Reformed Old Regime Parties		
Panel 2: New Regime Orientation Hypothesis			
More	Consistent Liberalizing New Regime Parties		
		See Table 6.7	New Regime Hypothesis
Less	Populist Leaning New Regime Parties		

the New Regime hypothesis across these two types. Specifically, the logic of the New Regime hypothesis that predicts support from economic winners and opposition from economic losers ought to apply more directly to those parties that continue to be closely associated with both the democratic and economic aspects of the transition, and might be mitigated a bit in the case of the parties that have moved in more populist directions. Thus, the *New Regime orientation hypothesis* predicts that there should be less empirical support for the New Regime hypothesis among more populist leaning New Regime parties than among New Regime parties that have stayed on a more consistently liberal path.

Table 2.4 concisely summarizes the prediction of both Party Orientation hypotheses. The specific rules employed to code these variants of New Regime and Old Regime parties are presented in Chapters 6 and 7, respectively; tables listing the parties coded in each category also can be found in those chapters.

Time-Based Hypotheses The next category of conditional hypotheses focuses on the passage of time as a predictor of where we ought to find more or less empirical support for the different standard economic voting hypotheses. It is distinguished from the previous categories in two important ways. First, two of the hypotheses yield the exact opposite prediction from one another, which was not the case with any of the other categories. Second, the entire approach is complicated by the fact that the means of distinguishing between categories is itself a fluid concept: how long should a "period" of time actually be? In the empirical tests that follow, I test the time-based hypotheses by breaking the twenty elections included in the study into three waves: those that took place between 1990 and 1992, 1993 and 1996, and 1997 and 1999. I use these periods because, with one exception, each country has at least one election in each wave, no country has more than a single presidential election in each wave, and four out of the five countries have one and only one parliamentary election in each wave.[47] Although this is certainly a defensible way in which to break up the time period between 1990 and 1999 to test support for time-based hypotheses, it may be that the true time frame for any (or some) of these hypotheses to find support is over decades or even lifetimes. Thus, the time-based hypotheses, while extremely interesting, must be introduced with the caveat that although it is possible to find evidence in support of these hypotheses, it is impossible to falsify them because the future may someday provide support over different types of time frames. For this reason, the strongest legitimate claim we can make is that within this particular time frame, there either is or is not empirical support for any of these hypotheses.

The first time-based conditional hypothesis is applicable to all three of the standard hypotheses. Based on the arguments regarding uncertainty presented earlier in this chapter, the ultimate expression of uncertainty might be that we should not expect to find any clear patterns of association between economic conditions and election results because voters are just too new to the democratic process to make any sense of it in the manner that voters in established democracies normally tend to do so. While the preceding statement is almost certainly overstated – and, indeed, functions as a sort of underlying null hypothesis for all three of the standard economic voting hypotheses tested in this book – we can derive a slightly milder conditional economic voting hypothesis from the argument by proposing that any reasonable standard hypothesis should generate more consistent empirical results as citizens become more familiar with democracy.

Another way to arrive at a similar hypothesis is to take the argument seriously that voters were primed by political leaders to expect economic

---

[47] The one exception is Russia, which has two parliamentary elections (1993 and 1995) in the second wave but none in the first wave.

failures in the first part of the decade as part of the costs of a transition to a market economy, and therefore politicians and parties were initially to have been given a free pass by voters in regard to the state of the economy.[48] If voters did indeed ignore the economy in the first round of elections, then we would expect to see a similar pattern to the one proposed in the preceding paragraph. Regardless of which scenario is at work, both provide justification for an *increasing support over time hypothesis*, whereby as the decade progresses and voters become more familiar with democratic participation or stop ignoring concerns with the state of the economy in making their vote choices, all three of the standard hypotheses should enjoy increasing empirical support. Perhaps one distinction between the two approaches is that the "free pass" scenario would predict practically no support for the standard hypotheses in the earliest elections, while the increasing familiarity with democracy scenario would just predict an increase in support over time without requiring an absence of support in the earliest time period, although this may be making too much out of a minor difference.[49]

---

[48] I want to thank Adam Przeworski for raising this point. Stokes (1996) takes this point even further, suggesting that in periods of economic reform voters might even reward incumbent parties for poor economic conditions (in particular, higher levels of unemployment) as a sign that reform is proceeding well. In particular, she cites a Czechoslovak finance minister (Vladimir Dlouhy) who stated that "Unless the unemployment rate grows to 8% to 10% this year, we will not be doing our job"(p. 505). Although I do not think that this hypothesis translates particularly well to the cross-regional level – it seems a bit of a stretch to assume that people in areas of the country that are particularly hard hit by the consequences of economic reform would be even more enthusiastic about the current government than people in areas of the country that are not as hard hit – there is also no evidence produced by this study to show that there was any empirical support for such a hypothesis at the cross-regional level. As an aside, it is interesting to note that the unemployment rate in the Czech Republic did not approach the 8 – 10% level in either 1992 (2.6%) or 1996 (3.9%), both years in which elections were held and the ruling party was returned to power, so apparently voters were not too bothered by the fact that unemployment had not increased as much as Dlouhy had hoped. It is also interesting to note that in the same *Financial Times* article where I found a version of Dlouhy's quote – the reporter cited him as saying that "it would be a sign that the reforms were not working" – the reporter also noted that Vaclav Klaus, who would go on to serve as the Czech Republic's Prime Minister for much of the 1990s, predicted much lower unemployment rates (4 – 6%) than Dlouhy (Colitt 1991; Przeworski 1992 also cites this article in note 1).

[49] The "free pass" scenario has a clearer link to the Incumbency hypothesis, as it is incumbents who are supposedly not being blamed for the state of the economy. But the logic holds for the New Regime and Old Regime hypotheses as well, albeit in a weaker form. If the earliest elections were held in a special environment in which economic conditions were somehow not as much of a factor as they would be later in the decade, then it should still hold that we would find less empirical support for the New Regime and Old Regime hypotheses in these periods as well.

Table 2.5. *Time-Based Conditional Hypotheses*

Predicted Support for Standard Hypotheses	Type of Variation	Coding	Applicability
Panel 1: Increasing Support over Time Hypothesis			
More	Late Elections	Elections in 1997–1999	New Regime, Old Regime, and Incumbency Hypotheses
↓	↓	Elections in 1993–1996	
Less	Early Elections	Elections in 1990–1992	
Panel 2: Decreasing Support over Time Hypothesis			
More	Early Elections	Elections in 1990–1992	New Regime, Old Regime, and Incumbency Hypotheses
↓	↓	Elections in 1993–1996	
Less	Late Elections	Elections in 1997–1999	
Panel 3: Time and Party Orientation Hypothesis			
More	Early Elections	Elections in 1990–1992	Old Regime-Reformed and New Regime – Populist parties
↓	↓	Elections in 1993–1996	
Less	Late Elections	Elections in 1997–1999	

However, it is also possible to arrive at a plausible theoretical story that predicts exactly the opposite effect for the passage of time. The arguments presented earlier in this chapter to justify both the Referendum and the Transitional Identity Models were predicated on taking uncertainty over the relationship between electing parties to office and resulting government policy seriously. Therefore, it holds that if the uncertainty used to motivate the standard economic voting hypotheses diminished significantly during the 1990s, there could be less empirical support for models that are explicitly designed to reflect the inherent uncertainty of the transitional context. So perhaps these models would be very useful for first- and second-wave elections, but much less useful by the time we arrive at the third wave of elections. In this case, a *decreasing support over time hypothesis* would predict diminished support for all three transition-based standard economic voting hypotheses as the decade progressed.

A more nuanced test of this proposition can be conducted by combining the idea that the passage of time might lead to more information about the distinctions between the different types of New Regime and Old Regime parties presented in the previous section. Consider first Old Regime parties. Perhaps early in the decade – when we would expect uncertainty to be higher – the distinction between reformed and unrepentant Old Regime parties might not be as apparent to voters as later in the decade, when they might have enough information to realize that the reformed Old Regime parties really had changed. Therefore, we could hypothesize that there should be the same level of support for the Old Regime hypothesis throughout the decade among unreformed Old Regime parties, but diminishing support for the Old Regime hypothesis as the decade progressed among reformed Old Regime parties. By a similar logic, there could be consistent support during the decade for the New Regime hypothesis among the liberal New Regime parties, but diminishing support for the New Regime hypothesis among the more populist New Regime parties as the decade progressed.

With the caveat that it is impossible to know *a priori* the appropriate time frame for testing these hypotheses, Table 2.5 concisely presents the different time-based hypotheses as they are tested in this book.

Interactive Hypotheses A final source for conditional economic voting hypotheses is to use each of the standard economic voting models as conditional hypotheses for explaining variation in the other. To do so, I take advantage of the fact that the two models make predictions for different classifications of parties that overlap in some, but crucially not all, cases. For example, for New Regime parties that are also incumbents, the Referendum and Transitional Identity models make the same predictions; both models predict that these parties should benefit where economic conditions are better. By contrast, the two models generate opposite predictions for Old Regime parties that are also incumbents; here, the Old Regime hypothesis predicts that the party should do better where economic conditions are worse, whereas the Incumbency hypothesis predicts that the party should do better where economic conditions are better.

We can therefore use the Referendum Model as a conditional hypothesis to predict where we ought to find more empirical support for the two standard hypotheses of the Transitional Identity Model. The interactive

Economic Conditions and Election Results

Table 2.6. *Interactive Conditional Hypotheses*

Predicted Support for Standard Hypotheses	Type of Variation	Coding	Applicability
Panel 1: Interactive Old Regime Hypothesis			
More	Opposition – Old Regime Parties		
		See Chapters 5 and 7	Old Regime Hypothesis
Less	Incumbent – Old Regime Parties		
Panel 2: Interactive New Regime Hypothesis			
More	Incumbent – New Regime Parties		
		See Chapters 5 and 6	New Regime Hypothesis
Less	Opposition – New Regime Parties		
Panel 3: Interactive Incumbency Hypothesis			
More	New Regime – Incumbent Parties		
↓	Other – Incumbent Parties	See Chapters 5, 6, and 7	Incumbent Hypothesis
Less	Old Regime – Incumbent Parties		

conditional hypothesis generated in this manner predicts that there should be more support for the New Regime hypothesis among New Regime incumbent parties than New Regime opposition parties, and, conversely, more support for the Old Regime hypothesis among Old Regime opposition parties than Old Regime incumbents.

Similarly, we can use the Transitional Identity Model as a conditional hypothesis to predict variation in support for the Incumbency hypothesis. To do so, I break down incumbents into three categories: New Regime-incumbent parties, Old Regime-incumbent parties, and other (defined as neither New Regime nor Old Regime) incumbent parties. We should then expect to find the most support for the Incumbency hypothesis among New Regime-incumbent parties (as the New Regime hypothesis predicts the same effect as the Incumbency hypothesis), the least support among

Old Regime-incumbent parties (as the Old Regime hypothesis predicts the opposite effect from the Incumbency hypothesis), and something in between these two extremes for the other-incumbent parties. Table 2.6 concisely presents the different interactive hypotheses as they are tested in this book.[50]

Conclusion

In this chapter, I have presented two standard economic voting models that predict the effect of cross-regional variation in election results on the distribution of votes for parties in post-communist countries. The Referendum Model produces the Incumbency hypothesis, which predicts that incumbent parties should perform better in areas of the country where economic conditions are stronger. The Transitional Identity Model produces two hypotheses: the New Regime hypothesis, which predicts that parties closely associated with the transition away from communism ought to perform better in areas of the country where economic conditions are better; and the Old Regime hypothesis, which predicts that parties closely associated with the prior ruling communist parties ought to perform better in areas of the country where economic conditions are worse.

I have supplemented these standard hypotheses with a number of conditional economic voting hypotheses that predict the circumstances in which we ought to find more empirical support for the standard hypotheses, or, more generally, the conditions in which economic conditions are more likely to have an impact on election results in the manner predicted by the standard hypotheses. Although there are too many of these conditional hypotheses to recount individually, most are based on one of five general approaches that reflect either anticipated responsibility for government policy, the importance of other noneconomic factors, distinctions between different New Regime and Old Regime parties, the passage of time, or the interaction of the two standard models. The remaining conditional

---

[50] One final word about the interactive hypotheses is in order. While all of the other conditional hypotheses presented in this chapter are assessed in terms of the variation they can explain for each appropriate standard economic voting hypothesis in Chapters 5, 6, and 7 before being assessed comparatively in Chapter 8, all empirical assessments of the degree of support for the interactive conditional hypotheses are held off until Chapter 8. I am presenting the results in this fashion because the interactive hypotheses by definition involve the simultaneous consideration of multiple standard hypotheses, which is a task left to Chapter 8.

hypotheses explore whether there is any basis for "intuitively" important distinctions, including parliamentary versus presidential elections and elections in East-Central Europe versus elections in Russia.

The goal for the remainder of this book is to test these hypotheses with empirical data from the twenty different elections included in the study. To do so, however, requires a method of comparative analysis, and it is to this task that I turn in the following chapter.

3

Comparative Cross-Regional Analysis

The purpose of this chapter is twofold. In the first half of the chapter, I introduce the method of analysis that I use to assess the empirical support for the models and hypotheses presented in the previous chapter. Although no specific component of the analysis represents a new analytic technique or statistical tool, the manner in which they are combined here – and applied to the substantive questions at hand – is novel, and thus warrants a systematic explication of the method. In this vein, the second half of the chapter considers in greater detail the advantages and disadvantages of the method of analysis.

The aims of the method are fourfold. First, it is intended to facilitate a comparative analysis of the effect of economic conditions on election results across multiple cases; in other words, it is explicitly designed for comparative study. Second, the method of comparison is intended to be as transparent and easily replicable as possible; faced with the same data and statistical results, others should be able to come to similar conclusions about the relative empirical support for different hypotheses, or at the very least understand exactly why I have drawn the conclusions that I did. Third, the method is explicitly designed to treat seriously issues of comparability of data, an especially important issue in new democracies. Finally, the method is intended to link the empirical tests of the data – and the conclusions drawn on the basis of these tests – as closely as possible to the actual hypotheses proposed in the previous chapter.

The method of comparison involves the following components. Separate data sets of regional level data are utilized to conduct statistical analyses of the effect of cross-regional variation in economic conditions on cross-regional variation in election results for each of the twenty elections in the dataset. Using these separate datasets, separate estimates for the effect of economic conditions on every party in which we have a theoretical interest – in other words all incumbent, New Regime, and Old Regime parties – are calculated. These effects are estimated using a compositional data model that is appropriate for working with multiparty election data. In all cases, the effects are calculated while controlling for a constant set of demographic variables in an effort to control for the other dominant explanation for cross-regional support for political parties, which is the existence of social cleavages. In order to compare the effect of the economy across the different elections, I focus not on individual coefficients and standard errors but, rather, on our overall level of confidence that the party in question either enjoyed more or less (depending on the hypothesis) electoral support in areas of the country where the economy was performing better. To measure this overall level of confidence by party, I use stochastic simulation to estimate a probability distribution of the substantive effect of a commensurate economic shock on each party in the study, and then calculate our confidence level that the effect of this shock on the vote for each party is in fact in the direction predicted by the relevant standard economic voting hypothesis. Support for the different hypotheses is then measured in two ways, first through an inspection of election by election results from the four sets of case studies and then in a more broadly comparative framework that looks at the results across all twenty elections simultaneously. Finally, a series of robustness tests (presented in Chapter 8) are also conducted that involve changing the specifications of the original statistical analyses, recalculating all of the measures of the effects of economic conditions on each party, and then assessing the comparative results in the same manner as in the original analysis.

In the following section, I present the method of analysis, detailing the variables included in the regressions, the statistical model used to analyze the data, the process by which I calculate my quantity of interest, and the manner in which I compare this quantity of interest across different parties and elections. In order to more fully illustrate the method of analysis, I use the 1996 Czech Republic election as a heuristic example. I chose this election because of the variety and clarity of results, as well as the fact that it is not included as one of the paired case studies. The election was the first in the Czech Republic following the dissolution of Czechoslovakia and resulted in the incumbent government of the Civic Democratic Party (ODS), the Civic Democratic Alliance (ODA), and the Christian Democratic Union (KDU) being returned to power with a higher proportion of votes than in the previous election but with a lower share of seats. While

Table 3.1. *1996 Czech Republic Parliamentary Election*

Party	Percentage of Party List Vote	Total Seats
Civic Democratic Party (ODS)	29.62	68
Czechoslovak Social Democratic Party (CSSD)	26.44	61
Communist Party of Bohemia and Moravia (KSČM)	10.33	22
Christian Democratic Union (KDU)	8.08	18
Republican Party (SR)	8.01	18
Civic Democratic Alliance (ODA)	6.36	13
Others	11.16	0
Total	**100**	**200**

Source: Czech Statistical Office: Volby do Poslanecke Snemovny Parlamentu Ceske Republikyv Roce 1996

the government had enjoyed a majority in the parliament from 1992 to 1996, it received only 99 out of 200 seats following the 1996 election.[1] As individual party coding decisions are not presented until the following chapters, please note that two of the incumbent parties that competed in the election, the ODS and the ODA, are also coded as New Regime parties. The KDU is the only other incumbent party, and is neither an Old Regime nor a New Regime party. The election also featured one Old Regime party, the Communist Party of Bohemia and Moravia (KSČM). The results of this election can be found in Table 3.1.

Method of Empirical Analysis

The goal of the empirical analysis is to as closely as possible test the standard economic voting hypotheses presented in the preceding chapter in an effort to explore the relative empirical support for the Referendum and Transitional Identity Models.[2] All three of the hypotheses generated from these models present predictions about the effects of variation in economic conditions on variation in election results. To assess these hypotheses accurately, therefore, we want to measure the effect of economic conditions while controlling for other potential explanations for distributions of votes at the regional level. It is important to note, however, that the

---

[1] For more on this election, see Fitzmaurice 1996; Fule 1997; Turnovec 1997; and Mateju and Vlachova 1998.

[2] As described in the previous chapter, the conditional hypotheses are assessed by looking for variation in the degree of empirical support for the standard hypotheses.

point of this study is *not* to attempt to assess the relative importance of economic conditions as opposed to other factors, but merely to control for these factors while measuring the empirical support for the economy-based hypotheses.

Two sets of factors appear paramount in this regard. The first are contemporary political developments that might affect the degree of support for different types of political parties, especially those currently in power. These could include, for example, foreign policy decisions, political scandals, or international developments. In time-series analyses of economic voting, such concerns have led scholars to include dummy variables for periods of war or, in the American case, the effect of Watergate.[3] Here, however, I draw on one of the first advantages of the comparative cross-regional approach, which is that by only including election results from one country at one point in time in any given regression analysis, I am able to control for all election-specific effects (and country-specific effects for that matter) in the statistical analysis. Thus, if the election is taking place in the immediate aftermath of the collapse of a communist region, that factor is constant across all of the regions in a country at the time of the election. The same holds for the distraction of a military conflict (e.g., Chechnya in Russia) or the presence of a political scandal (e.g., the Czech Republic in 1998).[4]

The second important explanation for variation in patterns of support for political parties is societal cleavages. There is, of course, a large literature on the topic from studies of Western European countries that points to the importance of labor patterns, rural-urban splits, center-periphery divides, and ethnic cleavages.[5] In addition, studies of voting behavior in postcommunist countries also have identified politically relevant socioeconomic cleavages, in particular highlighting the propensity of older voters

---

[3] See, for example, Chappell and Keech 1985; for a critique of this approach, see Fiorina 1981, Chapter 6.

[4] It is important to emphasize again that this study does not in any way argue that political factors cannot influence election results; to do so would clearly be problematic. But as the goal of my analysis is to produce as accurate an estimate of the effect of economic conditions as possible, limiting the pooling of data to a single election is valuable insofar as it allows us to estimate effects for economic conditions while controlling for national political developments. At the same time, the comparative framework of the study then allows us to assess politically based hypotheses like the supply-side conditional hypotheses by comparing the empirical support for the different standard hypotheses in different political contexts.

[5] See, for example, Lipset and Rokkan 1967 and the voluminous work that followed it.

to support Old Regime parties and urban voters to support New Regime parties.[6]

As opposed to national political developments, there is clearly variation in the presence of different demographic groups in different regions. Thus to control for the effects of societal cleavages on the distribution of vote shares, I include a constant set of control variables in all of the analyses, which, somewhat remarkably, were available at the regional level in all five countries for almost the entire period of the study.[7] These variables are the percentage of the workforce employed in agriculture, the percentage of the work force employed in industry, the percentage of the population living in urban areas, the percentage of elderly residents, and finally a control for the size of the region itself.[8] While these variables may not capture every possible societal cleavage, they do tap into most of the cleavages described in the preceding paragraph.[9] Again, I want to emphasize that this is not in

---

[6] For a summary of the role of cleavages in the voting literature in postcommunist countries, see Tucker 2002, 292. For specific examples, see Kopstein 1992; Clem and Craumer 1995c; Wyman, White et al. 1995; Clem and Craumer 1997; Szelenyi, Fodor, and Hanley 1997; Moser 1999 and especially Tworzecki 2003 and Colton 2000b. For a thorough review of the work on cleavages and postcommunist politics, see Whitefield 2002.

[7] In a small number of instances, it was necessary to use demographic data from a different year, although in almost all cases the data were off by no more than a year or two. However, as would be expected, all of the demographic variables are highly correlated across years because of the slow rate at which the demographic composition of a region changes. See Appendix II for the actual dates for all variables.

[8] The actual coding of each of these variables for each election can be found in Appendix II. Following convention, regional population is logged to take account of the sharp disparity between the size of capital cities (and occasionally other large cities) and other regions. In addition, the percentage of ethnic Hungarians is also included as a control variable in the Slovak analyses, as this is the only country in the study where an ethnically based party received a significant proportion of the national vote, with the main Hungarian party entering the parliament in all three elections. And in an early version of the analysis, robustness tests revealed different results when including the Hungarian party as a separate party in the analysis or in the base "other" category for analysis (see discussion later in this chapter of this robustness test); this disparity disappeared when the percentage of ethnic Hungarians was included in the analysis as a control variable. In two of the other countries – the Czech Republic and Hungary – I also tested whether including the percentage of ethnic minorities as a control variable had any effect on the assessment of the impact of economic conditions. In both cases, I found no meaningful effects.

[9] Moreover, as will be described in greater detail below, this method also allows me to measure the effect of economic conditions on election results directly, as opposed to imputing economic conditions on the basis of beliefs about economic disparities across demographic groups. For example, it is easy to claim that rural residents have been more disadvantaged by the transition than urban residents, and that therefore a link between the percentage of rural residents in a region and support for a political party is evidence that this party

any way meant to deny that there are demographic patterns to the vote for parties in my cases – and, indeed, a quick glance at the regression results will confirm this fact – but rather that the effects of economic conditions that I identify are not merely functioning as proxies for underlying demographic distinctions between regions.[10]

Economic Variables

In contrast to the demographic variables, different countries reported different economic variables at the regional level; moreover, there was also variation over time within countries as to what variables were reported at the regional level.[11] This situation presents two options for analysis. One option is to exclude all statistics that are not available for all twenty elections from all of the analyses, which would involve ignoring a great deal of information. The other option is to include the best available measure of economic conditions in each case – which necessitates comparing results from regressions with different sets of independent variable – and

---

enjoys more support where economic conditions are worse. While I do not doubt that in many cases economic conditions are worse in rural areas than urban areas, such a claim relies on an assumption about the economic implications of demographic characteristics of a region. In contrast, the analysis I employ relies only on measures of economic conditions to judge the impact of the economy and relegates demographic variables to control variables, thus allowing us to directly measure the impact of economic conditions and skipping the intermediary step of imputing economic attributes to demographic characteristics.

[10] One limitation of relying on aggregate-level sociodemographic measures is that they do not directly tap into possible cultural cleavages between voters on issues such as clericalism versus anticlericalism (see, in particular, Tworzecki (2003) in this regard). However, if such cleavages do not vary regionally, they will not introduce bias into the study of the effects of economic conditions. And as this study is not focused on testing the relative importance of economic versus cultural explanations for voting behavior, this should not prove to be much of a limitation. Moreover, to the extent that cultural cleavages may vary regionally, the complete collection of demographic control variables – and in particular the measures for the percentage of urban citizens, elderly citizens, and workers employed in agriculture – should function as a reasonable proxy for these types of differences. Finally, the fact that the study encompasses multiple countries also provides a bulwark against these types of concerns.

[11] Although it is possible that I may have missed some variables, I collected the data for this project in a series of trips to the national statistical offices of all five countries included in the study. In addition to searching publications available for sale and materials in the libraries of the statistical offices, I also met with officials of the statistical offices and statistical office librarians. While I cannot exclude the possibility that additional information may still be available, the effort extended to track down these data was constant across all of the countries and all of the elections.

to utilize a standardized method of comparison across the different set of results.

My response to this dilemma was to choose the latter option but to be extremely systematic in the manner in which I did so. Rather than eschew the use of available data, I included all available economic indicators in each individual statistical analysis. However, the decision of which economic indicators to include was guided by a fixed set of *a priori* rules – presented later – that were not in any way affected by the results of any analyses. So I did not in any circumstances drop economic variables because they did not seem to have a statistically significant effect on the outcome.[12] Finally, as a robustness test, I reran every analysis using only the three independent variables – unemployment, growth, and change in income – that were available for almost all of the cases. The results of this robustness test are presented in Chapter 8, but they clearly lead to the same overall conclusion regarding the relative strength of the Referendum and Transitional Identity Models as the original analyses. So although the analyses presented in Chapters 5–7 will be based on the use of the best available economic indicators, readers uncomfortable with this approach can rest assured that the conclusions reached by the study would be very similar had I relied only on the three variables noted here. Moreover, I employ a method of comparison across cases that focuses on a standardized measure of our overall confidence that the economy is helping or hurting particular parties – as will be explained shortly – and is therefore not dependent on a direct comparison of any particular coefficient from one regression with another.

My motivation for this solution came from the nature of the hypotheses presented in the preceding chapter. Were the hypotheses seeking to test the effect of particular economic conditions with one another – for example, to compare the effect of unemployment with the effect of growth – then it would be have been crucial to make sure that the analyses contained the same economic variables. However, the hypotheses simply predict that certain parties should enjoy more economic success when economic conditions are either better or worse. Therefore, the most prudent course seemed to be to make the best available estimate in each case of where economic conditions were better and where economic conditions were worse by taking advantage of the available data. This was especially so in the case of wage arrears, which were a major economic concern in Russia but were virtually

---

[12] For an example of this approach, see Wade, Groth, and Lavelle (1994).

nonexistent – and certainly were not reported regionally – in the Central-European cases.[13]

Turning to the question of which economic variables to include in the analysis, the existing literature on economic voting in established democracies clearly points to four important economic indicators: unemployment,[14] change in income,[15] growth,[16] and inflation.[17] In an ideal world,

[13] Again, the method of comparative cross-regional analysis is important in this regard. By limiting the individual statistical analyses to data from only one election, one can in fact include all available data without introducing problems of missing data to the analysis; in almost all cases, data reported in country X at time T were reported for all regions. Moreover, for a dataset of this size, there are remarkably few instances of missing data. In the majority of the twenty elections there are no missing observations, and in only one election – the 1991 Polish parliamentary election – are there more than two missing observations. In this one case, I am missing data on the vote for the Agarian Alliance (PL) in 1991 in five regions. To address this point I ran every model twice, once including the PL and excluding the missing regions, and once excluding the PL and including the missing regions. The results presented in the text for the PL are taken from the former set of analyses, while the results for the remaining parties contesting the elections are taken from the latter. There are two elections in which a single observation is excluded because of missing data in the dependent variable: Poland in 1991 and Hungary in 1990. In the 1999 Slovak presidential election analysis, there are two missing observations of one of the independent variables (change in growth), so the analysis is run using seventy instead of seventy-two observations. Finally, the number of observations in the analyses of the Russian elections varies from seventy-five to seventy-seven due to the availability of data from the breakaway republic of Chechnya and neighboring Ingushetia. It also should be noted that the Czech Republic added a region (Jesenik) following the dissolution of Czechoslovakia, so the regressions using the 1992 data have one fewer observation than the regressions using the 1996 or 1998 data.

[14] From studies of American elections, see Kramer 1971; Kinder and Kiewiet 1981; MacKuen, Erikson, and Stimson 1992; Goidel and Langley 1994; from OECD countries, see Whiteley 1980; Lewis-Beck and Bellucci 1982; Bellucci 1984; Powell and Whitten 1993; Feld and Kirchgassner 2000; and, for a cross-national study extending beyond the OECD, see Wilkin, Haller, and Norpoth 1997. Unemployment also has figured prominently in other cross-regional studies of postcommunist countries; see Pacek 1994; Wade, Groth, and Lavelle 1994; Gibson and Cielecka 1995; Bell 1997; and Fidrmuc 2000c.

[15] Change in income has been especially prominent in U.S.-based studies; see, for example, Tufte 1975; Kramer 1983; Markus 1988; and Erikson 1989, 1990. Other studies have relied on actual income levels as opposed to change in income; see, for example, Lewis-Beck and Bellucci 1982; Bellucci 1984 in the OECD context and Wade, Groth, and Lavelle 1994; Bell 1997; and Fidrmuc 2000c in the postcommunist context.

[16] From studies of American elections, see Chappell and Keech 1985; Kiewiet and Rivers 1985; Alesina and Rosenthal 1995; from OECD countries, see Powell and Whitten 1993; Whitten and Palmer 1999; from comparative studies of Latin American countries, see Remmer 1991; Roberts and Wibbels 1999.

[17] From studies of American elections, see Kramer 1971; Kinder and Kiewiet 1981; Chappell and Keech 1985; MacKuen, Erikson, and Stimson 1992; from OECD countries, see Whiteley 1980; Lewis-Beck and Bellucci 1982; Bellucci 1984; Powell and Whitten 1993;

therefore, we would include all four of these variables in any economic voting analysis. Inflation, however, does not lend itself to a cross-regional study, as the most substantial variation in inflation is usually across countries or over time within a single country as opposed to cross-regionally within a single country in a single time period, largely because of the importance of central bank policy in dictating national inflation levels. Moreover, it is very difficult to find inflation figures disaggregated to the regional level; indeed, I could only locate such data for four of the twenty elections included in the study. For these reasons, I use change in wages, growth, and unemployment as the three base economic variables in every regression analysis.[18]

Of the three, unemployment rates are relatively self-explanatory. The higher the unemployment rate, the more likely there are to be more people who are upset about the state of the economy for the many reasons discussed in the previous chapter.[19]

Change in income is calculated as the change in average salaries in the region since the previous year.[20] Note that this is not intended to function as a traditional retrospective measure whereby citizens are judging the competence of the government by whether or not they have a larger salary than when the government came to power; this would require measuring the change in salary since the previous election. Instead, it is intended to function as a measure of where the economy is performing better, on the basis of the assumption that all things being equal, people in areas of the

Chappell and Veiga 2000; and Feld and Kirchgassner 2000; from Latin America, see Remmer 1991; Roberts and Wibbels 1999.

[18] The one exception is the 1991 Russian presidential election, for which I was unable to locate any unemployment data.

[19] As discussed in the previous chapter, the "free pass" scenario could predict a different effect for unemployment early in the decade, although see the discussion of this implication at the regional level in note 48 in Chapter 2.

[20] I did not convert these figures to real income because of the lack of inflation figures disaggregated to the regional level. However, if we assume that inflation is relatively constant across the country because of the leading role of a centralized institution (the central bank) in dictating inflation levels, then changes in average income should be a relatively good proxy for changes in real income as well, as the period of the change is constant across all observations. It is worth noting that this would not be the case if data were pooled from more than one election. Moreover, although it is clear that, for example, a 100% increase in wages means radically different things in a low inflation and high inflation context, the fact that the analysis only involves pooling data from one country at one point in time means that the only assumption at work here is that people in the part of the country where salaries have risen by 100% are likely to be happier than those in areas where salaries have fallen by 50% in any overall inflation context.

country where average wages are rising are likely to be more satisfied with the state of the economy than those living in areas of the country where average wages are falling. One also could argue that average salaries growing at a faster rate might also signify the presence of new job opportunities at higher paying salaries, which would complement the original claim that people ought to be more satisfied with the state of the economy in areas of the country where salaries are rising at a higher rate.[21]

In some ways, economic growth represents the quintessential measure for establishing areas of the country where the economy is performing better and areas where it is performing worse. And for this reason, I have included a measure of growth in all the regression analyses. The ideal measure to use for regional growth is clearly change in regional GDP. Unfortunately, the situation is complicated by the fact that it proved very difficult to find measures of GDP disaggregated to the regional level in these countries, especially earlier in the decade.[22] As it turned out, I could only calculate figures for GDP growth for six of the twenty elections. For the remaining elections, I use change in industrial output as my measure of growth. While problematic, it is the best available proxy I could find, and the alternative was to have no measure of growth in a majority of the elections.[23]

In addition to these three standard variables, I also include measures of three other economic indicators when available that are more transition specific, two of which focus on positive benefits of the transition and one of which focuses on a negative consequence. The negative variable, mentioned earlier, is wage arrears, or the nonpayment of wages, which was a significant problem throughout the 1990s in Russia; these data are only included in the analyses of Russian elections. The two "positive" indicators are foreign direct investment and foreign trade, both of which were expected to be positive benefits of transitioning from a centrally planned to a market economy. The assumption here is that the economic contact with international

---

[21] One might object that in a transitional context, a rise in average salaries could also result from the closing of unprofitable enterprises and the firing of large numbers of lower income workers. Fortunately, the multivariate nature of the analysis ensures that the effect of change in income is estimated while controlling for unemployment rates.

[22] In fact, my attempts to secure such data led to one instance where an official of a statistical office actually laughed at me for suggesting that such data might be available.

[23] And keeping within the guideline of using the best available data, I always use change in GDP growth when it is available, and I always revert to change in industrial output when it is not; in no case where GDP growth was available was industrial output used instead.

actors, both in the form of trade and especially direct investment, would be additional indicators of better economic conditions. And in the few instances in which regional measures of inflation are available, they are included in the analyses as well.

Table 3.2 lists the variables included in each regression. The exact coding of each variable included in each regression can be found in Appendix II.[24]

Thus, to estimate the effect of economic conditions on election results for incumbents, New Regime, and Old Regime parties, I run a separate regression for each of these parties in each election in which the unit of analysis is the subnational region, the dependent variable is the share of the vote received by the party in question, the independent variables are regional measures of macroeconomic conditions, and regional demographic variables function as control variables, thus resulting in a separate set of regression results for each party in each election.[25] Regarding the unit of analysis, one would ideally disaggregate our data to the smallest possible observation, such as individual election districts. However, I was limited in this regard by the availability of commensurate economic data. Therefore, I use as my unit of analysis the smallest region for which I could obtain both electoral and economic data. Thus, the units of analysis in this study are the seventy-seven Russian oblasts, krai, and republics,[26] the seventy-six

---

[24] The decision of which dates to use for the variables also was guided by a constant set of *a priori* rules. For demographic variables, I used the date at which the data were available that was closest to the election. I followed the same rule for unemployment, which was often available at quarterly or even monthly intervals, and wage arrears, which was available monthly. For change in income and growth, I used the year of the election as the later year and the prior year's figure as the reference point; when data was available quarterly, I used the quarter closest to the election and the data from the same quarter of the previous year as the reference point. For inflation, foreign direct investment, and foreign trade, I used the data from the year of the election, on the assumption that this would do a better job measuring economic conditions at the time of the election than data from the previous year. One transition specific variable that was unfortunately not included in the study is private sector job creation, which Jackson, Klich, and Poznańska (2003a, 2003b, 2005) have now found to be an important determinant of electoral success for Polish reformist parties in cross-regional analyses of the 1993, 1995, and 1997 Polish elections. As there as is a good deal of overlap between their classification of reformist parties and my New Regime party category, my best guess is that including job creation data in the analyses would therefore have only strengthened support for the New Regime hypothesis, especially in Poland.

[25] So, for example, because the ODS competed in three separate elections, there is a separate result for the ODS in the 1992, 1996, and 1998 Czech elections.

[26] The Russian federation has three different types of subnational units, oblasts, krai, and republics, all of which are mutually exclusive. Moscow and St. Petersburg are also their own regions. Autonomous oblasts and autonomous krais – subsubnational units contained within some of these regions – are omitted from the analysis.

Table 3.2. *Independent Variables by Election*

Country	Year	% Unemp.	Δ Income	GDP Growth	Industrial Growth	FDI	Foreign Trade	Wage Arrears	Inflation
Czech Rep	1992	X	X		X				X
Czech Rep	1996	X	X		X				
Czech Rep	1998	X	X		X	X			
Hungary	1990	X	X		X	X			
Hungary	1994	X	X		X	X			
Hungary	1998	X	X	X		X			
Poland	1990	X	X		X				
Poland	1991	X	X		X				
Poland	1993	X	X		X	X			
Poland	1995	X	X		X	X	X		
Poland	1997	X	X	X		X	X		
Russia	1991		X		X		X		
Russia	1993	X	X		X		X	X	
Russia	1995	X	X	X				X	
Russia	1996	X	X	X				X	X
Russia	1999	X	X	X			X	X	X
Slovakia	1992	X	X		X				
Slovakia	1994	X	X	X		X			
Slovakia	1998	X	X		X	X			X
Slovakia	1999	X	X		X	X			X

FDI = Foreign Direct Investment; GDP = Gross Domestic Product

Czech okresy, the thirty-eight (1992–1994) and seventy-two (1998–1999) Slovak okresy,[27] the forty-nine Polish województwa,[28] and the twenty Hungarian megye. Finally, for reasons detailed in Chapter 5, only parties receiving greater than 2% of the overall vote are included in the analyses.[29]

The Statistical Model

Many previous aggregate level analyses of election results have relied on some form of standard least squares (LS) regression analysis.[30] There are many reasons why LS regression analysis has long been used to analyze election results, including the fact that electoral data are continuous and there is often no reason to expect a nonlinear relationship between any of the variables. However, there are methodological problems associated with using LS regression analysis in models that attempt to explain vote outcomes.

To assess these problems, consider first the nature of electoral data. If we think of each party's share of the vote as a proportion of the total vote, then there are two important characteristics of voting data. First, each party's share of the vote must be between 0 and 1. Second, the share of the vote earned by all parties must sum to 1. Stated more formally, the proportion of the Vote (V) for each party j ($j = 1, \ldots, J$) in district i ($i = 1, \ldots, I$) must meet the following criteria:[31]

$$V_{ij} \in [0, 1] \quad \text{for all } i \text{ and } j \tag{3.1}$$

$$\sum_{j=1}^{J} V_{ij} = 1 \quad \text{for all } i \tag{3.2}$$

[27] Slovakia changed its administrative regions in 1996; for information, see Krause 2000, 37.

[28] For the 1991 Polish parliamentary election, I rely on a breakdown of the vote by województwo provided in Gebethner (1995). For the 1993 and 1997 parliamentary elections, the national election commission reported the results for fifty-two electoral districts, forty-seven of which overlapped exactly with their corresponding województwo. Of the remaining five, three electoral districts were found in Katowice wojewodstwo (Sosnowiec, Katowice, and Gliwice) and two in Warsaw (m. st. Warszawa and warszaskie z wylacyeniem m. st. Warszawy). The votes from these districts were summed by the author to come up with vote totals for the entire województwo in both cases.

[29] The one exception to this rule, the Association of Slovak Workers (ZRS) in the 1998 Slovak parliamentary election, is also explained in Chapter 5. Parties receiving less than 2% of the vote are, however, included in the "other" category; see below for more information.

[30] See, for example, Tufte 1978; Lewis-Beck and Bellucci 1982; Paldam 1991; Powell and Whitten 1993.

[31] I adopt the notation of Katz and King (1999).

LS regression models, which generate continuous, unbounded predictions, do not guarantee that either of these conditions will be met. Predicted vote proportions for individual parties can be below 0 and above 1, and predictions for all parties are not constrained to sum to 1.[32]

For this reason, I use a statistical model to conduct the regression analyses in this study that is more appropriate for multiparty electoral data than LS analysis.[33] A full explication of this model can be found in Tomz, Tucker, and Wittenberg (2002), but the basic distinction from LS analysis is that the dependent variable is modeled as the log of the ratio of the vote for the party in question relative to a base category (the vote for one or more of the other parties) and that all of the equations for any given election are estimated simultaneously using a *seemingly unrelated regression* (SUR) model. As a result, all predicted vote proportions are bounded between 0 and 1, and the sum of all predicted vote proportions must equal 1; estimating the equations simultaneously using the SUR also allows the analysis to take advantage of the likely covariance across equations from the same election.[34] More technically:

- $V_i = (V_{i1}, \ldots, V_{i(J-1)})$ is a vector of vote proportions of party $j = (1, \ldots, J - 1)$ for each district i $(i = 1, \ldots n)$

[32] See Brandt, Monroe, and Williams (1999) for more on the topic.

[33] A widely noted attempt to address these issues in the political science literature was made in Katz and King (1999). In the following years, a number of alternative models building on similar insights but adding additional features were published; in addition to Tomz, Tucker, and Wittenberg 2002, see Honaker, Katz, and King 2002; Jackson 2002; and Mikhailov, Niemi, and Weimer 2002. Having worked with the model presented in the text since the beginning of this project, I chose to continue to do so, but this does not reflect a belief that it is in any way better than any of the available alternatives, and all are undoubtedly more appropriate techniques to use in modeling multiparty data than LS analysis. One strong advantage of the model I employ from the perspective of replication is that it is very easy to implement, as all of my analyses can be conducted using just three lines of code in STATA that have been automated into the (freely available) CLARIFY software package (Tomz, Wittenberg, and King 2003). A new approach to estimating multiparty data based on techniques of robust estimation utilizing a hyperbolic tangent (tanh) estimator is presented in Mebane and Sekhon (2004). Although early assessments of the method appear promising, it appeared too late in the life cycle of this current project for me to incorporate it into this book.

[34] As is noted in Tomz, Tucker, and Wittenberg 2002, "one could estimate the β_s via $J - 1$ separate linear regressions, but the SUR technique is more convenient, since it allows users to estimate the entire system of equations with one simple command. Moreover, the SUR is potentially more efficient, because it takes advantage of interesting information about covariance of the equations. . . . At a minimum, though, the SUR will be more convenient and no less efficient than equation-by-equation OLS" (p. 68).

- Y_i is a vector of $J - 1$ log ratios where $Y_{ij} = \ln(V_{ij}/V_{iJ})$ for party j $(j = 1, \ldots, J - 1)$ relative to party J
- Y_i is multivariate normal with a mean μ and a variance of Σ.
- Means can be estimated as a linear function of explanatory variables, whereby:

$$\mu_{ij} = X_{ij}\beta_j$$

- Equations are estimated simultaneously for all parties $j = (1, \ldots, J - 1)$ using a *seemingly unrelated regression*

Thus to return to the illustrative example, for the 1996 Czech Republic elections, the actual statistical model estimated is:

$$
\begin{aligned}
ln\,(\% &Vote_{ij}/\% Vote_{iJ}) \\
&= \alpha_j + \beta_{1j}UNEMPLOYMENT_i + \beta_{2j}\Delta WAGES_i \\
&\quad + \beta_{3j}INDUSTRIAL\_GROWTH_i + \beta_{4j}\%INDUSTRY_i \\
&\quad + \beta_{5j}\%ELDERLY_i + \beta_{6j}\%URBAN_i + \beta_{7j}\%AGRIGULTURE_i \\
&\quad + \beta_{8j}ln\,[POPULATION]_i + \varepsilon_{ij}
\end{aligned}
\tag{3.3}
$$

where

$i = $ region $(1, \ldots, I)$
$j = $ party $(1, \ldots, J-1)$ (ODS, ODA, KDU, KSČM)
$J = $ total of all other parties

Note that this equation estimates the effect of economic conditions on the vote for all of the parties for which the Incumbency (ODS, ODA, KDU), New Regime (ODS, ODA), and Old Regime (KSČM) hypotheses make predictions; the remaining parties that contested the election are included in the other ("J") category and function as the base category for the estimation of the model. All five control variables are included in the regression, and the independent economic variables are the three core variables: unemployment, change in wages, and growth. Table 3.3 presents the results of estimating Equation 3.3 for the 1996 Czech Republic elections.

These regression results presented in Table 3.3 reveal interesting findings about the effect of the economy on the vote for these four parties. But it is unclear how useful they are for the larger task of assessing whether or not each case provides support for the standard economic voting hypotheses presented in the previous chapter, or how we would compare these results

Table 3.3. *Estimated Coefficients (Standard Errors) of Effect on Party Vote for the 1996 Czech Parliamentary Election**

	ODS	ODA	KDU	KSCM
Unemployment Rate	−.087	−.113	−.087	.029
	(.013)	(.021)	(.033)	(.013)
Change in Income	.001	.008	.004	.000
	(.007)	(.011)	(.018)	(.007)
Industrial Growth	−.001	.002	−.006	.001
	(.001)	(.002)	(.003)	(.001)
Percent Agriculture	−.016	−.016	.082	.003
	(.006)	(.009)	(.015)	(.006)
Percent Industry	−.005	−.005	.018	−.009
	(.003)	(.005)	(.007)	(.003)
Percentage Elderly	.036	.052	.000	.007
	(.013)	(.020)	(.031)	(.012)
Percent Urban	.000	−.000	−.012	−.003
	(.002)	(.002)	(.004)	(.001)
Log Population	.050	.099	.806	−.069
	(.047)	(.073)	(.115)	(.045)
Constant	−1.266	−4.675	−11.418	−.531
	(1.038)	(1.628)	(2.564)	(1.008)
R-Squared	0.61	0.51	0.60	0.36
N	76	76	76	76

* Models estimated using seemingly unrelated regression (SUR) with logistic transformation of dependent variable.
Source: Okresy Ceske Republiky v roce 1996 and 1995, Vekove Slozeni Obyvatelstva Ceske Republiky v roce 1996, Volby do Poslanecke Snemovny Parlamentu Ceske Republiky v roce 1996 and Aktuality CSU: 1996 Duben, Kveten – 1.cast, Cesky Statisticky Urad.

with those found from another election. This would be a difficult enough task if we employed a model such as LS analysis, which would generate one intuitively logical set of coefficients and standard errors for each of the eighty-eight parties being analyzed. But an important feature of this model – and any multiparty election model that uses a logistic transformation of the dependent variable relative to a base category – is that coefficients need to be interpreted in the same manner as one would interpret a coefficient from a multinomial logit model, namely, as a predictor of the effect of the variable in question on the relationship between the vote for the party in question relative to vote for the base party. Thus, rotating the base party (e.g., including ODS as the base party and the "Other" category as one of the four dependent variables) will produce a different set of coefficients, standard errors, and r-squared values in exactly the same way as a multinomial logit analysis. Thus, the correct way to interpret the coefficient for unemployment on the ODS in Table 3.3 is not as the effect of unemployment on the overall vote for the ODS but, rather, as the effect of unemployment on the vote for the ODS relative to the composite "other" category (the vote for all parties besides the ODS, ODA, KDU, and KSČM).

Mathematically, however, the results are equivalent no matter what party is included as the base party. Thus, switching to a regression in which ODS is the base party will produce the exact same coefficients (with the opposite signs) and standard errors for the "Other" category regression from what is found for ODS with "Other" as the base category in Table 3.3. The same holds for all combinations of parties with one party in the set of estimated equations and one party included as the base category. What this means is that if we want to assess the empirical support for the different hypotheses on the basis of coefficients and standard errors, examining the results presented in Table 3.3 only presents one part of the picture. For a full sense of the effects of economic conditions, one would actually need to rotate through every party except one as the base party in turn in order to get a complete set of coefficients and standard errors.[35] This is complicated enough in the case of one election, but with an average of four economic variables per analysis and four and a half parties per election over twenty elections, any overall assessments of the empirical support offered from these different cases for the various standard hypotheses would have to be based on comparing close to two thousand coefficients and standard errors, which would quickly become an extremely subjective and very tedious enterprise. Moreover, with a log-transformed dependent variable, none of these coefficients would have any real intuitive meaning. Thus, in order to analyze the hypotheses comparatively, a much more compact estimate is needed of the effect of economic conditions on election results for each party that can be compared across cases.

An appropriate measure to use in this case is a first difference that calculates the change in the predicted share of the vote for each party when

---

[35] We would not need to rotate every party through because we can calculate the final party from the other regressions. For an example of a presentation of results from a multinomial logit analysis that reflects the complexity of interpreting results by rotating base parties, see Brader and Tucker 2001.

demographic variables are held constant and economic conditions are varied to simulate a standardized shift from a "bad" economic situation to a "good" economic situation.[36] To do this in practice, I calculate two estimates for the expected vote of the party in question: one with economic variables at their 10th percentile level and another with economic variables at their 90th percentile level.[37] In both cases, demographic variables are set at their means. Negative indicators, such as unemployment, are shifted from the higher value to the lower value, and vice versa for positive indicators, such as change in income.[38] When the expected vote in the "bad" economic situation (e.g., high unemployment, low wage growth) is subtracted from the expected vote in the "good" situation (e.g., low unemployment, high

---

[36] There are other options for solving this problem. One approach is to pick only one variable to be representative of the overall state of the economy. So, for example, Aguilar and Pacek (2000) use only change in GDP, Pacek (1994), Rattinger (1991), and Gibson and Cielecka (1995) all rely on unemployment to measure the state of the economy, and Posner and Simon (2002) utilize poverty. An alternative approach – although not widely employed – is to craft an index that attempts to capture multiple measures of economic conditions in a single variable; one example of this approach using individual level data is Nadeau, Niemi, and Yoshinaka (2002). Both approaches, however, require the analyst to make a *priori* decisions about the relative importance of different economic variables, either through excluding some variables to privilege others or in deciding on the relative weights of variables in the composition of an index. Another type of approach is to include multiple variables in different regressions, and then for the analyst to highlight particularly interesting coefficients and standard errors (see, for example, Bell 1997; Fidrmuc 2000c). While this method is clearly appropriate for providing thick description of individual election results, it is less clear how useful it is in assessing general support for the types of standard economic voting hypotheses presented in the previous chapter. Would two out of three variables in the correct direction provide support for the hypothesis? What about three out of five? Or two in the correct direction with small substantive effects, but one in the wrong direction with a large substantive effect? Ultimately, such a method rests on the subjective insights of the particular analyst for comparison across cases in a way that the method I utilize here does not require. Furthermore, comparing the significance of coefficients in this manner becomes increasingly difficult as the number of cases increases. Indeed, Bell (1997) takes pages to describe her findings, and she is only concerned with estimating the effect of two variables (unemployment and income) across four Polish elections. To adopt such an approach with twenty elections – especially if one hoped to conduct robustness tests such as the ones I describe later in this chapter and present in Chapter 8 – would be extremely, if not prohibitively, cumbersome.

[37] As is described later in this section, one of the robustness tests I employ involves changing the percentiles employed in the economic shock.

[38] For example, if there were one hundred regions, we would use the unemployment level from the region with the 10th highest rate in the first case and from the 10th lowest rate in the second case.

wage growth), the result is a single measure of the overall impact of better economic conditions on the vote for that particular party, which is exactly what is needed to analyze the Incumbency, New Regime, and Old Regime hypotheses. Moreover, not only do first differences have the advantage of producing a single, intuitive measure of the effect of economic conditions on the electoral fortunes of the party in question, they also are unaffected by mathematic definition by the choice of which party is included as the base party for the purpose of the regression analysis.

There is, however, one important shortcoming in comparing first differences. In moving from a set of betas with standard errors to a single point estimate of a first difference, however, we run the risk of losing information regarding our *uncertainty* in the quantity of interest being reported. Fortunately, this can be avoided by using stochastic simulation to simulate an entire distribution of first differences.[39] Such an approach has the added benefit of allowing us to quantify not only our best estimate of the first difference (e.g., the mean value of the simulations) but also our level of uncertainty surrounding that estimate (e.g., the standard deviation of the simulations). Moreover, we can easily generate confidence intervals surrounding substantively meaningful quantities of interest. For example, in the empirical analyses to follow, the crucial concern is whether we can be confident that the party in question either benefits from better economic conditions (incumbent and New Regime parties) or is hurt by better economic conditions (Old Regime parties). To assess this claim, we will want to know how confident we are that the first difference is greater than zero (in other words, that better economic conditions increase the expected vote for the party), or, in the case of Old Regime parties, less than zero. If 90 percent of the simulated first differences are greater than zero, then we can claim with 90 percent confidence that the party in question is helped by stronger economic conditions; the same holds in the reverse direction if 90 percent of the simulated first differences are less than zero. In this manner, calculating estimated probability distributions of first differences allows us to measure *exactly* what we need to test our

[39] More technically, I draw one thousand betas from the sampling distribution of the parameter estimates. From each set of betas, a separate first difference is calculated. The simulations were performed using *Clarify 2.1* (Tomz, Wittenberg, and King 2003). For a full treatment of the approach, see King, Tomz, and Wittenberg 2000. Thus in no way does relying on statistical simulation ignore the information contained in coefficients and standard errors; instead, it provides a substantively meaningful way for concisely summarizing this information.

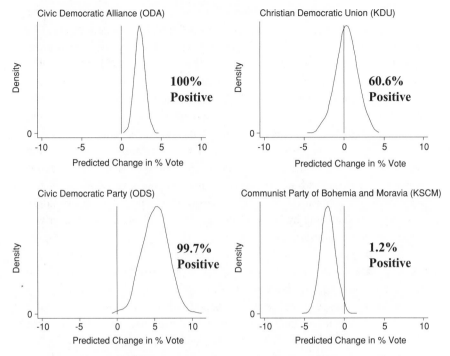

Figure 3.1 Estimated Probability Distribution of Effect of Economic Conditions on New Regime, Old Regime, and Incumbent Parties in 1996 Czech Republic Parliamentary Elections

hypotheses: how confident we should be that better economic conditions translated into better (or worse) election results for the party in question.

For ease of interpretation, these simulations can be plotted graphically, resulting in an estimated probability distribution of the first difference. Figure 3.1 plots these estimated distributions for the illustrative example, the 1996 Czech parliamentary elections.

From observing Figure 3.1, we find that this particular election provides clear empirical support for the New Regime and Old Regime hypotheses and mixed empirical support for the Incumbency hypothesis. We are very confident that both New Regime parties, the Civic Democratic Party (ODS) and the Civic Democratic Alliance (ODA), performed better in areas of the country where economic conditions were better, and that the one Old Regime party, the Communist Party of Bohemia and Moravia (KSČM), performed better where economic conditions were worse (as approximately

99 percent of the simulations predict a *decrease* in the vote for the party in the "good" economic region as compared to the "bad" economic region). The evidence in support of the Incumbency hypothesis is not quite as consistent. As noted above, we are confident that the incumbent ODA and ODS enjoyed more electoral support where economic conditions were better. The evidence provided by our analysis of the vote for the Christian Democratic Union (KDU), the third incumbent party, by comparison, is very weak. Although our best guess at the effect of the economic shock (the mean of the simulations) is positive, almost 40% of the simulations predict that the party's fortunes would decline as economic conditions improved. Thus, we have very little confidence that this particular party provides empirical support for the Incumbency hypothesis, as we are almost equally confident that the party was hurt by better economic condition as we are that it was helped by better economic conditions.

The primary quantity of interest – our level of confidence that the empirical data supports the hypothesis in question for the party in question –also can be concisely summarized in a table that lists the percentage of simulations for each party that are in the direction predicted by the particular hypothesis being analyzed. This is exactly how the results are presented for the paired case studies in Chapters 5–7 (see Tables 5.2, 6.2, and 7.2); full graphical presentations of all simulations can be found in Appendix III.

Using stochastic simulation to calculate our confidence that each party either performed better or worse under better economic circumstances has three important advantages as a method for assessing the degree of empirical support for the hypotheses presented in the previous chapter. First, it produces a concise and objective measure of the degree of support provided by each party for each hypothesis that can easily be compared across different elections and different countries. Moreover, as the measure is calculated according to an *a priori* set of rules, the assessment of whether or not the case provides support for the hypothesis in question can be made in an entirely transparent manner. (For example, it is not difficult to justify a claim that more support is provided for a hypothesis by Party A than Party B if Party A has 99% of the simulations in the correct direction and Party B has 55% in the correct direction. Compare this to an assessment of results based on looking at all of the coefficients and standard errors where Party A has two small statistically significant coefficients in the correct direction, one large but statistically insignificant coefficient in the correct direction, and one large statistically significant coefficient in the wrong direction and

Party B has three small and one large statistically insignificant coefficients in the wrong direction. It may very well be the case that there is more support for the hypothesis provided by Party A in both cases, but the former method allows for that conclusion to be drawn in a much more objective and transparent manner. This is evident even in the case of two parties, but clearly becomes much more important when comparing large numbers of parties.) Second, stochastic simulation of first differences produces unbiased estimates of the first differences regardless of which party is modeled as the base party in the analysis, thus eliminating the problem of needing to run multiple versions of each analysis that would be necessitated by direct comparisons of coefficients and standard errors.[40] Finally, the method produces a quantitative measure that directly assesses the degree of empirical support for the standard economic voting hypotheses presented in the previous chapter. These hypotheses speak to whether or not particular types of parties perform better or worse in areas of the country where the economy is stronger than in areas of the country where the economy is weaker, and this method measures the empirical support for exactly that proposition: based on our best measures of the strength of the economy after controlling for demographic indicators, what exactly is our confidence that a particular party did in fact perform better or worse where economic conditions were stronger?

Before concluding this section, it is important to reiterate that the quantitative analysis described here is not designed to provide inferences about the motivation for individual level behavior. Instead, the analysis assesses the degree to which regional variation in economic conditions affected regional variation in election results. This is an appropriate approach because, as noted in the previous paragraph, this is exactly what the standard economic voting hypotheses predict: whether particular types of parties enjoy more electoral success in parts of the country with different economic conditions. So although the motivation for these hypotheses presented in the previous chapter contained references to assumptions about how individuals would likely behave, it is important to note again that the empirical

---

[40] Although the estimated distribution may vary across repeated runs, all variance will be a result of the unbiased variance in the simulation procedure and not a result of the choice of base party. Put another way, repeatedly running simulations with the same base party will generate no less variation across sets of simulations than repeatedly running simulations while rotating the base party.

analyses included in the study test only the implications of these assumption – the aggregate level relationships between economic conditions and election results – and not the assumptions about individual level behavior themselves.

Robustness Tests

The final component of the method involves running a series of robustness tests on the overall findings produced by the statistical analyses. As anyone familiar with quantitative analysis is aware, changing variables in estimated equations can produce different results. Although it can be complicated enough to assess the degree to which results change when working with one regression from one dataset, the question of the robustness of findings is considerably more complex when working with findings from eighty-eight different regression using twenty different datasets. Thus, in order to assess the robustness of my findings, I adopt the following strategy. Rather than focus on the effect of various specifications of the model for any one particular party or election, I run the entire analysis from scratch on every single party using a standardized change from the original model and then compare whether or not the overall findings regarding the relative empirical support for the different standard economic voting hypotheses change in any appreciable manner. I do this four different times, using four different types of standardized changes.

In light of the concerns mentioned in the previous section, the first test is probably the most important, and involves running each of the regressions using only the five control variables and the three base independent variables that are available in (almost) all cases: unemployment, change in income, and growth.[41] Conversely, in the second robustness test I add an additional independent variable to each regression, which is a measure of poverty.[42]

---

[41] As mentioned previously, unemployment rates were not available at the regional level for the 1991 Russian presidential election. To deal with the peculiar case of wage arrears – important in the Russian context, and a non issue in the other four countries – I actually run this test twice for the Russian cases for which arrears were available, once with just the three base variables and once with the three base variables plus wage arrears.

[42] Ideally, one would use the percentage of people living below the poverty line – or some similarly low standard of living – to measure poverty. Unfortunately, such measures were only available in Poland and Russia, and even in these countries only in the second half of the decade. In the other cases, I have substituted either a per-capita measure of welfare spending, the percentage of people receiving social assistance, or the infant mortality rate. Thus, it would not be a particularly appropriate test for comparing the effects of poverty

The third robustness test focuses instead on the dependent variable, and involves increasing the number of parties for which the effects of economic conditions are being estimated in each election. Recall that because of the statistical model, all parties that are neither incumbent, New Regime, nor Old Regime parties are included in the "Other" category that serves as the base party for the logistic transformation of the vote for the parties included in the analysis. Therefore, as we estimate the effect of the vote on more parties, the composition of this base category changes. The purpose of this robustness test, therefore, is to see whether the results for the parties in which we are particularly interested – incumbent, New Regime, and Old Regime parties – change when the composition of the base category changes.[43]

The final robustness test involves the size of the economic shock. As noted earlier, the primary shock employed is one that shifts economic variables from the 10th percentile to the 90th percentile. As a robustness test, therefore, the size of this shock was decreased to a shock from the 20th to the 80th percentile.

The details and results of these different tests are all presented in Chapter 8. The net result of all these robustness tests, however, is exactly the same: in no way do any of these changes affect the overall conclusion of stronger empirical support for the Transition Model than the Referendum Model. In fact, given the number of cases involved, the aggregate findings remain remarkably similar across all of the robustness tests.

In addition to these specification-based robustness tests, recall that in the previous chapter I noted that one way of thinking about the conditional economic voting hypotheses was as theoretically oriented robustness tests of the analyses of the standard economic voting hypotheses. These

---

across different countries or elections. However, as the key point here is to see if the overall results change with an extra economic variable in the model, and not to make any particular assessments about the effects of poverty on election results, the fact that these measures are getting at different aspects of poverty is less of a concern in this particular instance.

[43] The extra parties included in the analysis were chosen based on substantive interest. This includes important parties that were neither New Regime, Old Regime, nor incumbent parties (e.g., the Czech Social Democratic Party or Fatherland-All Russia), the borderline New Regime parties discussed in the appendix to Chapter 5, and the nationalist parties analyzed in Chapter 6. When possible, agrarian, ethnic, and religious parties were also selected as well. As with the standard analyses, parties receiving less than 2% of the vote were not selected. At an earlier stage of the project, I also conducted a similar robustness test by decreasing the number of parties in each analysis and again found practically no effect on the remaining parties.

robustness tests do not change the specification of models, but rather the cases included in the overall assessments of the standard hypotheses. So readers interested in more robustness tests can turn to the analyses of the conditional hypotheses to examine what the overall findings of the book would have been had I changed the case selection to any of the subsets of categories in the conditional hypotheses (e.g., had I included only parliamentary elections, only high responsibility elections, only late decade elections, etc.).

Finally, in the chapters that follow I adopt a level of 90% of the simulations in the correctly specified direction as a threshold for identifying cases in which there appears to be "strong" empirical support for the hypotheses as a means of concisely summarizing my findings across cases. I use this level both because of the history of using 90% certainty in the discipline, and because it produced a fairly clean split in the data; the closest cases that did not reach the threshold were at least 5% away on both the positive and negative sides.[44] But the choice of 90% is of course arbitrary, so as the very first robustness test in Chapter 8, I present assessments of the standard hypotheses using different thresholds for "strong" empirical support.

To sum up, the method of comparative cross-regional analysis involves the following components. Cross-regional datasets from a single election are used to estimate the effect of economic conditions on the election results of each party individually for which one of the standard economic voting hypotheses makes a prediction. These regional economic voting effects are estimated by a compositional data model, and stochastic simulation is used to estimate the probability distribution of standardized economic shocks (first differences) on the vote for each party individually. On the basis of these estimates, the confidence that each party presents empirical support for the relevant hypothesis(es) is calculated, and these confidence levels are then compared across cases. Comparisons are conducted using both case studies of individual pairs of elections (which focus on the actual confidence level for each relevant party) and general comparisons across all twenty elections (which focus on the number of cases in which a threshold

---

[44] Noting whether 90% of the simulations are in the correctly predicted direction approximates a 90% confidence level because it is essentially a one-tailed test: all three of the standard hypotheses have a predicted direction in which the effect is expected to be. I thank Garret Glasgow for highlighting this point. Nevertheless, as is illustrated in Table 8.2, choosing a 95% threshold for claiming strong empirical evidence would have yielded the exact same results regarding the relative support for the Old Regime, New Regime, and Incumbency hypotheses.

of confidence is reached). Finally, these overall assessments are checked using a series of robustness tests that involve changing the specification of each equation in a standard format and then rerunning all of these analyses again from the start.

Advantages and Disadvantages of Comparative Cross-Regional Analysis

All methods of analysis in political science – be they quantitative or qualitative – have their advantages and disadvantages. Most books that are not explicitly focused on methodological topics usually do not take too much time to dwell on these concerns, in part because most studies rely on methodology that has been used before and because many excellent treatments of methodological questions exist in works devoted precisely to these tasks. However, as the method of comparison I employ in this book is novel, it is important to devote at least some attention to the tasks of highlighting the advantages and disadvantages of the method. Before doing so, I want to reiterate the point made in the introduction of this chapter, which is that none of the individual components of the method are new: there are other studies of the effects of economic conditions on election results that utilize regional level data in a comparative framework;[45] the statistical model has been analyzed in an article in *Political Analysis*;[46] and an emphasis in quantitative work on substantively meaningful quantities of interest as opposed to simply coefficients and standard errors has long been popular in certain quarters of political science.[47] However, with the exception of my own previous work on this project, the three have never before been combined in this manner, and so I devote the rest of this chapter to addressing some of the advantages and disadvantages of the method I have chosen to employ. Readers who are not particularly interested in methodological considerations are invited to skim or even skip this section entirely; there are no empirical results presented here, and the theoretical arguments are not advanced in any way beyond what was presented in the previous chapter.

---

[45] See note 25 in Chapter 1.

[46] See Tomz, Tucker, and Wittenberg (2002).

[47] And has certainly seen a renewed emphasis since the publication of "Making the Most of Statistical Analysis: Improving Interpretation and Presentation" (King, Tomz and Wittenberg 2000) in the *American Journal of Political Science* and its accompanying *Clarify* software.

I begin with the assumption that there is no silver bullet research strategy that is perfect for studying the effect of economic conditions on election results in a comparative context.[48] And although this section is largely focused on the method employed in this book, I do want to take just a moment to mention that other methods have concerns as well. Single country time-series analysis, which has played a crucial role in the development of the field of economic voting in the American context, faces the serious challenge of accounting for other over-time developments that are not included in the model, which is why we have seen the use of "war" and "Watergate" dummies and corresponding criticisms of this approach. Moreover, single country time-series analysis requires the presence of enough competitive elections to actually construct a large enough sample of observations, which is extremely problematic in countries with short histories of competitive elections. Cross-national time-series analysis, although increasing the number of observations, has the same time related problems as single-country time series analyses while also introducing questions of country-specific effects, comparability of data, and the question of how to correctly model cross-sectional time-series data. Comparative survey analysis, in addition to all of the standard methodological issues confronting single country survey analysis such as selection bias, question wording, and ordering of response items, also has to contend with the question of whether or not similar questions are interpreted differently in different countries, a topic that has recently attracted growing interest in the political science literature, and is especially consequential for surveys that are not explicitly designed to be compared.[49] And as will be discussed later in this section, pooling cross-regional data across time or countries introduces serious questions about the appropriate comparability of data, in addition to the previously mentioned concerns about the fact that different countries report different economic statistics at different periods of time.

---

[48] For a striking example of this, see the criticism of aggregate time-series models in Fiorina 1981, Chapter 6, as compared to the criticism of survey-based approaches leveled in Kramer 1983.

[49] See, for example, King, Murray et al. 2004. On selection bias, see Berinsky 2004; in the postcommunist context, see Berinsky and Tucker 2003. For an interesting recent methodological approach to comparative survey analysis, see Jusko and Shively 2005. Recent efforts to design surveys that are explicitly designed for cross-national analysis may help to alleviate these types of problems. See, for example, the Comparative Study of Election Systems (http://www.umich.edu/~cses/) and Huber, Kernell, and Leoni 2005 for a study utilizing these data.

This is not meant to imply that we cannot learn useful information about the relationship between economic conditions and election results in the postcommunist context by using one or more of these methods, but only that no approach is without its drawbacks. I have elected to use the comparative cross-regional approach because of its strength as a methodology; I leave it to others who choose to adopt alternative methodological strategies to make the case in this manner for their approaches as well. In the rest of this section, I highlight what I think are the most important benefits of the method that I use and then discuss what I think are its most serious drawbacks.

Advantages of Comparative Cross-Regional Analysis

Comparative Emphasis First and foremost, the comparative cross-regional approach is characterized by the fact that it is explicitly comparative: it is designed to compare findings both over time and across countries. Although this seems an almost trivial point to highlight at this point in the book, it is worth noting both the importance of comparative analysis and its relative paucity in the postcommunist electoral landscape. In the review I conducted of the 101 articles on elections and voting in postcommunist countries described in Chapter 1, fewer than half (forty) compared more than one election, and of these only thirteen explicitly compared elections from different countries.[50] And although studies of single elections are of course extremely valuable, most country-level experts armed with reliable survey data can always produce a multitude of compelling explanations for why the vote turned out the way it did in that particular election. Comparative analysis, by contrast, allows us to examine support for general hypotheses across different contexts and to present empirical analyses that move beyond a particular circumstance. Although one can of course test general hypotheses using data from just a single election, the possibility always remains that the results may in some way be a function of the peculiar circumstances surrounding that particular election. A comparative study – and a methodological approach designed to facilitate such a study – serves an important role in insulating one's findings from such a critique.

At the same time, most prior comparative studies of the relationship between economic conditions and election results reduce each election to

---

[50] For books that compare postcommunist election results across multiple countries, see Grzymala-Busse 2002 and Tworzecki 2003.

but a single observation, whether it is a single country time-series analysis,[51] cross-national analysis,[52] or cross-national time-series analysis.[53] Such a framework must contend with the possibility that election results are being influenced by election specific events that are not captured by the model. Moreover, as long as each national election is only one observation in the analysis, it is very difficult to learn anything about the effect of economic conditions on different parties within each election. Although less important in the two-party context of the United States, this is an issue worth considering in multiparty democracies. For example, if there are three incumbent parties competing in an election, any study that uses national election results as the unit of analysis must either code the incumbent vote from that election as all three parties, one of the three as the primary incumbent party (if there is an emphasis on a "primary" incumbent party), or some combination thereof.[54] Moreover, whatever results are returned from the regression analysis will speak to the findings across all of the elections, but will tell us little about the effects of economic conditions on the vote for the three political parties from the election in question.

Comparative cross-regional analysis, by contrast, addresses both of these issues. By only estimating equations from one election at one period of time, all election specific effects are controlled for when equations are estimated, as was explained in the previous section. Thus, there is no need for a "war" or "scandal" control in the statistical analysis, because these factors are shared contexts across the entire electorate. At the same time, comparative cross-regional analysis produces party by party estimates of the effect of economic conditions on each party included in the analysis. To return to the example of the 1996 Czech Republic election, we can learn from this method that the Incumbency Hypothesis is supported by empirical data for two incumbent parties, the ODS and the ODA, but not in the case of the third incumbent party, the KDU. With this information in hand, one can then begin to ask questions about what differentiates the ODS and the ODA

---

[51] See, for example, Tufte 1975; Rosa and Amson 1976; Lewis-Beck and Bellucci 1982; Bellucci 1984; Erikson 1989, 1990.

[52] See, for example, Wilkin, Haller, and Norpoth 1997.

[53] See, for example, Remmer 1991; Powell and Whitten 1993; Palmer and Whitten 1999; Roberts and Wibbels 1999; Whitten and Palmer 1999; Chappell and Veiga 2000; Royed, Leyden, and Borrelli 2000.

[54] For an interesting take on this problem, see Wilkin, Haller, and Norpoth 1997. In this article, the authors estimate their model twice, once using all incumbent parties and once using just the primary incumbent party.

from the KDU, such as, for example, that the ODS and ODA are both also New Regime parties, whereas the KDU is not a New Regime party. The ability to make this kind of distinction is even more illuminating when considering the 1998 Hungarian election. This election feature two incumbent parties, one that was a New Regime party and one that was an Old Regime party. By investigating the effect of economic conditions on each party individually, I find strong support for the Incumbency hypothesis in the case of the incumbent–New Regime party, but no support for the Incumbency hypothesis in the case of the incumbent–Old Regime party (see Chapter 5 for details). Without the ability to generate party by party estimates of the effect of economic conditions, this important distinction between the two incumbent parties would be obscured.

Indeed, generating party by party estimates addresses what is one of the more vexing problems in studying the effect of economic conditions on election results even in established democracies, which is the continued empirical evidence generated from these studies that the relationship between economic conditions and voting behavior varies over time and across contexts. To note just a few examples: Lin (1999) argues that economic voting is dependent on electoral context by examining American elections stretching back into the nineteenth century; Palmer and Whitten (1999) argue that the relationship between economic conditions and the vote for incumbent governments in OECD countries has become more volatile over time; and Alvarez, Nagler, and Willette (2000) report that economic conditions take on different levels of importance in the United States, Canada, and the United Kingdom. By generating party by party level estimates of the effect of economic conditions, I am able to examine the extent to which these concerns hold in my particular cases.

And although it is of course possible to build control variables into a cross-national model to control for variation in the relationship between economic conditions and election results, each new attempt to do so involves a new specification of the primary model for assessing the affect of economic conditions on election results. Comparative cross-regional analysis, by contrast, allows for one original specification of the statistical model for each election – which controls for any and all of these election specific effects – to generate the party by party estimates of the effect of economic conditions. Once generated, these results can be compared in a multitude of ways (e.g., all of the conditional economic voting hypotheses presented in the previous chapter), but without ever needing to respecify the original statistical model. We can therefore use the same set of original analyses to examine whether there is more support for the standard economic voting hypotheses earlier in the decade, in high responsibility election, or in East-Central European elections, for example. Moreover, as noted previously, we also can examine the degree of support generated for any hypothesis by any particular party, something that is not possible using a pooled cross-national model.

Availability and Appropriate Use of Data   Another advantage of comparative cross-regional analysis is that it vastly increases the amount of data that one can bring to bear upon the task of studying the effect of economic conditions on election results. A cross-national data set composed of these twenty elections would have only twenty observations. Moving to the regional level from the national level therefore allows us to drastically increase the number of observations on which we can base our conclusions. Of course, survey data also allow us to radically increase our number of observations from any aggregate study, but comparative analysis of survey data introduces all of the issues discussed previously about the availability and applicability of comparative survey analysis. Furthermore, it also moves us out of the realm of studying the effect of economic conditions on actual election results – in other words, the hypotheses presented in the previous chapter – and into the domain of individual voting behavior.

The question of the comparability of data raises another important advantage of the comparative cross-regional approach. When working with regional level data from the postcommunist context, the appropriateness of comparing regional data collected by different countries at different times is a legitimate question that warrants important consideration. Were I to pool all of my data into a single analysis, I would be making the assumption that a statistic from country A at time T in region X (e.g., unemployment in Bardejov, Slovakia, in 1992) measures the exact same economic reality as a statistic from country B at time T + 1 in region Y (e.g., unemployment in St. Petersburg, Russia, in 1999). This is a high level of assumption to put on regional data from established democracies, let alone data from countries undergoing the kinds of transitions found in the postcommunist world in the 1990s.

Conversely, the method that I have presented in this chapter only requires pooling data for statistical analysis within a single election. This type of analysis therefore relies only on the assumption that a statistic from country A at time T in region X (e.g. unemployment in Bardejov, Slovakia, in 1992) measures the same economic reality as a statistic from the same country A at the same time T in region Y (e.g., unemployment in Bratislava,

Slovakia, in 1992). Thus, we need only assume that statistics collected at the same time under the direction of the same statistical agency are measured in the same manner. Although it is likely that even this assumption is violated in certain instances – especially earlier in the decade – it is undoubtedly a much, much lower threshold for comparability of data than to assume that regional data collected under the direction of different statistical agencies at different periods of time are measured in the same manner.

A slightly different way of thinking about this issue is that it makes measurement error much less likely to introduce bias into the analysis. As is illustrated in King, Keohane, and Verba (1994, Chapter 5), systematic measurement error can introduce bias into analysis, whereas measurement error that is randomly distributed does not bias results.[55] If we believe that measurement error is likely to be present in economic statistics reported in transition countries, then the issue of measurement error has serious consequences for how we pool our data. If we think that measurement error is likely to vary either by country (e.g., Russia might systematically understate unemployment as compared to Poland) or within countries across time (e.g., Slovakia might have overstated growth earlier in the decade), then pooling data across these divides could introduce bias into the analysis. Pooling data within countries for a single time period, however, will only introduce bias if there is systematic variation in measurement error within a single country in a single time period (e.g., unemployment is systematically overstated in Western Hungary but understated in Eastern Hungary in 1994). Although we cannot dismiss out of hand the possibility that such patterns might exist, we certainly have no *a priori* reason to assume that measurement error will vary within individual countries in a single period; conversely, there are many reasons to think that we might find variation in measurement error across different countries and time periods. Or, to put it the same way as in the previous paragraph, the threshold necessary to assume that measurement error is randomly distributed within a single country at a single point in time is much lower than the threshold necessary to assume that measurement error is randomly distributed across countries.

Although the issue of comparability of data is serious when economic statistics are intended to measure the same phenomenon, such as unemployment rates, the issue is even more blatantly a problem when countries

---

[55] Randomly distributed measurement error can, however, influence the efficiency of one's results, and thus decrease the level of confidence we have in our results. This point is addressed in greater detail in the following section.

choose not to even report the same economic statistics at the regional level. Were all of the data to be pooled in a single analysis, we would either need to ignore all data that were not reported by all countries or else rely on some form of statistical procedure to impute entire series of missing data.[56] Moreover, even when countries choose to report the same statistic (e.g., the percentage of older citizens in a region) they may define this statistic differently (e.g., men over sixty and women over fifty-five in one country or everyone over sixty-five in another country). The comparative cross-regional approach, by contrast, both allows for the use of all available data in each individual statistical analysis without the need to impute nonreported data, and at the same time guarantees that the same definition of each statistic is being employed in each individual statistical analysis. With the data necessary for the current study, this would simply not be the case if the data were pooled across countries and elections.

For these reasons, comparative cross-regional analysis appears to be an especially appropriate method of analysis for studies of new democracies when different countries report different economic statistics and when there are questions about the comparability of data across elections. It allows us to greatly increase the data we can use to make our estimates of the effect of the economy on election results at a time when countries have had few elections while simultaneously leaning on these data only to the extent that is warranted. In doing so, it opens up a means of examining empirical support for general hypotheses about the relationship between economic conditions – as well as other factors that vary cross-regionally – and election results in areas of the world where it might not otherwise be possible to conduct comparative analyses.

Strategic Voting An additional benefit of comparative cross-regional analysis is that it largely insulates one's study from problems associated with the phenomenon of strategic voting. Although there are a number of different ways to think about strategic voting, the most common involves voters who shy away from their preferred party when it looks likely that the party (or candidate) is not likely to cross a minimum threshold necessary for the party (or candidate) to gain representation in the parliament (or win the contested seat, or make it into a second round of balloting). In an effort not to "waste" one's vote, the strategic voter is then posited to cast her ballot for another party (or candidate) with a more likely chance of actually making

---

[56] See, for example, King, Honaker et al. 2001.

it into the parliament.[57] Had I chosen a cross-national research design in which each election represented only one observation, then the fact that certain parties (e.g., those close to a minimum threshold for representation in the parliament) might see a drop off in their vote totals because of strategic voting whereas other parties (such as those safely above the threshold) would see an increase in vote totals could bias my results.

In a cross-regional framework, however, this problem disappears. Let us assume that an analysis of the vote for a particular party would show support for one of my hypotheses in the absence of strategic voting. For simplification, imagine a country with five regions, and this party would receive 10%, 10%, 8%, 6%, and 6% of the vote in each of these regions respectively, for an overall total of 8% of the national vote. Now assume that because of strategic voting, 3% of the electorate deserts the party. As long as the strategic voting occurs uniformly across regions – and as the strategic concern in question is a national threshold, these is no reason to assume it should not – the party will now receive 7%, 7%, 5%, 3%, and 3% of the vote in each of the regions, respectively. My analysis, which looks at the covariance between regional distribution of economic conditions and regional election results, will show the same result in either case. If the economy is performing best in the first two regions and worse in the last two regions, than either set of results will confirm that this particular party has performed better where the economy is better.[58]

Bridge between Methods Finally, the comparative cross-regional approach has the potential to function as a bridge between the two most popular means of studying the relationship between economic conditions and election results. Like survey analysis, cross-regional analysis can identify party specific effects for economic conditions within individual elections. And like cross-national analysis, comparative cross-regional analysis provides a method for testing the level of empirical support for general hypotheses across different contexts, including time and countries. At the same time,

[57] See, in particular, Cox 1997. For a concise summary of different approaches to strategic voting, see Meirowitz and Tucker 2004.

[58] If seats are distributed in particularly small districts – as is the case in parts of Poland – then the opportunity exists for strategic voting to have different effects in different regions. However, this requires that citizens know not only how popular a party was nationally, but also how close the party might be to passing the threshold necessary to gain a seat in an individual's home region. While it is not impossible to imagine some citizens in transition countries possessing this kind of information, it is difficult to see how such information would be broadly known.

it allows us to avoid problems with both of these methods. By relying on aggregate data, we avoid the need to compare results from different surveys in different countries. But conducting this aggregate analysis at the regional level allows us to avoid treating each election as only a single observation, and, consequently, to estimate the effect of economic conditions on multiple parties from a given election. As a result of these party-by-party estimates of the effect of economic conditions, we can then ask the interesting question of why we find different results for different parties, which I do throughout this book with the conditional hypotheses. This blending of focused analysis on individual elections and the assessment of the general level of support for hypotheses is further accentuated by the use of both paired cases studies and comparisons from the entire dataset to assess the empirical support for hypotheses. So while comparative cross-regional analysis is especially appropriate for new democracies, in the future it also may open up new avenues of research for established democracies as well, and especially in multiparty democracies.[59]

Drawbacks of Comparative Cross-Regional Analysis

As was noted in the beginning of this section, no method of studying the relationship between economic conditions and election results is without its drawbacks, and comparative cross-regional analysis is not distinct in that regard. The purpose of this section, therefore, is to highlight and address three potential drawbacks of the method: the potential for misattributing other effects to economic conditions; concerns over comparing confidence in estimates from datasets of different sizes; and the difficulty in assessing traditional models of retrospective voting using cross-regional approaches.

Correctly Attributing Economic Effects One of the defining features of the comparative cross-regional analysis approach is that all of the actual statistical analyses are conducted on aggregate-level datasets. As with any aggregate analysis of voting, we cannot identify the precise causal mechanism through which economic conditions affect the individual vote calculus, which in turn then aggregate up to the vote totals that we observe. Indeed, all our statistical analyses can confirm is whether or not there is a connection between patterns of votes for particular parties and patterns of

---

[59] See, for example, Rattinger 1991, who uses cross-regional analysis to study elections in Germany.

variation in macroeconomic conditions. Without going into too much of a digression into the philosophy of scientific inquiry, this is the reason we need the types of theoretical arguments presented in the previous chapter to predict exactly what types of patterns we should expect to find. With these *a priori* arguments in hand, we can then make the claim that the empirical evidence presented is either consistent with the observable implications of the theoretical arguments or suggests evidence to falsify these theoretical propositions.[60]

However, the possibility always exists that one's independent variable of interest – here cross-regional variation in macroeconomic conditions – could indeed be correlated with a true causal variable that is not measured by the model. This is, of course, the dreaded "omitted variable" problem faced by most quantitative analyses in political science.[61] What makes the problem particularly worrisome in the context of the relationship between economic conditions and election results at the regional level is that it is possible to produce an historical example that illustrates the problem. Imagine a comparative cross-regional study set up like the one in this book that used data from a number of elections in the United States from 1870 to 1920 to test a hypothesis that predicted that the Republican Party would perform better in areas of the country where economic conditions were better. If, as one might expect, economic condition were worse in the South in the half century following the Civil War, then a cross-regional analysis of the relationship between economic conditions and election results would find strong evidence to support the proposition that the Republican Party was performing better where economic conditions were better, when in fact the true cause of this relationship would be dislike of the Republican Party in the South due to fallout from the Civil War.[62]

Although it is impossible to ever control for all potential omitted variable bias, I would like to suggest a number of factors that should assuage concerns in this regard for this particular study.

First, as explained in detail earlier in this chapter, I have included a series of demographic control variables in every regression to control for the effect that societal cleavages might have on the distribution of votes. This includes both the types of cleavages associated with the long-standing

---

[60] For more, see King, Keohane, and Verba 1994.

[61] See, for example, King, Keohane, and Verba 1994, 168–82; Greene 1993, 246–7.

[62] I thank Donald Kinder for highlighting this example specifically and this issue more generally.

development of political parties in Western Europe, such as labor patterns, rural–urban splits, and center–periphery relations, and those that have been privileged in discussions of postcommunist politics, such as the popularity of Old Regime parties among older voters and in areas with more industrial development and the appeal of New Regime parties in more urban areas. All of these factors are controlled for in the original statistical analyses,[63] and therefore cannot be the source of omitted variable bias in my results.[64]

In addition to the demographic control variables within individual elections, the presence of multiple countries in the study also serves as an important control for the effect of larger macrohistorical factors. For example, if one were to argue that voting behavior in the postcommunist era were to some extent a function of the history of which empire the country had been a part of, the sample includes countries from the Russian empire (Russia) the Austro-Hungarian empire (Hungary, Slovakia, and the Czech Republic) and parts of multiple empires (Poland). Similarly, if one felt the true story was one of religious orientation, the study includes an Eastern Orthodox Country (Russia), an almost entirely Catholic country (Poland), two majority Catholic countries (Hungary and Slovakia), and a country with a plurality of atheists (Czech Republic).[65]

Another factor besides the presence of both within country and across country control variables is the centrality of the economic transition that was occurring in these countries during the 1990s. As mentioned in the previous chapter, it is difficult to overstate the degree to which economic life changed across all of these countries during the transition period. Economies that were characterized by fixed prices, massive shortages of goods, full employment, and cradle to grave social entitlement programs were replaced, often in exceedingly short periods of time, by economies featuring wide-scale unemployment, serious inflation, and loss of entitlement programs, but also all sorts of new opportunities for employment, travel, and purchasing goods. In short, if anything was going to be the postcommunist version of the Civil War – in other words, a salient focal point around which we

---

[63] They are also controlled for in the estimates of the effects of the economic shocks; recall that demographic variables are held at their means when estimates of the vote for parties in regions with "bad" and "good" economic conditions are calculated.

[64] Indeed, to return to the example of the United States and the Civil War, the percentage of workers employed in agriculture control variable might actually have picked up some of the distinctions between the South and other parts of the country.

[65] For information on religious adherents by country, see the CIA World Factbook (http://www.cia.gov/cia/publications/factbook/).

might expect political behavior to revolve – the economic transformation would be as good a guess as any. Thus, far from being likely that there might be some underlying causal factor that is independent of economic factors affecting the vote, any such alternative explanation would require a theoretical argument for why economic factors would not prove equally or more salient in the context of the postcommunist transitional period.

Another factor mitigating against the likelihood that some omitted variable can explain long-standing patterns of support for parties is the *de novo* status of most of the political parties competing in these elections. With the exception of the Old Regime parties, almost all of the other parties analyzed in this study were formed during the transition era. Moreover, even if some of these parties claimed to trace their lineage back to the precommunist era, the single-party communist era had lasted over forty years in East Central Europe and over seventy years in Russia.[66] So for most political parties, their popular support was developing concurrently with the transition itself. The one major exception here, the existence of Old Regime parties, is built directly into the theoretical argument of the Transitional Identity Model, as it is precisely the fact that we expect voters to have more information on and a certain set of beliefs about these parties that produces the Old Regime hypothesis.

Taking these three points together, in order to have a Civil War–type omitted variable problem in the analysis, we would need the following conditions to hold. Strong support for political parties would have had to have developed almost immediately in the life span of these parties that was *independent* of the social-demographic control variables included in the study and was *independent* of the economic developments during the transition as measured by the explanatory variables in the different models, but at the same time was *highly correlated* with patterns of variation in these same macroeconomic variables.

Again, this is not to say that other factors do not matter, but, rather, that because of the structure of the analysis in this book, the effects that I am reporting are due to economic conditions are unlikely to be serving merely as a proxy for another underlying variable. Moreover, the fact that multiple countries are included in this study again functions as a relevant buffer against this type of problem. Even if all of these conditions did hold in one particular country, it is that much more unlikely that they

---

[66] Although for an analysis of town-by-town variation in the transmission of political identities from the pre to postcommunist eras in parts of Hungary, see Wittenberg 2006.

would be replicated across all of the countries in the study in the same manner.[67]

Different Sized Datasets A second issue of concern with comparative cross-regional analysis stems from the method of comparison of results across elections. As explained in the chapter, my primary quantity of interest for the purpose of comparison in this study is the degree of confidence that each party either performed better or worse in parts of the country where economic conditions were stronger. This measure is in a large part a function of two factors: the size and direction of the effects for each of the independent variables, and our underlying uncertainty in these effects. All things being equal, more data allows us to reduce uncertainty, which means that to a certain extent the quantity of interest is a function of the number of observations in the dataset. In other words – again all things being equal – the parties from countries with a larger number of regions should be more likely to generate estimated first differences with higher confidence levels than parties from countries with a smaller number of regions.[68]

As this concern is a mathematical fact, there are two ways of addressing it in a study. The first is an *a priori* question of research design; the second is to *ex post* examine one's results to see if there seems to be any correlation between the number of observation in each dataset and the results generated for parties in that country.

From an *a priori* perspective, there are two features that need to be considered: the number of observations in each data set and the research

---

[67] The most common suggestion I have heard in this regard concerns the Polish case and the possibility that the legacy of the different imperial empires that ruled different parts of the country before World War I could have affected both economic developments and the political proclivities of citizens differently in different parts of the country (e.g., Jackson, Klich, and Poznańska 2003a use control variables for to identify Polish regions included in the former Russian or Austrian partition, see p.103). Another potential concern is the salience of religion in Polish politics, which is likely only partially captured through the socio-demographic variables I employ (see, for example, Jackson, Klich, and Poznańska 2003b, note 11). Although testing hypotheses based on either of these factors is beyond the scope of this study, it is important to note that, as will be demonstrated in Chapters 5–8, there is no more support found for any of the standard hypotheses in the Polish case than in the other four cases, none of which faced similar split imperial empire experiences. Again, this is not in any way meant to function as a test of the importance of history or religion in contemporary Polish politics – to do so would require a fundamentally different research design – but only to illustrate the manner in which conducting a comparative cross-regional analysis makes it much harder to argue that the overall results are being driven by omitted variables.

[68] I thank Nathaniel Beck for raising this point.

design. One could imagine that there would be more serious concerns in this regard if one were comparing results from a dataset with twenty observations with results from a dataset with two thousand observations. For my study, however, the variation in the size of the datasets is not that great. Indeed, fifteen of the twenty elections are from datasets with between forty-nine and seventy-seven observations.[69] The remaining five elections did involve smaller datasets, with two elections (the 1992 and 1994 Slovak parliamentary elections) having thirty-eight observations and three elections (all three Hungarian parliamentary elections) having only twenty observations.

Fortunately, *ex-post* observations show no relationship between the number of observations in each country and the prevalence of strong confidence in empirical results. Hungary, with the smallest number of observations, did not generate noticeably fewer cases of empirical support for any of the three standard hypotheses, whereas parties from Russia, which had the largest number of observations, actually generated the least empirical support for the Old Regime hypothesis (a point that is discussed in great detail in Chapter 7). Moreover, as is discussed in Chapter 8, there were two elections in the sample that generated especially poor empirical support for all three of the hypotheses. Neither was a Hungarian election; one was a Russian election with seventy-six observations and one a Slovak election with thirty-eight observations. Finally, although all of the regressions with an $N < 40$ were for parliamentary elections, there is actually more empirical evidence to support all three standard hypotheses in the parliamentary elections than in the presidential elections (as is discussed in detail in Chapters 5–8). So while there certainly is some discrepancy in the size of the datasets, in no way do the overall findings of the book seem to be a function of this variation in size of dataset.

Moreover, the *a priori* research design of the study mitigates against such a concern, especially for the standard hypotheses. Indeed, the comparative design of the study requires that each standard hypothesis be tested using each different dataset.[70] So even if there were some meaningful "advantage" to returning empirical results with a higher confidence level to be gained from analyses in countries with a larger number of regions, each hypothesis

---

[69] This includes all the Polish, Czech, and Russian elections, and the Slovak elections that occurred after the 1996 administrative reorganization.

[70] The one exception to this rule is the 1999 Slovak presidential election, which did not have an Old Regime candidate.

would still have the opportunity to perform exceptionally well in each larger N context and face the same challenge of generating empirical support in each smaller N context. So although a direct comparison of results from Hungary and Russia might be of more concern in this regard, the assessment of the three standard hypotheses is less likely to be biased in any meaningful way because each hypothesis was tested across all of the different datasets.[71]

Variation in measurement error also can lead to a similar problem. While randomly distributed measurement error does not bias results, it can introduce inefficiency into the analysis (King, Keohane, and Verba 1994, 157–67). If we accept the proposition that measurement error might vary by country, then the possibility exists that countries with less measurement error in their statistical measures might be more likely to yield analyses with – all things being equal – greater confidence in the findings of empirical support for the standard economic voting hypotheses. Thus, we have a similar concern as with the number of regions: that some countries might have an unfair advantage over others in producing results with greater confidence in the findings.[72] Fortunately, both the *ex-ante* research design and *ex-post* findings discussed here mitigate against this type of factor having unduly influenced the conclusions of the study as well.[73]

---

[71] The conditional hypotheses, however, are not necessarily insulated from such a concern in this manner, as many of the conditional hypotheses do not include at least one election from each country in each category. As specified in this study, though, there is no example of conditional hypothesis that groups the low N countries (Hungary, pre-1996 Slovakia) in one category and the high N countries (Czech Republic, Russia, post-1996 Slovakia) in another category. In fact, almost all of the categories across all of the conditional hypotheses include cases from multiple countries; the only exception from the theoretically motivated conditional hypotheses is the institutional responsibility hypothesis, which includes only Polish elections in one category. But that being said, Poland, with forty-nine regions, is not at either extreme in terms of the number of regions.

[72] Although it should be noted that if we are most suspicious of measurement error in Russia, then this concern yields the opposite prediction from the number of regions concern. Measurement error might lead us to anticipate the least confidence in the Russian analyses, but the fact that Russia (along with the Czech Republic) has the largest number of regions in the study would lead us to expect comparatively more confidence in the Russian results.

[73] The one exception to this claim concerns the time-based conditional hypotheses. If we think that measurement error was in general decreasing across all five countries as time passed – which is an intuitively plausible claim – then there is no way to reject the claim that variation in measurement error could be accountable for findings of more support for the standard economic voting hypotheses later in the decade. As was noted in the previous chapter, there are also theoretical reasons why we might expect this to be the case, but we cannot rule out the methodological explanations either. Accordingly, I return to this point in Chapter 8 when assessing the overall support for the time-based conditional

It is also important to note that this issue of comparing results from datasets of different sizes or with different levels of measurement error is not in any way a function of the decision to use simulated economic shocks (first differences) to generate the quantity of interest; any attempt to compare the statistical significance of individual coefficients would be subject to the same criticism.[74] This does, however, raise the question of why I chose to focus on the confidence that the estimated effect of economic conditions is either positive or negative as opposed to the magnitude of the predicted effect (e.g., the size of the mean or median predicted effect from the simulated distribution).

The simplest answer to the question is that the confidence that the effect of the economy is either positive or negative is the most appropriate measure to test the standard hypotheses, which predict exactly that: the types of parties that ought to do better where economic conditions are better or worse. By focusing on our confidence that the party either did do better or did do worse, I am able to present evidence that precisely speaks to the hypothesis.

However, there is also a large methodological concern in comparing the predicted size of the first difference across different parties because it is highly correlated with the size of the overall national vote received by the party. Indeed, across the eighty-eight incumbent, New Regime, and Old Regime parties, the correlation between the absolute value of the mean predicted effect for economic conditions on parties (e.g., a predicted improvement of 5.1% in the "good" economic region as opposed to the "bad" economic region, as was the case for the ODS in the illustrative example) and the proportion of the vote they received nationally in the election (e.g., 29.62% of the vote for the ODS, see Table 3.1) is +0.46. Therefore, any analysis comparing the *size* of the predicted economic effect across parties would first have to account for the difference in the overall percentage of the vote received by the different parties. This is a step that is not necessary when comparing confidence levels, as there is almost no relationship between the degree of confidence that we have that a party either performs better or worse following the economic shock and the percentage of the

---

hypotheses. Moreover, it should be noted that this does *not* affect our assessment of the standard economic voting hypotheses, as these are tested using elections from all three periods.

[74] Nor would pooling the data across countries solve the problem, as this would still generate results on the basis of an unequal number of observations from each country.

vote received nationally in the election (correlation $= +0.05$).[75] However, there is a strong correlation between the degree of confidence we have that the party has performed better or worse following the economic shock and the size of the predicted effect (correlation $= +0.52$). This makes sense, because as our level of confidence that an effect is either positive or negative approaches its lowest level (50 percent of positive simulations), it becomes more and more likely that the distribution straddles 0, and thus that the absolute value of the mean predicted effect also will be close to 0. So one way to think about the size of the predicted effect for economic conditions is that it is a function of both the overall popularity of the party and our confidence that the party is indeed performing better or worse where economic conditions are better. In this sense, by just focusing on the confidence level, which is what I do in this book, I am able to tap into the size of the economic effect (recall the $+0.52$ correlation) but only after having stripped out the component of the measure that is a result of the overall popularity of the party. And this is exactly what is needed to assess the degree of empirical support for the standard hypotheses: a measure of the effect of the economy on election results that is independent of the overall popularity of the party.

Appropriateness for Measuring Traditional Retrospective Voting
Although this is a study of the relationship between regional economic conditions and election results in postcommunist countries, I have attempted as much as possible to link the work to the larger literature on the relationship between economic conditions and election results. As noted in the preceding chapters, this literature has been dominated by work on elections in established democracies, has relied almost entirely on national level election results as the unit of analysis, and for the most part has focused primarily on the question of the relationship between economic conditions and the vote for the incumbent party. The theoretical framework adopted to motivate this empirical question in the existing literature has largely been one of retrospective voting: did voters react to economic conditions by punishing or rewarding incumbents for how the economy had performed on their watch? My study includes a hypothesis with a similar empirical prediction, the Incumbency hypothesis, which predicts that incumbent parties should perform better in areas of the country where economic conditions are stronger

---

[75] Confidence here is calculated as | *positive simulations*-50|, (where *positive simulations* = the percentage of simulated effects that are greater than zero) to take account of the fact that we can have high certainty in either a positive or negative direction.

than in areas of the country where economic conditions are worse. I did not, however, use a retrospective voting model to motivate this hypothesis; instead, I used the information-based model presented in the previous chapter that relied on predictions about how concentrations of people who were more or less satisfied with the state of the economy at the time of the election might be likely to behave. So while the hypothesis is very similar to the standard one found in the literature, its theoretical implications are different.

This highlights a final shortcoming of the comparative cross-regional approach, which is that it is not particularly well suited for assessing theories of retrospective voting, especially in a transitional context. The primary reason for this conclusion is because it is unclear whether we ought to expect residents of regions where economic conditions have changed more in the period of time since the previous election to be more upset or happy with the current government than residents of regions where economic conditions have remained at a more extreme level throughout the period. Consider as an example unemployment in two regions. In region A, unemployment rises from 2% to 4% between two elections. In region B, unemployment remains at 15% between both elections. By any retrospective measure, unemployment has gotten worse in region A while staying the same in Region B. Therefore, any analysis that attempts to build changes in economic conditions under the watch of the current government into its model would end up predicting that citizens of region A ought to "punish" the incumbent government more than citizens of region B.[76] And as retrospective voting models are used to assess whether citizens are holding the government accountable for their behavior, any finding that citizens in region B had "punished" the government more than citizens in region A would need to be interpreted as evidence that voters were *not* holding the government accountable for economic behavior, when in reality it is easy to imagine citizens in region A being thrilled that the unemployment rate in their region – even though it had doubled – was still incredibly low whereas citizens in region B would be furious that after X number of years in office, the government had done nothing to lower unemployment in their region.

As a result, it is difficult to conclude anything other than that cross-regional data are not particularly suitable for assessing classic arguments

---

[76] Punishment here could either be interpreted as citizens of region A giving a lower proportion of the vote to the incumbent government than citizens of region B or as decreasing the proportion of the vote given in region A compared to the previous election by a larger amount than in region B; either way, the points that follow about the difficulty in interpreting this result hold.

about whether or not voters use elections to hold the government accountable for economic developments under its watch.[77] But this is not to say that one cannot test whether or not incumbent parties perform better in parts of the country where economic conditions are better, but only that it is important to think about this in terms of the effects of having more people in certain areas that are likely to be satisfied with the state of economy generally than in other areas, as I have done in the previous chapter. Moreover, this is not to say that such a test does not have a retrospective feel to it, but only that it is crucial to realize that, to the extent that I test a model of accountability, it is the degree to which voters hold incumbents accountable for the state of the economy *at the time of the election*, as opposed to in terms of how it has changed since the previous election.[78]

Finally, I want to conclude by addressing the question of why I have not chosen to include control variables for the previous vote in my regression equations, as is often done in cross-national time-series analyses. The simplest answer to the question is that the hypotheses presented in the previous chapter do not make predictions about the change in vote from previous elections, but instead make predictions about where in the country parties are expected to enjoy more or less electoral support. Therefore, to include a control variable for vote in the previous election would mean that the analysis was not directly testing the hypotheses.

But there are also other logistical, theoretical, and methodological concerns with including controls for the previous vote in the analysis. Logistically, the presence of so many parties that appear and disappear and move in and out of different electoral coalitions between different elections raises the very serious question of how one would in fact determine the correct vote for the "previous" vote total. For starters, one would almost certainly need

---

[77] There is one potential exception to this claim, although it involves a reinterpretation of the traditional definition of incumbency; this point is discussed in detail in Chapter 9.

[78] The question of where microlevel studies of economic voting fall in this regard is an interesting one. Although such studies are usually designed to test a traditional retrospective approach, the question most often used in actual statistical analyses – especially in the American context – is some variant on the degree to which the respondent thinks either the country's or their own economic situation has changed over the *past year*, as opposed to since the previous election. Moreover, it would be interesting to know the extent to which answers to this type of question reflect an assessment of the respondent's view of the economy (or her own economic situation) at the time of the survey, or an assessment of how the economy (or her own situation) has changed under the entire period of rule of the current government. To the extent that it is the former, the similarities with cross-regional analysis may be stronger than at first glance.

to eliminate the 1991 Russian presidential election, the 1990 Hungarian parliamentary election, and the 1993 Russian parliamentary election from the study because of a lack of any appropriate "previous" vote total. Similarly, the 1992 Slovak, 1991 Polish, and 1992 Czech parliamentary elections would face the challenge of the appropriate "previous" vote for umbrella movements that had subsequently disintegrated. The 1992 and 1994 Slovak elections and the 1998 Czech elections would need to face the question of controlling for the "previous" vote for new parties that were formed when they split from existing parties against which they were then explicitly competing in the new election. The 1997 Polish parliamentary election would raise the question of which parties to control for when newly merged and newly formed electoral coalitions play a prominent role in the election. The 1995 and 1999 Russian parliamentary elections both featured prominent parties that had not participated in the previous election. Moreover, none of these points even touch on the question of whether presidential elections can reference parliamentary elections for "previous" vote totals or vice versa. Thus, regardless of the theoretical desirability of testing hypotheses that include controls for previous vote totals as part of the analysis, the reality of doing so in the postcommunist context would most likely result in (1) the dropping of numerous elections from the analysis and (2) the introduction of a tremendous number of *ad hoc* coding rules to figure out how to do this in each individual case. The first point would lead to the arbitrary discarding of important and useful data, whereas the second point would have a severe impact on the robustness of results, as it is impossible to imagine a set of coding decisions that could not be exchanged for multiple other plausible ways of coding the "previous" vote.[79]

Moreover, it is far from certain that it would be desirable to test cross-regional models by controlling for the previous vote for theoretical reasons. The decision to control for previous vote totals in these types of analyses is based on the presence of three assumptions: that voters have partisan loyalty, that this partisan loyalty affects their voting calculus, and that the prior vote totals received by the party represent a good proxy for estimating this unobservable regional party loyalty. The final assumption is based on the idea that the previous vote total represents a draw from a distribution of all possible

---

[79] Not surprisingly, the precedent in cross-regional studies of the effect of economic conditions on election results in postcommunist countries has been to do exactly what I have done in this book, which is to focus on the distribution of votes in the current election as opposed to the change in the distribution of votes since the previous election, although see Fidrmuc 2000a and Pacek 1994.

prior vote totals, and that the draw itself is a good approximation of that distribution. This is likely to be the case only if the distribution is normally distributed with a small level of variance. Even within stable democracies, scholars often doubt whether one single election represents a suitable proxy for this distribution, and instead they use a running average from multiple previous elections.[80] In transition countries, there is no reason to assume that any of these propositions are true. We do not know the degree to which partisan loyalty is present from the start in transition; and the idea that there could be full partisan loyalty of the Western variety seems unlikely given the proliferation of new parties, especially in the earlier elections. In most cases, there are at best one or two elections on which to base a "proxy" measurement of this loyalty, and these are elections that have occurred under rather extraordinary circumstances. In many cases – as has been discussed earlier – there is not even a single appropriate prior election. Moreover, given the nature of the postcommunist transitional experience, it is very likely that the state of the economy had an important effect on the vote for whatever party is being analyzed in the previous election. Thus, it would seem theoretically problematic to claim that this measure captures party loyalty that is somehow independent of concern over economic conditions.

Additionally, at least one recent paper raises the point that there may be methodological concerns with including lagged dependent variables in time-series analyses – especially when there are theoretical reasons to suspect whether the value of the dependent variable in the previous period has actually had a causal effect on the value of the dependent variable in the current period – noting that doing so can result in statistically significant coefficients appearing in regression results with signs in the wrong direction.[81]

---

[80] See, for example, Erikson 1990. Of course, given the difficulties of correctly identifying even an appropriate single "previous" vote total in the postcommunist context, trying to use a running tally of this nature with the data currently available is practically impossible.

[81] For more details, see Achen 2000. The author uses budget expenditures as an example of a case in which the dependent variable may look similar from year to year, but which in no way implies that legislators simply adopt the same figure as the previous year because of inertia. Instead, it may be that the causal factors that actually determine budget allocations themselves do not change much over time. In this case, including a lagged version of the dependent variable may simply obscure the real causal variables, and, as noted above, the results can even be more pernicious. This seems a useful analogy to election results in the postcommunist context, whereby economic conditions may have had a very large impact on why a party performed better in particular areas of the country in an election at time T, and then continued to have a similar effect in time T + 1. Such a pattern does not mean that voters in the region have simply become blind followers of that party oblivious to

Taken together, controlling for the previous vote in the types of regressions included in this study is logistically problematic, theoretically questionable, and may be methodologically suspect. And, most importantly from the point of view of this study, it would not result in an appropriate test of the hypotheses presented in the previous chapter.[82]

economic concerns but may instead just reflect the importance of economic factors across both elections.

[82] That is not to say that hypotheses that make predictions about the change in vote since the previous election would not be interesting to consider. Nevertheless, testing such hypotheses in a comparative framework using regional level data from the countries and time periods included in this study would be an inherently problematic task for all of the reasons outlined in the previous paragraphs.

4

Paired Case Studies

The purpose of this chapter is to present background information on the nine elections included in the four paired case studies, including which parties were in power leading up to the election, major issues that came up during the campaign, the most important parties contesting the election, and the election results. I also include references to works in which interested readers can find more information on each of these elections.[1]

The chapter is included in the book for three reasons. First and foremost, I hope to familiarize those who are not well versed in the peculiarities of postcommunist electoral politics with some basic facts about each election in an effort to make the case studies more widely accessible. Second, I want to highlight why exactly I think it is interesting to consider these elections as substantively meaningful "pairs." Finally, in a comparative study such as this one, it is impossible to do justice to the full panoply of issues at work in any one particular election, and I very consciously leave that task to others who are able to devote entire articles or even books to single-election analyses. Nevertheless, the danger is that in doing so we can lose sight of how interesting and important these elections were for the development of these countries in the postcommunist era. Thus, the final purpose of the chapter is to attempt to share with readers a bit of the richness of the electoral experiences that provide the data for my analyses.

The first paired case study is the 1992 Czech and Slovak parliamentary elections. These are examples of early parliamentary elections, as both took place in the first wave (as defined in Chapter 2) of elections. Moreover, these

---

[1] In particular, I recommend the "Election Notes" section of *Electoral Studies* for concise and informative descriptions of each election.

126

are the only two elections in the dataset that took place at the same time, as both elections were held before the breakup of Czechoslovakia; these also were the last elections before the two republics became independent countries.

The second paired case study is the 1995 Polish and 1996 Russian presidential elections, and these are the only presidential elections included in the case studies. Both took place in the middle of the decade, and both were the second competitive presidential election in their respective countries. Both also featured tight contests that required a second round to determine the eventual winner. In the Russian case, the incumbent Boris Yeltsin was reelected, but in the Polish case the incumbent Lech Wałęsa was defeated.

The third paired case study actually contains three elections, the 1993, 1995, and 1999 Russian parliamentary elections. This case study is distinct from the others as it compares elections from only one country and because it includes elections from throughout the decade, thus providing an opportunity to examine within one country how results changed over time. Moreover, given the general lack of comparative analysis of Russia with East-Central European countries in the postcommunist elections literature, it seemed prudent to examine the results from the Russian elections in depth.

The final paired case study focuses on the 1997 Polish and 1998 Hungarian parliamentary elections. These elections both featured an incumbent coalition government dominated by an Old Regime party running for reelection. Thus, they each provide a case where the Referendum and Transitional Identity Models produce contradictory predictions. As incumbents, the Referendum hypothesis predicts that these parties should perform better in parts of the country where economic conditions are better, but as Old Regime parties, the Old Regime hypothesis predicts that they would do better in areas of the country where economic conditions are worse. Thus, this final case study allows us to compare the Referendum and Transition Models in a head-to-head framework.

Case Study #1: Early Decade Parliamentary Elections: 1992 Czech and Slovak Elections

Following the collapse of communism but prior to its dissoluation, Czechoslovakia had a federal structure with shared power between the

127

federal government and two republic level governments, one in Slovakia and one in the "Czech lands," which included the rest of the country. On June 5–6, 1992, Czechs and Slovaks voted in three separate elections, one for each of the two houses of the Federal Parliament, and one for their respective republic level parliaments. As it was the republic level parliaments that would become the respective national parliaments of the independent Czech and Slovak Republics following the breakup of Czechoslovakia at the end of 1992, these are the elections included in this study.[2]

The 1990 Czechoslovakian elections had been dominated by two anti-communist umbrella movements, the Civic Forum in the Czech Republic and the Public Against Violence movement in the Slovak Republic. Although the 1992 elections were in fact regularly scheduled elections – the 1990 elections were for a special one-shot two-year term – both of these broad umbrella movements had disintegrated into a number of successor parties by the early part of 1991.[3] At the time of the June, 1992 elections, coalitions dominated by these successor parties were running both the Czech and Slovak republic governments.

Both elections were dominated by two major issues: the future of economic reforms and the future of the Czechoslovakian federation. However, the relative importance of these two issues within the two republics was different. In the Czech Republic, the commitment to economic reform was the more important campaign issue, while the status of of the Slovak Republic within the federation was the dominant issue in Slovakia.[4] Both elections were conducted using proportional representation with minimum thresholds (5% for parties, 7% for coalitions of two to three parties, and 10% for coalitions with more than four parties), and the opportunity for citizens to cast preferential ballots for up to four candidates on the party list.[5] At the time of the election, economic conditions were significantly worse in Slovakia than in the Czech Republic, with an unemployment rate of 11.4% in the former and only 2.6% in the latter; moreover, while Czech

---

[2] As it turned out, the vote for parties in the different houses of the Federal Government was fairly similar; see, for example, Rose and Munro 2003, Chapters 7–9; Krejcí 1995, Chapter 10. Moreover, most of the parties only campaigned in one of the two republics; see Obrman 1992a.

[3] The Civic Forum collapsed in February, Public Against Violence in April; see Kostelecky 1995.

[4] See, for example, Wightman 1993b, although for a more nuanced take, see Innes 1997, 2001.

[5] For details of the electoral law, see Krejcí 1995, Chapter 7; Birch, Millard et al. 2002, Chapter 4; and Kopecký 2001.

GDP would only drop by 0.5% in 1992, Slovak GDP would fall 6.7% that year.[6]

In both republics, the winning party was the largest splinter group of the now defunct anticommunist umbrella movements. In the Czech Republic, this was the Civic Democratic Party (ODS), which received almost 30% of the vote and ended up with more than twice as many seats in the parliament as its nearest competitor, although it was still twenty-five seats short of an outright majority. The party was led by Vaclav Klaus, who would go on to become the prime minister of the Czech Republic and would become largely synonymous with the evolution of Czech economic reform. The other successor parties to the Civic Forum did not perform as well as expected in the election. The Civic Democratic Alliance (ODA), which ran on a very similar platform to the ODS, just managed to clear the 5% threshold and the Civic Movement (OH), which tried to lay claim to the Civic Forum's non-ideological mantle and boasted the largest number of the Czech Republic's most popular politicians, fell just short of the threshold at 4.6%.[7] All told, eight parties cleared the threshold and entered the parliament, with the communist-based Left Bloc coalition receiving the second highest proportion of the vote at 14%. The Czech Social Democratic Party (CSSD), which would become the principal rival to the ODS as the decade progressed – eventually coming into power following the 1998 parliamentary elections – placed third, but with only 6.5% of the vote. Following the election, the ODS became the senior partner in a ruling coalition with the ODA and the Christian Democratic Union (KDU), which had received 6.3% of the vote.

In the Slovak Republic, the election also was won by the largest splinter group, but, unlike the ODS, which was primarily organized around an ideological position related to market reform, the Movement for a Democratic Slovakia (HZDS) put forward populist and patriotic pro-Slovak appeals with a clear emphasis on Slovak nationalism. HZDS dominated the voting in Slovakia even more than the ODS did in the Czech Republic, winning 37.3% of the vote and falling just one seat short of a majority in the Slovak parliament. As in the Czech Republic, the communist successor party, here the Party of the Democratic Left (SDL'), finished with the second highest

---

[6] Not surprisingly, inflation was fairly similar in both republics, with a 10.1% increase in the consumer price index in Slovakia and an 11.1% increase in the Czech Republic. The sources for all of the national economic statistics cited in this chapter are listed in Table 1.2 in Chapter 1.

[7] See Pehe 1992a, 23.

vote total, winning 14.7% of the vote.[8] In addition to the HZDS, another explicitly nationalist party, the Slovak National Party (SNS), also faired well in the election, coming in fourth place with 7.9% of the vote.[9] In sharp contrast to the Czech Republic, the standard bearer of the pro-market reform position in Slovakia, the Civic Democratic Union (ODU), received only 4% of the vote and failed to make it into the parliament, as did the Social Democratic Party of Slovakia, despite the presence of the hero of the Prague Spring, Alexander Dubček, on its party list. Following the election, the leader of the HZDS, Vladimír Meciar, put together a government composed largely of members of his own party.[10]

The aftermath of these elections is now well known to history. With both Klaus and Meciar refusing to join the federal government and choosing instead to assume the mantle of prime minister in their respective republics, discussions regarding the dissolution of Czechoslovakia began within a week after the 1992 election concluded. By the end of the year, Czechoslovakia would cease to exist, having been replaced by the independent Czech and Slovak Republics.[11]

Case Study #2: Mid-Decade Presidential Elections: 1995 Polish and 1996 Russian Presidential Elections

Lech Wałęsa's role in bringing about the collapse of communism in Poland – and some would say all of Eastern Europe – is by now well

---

[8] It is interesting to note the similarity in the proportion of the vote won by the Left Bloc and the SDL' in light of the fact that, as will be discussed in Chapter 6, the SDL' had already begun to consciously recast itself as a social-democratic party while the party at the heart of the Left Bloc, the Communist Party of Bohemia and Moravia, continued to run as an unreformed communist party.

[9] This did, however, represent a drop off from the 1990 election, in which the SNS had received 13.9 percent of the republic vote. In part, this may have been because of the proliferation of nationalist parties contesting the 1992 election; one commentator put the number at eight separate parties (Obrman 1992a, 12). For more on the SNS, see Bugajski 2002, 313–15.

[10] Out of fourteen ministers in the government, twelve were from the HZDS, with one independent and one member of the SNS rounding out the cabinet. The SNS was not technically part of the coalition, but it generally provided tacit support for the government (Pehe 1992d; Szomolanyi 1999). However, by March 1993, a split in the HZDS had already occurred – eight MPs left the party – and the HZDS was forced to enter into a coalition with the SNS.

[11] Readers interested in learning more about these elections are encouraged to see Pehe 1991a; Obrman 1992a; Pehe 1992a, b; Olson 1993; Wightman 1993a; Wolchik 1993; Cepl and Gillis 1994; Kostelecky 1995; Krejcí 1995; Innes 1997; Leff 1997; Innes 2001; and Kopecký 2001.

known.[12] Not surprisingly, in 1990 he was elected president of Poland in the nation's first postcommunist presidential election.[13] However, his performance as president did not generate nearly as many accolades as his prior career as a leader of the anticommunist Solidarity movement. His time in office was marked by conflict with those around him, including the parliament, the government, and even his own advisors.[14] As one noted Polish scholar wrote, "Many Poles seemed to expect that, once elected, Wałęsa would miraculously turn from a rough-edged electrician and union leader to a dignified statesman, with noble manners, speaking flawless Polish. This transformation could not take place, of course, and the symbolic function of the presidency seemed undermined by Wałęsa's slips of tongue and conduct. . . . [as well as] his actions and bellicose attitude towards other political actors" (Jasiewicz 1997, 156). Wałęsa's propensity for political conflict was further accentuated by the fact that following the 1993 Polish parliamentary elections, a government dominated by Solidarity successor parties was replaced by a government led by the communist successor Democratic Left Alliance (SLD) in coalition with the Polish Peasant Party (PSL).[15] All told, Wałęsa watched his approval ratings drop sharply over the course of his years in office, falling to around 10% in the first few months of 1995.

The 1995 Polish Presidential election was held according to a two-round majoritarian rule. If a candidate received more than 50% of the vote in the first round, then he or she was elected president; otherwise the top two candidates advanced to a second round. Wałęsa's primary competition in his reelection bid was the leader of the SLD, Aleksander Kwaśniewski. In contrast to Wałęsa, Kwaśniewski presented a thoroughly professional image, including his language, manner, and even dress. But Wałęsa also faced competition from other Solidarity successor candidates, including Jacek Kuron of the Freedom Union (UW), and Hanna Gronkiewicz-Waltz, the president of Poland's National Bank.[16] The nationalist Jan Olszewski and the the

---

[12] For more on Wałęsa's role in Polish history, see Ash 1999; Biskupski 2000; and Lukowski and Zawadzki 2001.

[13] For more on the 1990 Polish presidential election, see Sabbat-Swidlicka 1990; Vinton 1990b; Weydenthal 1990; Zubek 1991b; and Jasiewicz 1992a.

[14] For details, see Jasiewicz 1997, who labels the subsections of his chapter "Round One: Wałęsa versus a postcommunist parliament"; "Round Two: Wałęsa versus an anticommunist parliament"; and "Round Three: Wałęsa versus a neo-communist parliament."

[15] For more on the 1993 parliamentary election, see Jasiewicz 1993; Lipinski 1993; Zubek 1993; Millard 1994b; Chan 1995; and Gibson and Cielecka 1995.

[16] More information on Kuron and Gronkiewicz-Waltz is provided in Chapter 6.

PSL's Waldemar Pawlak, by now a former prime minister, also contested the election.

Despite the depths to which Wałęsa's approval ratings had fallen, his popularity began to steadily increase throughout the summer and especially the fall of 1995. Although at various times both Kuroń and Gronkiewicz-Waltz looked likely to surpass Wałęsa, by the time of the actual election he ended up easily taking second place in the first round of voting, earning three times as many votes as his nearest competitor. As had been predicted by opinion polls throughout the year, Kwaśniewski earned the highest number of votes in the first round, although the gap between his vote percentage (35%) and Wałęsa's vote percentage (33%) was much smaller than expected. Gronkiewicz-Waltz in particular seemed to suffer from a large number of election day defections, and ended up with only 2.8% of the vote.

In the period leading up to the first round of the election on November 5, 1995, a number of topics were prominently featured in the campaign, including the state of the economy – and especially issues related to privatization and reform – the role of the Catholic Church, Europe, and the question of how to deal with former communists. In the two weeks between the first and second rounds of voting, however, the debate focused much more heavily on the character of the two candidates. In particular, Kwaśniewski noticeably outperformed Wałęsa in two nationally televised debates – where the primary message of Wałęsa seemed to be that only he could prevent the return of communism in Poland – further highlighting the sense that his campaign was much less "professional" than Kwaśniewski's campaign.[17] And on November 19, 1995, Kwaśniewski defeated Wałęsa in the second round of the election in a close contest, winning 51.7% of the vote.[18]

The 1996 Russian presidential election followed a very similar pattern: a hero of the overthrow of the Communist Party entered the election as a beleaguered incumbent who was not expected to make it out of the first round – Russia also employed a two-round majoritarian electoral system – and yet somehow managed to resurrect his candidacy to the point at which he did in fact get into the second round to face an opponent who represented

---

[17] See Jasiewicz 1997, 159–60.
[18] For more information on the 1995 Polish presidential election, see Karpinski 1995a, 1995b; Osiatynski 1995; Tworzecki 1996; Bell 1997. For more on Wałęsa in particular, see Kurski 1993; Jasiewicz 1997.

the communist successor party. The biggest difference in the story, however, is that in the 1996 Russian presidential election Boris Yeltsin handily defeated his communist opponent, Gennadii Zyuganov, in the second round, winning 54% of the vote as compared to Zyuganov's 40% of the vote (6% of the voters cast their ballot against both candidates).[19]

The 1996 Russian presidential election is perhaps the most studied and most analyzed election of the postcommunist era.[20] It took place in the aftermath of a disastrous showing for pro-government and pro-reform parties in the 1995 Russian parliamentary election – which will be discussed in the following section – with postcommunist and authoritarian oriented parties capturing almost two-thirds of the parliament. Yeltsin's primary opponents in the election were the communist Zyuganov – whose party had received the highest percentage of list votes and the largest number of seats in the 1995 parliamentary election – the nationalists Aleksandr Lebed and Valdimir Zhirinovskii, and the more reformist-oriented Grigorii Yavlinskii.

At the time of the election, national economic conditions were far from ideal. Since Yeltsin had come to power in 1991, GDP had declined every single year,[21] unemployment had increased every year and was approaching 10%, inflation had been in the triple digits from 1993 to 1995 and still remained high at 48% in 1996, and workers were suffering from chronic nonpayment of wages. Six months before the elections, Yeltsin had an 8% approval rating, and all signs "heralded Yeltsin's crushing defeat in the June 1996 presidential election, a conclusion reached by many in Russia and the West" (Brudny 1997, 255). Following the 1995 parliamentary election, Yeltsin himself wrote that "At that time my whole life seemed under assault, battered about by all sorts of storms and strife. I stayed on my feet but was almost knocked over by the gusts and blows. My strong body had

---

[19] For an article length biography of Zyuganov, see Otto 1999.

[20] For analyses focusing on just this election, see Clem and Craumer 1996; Gershanok 1996; Hough, Davidheiser, and Lehmann 1996; McFaul 1996; Rose and Tikhomirov 1996; Brovkin 1997; Brudny 1997; Mason and Sidorenko-Stephenson 1997; McFaul 1997b; Hough 1998; Miller 1998; and Colton 2002. For examples of studies that include it in a comparative framework with other Russian elections, see Clem and Craumer 1997; Myagkov, Ordeshook, and Sobyanin 1997; O'Loughlin, Kolossov, and Vendina 1997; White, Rose, and McAllister 1997; Wyman 1997; Treisman 1998; Colton 2000b; Marsh 2002; and Rose and Munro 2002.

[21] Although the rate of decline was slowing at the time of the election, down from a low of −12.6% growth in 1994 to −4.1% growth in 1995 and −3.6% growth in 1996.

betrayed me. . . . And the people could not forgive me for economic 'shock therapy' or for the humiliation of Budyonnovsk and Grozny. It seemed as if all were lost" (Yeltsin 2000, 17).

As late as March 1995, Yeltsin himself was still considering canceling the elections entirely, a position advocated by his security chief Aleksandr Korzhakov, who reportedly stated, "Why risk everything just to have some people put pieces of paper into something called a ballot box?"[22] But that same month, Yeltsin made the crucial decision to replace his campaign team, then headed by Korzhakov ally Oleg Soskets, with a team led by Anatolii Chubais that enjoyed the financial backing of Russia's oligarchs, in particular Vladimir Gusinskii and Boris Berezovskii, who had agreed to put aside their own rivalries in an effort to ensure Yeltsin's reelection.[23]

In the remaining months before the election, Yeltsin's popularity began to climb dramatically. Many arguments have been put forward to account for this rise: the slick Western-style campaign; control of the media provided by the oligarchs; Yeltsin's attempt to demonstrate his vitality to the population through an active campaign including visits to two dozen different cities, touring mine shafts, and appearing on stage with rock stars;[24] public announcements regarding the back payment of wages; a cease-fire in the Chechen conflict that was announced at the end of May; the then-secret agreement of the Yeltsin camp to support Lebed in the first round in return for an endorsement before the second round; and the strategic decision to attempt to reframe the election as a two-man race between Yeltsin, representing the path forward, and Zyuganov, representing the return to communism.[25] Regardless of which of these may have been the most important, the net result was one of the more impressive electoral comebacks in recent memory, with Yeltsin winning the first round with 35% of the vote compared to Zyugaov's 32% of the vote. But, unlike Wałęsa, Yeltsin went on to win the second round handily as well.[26]

[22] According to David Remnick, Korzhakov made the comment to Duma deputy Galina Starovoitova; cited in White, Rose, and McAllister 1997, 254.

[23] For details, see in particular McFaul 1997b, 18–19; Brudny 1997, 259; and Yeltsin 2000, Chapter 2, where Yeltsin highlights the importance of his daughter Tatyana Dyachenko in convincing him to make the switch.

[24] See McFaul 1997b, 26–27.

[25] This strategy included showing the Academy Award – winning film *Burnt by the Sun*, which highlighted the horrors of the Stalinist era, on television the night before the first round of voting (Brudny 1997, 260).

[26] For work focused on Yeltsin, see Colton 1995; White 1997; Shevtsova 1999; Brown and Shevtsova 2001; Colton 2002; as well as his autobiographies, Yeltsin 1990, 1994, 2000.

Case Study #3: Russian Parliamentary Elections: 1993, 1995, and 1999

The background against which the December 12, 1993, Russian parliamentary elections occurred was far from ideal for a nation holding its first competitive legislative elections of the postcommunist era. Seemingly since his election to the presidency of the Russian Federation in the summer of 1991, Yeltsin had quarreled with the Soviet-era holdover Russian parliament over such fundamental issues as the pace and manner of economic reform, the composition of the government, the timing of elections, and the division of powers between the executive and the legislature. Despite numerous attempts to resolve these issues, including the replacement of Yeltsin's reformist prime minister Yegor Gaidar with the more conservative Viktor Chernomyrdin in December 1992 and the holding of a national referendum in April 1993, the conflict between the two bodies continued to escalate, culminating in the unilateral dismissal of parliament and calling of early elections by Yeltsin on September 21, 1993. Members of parliament responded by impeaching Yeltsin, appointing his vice president Alexsandr Rutskoi in his place along with a shadow government, and barricading themselves in their building. The showdown became violent on October 3, with anti-Yeltsin forces attacking the Ostankino television tower, and – after much uncertainty – was resolved the following day only when the Russian Army and troops from the Interior Ministry attacked the parliament and arrested its leaders.[27]

Two months later, the 1993 Russian parliamentary elections were held. Delegates to the parliament were elected through a mixed electoral system. Half of the 450 delegates were elected in single member districts, while the other 225 were selected on the basis of proportional representation using closed-list voting rules; parties needed to receive at least 5% of the party list vote to receive any of the proportional representation seats.[28]

---

[27] For a concise summaries of these events, see Colton 1998b, 4–7, and White, Rose and McAllister 1997, 87–94. For a more detailed description of the conflict between Yeltsin and the parliament, see Nichols 2001, Chapter 3; Moser 2001, 76–83; Huskey 1999, 25–34, and, for a more focused look at the struggle over the constitution, Ahdieh 1997. For an insider's take on the struggle, see Gaidar's autobiography, *Days of Defeat and Victory* (Gaidar 1999).

[28] Two deputies per administrative region were simultaneously elected to an upper house of the Russian parliament, the Federation Council, on a first-past-the-post basis. This upper house election was "in effect a 'no party' contest, in which candidates stood on local or regional or personal grounds" and were even prohibited from listing a party affiliation on the ballot (White 1997, 125).

Despite the chaos preceding the elections – which in addition to the October events included the suspension of newspapers (including *Pravda*) and the banning (and in some cases unbanning) of political parties and candidates – numerous parties managed to register, compete, and surpass the 5% threshold. One of the defining characteristics of the election was the newness of the parties; indeed, of the eight parties receiving seats from the party lists, five were formed in 1993, three of which were actually founded in October 1993.[29]

As one noted scholar observed, the 1993 Russian parliamentary elections "were intended to put the final nail in the coffin of communism and set Russia on the path of irreversible democratic development" (Sakwa 1995, 195). To this extent, the election was expected to produce a victory for the "party of power" (*partiya vlasti*), Russia's Choice (VR), led by the ex-prime minister and architect of economic reforms, Yegor Gaidar.[30] However, as would often be symptomatic of pro-democracy forces in Russia, not all of the democratic forces were able to unite under the same electoral banner. Numerous other parties that could be described as democratic contested the election, the most notable of which were the Party of Russian Unity and Concord, which contained a number of current government ministers, Nikolai Travkin's Democratic Party of Russia, the "oldest" democratic party in Russia, having been founded in 1990, and Grigorii Yavlinskii's Yabloko party.[31] Russia's Choice also faced competition from the Communist Party of the Russian Federation (KPRF), which, although briefly banned in October, was allowed to participate in the election, and the ironically named far right nationalist party, the Liberal Democratic Party of Russia (LDPR), under the leadership of Vladimir Zhirinovskii.[32] Zhirinovskii was known

---

[29] The three were Yabloko, Women of Russia, and the Party of Russian Unity and Concord; the Agrarian Party of the Russian Federation and Russia's Choice had been founded earlier in 1993; see White 1997, Table 6.1.

[30] The use of the phrase "party of power" in the Russian context is discussed in the following chapter.

[31] The party was actually called the Yavlinskii-Boldyrev-Lukin bloc after its three founders, Grigorii Yavlinskii, Yurii Boldyrev, and Vladimir Lukin, but quickly became known as Yabloko (which means apple in Russian) and over time became associated exclusively with Yavlinskii. For an article-length biography of Yavlinskii, see Rutland 1999.

[32] Other communist successor parties chose to boycott the election, but the KPRF "participated on the grounds that a boycott would be counter-productive and inhibit the development of an opposition" (Sakwa 1995, 204). The topic of the evolution of communist forces in Russia during this time period is addressed in greater detail in Lentini 1992; Urban 1996; Sakwa 1998; Flikke 1999; Sakwa 2002a; and especially Urban and Solovei 1997.

not only for traditional nationalist positions – such as blaming Jews and foreigners for Russia's problems – but also for the outlandishness of his proposals, including "'new Hiroshimas and Nagasakis on Japan' and 'another Chernobyl' on Germany" (White, Rose, and McAllister 1997, 114) or that Uzbeks and Tajiks should be used as cannon fodder in a renewed war in Afghanistan.[33] In contrast, the image many had of Russia's Choice was one of arrogance and confidence of victory by intellectuals out of touch with the average Russian; in particular their campaign theme that "everything was on course and nothing needed to be changed" (Wyman, Miller et al. 1994, 265) revealed a serious disconnect with Russian citizens.[34] It is also important to note that despite the clear association of Russia's Choice with the Yeltsin administration, Yeltsin never officially endorsed Russia's Choice and did not campaign on its behalf.[35]

In view of lofty expectations for a certain victory, supporters of Russia's Choice (as well as much of the Western world) were stunned when results showed that the LDPR had won the largest number of PR list votes with 22.9% of the vote.[36] Although Russia's Choice ended up as the single largest party in the parliament as a result of victories in single member districts – although even here the party's success can hardly be called impressive as 141 of the single member district mandates were claimed by independent candidates (White, Rose, and McAllister 1997, 123) – the results were viewed as a serious setback for the Russian reform movement. Moreover, the sense of failure was exacerbated by the fact that the recently vanquished KPRF received almost as many votes on the PR list as Russia's Choice, with 12.4% of the vote for the former compared to 15.5% of the vote for the latter. None of the other parties received more than 10% of

---

[33] *New Yorker* 1993. Wyman, Miller et al. also point out that in addition to being outlandish, Zhirinovskii was also at times genuinely funny, such as when "he compared the Soviet period to a variety of sexual acts: the revolution was a rape, the Stalin period homosexual, Khrushchev – masturbation, the Brezhnev and Gorbachev years political impotence, and of course his own victory would be orgasm" (Wyman, Miller et al. 1994, 258).

[34] See as well Tsygankov 1995.

[35] See Colton 1998b, 13. To this day, analysts often speculate on how Russian political development would have evolved had Yeltsin opted to join a political party.

[36] The election results were also accompanied by accusations of electoral fraud, in particular to assure the 50% turnout required for the constitutional referendum that accompanied the vote (White, Rose, and McAllister 1997, 127–8), although see Filipov and Ordeshook 1997 for a qualified rebuttal of these claims, especially regarding the magnitude of potential vote fraud.

the vote, although five more did surpass the 5% threshold and enter the parliament.[37]

If there was any consolation for the leadership of Russia's Choice at the conclusion of the election, it was that the 1993 parliament was only intended to serve as a temporary parliament, with the next elections already scheduled for December 1995. However, by the time of the 1995 elections, Russia's Choice – now renamed Russia's Democratic Choice (DVR) – was no longer the party most closely associated with President Yeltsin and his government. Instead, Yeltsin had tasked Chernomyrdin, who remained prime minister throughout the period between the two elections, with forming a new pro-government party, which would subsequently be named Our Home is Russia (NDR).[38] Most of the cabinet members also joined the party, and it enjoyed the "overt support of the president," as well as the "vast financial and political resources" at the disposal of the government (Belin and Orttung 1997, 34–5).[39] NDR, by conscious design, portrayed a much more centrist image than Russia's Choice had in the previous election, emphasizing its commitment to stability and its links to bureaucratic competence through such inspiring slogans as, "On a firm foundation of responsibility and experience."[40]

Given the calm manner in which the 1995 Russian parliamentary elections were carried out, NDR faced a surprisingly similar electoral landscape

---

[37] For more on the 1993 Russian parliamentary elections, see Clem and Craumer 1993; Slider, Gimpelson, and Chugrov 1994; Wyman, Miller et al. 1994; Zlobin 1994; Clem and Craumer 1995b, 1995c; Sakwa 1995; Wyman, White et al. 1995; Barnes 1996; Filipov and Ordeshook 1997 and especially Lentini 1995 and Colton and Hough 1998.

[38] Originally, the plan had called for not one but two "parties of power." One – NDR – was to represent the center right and be the governing party, while the other – the Bloc of Ivan Rybkin – would anchor the center left and serve as the loyal opposition. The net result was to be a crowding out of other parties to the fringes of Russian politics, which would now revolve around a stable center of pro-government parties (Kolesnikov 1996). Even putting aside the obvious contradictions of trying to build a party system around two pro-government parties, the plan stumbled from the start when the Bloc of Ivan Rybkin "failed miserably through defections, a lack of organization, and no clearly defined purpose. Russians found it difficult to accept a loyal opposition bloc that had been created by the government itself" (Grigoriev and Lantz 1996, 360).

[39] Oft-cited evidence in this regard is the lavish spending by NDR to involve celebrities such as supermodel Claudia Schiffer and American pop star Hammer in the campaign in an attempt to appeal to younger Russians (Grigoriev and Lantz 1996, 163).

[40] NDR's links to the bureaucracy led to the charge from Vitallii Tretyakov, then editor of *Nezavisimaya Gazeta*, that the party's Russian acronym NDR really stood for "Nomenklatura Dom Rossiya," (The Nomenklatura's Home is Russia.) The party's close ties to Gazprom, the behemoth Russian gas giant, were also mocked by the nickname "Nash Dom – Gazprom!" (Our home – Gazprom!) (Belin and Orttung 1997, 34–5).

to the one Russia's Choice had contested. The KPRF was the primary challenger on the left, the LDPR was the primary nationalist challenger, and the democratic camp remained highly fractured and split across different parties and movements. The economy continued to perform poorly (see preceding section) – if not quite as badly as in the first third of the decade – and Yeltsin and the policies of economic reform pursued by his government remained a lighting rod for opposition criticism.[41] Furthermore, the electoral system was practically the same as the one used in 1993, with all of the fundamental components – mixed system split between SMD and PR, closed list voting, and a 5% threshold for receiving PR seats – remaining in place.[42]

At the same time, there were a number of significant differences from the 1993 elections, in addition to the obvious contrast between a regularly scheduled election and one that followed armed conflict on the streets of Moscow by two months. The most important of these may have been the sheer number of political parties competing in the election, which jumped to forty-three. As all parties were given equal access to free television time, parties such as the Beer Lovers Party and the Subtropical Russia Movement proved more distracting to voters than they might otherwise have been. And potentially more seriously, the proliferation of parties led to almost half of the ballots in the list voting being "wasted" on parties that did not cross the 5% threshold.[43] Another difference was the obvious influence of the LDPR's success with a nationalist message in 1993, which was felt in two ways. First, a number of new nationalist parties competed with the

---

[41] See, for example, Tsipko 1996, 186; Grigoriev and Lantz 1996, 160; and Belin and Orttung 1997, Chapter 5.

[42] The biggest change was that the upper house of the Russian parliament, the Federation Council, was no longer to be popularly elected, and instead the governor and head of each regional legislature would represent their region. Regarding the lower house elections, the primary change affected the composition of the party lists so as to increase the likelihood of representatives from outside of Moscow being elected to the parliament. The change had little effect on voters, who continued to cast their ballots in the proportional representation component of the election for a party as opposed to for individuals on the party list. For details, see White, Rose, and McAllister 1997, 194–5.

[43] Although many of these parties did receive some seats in the parliament from the SMD contests, only three gained more than five seats in this manner. And the four parties that most closely missed passing the 5% threshold, the Congress of Russian Communities, Women of Russia, the Communist Workers of Russia – For the Soviet Union, and Workers Self-Government, received only five, three, one, and one seat(s), respectively. The fact that even the last party to exceed the threshold (Yabloko), which had only 6.9% of the vote, still received thirty-one list seats demonstrates just how consequential falling below the 5% threshold turned out to be.

LDPR for the nationalist vote. Indeed, before the election, the Congress of Russian Communities (KRO), featuring the popular ex-general Aleksandr Lebed and a somewhat more toned down nationalist message – stressing law and order, a strong state, and a strong military but avoiding the ethnic baiting practiced by the LDPR – was widely expected to do very well in the election.[44] Second, the KPRF also adopted a more nationalist tone, offering what one scholar called "Red Patriotism" (Tsipko 1996, 187). A final new feature of the political landscape was the ongoing presence of military conflict with the separatist Chechen Republic following Yeltsin's decision to invade in December, 1994.[45]

In a manner reminiscent of the 1993 elections, the results of the 1995 parliamentary election were again a huge disappointment for the pro-government party. Despite the vast resources at its disposal, NDR received only slightly more than 10% of the party-list vote.[46] But NDR was not the only party to suffer a disappointing result in the election. The LDPR saw its vote proportion cut in half from the previous election, receiving only 11.2% of the vote. But even that was a more successful result than the KRO enjoyed, as the party received only 4.3% of the vote and failed to cross the 5% threshold.[47] Russia's Choice, now no longer associated with the current government but still one of the best-known democratic parties, suffered the same fate of failing to cross the 5% threshold with only 3.9% of the vote. The one party undoubtedly satisfied with its performance was the big winner, the resurgent KPRF, which won 22.3% of the list votes, but, because of the large number of wasted votes in the party-list voting and its strong performance in the single member districts, entered the parliament with nearly three times as many deputies (157) as its closest competitor. It emerged as by far the strongest party in the new parliament, and its leader, Zyuganov, seemed a likely choice to succeed Yeltsin as president of Russia

---

[44] See Grigoriev and Lantz 1996, 162. For an article-length biography of Lebed, see Kipp 1999.

[45] For a thorough recounting of the struggle over Chechnya, see Gall and De Waal 1998. For a discussion of the dilemma faced by political parties – and Russia's Democratic Choice in particular – in opposing the war, see McFaul 2001, 257–61.

[46] One argument for the low vote is that Russians were using the parliamentary election to "send a message" to Yeltsin prior to the presidential election (Colton 1996b; Meirowitz and Tucker 2004).

[47] In the forthcoming presidential election, however, the positions of Lebed and Zhirinovskii would be reversed, with Lebed winning more than twice as many votes. This would prompt Zhirinovskii to complain that "Lebed stole my act and he stole my votes. I should take him to court" (as cited in White, Rose, and McAllister 1997, 253).

(although, as described in the previous section, this did not end up happening). Perhaps the only other party that could claim to have had a positive performance in the election was Yabloko, which was the only one of the democratic parties to surpass the 5% threshold, although it too received a smaller proportion of the vote (6.9% vs. 7.9%) than it had in 1993.[48]

If the 1995 parliamentary elections served as a wake-up call to Boris Yeltsin as he prepared for his reelection campaign, the 1999 parliamentary election was dominated by the question of who would succeed Yeltsin as president.[49] Yeltsin was limited by law to two terms, and as the 1999 elections approached almost all indications were that he intended to abide by that law and step down following regularly scheduled presidential elections in the summer of 2000. Before being dismissed as prime minister on March 23, 1998, it seemed likely that Viktor Chernomyrdin would enter the race as the favorite candidate. However, with his dismissal, Russia entered an era of rotating prime ministers that would see five different men hold the office in a span of sixteen months, culminating in the appointment of the relatively unknown Vladimir Putin on August 9, 1999, mere months before the December 1999 parliamentary elections and only a year removed from the August 1998 economic collapse, which had been triggered by default on Russian debt and led to a precipitous decline in the value of the ruble.[50]

Chernomyrdin's dismissal signaled the end of NDR as a viable political party, opening a hole in the middle of the political spectrum for a new "party

---

[48] For more on the 1995 Russian parliamentary elections, see Clem and Craumer 1995a; Moser 1995; Colton 1996a, 1996b; Grigoriev and Lantz 1996; Tsipko 1996; Urban 1996; Fish 1997; Rose, Tikhomirov, and Mishler 1997; White, Wyman, and Oates 1997; Wyman 1997 and especially Belin and Orttung 1997. For work that analyzes both the 1993 and 1995 parliamentary elections, see Myagkov, Ordeshook, and Sobyanin 1997; O'Loughlin, Kolossov, and Vendina 1997; Treisman 1998; Moser 1999 and especially White, Rose, and McAllister 1997; Colton 2000b; and Marsh 2002.

[49] Although in retrospect Vladimir Putin's election as president of Russia in March, 2000 seems almost inevitable, it is impossible to overstate the degree to which this was not the case in the years leading up to the election. Indeed, during a series of interviews that I conducted with academics, political consultants, members of think tanks, and representatives of political parties in the summer of 1998, not a single person once mentioned Putin's name in response to questions I posed regarding the forthcoming presidential contest.

[50] Chernomyrdin was replaced by Sergei Kirienko, who was followed by Yevgenii Primakov in September 1998 (although only after the parliament twice rejected Chernomyrdin, whom Yeltsin had attempted to reappoint.) Primakov was in turn replaced by Sergei Stepashin in May 1999, who would give way to Putin that summer. For a concise summary of information on all of Yeltsin's prime ministers, see Sakwa 2002b, 112–21.

of power."[51] As opposed to in 1995, however, the first party to attempt to fill this void was not organized by the Kremlin but, rather, in opposition to the Kremlin. As one analyst wrote at the time, "Never before has Russia seen such a coalition drawn from the grass-roots level without anyone's blessing. The Kremlin, in fact, is working against Fatherland-All Russia. For the first time in the country's history, the 'party of power' is headed by politicians with the highest popularity ratings; for the first time, its leader are launching an election campaign without being burdened by a responsibility for the the incumbent executive's records" (Makarenko 1999, 61). The Fatherland-All Russia (OVR) bloc was formed in the summer of 1999 by unifying the Fatherland movement organized around Moscow Mayor Yuri Luzhkov with the All-Russia bloc, which was based around regional governors.[52] OVR was also aided immeasurably by the decision of Yevgenii Primakov, the still popular ex-prime minister, to agree to become its head (and its likely presidential candidate).[53] The party promised voters people with practical experience in economic reform and running the country, but who knew how to do it better than those currently inhabiting the Kremlin; it was to be a party of *liudi dela*, or people of action.[54] Even before the merger between the different forces was complete, the hypothetical party was the most popular in Russia by the end of July (Makarenko 1999, 73), and immediately following the merger, one scholar wrote that "the formation last week of a new electoral bloc, Fatherland-All Russia, might be the most important development in Russian politics since the 1996 elections. . . . [T]he new, left-of-center coalition has the potential to dominate the post-Yeltsin era."[55]

The creation of OVR prompted a counter response from the Kremlin that took two forms. First, the Kremlin produced yet another government sponsored party of power, the Inter-Regional Movement Unity, commonly

---

[51] NDR would go on to compete in the 1999 election and receive only 1.2% of the vote after attempts at alliances with Russia's Democratic Choice (in August 1999) and Unity (October 1999) both failed. (Interview by author with Boris Makarenko, Deputy General Director, Center for Political Technologies, Moscow, Russia, March 30, 2000). Chernomyrdin himself, however, would enter the parliament from a single member district seat (Oates 2000, 6).

[52] For an article-length biography of Luzhkov, see Colton 1999.

[53] See Colton and McFaul 2000, 203. For an article-length biography of Primakov, see Daniels 1999.

[54] Interview by author with Yury Ushanov, Executive Secretary of the Program Council of Fatherland, Moscow, Russia, March 31, 2000.

[55] Cited in McFaul 2000, 9–10.

referred to as Unity. Headed by Sergei Shogui, the Minister of Emergencies, Alesksandr Karelin, a former international wrestling champion, and Aleksandr Gurov, former head of the organized crime department of the Interior Ministry of the USSR, the party was given little chance of crossing the 5% threshold, let alone playing a major role in the election.[56] During the campaign, Unity emphasized little more than its own newness, its rejection of ideology, its disdain for OVR, and, above all, its connection to Prime Minister Putin, who, while following Yeltsin's pattern of not explicitly endorsing a party, announced that "I, personally, as a citizen, will vote for Unity."[57] The second response of the Kremlin was to engineer an extremely negative portrayal of OVR, and especially of Primakov and Luzhkov, on state-controlled TV. These attacks emanated from numerous sources, but in particular the popular political *Sergei Dorenko Show*. Some of the more notorious of these attacks included bloody footage of Primakov's hip operation (to suggest he was too old to govern), accusations that Luzhkov had been involved in the 1996 murder of an American businessman, and claims that OVR was willing to undermine both the economy and the war in Chechnya to get rid of Putin.[58]

Other aspects of the 1999 election, however, were similar to those preceding it. The electoral rules governing the election were largely similar – the key features remained the same – with just some minor modifications in an attempt to reduce the number of parties competing in the election.[59] These attempts met with some success, as the number of parties dropped from forty-three to twenty-six. And with the exception of the two competing parties of power, the political landscape otherwise looked fairly similar, with competition from the LDPR (running under the name of the Zhirinovskii Bloc in this election), the KPRF, and Yabloko, although it is worth noting

---

[56] Interview by author with Vladimir Avarchev, member of parliament 1995–99 (Yabloko), Moscow, Russia, March 27, 2000. See as well Colton and McFaul 2000, 203, which cites a noted Russian political analyst as predicting "as late as October that Unity would harvest '1–2%, a maximum of 3%' of the vote." Indeed, even the Carnegie Endowment for International Peace's *Primer on Russia's Duma Elections*, with a release date of November, 1999, predicted that "the level of disgust with the current Yeltsin regime is so high that a bloc openly affiliated with the Yeltsin regime is unlikely to perform well in the upcoming vote" (Petrov and Makarkin 1999, 125).

[57] Cited in Colton and McFaul 2000, 211.

[58] See Belin 1999c, for an exhaustive list of these and other attacks made against OVR by the media. Often lost in the recounting of these criticisms, however, is the fact that OVR did have the overt support of the Moscow funded TV-Center (Channel 3) and received favorable coverage from NTV (Channel 4); for details, see Oates 2000, 11.

[59] For details, see McFaul and Petrov 1999, 3–4.

that none of these parties faced the kind of attacks the media leveled at OVR. The LDPR in particular received surprisingly positive coverage in the media, especially as compared to during the two previous parliamentary election campaigns.[60] One change in the electoral landscape, however, was provided by the fact that many of the democratic forces, including the remnants of Gaidar's Russia's Democratic Choice party, finally managed to unify under the banner of the Union of Right Forces (SPS), led by ex-prime minister Sergei Kirienko, former deputy prime minister Boris Nemtsov, and former minister of small business Irina Khakamada. The party presented itself as an advocate of democratic capitalism but opposed to the current crony-capitalism prevalent in Russia.[61] This message, however, was balanced by explicit support for Putin – one ad featured the slogan "Putin for President; Kirienko for the Duma" – which in turn was reciprocated in what amounted to a tacit endorsement of the party by Putin; campaign ads in the final week of the campaign featured Putin meeting with Kirienko.[62] Additionally, the party highlighted its youthful leaders and presented itself as the party of the future.

Unlike the 1995 election, the 1999 election took place against the backdrop of improving economic conditions. After a disastrous year in 1998 in which GDP – after having finally posted a modest gain in 1997 – fell by 5.3%, GDP actually rebounded to grow by 6.4% in 1999 (and would increase by 10% the following year), and polls showed increasing optimism about future economic conditions.[63] Chechnya also played a completely different roll in the 1999 election. Whereas the Chechen conflict had been seen as a drag on Yeltsin's popularity, Putin's decisive actions regarding the war in Chechnya were seen as a key to his skyrocketing popularity, which reached 80% approval ratings as the elections approached.[64]

---

[60] Two explanations have been put forward for this positive coverage. First, despite its outsider status, the LDPR actually had a remarkably strong track record of supporting the government on most major votes, and the Kremlin may have decided that the LDPR needed a boost after early opinion polls suggested that the LDPR might not clear the 5% threshold. Second, Zhirinovskii seemed to spend a great deal of the time that he was being interviewed in the media attacking OVR, which was actively courting the "patriotic" electorate. See Belin 1999b, for details.

[61] Interview by author with Boris Nemtsov, Moscow, Russia, March 31, 2000.

[62] See Belin 1999d.

[63] See McFaul 2000, 8.

[64] See McFaul 2000, 17–18. For a thorough analysis of voters' opinions of Putin, see Colton and McFaul 2003, Chapter 7.

144

The most important result of the December 19, 1999, election also represented a sharp break with the previous two parliamentary elections, as the Kremlin-sponsored party of power finally exceeded expectations. Although the KPRF still received the single largest number of votes on the PR list (24.2%), Unity, despite its late September formation, finished a very close second, with 23.2% of the vote. More important, it easily outdistanced OVR, which received only 13.3% of the vote, and as a result virtually collapsed as an opposition movement. Following its poor showing in the parliamentary election, OVR chose not to run a candidate in the presidential election, many of its regional supporters quickly defected to Unity, and by 2001 the two parties would merge. Both democratic forces surpassed the 5% threshold, with SPS (8.5%) surprisingly outpolling Yabloko (5.9%); much of SPS's late surge was attributed to the "Putin" bounce, with even Nemtsov estimating that Putin's tacit endorsement may have been worth a 2 percentage point increase in their share of the vote.[65] The LDPR rounded out the list of parties surpassing the threshold, but again saw its share of the vote cut almost in half, receiving just 6% of the vote.[66]

Finally, the election neatly solved the dilemma of who would serve as Russia's next president. On New Year's Eve 1999, Yeltsin again showed his capacity for surprise and capturing world attention by resigning and transferring power to the new interim president, Vladimir Putin, who would go on to be elected to his own four-year term on March 26, 2000, in a landslide victory.[67]

Case Study #4: Late Decade Incumbent-Old Regime Elections: 1997 Polish and 1998 Hungarian Parliamentary Elections

The 1997 Polish and 1998 Hungarian parliamentary elections shared a number of features in common. Both involved a communist successor party running for reelection at a time of generally improving economic conditions after having ruled in coalition with one other party for almost the entire

---

[65] Interview by author with Boris Nemtsov, Moscow, Russia, March 31, 2000.

[66] The LDPR would rebound in 2003, however, and receive 11.5% of the vote.

[67] For more on the 1999 Russian parliamentary election, see Colton and McFaul 2000; McFaul 2000; Oates 2000; Clem and Craumer 2001; Myagkov and Ordeshook 2001; Rose, Munro, and White 2001; Clem and Craumer 2002; Rose and Munro 2002 and especially Colton and McFaul 2003, as well as the thirteen election reports compiled by Radio Free Europe/Radio Liberty and posted at http://www.rferl.org/specials/russianelection/pastreports.asp.

period of time since the preceding election. In both cases, a party that had not previously led a government played an important role in unifying a fractured opposition and emerged from the election with the largest number of seats in the new parliament and control of the government. Moreover, in both cases a party that had led the government in the earlier part of the decade before the accession of the communist successor party to power entered the new coalition as a junior partner. Finally, both elections saw the emergence of a nationalist party that gained seats in the parliament for the first time.[68] These elections are also particularly valuable from a theoretical perspective because they provide an opportunity to directly contrast the predictions of the Referendum and Transitional Identity models since they feature important Old Regime parties that are running for reelection as incumbent parties. Thus, the Referendum Model predicts that as incumbent parties these parties should perform better in areas of the country where economic conditions are better, whereas the Transitional Identity Model predicts that as Old Regime parties these same parties should perform better in areas of the country where economic conditions are worse.

In Poland, the Old Regime incumbent party was the Democratic Left Alliance (SLD), which had come to power in 1993 and ruled in coalition with the Polish Peasant Party (PSL) for almost the entire period leading up to the 1997 election. Although the coalition was rocky, it had held until the month before the election – when it finally collapsed over the issue of agricultural subsidies – something no prior postcommunist Polish government had managed.[69] As the election approached, the Polish economy was improving in many regards; GDP growth would be between 6 and 7 percent for the third straight year, and unemployment and inflation had both been falling since the SLD-PSL government came to power.[70] Not surprisingly, the SLD stressed its own economic competence during the campaign, using

---

[68] One difference between the two elections, however, was the electoral systems employed by both countries. Poland utilized an open list PR system with both regional and national components, whereas Hungary employed a mixed electoral system with single member districts, regional party lists, and national list seats that were awarded on the basis of "wasted" votes from both the single member districts and regional party lists. For a detailed accounting of what some have called the most complicated set of electoral rules in the world, see Benoit, Csalotzky, et al. 1998.

[69] See Chan 1998, 564. For more on the struggles between the SLD and PSL, see note 22 in Chapter 5.

[70] Not everything about the economy was rosy, though, as the country had suffered through serious floods the previous summer and strike activity seemed to be on the rise (Curry 1997, 75–6).

slogans such as "We kept our word" and "Good today, better tomorrow."[71] The party also stressed social issues such as women's reproductive rights and the fact that it was less confrontational than its right-wing opponents.[72]

The SLD's primary opposition was the Solidarity Electoral Action (AWS) coalition, a grouping of over thirty right-wing parties and movements under the leadership of the Solidarity Trade Union.[73] The impetus behind bringing all of these parties together was the fact that in the 1993 parliamentary election, the existence of a 5% threshold and a plethora of right-wing parties that failed to clear this threshold meant that right-wing parties were severely underrepresented in the parliament compared to the percentage of votes they had received nationally; by contrast the SLD had received 20% of the vote and 37% of the seats in the parliament. In the campaign, AWS – perhaps not surprisingly given its composition – tended to avoid overly specific policy proposals and instead stressed a values-based message that centered on putting the family first.[74] AWS also played heavily on its links to the original Solidarity movement and the forces that had overthrown the communists in 1989.[75]

Competing with both the AWS and the SLD was the Freedom Union (UW), which had been created by a merger in April 1994 of the Democratic Union and the Congress of Liberal Democrats, the two parties that had led most of Poland's governments from 1989 to 1993 and were most closely associated with Poland's original shock therapy economic reform program. Like Russia's Choice, the importance of these two parties had seemed to be waning following the 1993 parliamentary election when they lost control of the government; the Congress of Liberal Democrats had not even made it into the 1993–97 parliament. Unlike AWS and SLD, which put forward very broad-based platforms, the UW had a focused campaign

---

[71] Interview by the author with Dariusz Klimaszewski, Member of the Central Executive Committee of SdRP, Warsaw, Poland, August 12, 1997.

[72] See Szczerbiak 1999, 1411–12. The question of relations between the state and the Catholic Church played an important role in the campaign generally, as did the question of the new constitution and the issue of lustration. See Chan 1998, 562–3.

[73] See Szczerbiak 1999, Appendix I, for a list of the parties comprising the movement.

[74] As the head of their analysis office for the coalition's program told me, this involved emphasizing the economic, social, and political rights of families. When I pressed for more details, I was told that while the priorities of the current coalition were budget, then GDP, then citizen, AWS would emphasize family, then GDP, then budget (interview by the author with Witold Nieduszynski, Director of the Office of Program Analysis, Solidarity Electoral Action [AWS], Warsaw, Poland, August 27, 1997). This inevitably became tinged with a quasi-populist appeal as well (Wenzel 1998, 145).

[75] See Szczerbiak 1999, 1407; Wenzel 1998.

message centered on the same pro-reform policies they had pursued in the past, which included finishing the reforms initiated by the first postcommunist government and completing the privatization process. Moreover, the party also tried to make the argument to voters that it was not the policies of the current government that were responsible for the improving economic outlook, but, rather, the policies of the original postcommunist governments.[76]

When the results were in, the SLD had actually increased its share of the vote since the previous election – winning 27.1% of the vote in 1997 as compared to 20.4% of the vote in 1993 – but had lost control of the government. AWS won almost 34% of the vote, which translated into 201 seats in parliament as opposed to 164 seats for the SLD. The UW performed better than it had in 1993 as well, increasing its share of the vote from 10.6% to 13.4%, and entered the parliament as the third largest party with sixty seats. The big loser in the election was the PSL, which saw its share of the vote drop by more than half – from 15.4% to 7.3% – and its number of seats plummet from 132 to only 27. The election also saw the rise of a nationalist party, the Movement for the Reconstruction of Poland (ROP), which managed to surpass the 5% threshold and enter the parliament.[77] After a protracted period of negotiation, AWS and the UW agreed to form a coalition government under the leadership of Jerzy Buzek, and the UW, the leader of Poland's first postcommunist government, became the junior coalition partner.[78]

In Hungary, the communist successor party was the Hungarian Socialist Party (MSzP), which had been in power since 1994. Similarly to Poland, Hungary also had enjoyed a period of improving economic conditions while the communist successor party was in power. GDP had grown every year and reached a rate of 4.6% growth in 1997, the highest figure of the

---

[76] Interview by the author with Krzystof Andracki, Director of the Press Bureau of National Election Headquarters of Freedom Union, Warsaw, Poland, August 27, 1997.

[77] The party stressed issues such as reprivatization, the decommunization of the state, and lustration of former Communist officials (interview by author with Jan Polkowski, Press Secretary of the Natonial Election Staff of ROP, Warsaw, Poland, August 12, 1997; see as well Szczerbiak 1999, 1413; Wenzel 1998, 144). And although ROP did not survive to contest the 2001 parliamentary elections, its showing in 1997 may have been a sign of things to come in 2001, when two other populist/nationalist parties, Self Defense of the Republic of Poland and the League of Polish Families, would capture almost a fifth of the total vote.

[78] For more on the 1997 Polish parliamentary election, see Curry 1997; Karpinski 1997a; Chan 1998; Wenzel 1998; Markowski 1999; and Szczerbiak 1999.

postcommunist era, inflation had remained stable and would drop in 1998 to 14.2%, the lowest rate since 1987, and unemployment had fallen every year that the MSzP was in power. Unlike Poland's SLD, however, the MSzP, which had actually won a majority of the seats in the parliament on its own in 1994, had ruled in coalition with a liberal party that had a been a prominent member of the anticommunist opposition that helped bring about the transition in Hungary in 1990, the Alliance of Free Democrats (SzDSz). The MSzP's campaign message, though, was similar to the message put forth by the SLD. First and foremost, the party stressed its successes in managing the economy and urged voters to stick with the current coalition and its policies.[79] It also highlighted the danger of turning the country over to right-wing forces that it viewed as extreme.[80]

The MSzP's primary competition in the election was FIDESZ-Hungarian People's Party. (Fidesz-MPP). Fidesz-MPP was distinguished from the AWS in Poland in two important ways. First, Fidesz-MPP was not a new party. It had run in both the 1990 and 1994 elections as a liberal anticommunist party of young people. Indeed, "Fidesz" was the acronym from the party's original name, the League of Young Democrats (Fiatal Demokraták Szővetsége). Second, Fidesz-MPP did not attempt to consolidate the anticommunist successor vote by forming an electoral coalition, but, rather, by establishing itself as the premier opposition party. Following a disappointing showing in the 1994 election in which Fidesz clearly lost the the liberal-centrist vote to the SzDSz, which received 19.7% of the vote compared to 7% for Fidesz, Fidesz made a concerted effort to move to the right of the political spectrum and establish itself as the dominant right-wing party.[81] Indeed, its goal before the election was not to join other

---

[79] In particular, the party argued that it needed more time to continue its economic changes, including finishing privatization, construction of a social safety net, and reducing inflation below 10%. Interview by the author with Vilmus Szabo, Head of the International Secretariat of the MSzP, Budapest, Hungary, May 8, 1998.

[80] Interview by author with Dr. Gyorgy Hegyi of the International Secretariat of the MSzP, Budapest, Hungary, May 7, 1998. For example, during the interview Hegyi stated that although Fidesz-MPP claimed it would not cooperate with the far right Hungarian Party of Truth and Life (MIEP), in reality they were cooperating and would continue to do so. And because MIEP was anti-EU and anti-NATO, by extension this meant that Fidesz-MPP would threaten Hungary's movement toward Europe. Similarly, he claimed that the economic promises made by Fidesz-MPP were unrealistic and would fall before the reality of budget constraints.

[81] See, for example, Fowler 1998, 257.

right-wing parties in the parliament and govern, but, rather, to defeat the other right-wing parties during the election.[82] It argued in the campaign that although the MSzP government had achieved 4–5% growth rates, what Hungary really needed was 7% growth rates, which it would deliver through tax reduction. Concurrent with its program of liberal economic reform, Fidesz-MPP also stressed a conservative pro-family message, the defense of Hungarian interests in foreign relations, and a strong state to tackle crime and corruption.[83]

Seemingly stuck between the two was the SzDSz, which found itself in the unenviable position of needing to both defend the status quo and present itself as an alternative to the main party responsible for the status quo, its coalition partner the MSzP. Unlike the UW in Poland, SzDSz could not simply attack the current government but had to manage a more nuanced campaign. This involved arguing for continuing the policies of the current government while at the same time suggesting that the party most responsible for those policies, the MSzP, would not have implemented these policies without the presence of the SzDSz in the government.[84] As a consequence, despite similarities in economic goals with Fidesz-MPP, SzDSz as well made the argument that Fidesz-MPP would be forced to cooperate with more extreme right-wing parties and could not be trusted to implement the policies it promised.[85]

---

[82] Interview by the author with Gyurk Andras, Fidesz-MPP Candidate for Parliament in 1998 Hungarian parliamentary election, Budapest, Hungary, May 5, 1998. Although Fidesz-MPP did cooperate with another right-wing party, the Hungarian Democratic Forum, by jointly nominating seventy-eight candidates in single member districts, the latter would emerge from the election as the clear junior partner to Fidesz-MPP. See Fowler 1998, 258, for details.

[83] Interview by the author with Kiraly Andras, International Secretary of Fidesz-MPP, Budapest, Hungary, May 5, 1998. See, as well, Fowler 1998, 258–9. As an aside related to the discussion in Chapter 2 of the difficulty in using partisan orientation as part of a model in the postcommunist context, consider Fidesz-MPP as an example. It shared an economic outlook common with pro-reform parties, an almost conservative/nationalist approach to social issues and foreign policies, and claimed that it was a right-wing party. Where would this party be placed on a left-right spectrum? In the same place as the UW in Poland, which shared a similar economic message but none of the nationalist positions? In the context of this book, however, Fidesz-MPP is clearly a New Regime party, albeit one in the populist leaning category.

[84] Interview by the author with Varga Kristof, Campaign Manager for SzDSz, Budapest, Hungary, May 7, 1998.

[85] Interview by author with Forgas Andras, Secretary for Foreign Affairs, SzDSz, Budapest, Hungary, May 5, 1998 and interview by the author with Varga Kristof, Campaign Manager for SzDSz, Budapest, Hungary, May 7, 1998.

When the votes were counted, the MSzP had received almost the exact same proportion of the PR list votes as it had in the previous election, with 32.3% of the vote in 1998 as compared to 33.0% of the vote in 1994. Unlike in Poland, however, this share of the vote was the most received by any party, topping Fidesz-MPP, which received 28.2% of the vote. However, Fidesz-MPP significantly outperformed the MSzP in the single member district component of the election, and entered the parliament as the single largest party, receiving 148 seats to the MSzP's 134 seats.[86] And while in Poland the liberal opposition party (the UW) saw its share of the vote increase and the agrarian junior coalition partner (the PSL) saw its share of the vote drop, in Hungary the liberal coalition partner (the SzDSz) saw its vote drop precipitously, from 19.7% of the vote and sixty-nine seats to 7.9% of the vote and twenty-four seats, whereas an agrarian opposition party, the Independent Smallholders Association (FKgP), saw its share of the vote increase significantly, from 8.8% of the vote in 1994 to 13.8% of the vote in 1998. Like Poland, the 1998 Hungarian election also witnessed a nationalist party surpassing the 5% threshold; in the Hungarian case, this was the far-right Hungarian Party of Truth and Life (MIEP). However, despite claims by the MSzP-SzDSz coalition that a Fidesz-MPP victory would necessitate bringing MIEP into the government, this did not come to fruition as Fidesz-MPP instead formed a government with the leading party in Hungary's first postcommunist government, the Hungarian Democratic Forum (MDF), and the agrarian FKgP.[87]

* * *

As the previous sections demonstrate, none of these elections occurred in a vacuum. Economic issues played an important role in all of the campaigns, but they were clearly not the only factors that affected the election outcomes. So the question now stands as to whether – against this panoply of different issues, contexts, countries, and times – it is possible to find systematic evidence to either support or falsify the hypotheses presented in the second chapter. It is to this task that I now turn in the following four chapters.

[86] Indeed, had it not been for the final compensatory tier of Hungary's electoral system, which included votes "wasted" in both the PR and SMD components, Fidesz-MPP would have had an even larger lead in the parliament, as the MSzP received thirty compensatory seats as compared to ten for Fidesz-MPP.

[87] For more on the 1998 Hungarian parliamentary election, see Benoit, Csalotzky et al. 1998; Fowler 1998; Haraszti 1998; Körösényi 1999; Agh 2000; Fricz 2000.

5

The Incumbency Hypothesis

The Incumbency hypothesis predicts that incumbent parties should enjoy greater electoral success in regions of the country where the economy is performing better than in regions of the country where the economy is performing worse. Of the three standard economic voting hypotheses tested in the book, the empirical support for the Incumbency hypothesis is the weakest. This is not to say that there is no support for the hypothesis, but of the forty-nine incumbent parties that contested the twenty elections examined in this book, we are only confident that economic conditions had the expected effect on the vote for twenty of these parties; in other words, the hypothesis is strongly supported by the data in only slightly more than 40% of the cases.

With over half of the cases considered in the study failing to provide support for the Incumbency hypothesis, turning to the conditional economic voting hypotheses to try to provide an explanation for the variation in support for this hypothesis is particularly instructive. In terms of the intuitive conditional hypotheses, neither the East-Central Europe versus Russia nor the Presidential versus Parliamentary distinctions provide much leverage in explaining the variation in empirical support for the Incumbency hypothesis. However, I do find modest levels of support for some of the more theoretically oriented conditional hypotheses. In particular, I find stronger empirical support for the Incumbency hypothesis as the decade progresses and among parties that received a larger percentage of the overall national vote. I also present some preliminary evidence suggesting that variation in empirical support for the Incumbency hypothesis is in part a function of each incumbent party's classification vis-à-vis the Transitional Identity Model (in other words, whether the party is also a New Regime party, an Old Regime party, or neither).

In the following section, I present the coding rules for classifying parties. I then discuss the coding decision for each of the elections included in the paired case studies. This is followed by a presentation of the party-by-party results for the case studies. The rest of the chapter then addresses the comparative results from across the entire study, first for all twenty elections as a whole and then disaggregated into the different categories proposed by the conditional hypotheses.

Defining Incumbency

In this section, I present the rules governing the coding of parties as incumbent parties for the purpose of testing the Incumbency hypothesis. Although I refer to numerous examples of applications of these rules (and go into greater detail on many of them in the footnotes), I want to reiterate that the goal of this section is *not* to provide a justification for every single coding decision. As mentioned previously, I do provide explanations for all of the coding decisions included in the case study elections in the following section, but in the interest of time and space I have elected not to do so for all forty-nine incumbent parties.

Defining incumbency in the stable two-party atmosphere of U.S. elections is usually a fairly simple task. The incumbent party is the party of the person who holds the office under consideration. In almost all instances, even if the current holder of that office is not running for reelection to that seat, someone from his or her party is. About the only complication faced in coding incumbents in studies of legislative elections is whether to classify incumbents as the party of the current office holder of each individual seat or as those people competing for office who are in the same party as the incumbent president; most models of economic voting do the latter (see, for example, Erikson 1990).

In new democracies, defining incumbency can be a much more complicated task. How does one code the incumbent party when there are multiple governments between elections, such as between the 1992 and 1994 Slovak parliamentary elections?[1] Or when different parties rotate in and out of the government, such as in the two years preceding the 1991 Polish parliamentary elections when no fewer than six different parties participated in the

---

[1] For more on the 1994 Slovak parliamentary election, see Pehe 1992d; Fisher 1996; Leff 1997; and Szomolanyi 1999.

government at different times?[2] Furthermore, the relationship between legislative and executive power is often less than clear and continually evolving, which also complicates coding decisions regarding incumbent parties.

In an effort to tie the definition of incumbency as closely as possible to the theoretical arguments underlying the Referendum Model, I adopt a fairly inclusive definition of incumbency.[3] In the following paragraphs, I detail the specifics of this definition on an institution-by-institution basis, but the underlying idea is that all parties that voters could consider responsible for government policies since the previous election should be classified as incumbents.

Presidential elections in presidential systems present perhaps the simplest coding decisions. When a sitting president runs for reelection, he or she is coded as the incumbent. If the sitting president chooses not to run, then the representative of his or her party who does run is considered the incumbent. If the president is an independent, then the candidate with the explicit backing of the sitting president would be considered the incumbent. Finally, in the initial competitive election of the postcommunist era, the incumbent is defined as the candidate (or candidates) that represents the party in power before the transition began (in other words, the communist successor parties, or, as they are referred to in this book, the Old Regime parties).[4] If in one of these initial elections the representatives of the Old Regime are split and hard- and soft-line factions both nominate a candidate for president, then both candidates are considered incumbents; in this book, this rule is invoked in the case of the 1991 Russian Presidential election,

---

[2] For more on the 1991 Polish parliamentary election, see Jasiewicz 1992a; Vinton 1993b; and Gebethner 1995.

[3] This of course increases the scope of the model as compared to a more restrictive definition, one of the factors considered in the comparison of the Referendum and Transitional Identity Models in Chapter 8. Later in this chapter, I consider a much more restrictive definition of incumbents in parliamentary elections while assessing whether more empirical support for the Incumbency hypothesis is found among lead members of coalition governments than their junior partners.

[4] In this book, this rule is applied in the 1991 Russian and 1990 Polish presidential elections. In Russia, this was clearly appropriate because the Communist Party of the Soviet Union was still in power. In Poland, the 1989 elections were actually the first competitive elections of the postcommunist era, but as these elections were not fully competitive and were predicated on prearranged power sharing arrangements, I elected to code the representative of Poland's Old Regime party as the incumbent for the 1990 presidential election as well.

the only presidential election in the study with more than one candidate coded as an incumbent. [5]

For parliamentary elections in a presidential system when the president is a member of a political party, that party is coded as the incumbent party.[6] If the president is an independent, then the parties in the parliament that are most closely tied to the president and come closest to representing the "party of power" are coded as incumbents. As will be discussed in the next section, the three Russian parliamentary elections (1993, 1995, 1999) are the only cases covered by this coding rule in the study.

For presidential elections in a parliamentary system, the candidate nominated by the current governing coalition is considered the incumbent. If the sequence of elections is such that presidential elections follow the parliamentary elections, however, then the candidate of the ruling party before the parliamentary election is considered the incumbent in the presidential election. Here, this rule is applied in the 1999 Slovak presidential election.[7]

---

[5] Vadim Bakatin was supported by Mikhail Gorbachev and the more moderate communists, while Nikolai Ryzhkov represented the hard-line communists. Bakatin was "understood to be Gorbachev's own choice for the Russian presidency" (White, Rose, and McAllister 1997, 37); see as well Rahr 1991; Urban 1992. There are other candidates besides Ryzhkov who also could be considered hard-liners, such as Albert Makashov. Urban writes "those associated with the old order fielded a spate of candidates, all of whom ran *against* El'tsin" (Urban 1992, 187). However, it seemed like a mistake theoretically to code all of the candidates besides Yeltsin (and Vladimir Zhirinovskii) as incumbents. In reality, the race had boiled down to a contest between Yeltsin and the hard-line Ryzhkov, who received close to 17% of the vote, so Ryzhkov seemed a logical choice to be "the incumbent" of the hard-liners. However, given Gorbachev's leadership position in the Soviet Union at the time of the 1991 Russia presidential election, it also appeared prudent to code Gorbachev's preference, Bakatin, as an alternate incumbent (see Rahr 1991, 29, and White, Rose, and McAllister 1997, 37).

[6] This follows a similar logic of coding members of the U.S. Congress as incumbents if they are of the same party as the president, as opposed to the actual people in office at the time of the election; see, for example, Erikson 1990.

[7] Thus, Vladimír Meciar is coded as the incumbent for this election. Although his party – the Movement for a Democratic Slovakia – was no longer in power at the time of the 1999 Slovak presidential elections, his party had been in power for the period of time between the September, 1994 and September, 1998 parliamentary elections and he personally had served as prime minister for the duration of the government. One way to conceptualize this is to think of the 1998/1999 sequence of Slovak elections as an election cycle, in which case the incumbent party should be the same in both elections. The alternative option would have been to code Rudolf Schuster, the eventual winner of the election and the candidate of the new ruling coalition following the 1998 election, as the incumbent. However, this coalition had only been in power for six months at the time of the presidential election, and with Schuster himself not yet serving as president, it seemed quite a stretch to code him as the incumbent candidate. As it turns out, there is no empirical support for either Schuster

The remaining category is parliamentary elections in parliamentary or mixed systems. If a single coalition has ruled since the previous election, then the members of that coalition are obviously coded as the incumbent parties. If multiple coalitions have ruled since the previous election then the members of the most recent coalition government are coded as the incumbent parties, with two exceptions. First, if a previous coalition government has ruled for a significant period of time before the election, then members of both coalitions are coded as incumbents. The precise definition of significant is clearly open to interpretation, but a rough guide is if the first coalition ruled for as long as the more recent coalition has been in power. This rule is important for four of the elections in the dataset, all of which featured at least two coalition governments between elections; in the 1991 Polish and 1992 and 1994 Slovak parliamentary elections, members of both coalitions are coded as incumbents, whereas in the 1993 Polish elections only the members of the last coalition led by Hanna Suchocka are coded as incumbent parties.[8] Second, if a caretaker government is appointed in

or Meciar performing as the Incumbency hypothesis predicts, so those who disagree with this coding decision can rest assured that it had no impact on the overall results. Had the definition for incumbents in a presidential election in a parliamentary system been expanded to include representatives of all parties that participated in the prior governing coalition, then the nationalist Ján Slota (head of the Slovak Nationalist Party) also would have been coded as an incumbent. As it turns out, the data does not support the Incumbency hypothesis in the case of Slota either, so including him in the dataset would only have made the Incumbency hypothesis perform worse overall. For more on the 1998–1999 Slovak election cycle, see Butorova, Meseznikov et al. 1999; Fish 1999; Fitzmaurice 1999; Szomolanyi 1999; and Fitzmaurice 2001.

[8] Following the 1991 Polish election, Jan Olszewski of the Center Alliance became prime minister in December 1991 at the head of a very unsteady coalition of five parties that was generally opposed by an active President Wałęsa. The coalition soon dropped to three parties, and by May 1992, the Polish parliament had already passed a vote of no confidence in the government. Not surprisingly, the government did not survive past June. Wałęsa then asked Waldemar Pawlak, the head of the Polish Peasant Party, to form a government, which he was unable to do. Finally, in July 1992, Hanna Suchocka of the Democratic Union put together a seven-party coalition that ruled until the September 1993 parliamentary elections. Because the Olszewski government only ruled for a short period of time in the beginning of the electoral cycle and the Pawlak government never even took office, parties are not coded as incumbents based on participation in either of these governments. From the Suchocka government, there were four parties that competed in the 1993 elections that received at least 2% of the vote – the Democratic Union (UD), the Congress of Liberal Democrats (KLD), the Agrarian Alliance (PL), and the Catholic Electoral Committee "Fatherland" (KKW) – and these are the four parties that are coded as incumbents. For more on this period in Poland, see Koldys 1992; Jasiewicz 1993; Sabbat-Swidlicka 1993; Vinton 1993b; Lewis 1994; and Sabbat-Swidlicka 1994.

conjunction with plans for new elections, then only the members of the previous government are coded as incumbents.[9]

Similarly to the rule for presidential elections in a presidential system, the incumbent in an initial competitive parliamentary election in a parliamentary system is also defined as the party (or parties) that represent the party in power before the transition, or what I have labeled the Old Regime parties. The only election in this study where this coding rule needs to be applied is in the 1990 Hungarian elections, where both the hard line Hungarian Socialist Workers Party (MSzMP) and the reformed Hungarian Socialist Party (MSzP) are coded as incumbents.[10]

The final coding decision for parliamentary elections in a parliamentary system concerns parties that break up between two elections. Essentially, this takes one of two forms. First, an umbrella party/movement that competes in an initial election can completely collapse before the subsequent election. When this occurs, such as before the 1992 Czech elections, the incumbents are coded as the parties that emerge directly from this umbrella organization. The second scenario involves a defection from a political party between elections, such as when the Freedom Union split off from the Civic Democratic Party before the 1998 Czech elections. In this case, both parties are coded as incumbents based on the assumption that voters know that the new party was part of the prior government.

---

[9] The 1998 Czech election had the potential to present a difficult case for this rule. A caretaker government was appointed in November 1997, but the election did not take place until June 1998. And although the government was led by the nonpartisan Josef Tosovsky, a former governor of the Central Bank and a very reluctant politician, the rest of the government was made up of members of three political parties: the Freedom Union, and Christian Democratic Union, and the Civic Democratic Alliance. The coding decision in this particular case is greatly simplified by the fact that the latter two parties had been part of the original coalition, and the Freedom Union was made up of deputies that had defected from the other member of that coalition, the Civic Democratic Party. Thus, all three parties can be coded as incumbents based on their participation in the first coalition, and no decisions need to be made as to whether the Tosovsky government warrants incumbent status. As it turned out, the Civic Democratic Alliance chose not to participate in the 1998 election following a series of financial scandals (interviews by author with Ondrej Turek, Head of Public Relations for the Freedom Union, Prague, Czech Republic, June 16, 1998, and Miroslav Macek, Vice-Chairman of Civic Democratic Alliance, Prague, Czech Republic, June 18, 1998). For more on the 1998 Czech parliamentary election, see Pehe 1998; and Kopecký and Mudde 1999.

[10] See Chapter 6 for a more detailed discussion of the evolution of these two parties. For more on the early stages of Hungary's transition in general, see Schopflin 1991; Bigler 1992; Oltay 1994; and Szelenyi, Fodor, and Hanley 1997.

As is the case with both New Regime and Old Regime parties, successor incumbents – be they from collapsed umbrella parties or defections from existing parties – are only included in the analysis if they have received at least 2 percent of the vote. This rule was primarily adopted to deal with early elections where large numbers of tiny parties – especially in the 1991 Polish elections, which was contested by over one hundred parties – could legitimately be described as having sprung from the original anticommunist umbrella movement. Were all these parties to be included, a large proportion of the analysis would be dominated by essentially meaningless parties. Although the 2% threshold is somewhat arbitrary, it seems to work very well in practice, keeping all of the well-known parties in the analysis without really eliminating any parties of importance, while at the same time excluding a number of small, irrelevant parties.[11]

To summarize, the goal of these coding rules has been to try to give the Incumbency hypothesis as wide a scope as possible by allowing for the possibility that voters might choose to support or oppose any of the parties that were part of the government – or were perceived as the party of the government in a presidential system – since the previous election. My goal in laying out these rules in this manner is to allow researchers attempting to replicate my coding decisions to do so with a minimum amount of confusion. While the coding rules were clearly drafted with the postcommunist context in mind, my hope is that they are sufficiently general so as to allow their use in other regions of the world.

Coding the Case Studies

Table 5.1 presents the coding of incumbent parties for all twenty elections. In this section, I discuss in detail the coding decision for the parties contesting elections included in the paired case studies. Although not every coding scenario is considered in these case studies, they do provide illustrations of most of the different types of coding decisions.

---

[11] The one exception to this rule is that when an important incumbent party (e.g., one of the two or three main members of a coalition) survives between elections but fares so poorly in the subsequent election that it does not receive 2% of the vote in that second election, it is still included in the analysis as an obvious incumbent. There is but one case across all twenty elections in which this rule is invoked: the Union of Slovak Workers, which dropped from 7.3% of the vote in the 1994 Slovak parliamentary election to 1.3% of the vote in the 1998 parliamentary election.

Table 5.1. *Coding of Incumbent Parties*

Country	Date*	Incumbent Parties
Czech Republic	June 5–6, 1992 (L)	ODS, ODA, OH
Czech Republic	May 31–June 1, 1996 (L)	ODS, ODA, KDU
Czech Republic	June 19–20, 1998 (L)	ODS, KDU, US
Hungary	April 8, 1990 (L)	MSzP, MSzMP
Hungary	May 8, 1994 (L)	MDF, FKgP, KDNP
Hungary	May 10, 1998 (L)	MSzP, SzDSz
Poland	November 25, 1990 (P)	Cimoszewicz
Poland	October 27, 1991 (L)	UD, KLD, PSL, PL, PC, WAK
Poland	September 19, 1993 (L)	UD, KLD, KKW, PL
Poland	November 5, 1995 (P)	Wałęsa
Poland	September 21, 1997 (L)	SLD, PSL
Russia	June 12, 1991 (P)	Ryzhkov, Bakatin
Russia	December 12, 1993 (L)	VR, PRES
Russia	December 17, 1995 (L)	NDR
Russia	June 16, 1996 (P)	Yeltsin
Russia	December 19, 1999 (L)	Unity
Slovakia	June 5–6, 1992 (L)	HZDS, KDH, ODU
Slovakia	September 30–October 1, 1994 (L)	DU, KDH, SV, HZDS, SNS
Slovakia	September 25–26, 1998 (L)	HZDS, SNS, ZRS
Slovakia	May 15, 1999 (P)	Meciar

* L = Legislative, P = Presidential; For two-round elections, date refers to first round.

Case Study #1: 1992 Czech and Slovak Parliamentary Elections

The 1992 Czech and Slovak republic level elections occurred concurrently with the elections for the Czechoslovakian parliament, seven months before the dissolution of Czechoslovakia and the creation of the independent Czech and Slovak Republics. Coding decisions here are complicated by the need to consider the leadership of both the federal Czechoslovakian and the republic level governments, but are eased somewhat by the large overlap between the participation by parties in the republic and federal governments.

In the 1990 Czechoslovak elections, the Civic Forum – a broad anticommunist movement – received approximately 50% of the vote in the regions of Czechoslovakia that would become the Czech Republic for both the federal parliament and the republic level parliament, more than three times the proportion of the closest runner-up, the Communist Party of Bohemia and Moravia. The Civic Forum therefore dominated the composition of Czech republic-level government, with eleven out of the twenty-one ministers in the government.[12] At the federal level, Civic Forum was the only Czech party to have ministers in the government, controlled more ministries than any other party, and controlled the prestigious Ministries of Foreign Affairs (Jiri Dienstbier) Finance (Vaclav Klaus) and Economy (Vladimir Dlouhy).[13] Had Civic Forum survived until the 1992 elections, it undoubtedly would have been coded as the incumbent party in the 1992 elections.

However, "by the end of 1990 it had become clear that Civic Forum and the Public against Violence [the Civic Forum's Slovak counterpart] had fulfilled their role as provisional anticommunist alliances of people with divergent political philosophies and that they would break up into political groups with more clearly defined political orientations" (Pehe 1991c, 2). By the 1992 elections, Civic Forum had effectively disintegrated into three parties: the Civic Democratic Alliance (ODA), the Civic Democratic Party (ODS), and the Civic Movement (OH).[14] As all three parties were clearly linked to the Civic Forum and were represented in the parliaments and governments at the time of the 1992 elections, all three are coded as incumbents in the 1992 election.

The 1990 elections to the Slovak parliament saw a slightly more equitable distribution of votes than the Czech Parliament. Although an umbrella anticommunist movement – called the Public Against Violence (VPN) movement – still clearly won the election, it took closer to 30% of the vote, as opposed to the close to 50% won by Civic Forum in the Czech Republic. Moreover, three additional parties received between 10 and 20% of the vote: the Christian Democratic Movement (KDH), the Slovak National Party (SNS), and the communists (still running as a unified party with their Czech counterparts).[15] The Slovak government that emerged following the election was dominated by the VPN, which had thirteen out of the twenty-three ministers in the government, including the Prime Minister Vladimír Meciar; seven of the remaining ten ministers came from the

---

[12] Indeed, only three other ministers were affiliated with any other parties; seven of the twenty-one were independents (Martin 1990).

[13] For more details, see Martin 1990.

[14] The Civic Forum officially split into the Civic Democratic Party and the Civic Movement on February 23, 1991. Shortly thereafter, the Civic Democratic Alliance split off as well, holding its founding conference on April 20, 1991. There were several other smaller groups that emerged from the Civic Forum, but none captured over 2% of the vote in the 1992 elections (Pehe 1991c, 2; see as well Wightman 1993a).

[15] See Innes 1997, 396.

KDH.[16] Like Civic Forum, VPN began to disintegrate in the spring of 1991, when Meciar formed his own group within VPN in March 1991. By the end of April, VPN had officially split and Meciar had been dismissed as the Slovak prime minister. Meciar's group went on to become the political party Movement for a Democratic Slovakia (HZDS). Meciar was replaced as prime minister by Jan Carnogursky of the KDH in April 1991. In addition, once VPN split, KDH became the strongest party in the Slovak parliament. The remaining part of VPN continued to support the Carnogursky government, and it entered the 1992 campaign as the Civic Democratic Union (ODU). Because all three parties played a clear role in the government in the period between the 1990 and 1992 elections, all three are coded as incumbents.

Case Study #2: 1995 Polish and 1996 Russian Presidential Elections

In both of these mid-decade presidential elections, a president elected in the early 1990s was running for reelection, so there is absolutely no confusion about the coding decision. In Poland, the Solidarity hero Lech Wałęsa had become Poland's first democratically elected president in December 1990 by receiving almost three-quarters of the vote in a second round runoff against Stanislaw Tymiński, an émigré Canadian businessman who had shocked pundits by finishing second in the first round of the election behind Wałęsa.[17] Wałęsa chose to run for reelection in 1995, and therefore is coded as the incumbent candidate.[18] In Russia, Boris Yeltsin had avoided

[16] The remaining three ministers were from the Democratic Party (DS), which would normally qualify the DS as an incumbent party as well. However, in the 1992 elections, the DS ran as part of a coalition with the Czech ODS, which clearly was not an incumbent party in Slovakia (Obrman 1992a). Indeed, the ODS was not even really a Slovak party, which makes the coding decision that much more difficult. As the DS also only played a small part in the government (three out of twenty-three ministries), I made the decision not to code it as an incumbent party for the 1992 election.

[17] In the first round, which took place in November 1990, Tymiński received 22.7% of the vote, finishing ahead of the reformist prime minister Tadeusz Mazowiecki (17.8%), the Democratic Left Alliance's candidate, Wlodzimierz Cimoszewicz (9.1%), and the Peasant Party's Roman Bartoszcze (7%); Wałęsa had received 39.4% of the vote, far short of the majority needed to avoid a second round. For more on the 1990 Polish presidential election, see Vinton 1990b; Weydenthal 1990; Kurski 1993; and Taras 1995.

[18] By the time Wałęsa ran for reelection, the parliament was controlled by the Democratic Left Alliance (SLD), as was described in Chapter 4. Had Poland been classified as a parliamentary system instead of a mixed system, then the coding rules would have called for Aleksander Kwaśniewski, the SLD's candidate in the presidential election and the eventual victor, to

the need for a second round in his initial presidential election when he was overwhelmingly elected president of the Russian Federal Republic of the Soviet Union in June 1990. In the election, which preceded and in part led to the collapse of the Soviet Union, Yeltsin had received almost 60% of the vote, which was more than three times his closest rival, Nikolai Ryzhkov. Yeltsin, too, chose to run for a second term, and therefore is coded as the incumbent candidate in the 1996 Russian presidential election.

Case Study #3: 1993, 1995, and 1999 Russian Parliamentary Elections

Russia is the only country in the study that is a presidential system, and as such the Russian parliamentary elections are the only elections in which incumbent parliamentary parties are coded based on their relationship to the incumbent president. Fortunately, the tradition in Russia during this period of time of a party emerging in each electoral cycle as the clear " party of power" (*partiya vlasti*) because of its connections to the president and government – and the widespread consensus among observers regarding the identity of this party – makes this task fairly simple.[19] As described in detail in Chapter 4, the party of power was very clear in both the 1995 and 1999 parliamentary elections, with Our Home is Russia (NDR) and Unity filling the role in these two elections, respectively. In both elections, these are the only parties coded as incumbent parties because of the fact that each possessed such clear ties to the president and his government in a manner that no other party even vaguely approached.[20]

The 1993 election presents a slightly different situation. Although Russia's Choice "represented the official face of the government" (Sakwa 1995, 199) and "was the closest approximation to a 'party of power'" (McFaul and Markov 1995, 39), there also were a number of important government ministers running under the banner of the Party of Russian Unity

be coded as the incumbent. However, because Poland is classified as a mixed system, the current occupant of the presidency, in this case Wałęsa, is coded as the incumbent.

[19] For more on the term "party of power" and its use in the context of Russian politics, see Colton and McFaul 2003, Chapter 3, and especially note 2 of that chapter (p. 266).

[20] Had Russia employed a parliamentary form of government, then NDR would have been coded as an incumbent in 1999 as well because of its presence in the government for a significant period since the 1995 and 1999 parliamentary elections. But because Russia is coded as a presidential system, the goal is to ascertain the party that best represents the president at the time of the election, which clearly excluded NDR by 1999.

and Concord (PRES). Both parties are therefore coded as incumbent parties for this election, reflecting the same general spirit that dictates that all members of a coalition government are coded as incumbent parties.

Case Study #4: 1997 Polish and 1998 Hungarian Elections

Here as well, the coding decisions are fairly simple because of the stability of governments between elections and the fact that none of the parties involved splintered into different successor movements. In Hungary, the unlikely Old Regime–New Regime coalition of the Hungarian Socialist Party (MSzP) and the Alliance for Free Democrats (SzDSz) stayed together for the duration of the period between the 1994 and 1998 elections, and thus both are coded as incumbents.[21]

In Poland, the Old Regime Democratic Left Alliance (SLD) and the agrarian Polish Peasant's Party (PSL) maintained an uneasy coalition for almost the entire period between the 1993 and 1997 elections. While there were three different prime ministers during this period, the coalition between the parties held together until practically the end of the term, which resulted in Poland's first ever regularly scheduled postcommunist parliamentary election.[22] So, although the coalition members were more confrontational with one another than most stable coalitions, both parties clearly fall within the definition given above for incumbent parties.

---

[21] For more on the 1998 Hungarian election, see Benoit, Csalotzky et al. 1998; Fowler 1998; Körösényi 1999; Agh 2000; and Schmidt and Tóth 2000.

[22] Although the SLD was the larger of the coalition partners, it originally chose to allow a member of the PSL, Waldemar Pawlak, to occupy the position of prime minister in part to allay fears that its return to power heralded a return to the old ways of communism (Curry 1995). However, following repeated clashes, the SLD reclaimed the position through a constructive vote of no confidence in March 1995 and installed József Olesky as prime minister (Karpinski 1996). Olesky, however, was forced to resign in February 1996 because of a scandal over whether he had provided information to Soviet and then Russian intelligence agents from 1983 through 1995 (Karpinski 1996; Castle and Taras 2002). The SLD held on to the post, however, replacing Olesky with Woldzimierz Cimoszewicz, who stayed in power until the end of the term. Readers will note later in the chapter that even though the first of these prime ministers was from the PSL, the SLD is coded as the primary coalition member while the PSL is coded as the junior partner. This decision was made because of both the numerical superiority of the SLD, which held 171 seats in the parliament as opposed to the PSL's 132 seats, as well as the fact that the PSL's Pawlak only held the premiership for a year and a half, as compared to the SLD's Olesky and Cimoszewicz, who combined to hold the post for two and a half years.

Table 5.2. *Empirical Support for Paired Case Studies: Incumbency Hypothesis*

		Party	Confidence in Predicted Effect
Czech Republic / Slovakia 1992			
Czech Republic	1992	Civic Movement (OH)	100.0
		Civic Democratic Party (ODS)	100.0
		Civic Democratic Alliance (ODA)	99.7
Slovakia	1992	Movement for a Democratic Slovakia (HZDS)	34.0
		Christian Democratic Movement (KDH)	54.9
		Civic Democratic Union (ODU)	81.8
Mid-Decade Presidential Elections			
Poland	1995	Lech Wałęsa	95.1
Russia	1996	Boris Yeltsin	98.0
Russian Parliamentary Elections			
Russia	1993	Russia's Choice (VR)	96.8
		Party of Russian Unity and Concord (PRES)	30.9
Russia	1995	Our Home is Russia (NDR)	92.6
Russia	1999	Inter-Regional Movement Unity	100.0
Late Decade Incumbent–Old Regime Elections			
Poland	1997	Democratic Left Alliance (SLD)	1.2
		Polish Peasant Party (PSL)	50.7
Hungary	1998	Hungarian Socialist Party (MSzP)	0.4
		Alliance of Free Democrats (SzDSz)	100.0

Empirical Results: Paired Case Studies

Table 5.2 presents our level of confidence – based on the method described in Chapter 3 – that the empirical data support the prediction of the Incumbency hypothesis for all of the incumbent parties contesting an election in the paired case studies. In the remainder of this section, I consider each case study in turn.

The 1992 Czech and Slovak parliamentary elections reveal sharply different patterns. The empirical results almost perfectly support the Incumbency hypothesis in the Czech case, but largely fail to do so at all in the Slovak case. Indeed, we are very confident that all three Czech incumbent parties performed better where the economy was stronger, as in all cases at least 99% of the predicted effects are positive. In contrast, none of the Slovak parties approach the 90% cutoff. In fact, our best guess is that the effect works in the opposite direction for HZDS, and we really are unable to make an informed guess one way or another for the KDH, with close to 50% of simulated first differences in each direction. Of the three, only the ODU is even close to approaching a reasonably significant level of confidence in an effect in the direction predicted by the Incumbency hypothesis.

What could account for these sharp distinctions in elections taking place at the same time in what was still the same country? Two possible explanations can be found in the conditional economic voting hypotheses. First, the regime future hypothesis predicted that the economy would have less of an impact on election results when the future of the regime is a significant part of the election rhetoric. As noted in Chapter 2, the 1992 Slovak election is one of the two elections in the study coded as a regime future election. Seen from this perspective, the fact that there is no support for a standard economic voting hypothesis – here the Incumbency hypothesis – in the 1992 Slovak election makes sense. Another possible explanation is suggested by using the Transitional Identity Model to predicted variation in support for the Incumbency hypothesis. As illustrated in Panel 3 of Table 2.6, the interactive conditional hypothesis predicts more support for the Incumbency hypothesis among incumbent–New Regime parties than incumbent parties that are not also New Regime parties. In the Czech case, all three incumbent parties are also New Regime parties (see Table 6.1), and in all three cases the data are very supportive of the Incumbency hypothesis. In the Slovak case, only the ODU is also coded as a New Regime party (see Table 6.1), whereas the other two are neither New Regime nor Old Regime parties. Although the ODU does not cross the 90% confidence threshold, it is clearly provides the best empirical support for the Incumbency hypothesis of the three Slovak incumbent parties. This suggests some preliminary evidence that the Transitional Identity Model can explain variation in support for the Incumbency hypothesis in the manner pedicted by the interactive conditional hypothesis (see Table 2.6).

Turning to the pair of mid-decade presidential elections, the Incumbency hypothesis is well supported by the data in the reelection bids of both Lech Wałęsa and Boris Yeltsin. This leads to three observations. First, there is preliminary evidence that the Incumbency hypothesis is not only appropriate for parliamentary elections but also can aid our understanding of regional economic voting patterns in presidential elections. Second, we now have our first example of a standard economic voting hypothesis being supported by data from Russia, here in a presidential election. Finally, it should be noted that both of these candidates are also coded as New Regime candidates , which suggests that the findings are consistent with the support for the interactive conditional hypothesis noted above in the 1992 Czech and Slovak case study.

In examining the three Russian parliamentary elections, we find further evidence of empirical support for the Incumbency hypothesis in Russian elections. Of the four incumbent parties that competed in these three elections, the empirical results only fail to support the hypothesis in one case: the Party of Russian Unity and Concord (PRES) in 1993, in which we have absolutely no confidence that economic conditions have had the effect predicted by the Incumbency hypothesis. Although PRES undoubtedly should be coded as an incumbent party based on the coding scheme employed here, it is worth noting that Russia's Choice was clearly the primary "party of power" in the 1993 election (and is coded as such later in the chapter for the analysis of the coalition conditional hypothesis). Thus, the case provides an election-specific example in which the Incumbency hypothesis is well supported by the primary coalition partner and not supported by another coalition partner, at least insofar as this plays out in a presidential system.

As noted previously, the last case study features two elections with Old Regime parties as lead coalition members. This results in a direct conflict between the predictions of the Incumbency hypothesis, which predicts incumbents should perform better where economic conditions are stronger, and the Old Regime hypothesis, which predicts that Old Regime parties should perform better where economic conditions are weaker. Strikingly, the results from both the 1997 Polish and 1998 Hungarian parliamentary elections are unequivocally supportive of the Transitional Identity Model as opposed to the Referendum Model. Contrary to the predictions of the Incumbency hypothesis – but completely consistent with the Old Regime hypothesis – we are extremely confident (more than 98% certain in both cases) that both Old Regime incumbent parties performed *worse* where economic conditions were better.[23] Furthermore, the one New Regime party among the four incumbent parties in this paired case study, the SzDSz in Hungary, is the only example in which the Incumbency hypothesis works as expected; we have very strong confidence that this party benefited from better economic conditions. Finally, the incumbent party in these cases which

---

[23] Although both analyses are clearly cross-sectional and thus do not measure over-time trends at all, one can not help but speculate that this might provide some insight as to why both parties were voted out of office despite improved economic conditions during their four-year reigns. I return to this point in Chapter 9.

is classified neither as an Old Regime nor as a New Regime party, the PSL in Poland, is the one case in which we cannot make any claim as to whether the economy either helped or hurt the party's electoral performance, as the simulated effects of the economic shock is approximately evenly distributed in both directions.

Thus, we can make two important conclusions from this final paired case study. First, for the parties for which the Transitional Identity and Referendum Models have conflicting predictions, there appears to be little empirical support for the predictions of the Referendum Model. Second, similarly to the 1992 Czech/Slovak case study, the Transitional Identity Model appears to be a strong predictor of the cases in which the Incumbency hypothesis is likely to be well (or poorly) supported by the empirical data in the manner suggested by the interactive conditional hypothesis.

Comparative Analysis

As the purpose of a comparative study is to avoid reliance on any one particular case for drawing general conclusions, I now turn to comparative results drawn from all forty-nine incumbent parties that contested the twenty elections included in the study. And although the Incumbency hypothesis was well supported by the empirical data in over half of the cases examined as part of the case studies, it did not fare as well across the entire sample. Using a 90% threshold for "strong" empirical support reveals that the prediction of the Incumbency hypothesis is strongly supported by the empirical data in twenty out of forty-nine cases, or 41% of the time.[24] In eight cases, or 16% of the time, we are actually strongly confident that the effect is in the opposite direction from what is predicted by the model (as was the case for the MSzP and the SLD in the final paired case study).

Moreover, this overall finding is quite robust to the different specifications of the estimate as discussed in the previous chapter. To reiterate, all of the estimates were recalculated using just the three core independent economic variables, with an additional independent variable (poverty), with additional parties included in the analysis, and with a smaller-sized economic shock. But no matter how the analysis was conducted, the overall finding was remarkably constant: the number of cases in which the

---

[24] The rational for employing a 90% threshold is described in the previous chapter. Results based on other thresholds for "strong" empirical support are presented as part of the comparative analysis in Chapter 8; see especially Table 8.2.

Incumbency hypothesis was strongly supported by the empirical evidence varied from a low of eighteen out of forty-nine parties (or 37%) to a high of twenty out of forty-nine parties (or 41% of the cases); see Table 8.3 in Chapter 8 for more details. Of course, the possibility remains that the hypothesis could enjoy more empirical support in subsections of the cases in which we expect the economy to be more important. Thus, in the remainder of this chapter, I examine whether or not any of the conditional economic voting hypotheses presented in Chapter 2 identify subsections of the cases in which there is more empirical support for the Incumbency hypothesis than across the entire study.

Intuitive Explanations

The three intuitive conditional hypotheses presented in Chapter 2 highlight the distinction between parliamentary and presidential elections, elections in Central Europe and Russia, and country-by-country distinctions across results. Based on Panel 1 in Table 5.3, we can clearly reject the claim that the Incumbency hypothesis is only supported by empirical evidence in either parliamentary or presidential elections but not in elections to the other institution. While the Incumbency hypothesis seems to be slightly better supported by data from parliamentary elections, the distinction is slim at best and undoubtedly in part a function of the small number of cases from presidential elections.[25] But we do find the telling result that if we had eliminated presidential elections from the study altogether, the overall conclusion concerning the degree of support for the Incumbency hypothesis would have remained practically the same, with 42% of the cases surpassing the 90% confidence threshold as opposed to 41% in the study as it now stands. Therefore, any concern that the overall finding regarding the lack of strong support for the Incumbency hypothesis was being driven by the decision to include presidential elections in the study should be laid to rest by this finding.

To a large part, the motivation for examining the East Central Europe versus Russia distinction is to explore whether the different regional

---

[25] To illustrate just how sensitive this makes the results, if only one presidential candidate had been coded as an incumbent in the 1991 Russian presidential election instead of both Bakatin and Ryzhkov, then the percentage of successes for the Incumbency hypothesis in presidential elections would be 40% (two out of five instead of two out of six), or practically identical to the 42% of the parliamentary cases.

Table 5.3. *Intuitive Explanations of Variation in Support for Incumbency Hypothesis*

Panel 1: Parliamentary vs. Presidential Elections

	All	Parliamentary	Presidential
90% Confident in Predicted Direction	20	18	2
90% Confident in Wrong Direction	8	7	1
Total Cases	49	43	6
Percentage with 90% Confidence in	**41%**	**42%**	**33%**
Predicted (Wrong) **Direction**	(16%)	(16%)	(17%)

Panel 2: East-Central Europe vs. Russia

	All	East-Central Europe	Russia
90% Confident in Predicted Direction	20	16	4
90% Confident in Wrong Direction	8	8	0
Total Cases	49	42	7
Percentage with 90% Confidence in	**41%**	**38%**	**57%**
Predicted (Wrong) **Direction**	(16%)	(19%)	(0%)

Panel 3: Country by Country Variation

	All	Czech R.	Hungary	Poland	Slovakia	Russia
90% Confident in Predicted Direction	20	7	2	3	4	4
90% Confident in Wrong Direction	8	0	3	3	2	0
Total Cases	49	9	7	14	12	7
Percentage with 90% Confidence in Predicted (Wrong) **Direction**	**41%** (16%)	**78%** (0%)	**29%** (43%)	**21%** (21%)	**33%** (17%)	**57%** (0%)

economic voting models might somehow work well in the East-Central European cases but be inappropriate for Russia. The evidence suggests that if anything, there is actually more empirical support generated for the Incumbency hypothesis in the Russian cases than in the East-Central European cases. As Panel 2 of Table 5.3 illustrates, the Incumbency hypothesis is supported by the data for a higher proportion of the Russian parties (57%) than East-Central European parties (38%). Although we should probably refrain from reading too much into this based on the much smaller number of Russian cases, it should suffice to refute the critique that the Referendum Model is somehow *a priori* inappropriate for Russia.

Moreover, Panel 3 of Table 5.3 illustrates the dangers of falling into the trap of just thinking of the distinction between countries as based on the old East-Central Europe versus former Soviet Union split. By disaggregating the results across all countries, we uncover a pattern that is not based on this distinction at all. Instead, we find that the model enjoys the most empirical support in the Czech Republic and, to a lesser extent, Russia, and has significantly less support in Hungary, Poland, and Slovakia.

What might explain this distinction? Traditional claims of Czech exceptionalism in matters related to the development of democratic behavior usually draw on the Czechoslovakian interwar experiences with democracy.[26] Were this explanation to be the key to understanding why the Incumbency hypothesis has so much more support in the Czech case, however, we would expect the hypothesis also to be well supported in the Slovak case and not particularly well in the Russian case.[27] The results, however, are the opposite, with the hypothesis having more empirical support in Russia than Slovakia.

Following on the line of reasoning developed in the case study section, however, we can observe a very interesting pattern. Both the Czech Republic and Russia are distinguished by the fact that a large proportion of their incumbent parties are also New Regime parties. The definition of New Regime parties is discussed in great detail in the next chapter, but for the time being it is illustrative to note that across the three Czech elections, seven of the nine incumbent parties are New Regime parties; in the five Russian elections, five out of the seven incumbent parties are New Regime parties.[28] The pattern is quite different for Hungary (two out of seven), Poland (five out of fourteen), and Slovakia (two out of twelve).[29]

---

[26] For more on elections in Czechoslovakia in the interwar period, see Krejčí 1995, Chapter 3; for more on the Czechoslovakian interwar experience generally, see Leff 1997, Chapter 1, and Wolchik 1992, 120–7.

[27] Slovakia was part of Czechoslovakia in the interwar period as well, whereas Russia had been under Communist rule for most of the twentieth century. Thus, any argument based on interwar democratic experiences would likely need to have Slovakia ahead of Russia on this score.

[28] In the Czech Republic, the exception is the Christian Democratic Union, which is coded as an incumbent in both 1996 and 1998. In Russia, the exceptions are the two Old Regime–incumbent candidates in the 1991 presidential election, Bakatin and Ryzhkov. For the remaining Russian elections, all of the incumbent parties are also New Regime parties.

[29] The primary reason for this distinction is because the New Regime parties that came to power in the Czech Republic in 1990 essentially remained in power through the 1998 election. Thus, there is not a Czech election in the study where either an Old Regime party

The Incumbency Hypothesis

Table 5.4. *Support for the Incumbency Hypothesis in Russia and Czech Republic by New Regime Party Status* (Parties with 90% confidence of effect/Number of incumbent parties)

	New Regime	Other	Total
Czech Republic	7/7	0/2	7/9
Russia	4/5	0/2	4/7
Total Cases	11/12	0/4	11/16

Further evidence that the improved success of the Incumbency hypothesis in the Czech and Russian cases is a function of the prevalence of New Regime incumbents is demonstrated in Table 5.4. Here we note that of the twelve incumbent parties in the Czech Republic and Russia that are also New Regime parties, the empirical evidence supports the prediction of the Incumbency hypothesis in eleven of these cases (PRES in Russia is the sole exception). However, the Incumbency hypothesis is not supported by the empirical data in any of the four remaining non–New Regime incumbent parties across both countries.

Thus, although this line of inquiry began on the basis of an atheoretical motivation – to explore whether the intuition that the model might work well in East-Central Europe but not in Russia was substantiated by the data – it is now possible to use a theoretically motivated explanation to explain an interesting anomaly in the data. In line with observations made on the basis of the assessments of the paired case studies, we now have additional evidence to support the prediction that there should be more support for the Incumbency hypothesis among incumbent parties that are also New Regime parties than other incumbent parties. Or, put more succinctly, there is now more evidence to support the claim that an incumbency effect in regional economic voting is conditional on a party's Transitional Identity.

---

or a party that was neither a New Regime nor an Old Regime party anchored the governing coalition heading into the election. Similarly, following Yeltsin's election to the presidency in 1991, the incumbent parties in Russia are also always New Regime parties, as Yeltsin remained in office until the end of the decade and the coding rules for incumbency in Russia's presidential republic are contingent on parties' relationship to the president. In Poland, Hungary, and Slovakia, however, there was much greater turnover in the government, both between election cycles and because of election results, thus leading to a wider variety of types of incumbents contesting elections.

Responsibility Hypotheses

In Chapter 2, three responsibility-based conditional hypotheses were proposed to predict variation in the level of empirical support for the Incumbency hypothesis. The institutional responsibility hypothesis posited that there should be more empirical support for the Incumbency hypothesis in elections for more important institutions than for less important institutions. The coalition hypothesis predicted more support for the Incumbency hypothesis for the primary member of a coalition in parliamentary elections than for their junior partners. Finally, the size of vote hypothesis predicted more support for the Incumbency hypothesis among incumbent parties that received a larger share of the overall vote in the election.

Table 5.5 suggests that the institutional responsibility hypothesis cannot offer much leverage over the variation in support for the Incumbency hypothesis. Our expectation was to find the percentage of cases in which we were confident that the empirical results supported the Incumbency hypothesis decline as we moved from the high responsibility category (dominant elections, defined as presidential elections in presidential systems and parliamentary elections in parliamentary systems) to the low responsibility category (dominated elections, defined as parliamentary elections in presidential systems and presidential elections in parliamentary systems). A quick glance at Panel 1 of Table 5.5, however, demonstrates little evidence to support the hypothesis. Although there is more support for the Incumbency hypothesis in dominant elections than in mixed elections, we actually see the highest proportion of support coming out of the dominated category, which was predicted to have the lowest levels of support. At the same time, this is an admittedly a weak test, with the most damaging evidence for the hypothesis coming from a category with only five parties. So it may be the case that with more data, the results would begin to look more supportive of the hypothesis, but for now all we can conclude is that there is not sufficient evidence from these cases to support the institutional responsibility hypothesis.

Turning to the coalition hypothesis, the breakdown of all incumbent parties into either primary or junior coalition partners is listed in Table 5.6 (see the appendix to this chapter for a detailed explication of the coding rule as well as explanations of individual coding decisions). Note that only one party is listed as the primary coalition member for each election, resulting in a total of fifteen primary coalition members and twenty-eight other coalition members.

Table 5.5. *Responsibility Explanations of Variation in Support for Incumbency Hypothesis*

Panel 1: Institutional Responsibility

	All	Dominant	Mixed	Dominated
90% Confident in Predicted Direction	20	14	3	3
90% Confident in Wrong Direction	8	5	3	0
Total Cases	49	30	14	5
Percentage with 90% Confidence in	**41%**	**47%**	**21%**	**60%**
Predicted (Wrong) **Direction**	(16%)	(17%)	(21%)	(0%)

Panel 2: Coalitions in Parliamentary Elections

	All	Primary Coalition Member	Other Coalition Member
90% Confident in Predicted Direction	18	8	10
90% Confident in Wrong Direction	7	3	4
Total Cases	43	15	28
Percentage with 90% Confidence	**42%**	**53%**	**36%**
in Predicted (Wrong) **Direction**	(16%)	(20%)	(14%)

Panel 3: Size of National Vote

	All	<5%	≥5%	≥10%	≥20%
90% Confident in Predicted Direction	20	1	19	11	8
90% Confident in Wrong Direction	8	3	5	4	2
Total Cases	49	7	42	21	12
Percentage with 90% Confidence in	**41%**	**14%**	**45%**	**52%**	**67%**
Predicted (Wrong) **Direction**	(16%)	(43%)	(12%)	(19%)	(17%)

Panel 2 of Table 5.5 illustrates that there is more support for the Incumbency hypothesis among the primary members of coalitions than among their junior partner(s). Although the size of the effect is not that dramatic, there is strong empirical support for the Incumbency hypothesis in over half of the cases of the primary coalition partners but only in slightly more than a third of the cases of other coalition parties. That being said, the small number of primary coalition partners (15) should caution us not to make too much of this finding; a switch in the results for only two primary coalition members would make the results nearly identical. It is interesting to note that if we eliminate incumbent Parties that are also Old Regime parties – which we know from the final case study did not fare well in producing strong support for the Incumbency hypothesis – then the

Table 5.6. *Coding of Primary and Junior Coalition Partners*

Country	Year	Primary Coalition Party	Junior Coalition Parties
Czech Republic	1992	ODS	ODA, OH
Czech Republic	1996	ODS	ODA, KDU
Czech Republic	1998	ODS	US, KDU
Hungary	1990	MSzP	MSzMP
Hungary	1994	MDF	FKgP, KDNP
Hungary	1998	MSzP	SzDSz
Poland	1991	UD	KLD, PSL, PL, PC, WAK
Poland	1993	UD	KLD, KKW, PL
Poland	1997	SLD	PSL
Russia	1993	VR	PRES
Russia	1995	NDR	
Russia	1999	Unity	
Slovakia	1992	KDH	HZDS, ODU
Slovakia	1994	DU	KDH, SV, HZDS, SNS
Slovakia	1998	HZDS	ZRS, SNS

Incumbency hypothesis is supported by the data in 67% of the cases (eight out of twelve) for the primary coalition partners as compared to 40% of the cases (ten out of twenty-five) for the junior coalition partners, which is a larger gap than found in the overall results in Panel 2.

Of the three responsibility hypotheses, the size of vote hypothesis is clearly the best supported by the data. Readers should note that Panel 3 of Table 5.5 is organized slightly differently than the first two panels. The second (<5% of the vote) and third (≥5% of the vote) columns are mutually exclusive and exhaust the universe of cases, but the fourth (≥10% of the vote) and fifth (≥20% of the vote) columns are subsets of the third column. Viewed together, though, they reveal a clear pattern: the larger the percentage of the overall vote received by a party, the more likely we are to find support for the Incumbency hypothesis. This is most apparent at the extremes. For incumbent parties that received < 5% of the vote, the Incumbency hypothesis is well supported by the data in only one out of seven cases (14%). But for incumbent parties that received over 20% of the vote, the Incumbency hypothesis is well supported by the empirical evidence in eight out of twelve cases (67%). Thus, if we were willing to limit our tests of the Incumbency hypothesis only to parties that received at least 20% of the overall vote, we would have a hypothesis that was substantially

Table 5.7. *Supply-Side Explanations of Variation in Support for Incumbency Hypothesis: Personality Hypothesis*

	All	Presidential Elections	Open-List PR Elections	Closed-List PR Elections
90% Confident in Predicted Direction	20	2	13	5
90% Confident in Wrong Direction	8	1	4	3
Total Cases	49	6	32	11
Percentage with 90% Confidence in Predicted (Wrong) **Direction**	**41%** (16%)	**33%** (17%)	**41%** (13%)	**45%** (27%)

better supported by the empirical data. The flip side of such a decision would be a model with extremely small scope, as there were only twelve incumbent parties across all twenty elections that received at least 20% of the national vote.

Supply-Side Hypotheses

The basic idea underlying the supply-side hypotheses is that there should be less empirical support for the Incumbency hypothesis when other, noneconomic factors are more important. Here, I consider the support for one supply-side hypothesis, the personality hypothesis, which predicts less empirical support for the Incumbency hypothesis as electoral rules place greater emphasis on the personal identity of candidates for office.

More specifically, the personality hypothesis predicts that the strongest support for the Incumbency hypothesis should be found in closed list proportional representation (PR) parliamentary elections, the least support in presidential elections, and a level of support somewhere between these extremes for open-list PR parliamentary elections. As both Hungary and Russia used closed-list PR voting and Poland, Slovakia, and the Czech Republic employed open-list PR voting, there is variation across the three categories. The results in Table 5.7 can best be described as providing lukewarm support for the personality hypothesis. The percentage of cases in which the Incumbency hypothesis is supported by the empirical data does increase in the manner predicted by the hypothesis as we move from presidential elections to open-list PR elections to closed list PR elections. However, this finding should be greatly tempered by both the small number of cases of incumbents in presidential elections and the fact that the percentages of cases supported by the data – albeit while increasing in the

Table 5.8. *Time-Based Explanations of Variation in Support for Incumbency Hypothesis*

	All	90–92	93–96	97–99
90% Confident in Predicted Direction	20	3	11	6
90% Confident in Wrong Direction	8	3	2	3
Total Cases	49	17	20	12
Percentage with 90% Confidence in Predicted (Wrong) **Direction**	**41%** (16%)	**18%** (18%)	**55%** (10%)	**50%** (25%)

correct direction – are in reality fairly close to each other. So although the result is in the expected pattern, it is clearly a very tenuous result that at best can be taken as an indication that the hypothesis deserves continued investigation.

Time-Based Hypotheses

The final category of conditional economic voting hypotheses that we can apply to the Incumbency hypothesis concerns the effect of the passage of time. Recall that I presented two contradictory time-based hypotheses in Chapter 2, one of which predicted more support for Incumbency hypothesis as the decade progressed, and one of which predicted less support. The results, presented in Table 5.8, demonstrate a clear pattern. In the first wave of elections that took place between 1990 and 1992, there is much less support for the Incumbency hypothesis than in elections that took place from 1993 to 1999; while there is actually a drop between the second wave and the third wave, this difference appears trivial and pales in comparison to the distinction between the first wave and the two other waves. What exactly is the root cause of the pattern is something that cannot be definitively solved by examining these aggregate level results. But the finding is consistent with both of the ideas used to motivate the increasing support over time hypothesis. It may be that the earliest elections were too chaotic for even the low information Incumbency hypothesis to generate much empirical support (although findings in the next two chapters will cast doubt on this interpretation), and it may be that voters were not yet looking to the state of the economy as a determinant of whether to vote incumbent parties out of office. It also may be the case the same factors that have led the Referendum Model to generate less support than the Transitional Identity Model generally contribute to the lack of support in the first wave of elections. Moreover, the fact that there was such a sharp change between the first and second wave and then practically no change between the second and third waves again raises the question of whether testing the hypothesis using "waves" that are only of a few years' duration is even the appropriate time frame. But regardless of the explanation as to why the results hold, there is a certainly a pattern here: from 1993 on, the empirical data is much more likely to support the Incumbency hypothesis than during the first wave of elections.

Conclusions

Overall, the empirical support for the Referendum Model and the Incumbency hypothesis is of modest strength. Across the entire decade, the empirical evidence only supports the claim that incumbent parties received a higher proportion of the vote in regions of the country where the economy was doing better with a reasonable degree of confidence for roughly 40% of those parties.

There are, however, a number of interesting points to be learned about those cases where the model is well supported by the data. First, it is possible to find empirical support for the hypothesis in both presidential and parliamentary elections, as well as in both East-Central European and Russian elections. Second, there is some evidence that the Incumbency hypothesis is better supported by the data in the manner predicted by some of the conditional hypotheses. Perhaps the most substantial finding is that the Incumbency hypothesis seems to do a better job predicting regional economic voting patterns for parties that receive a larger share of the overall vote than for those receiving a smaller share. As noted in Chapter 2, this is one of a number of ways of testing the responsibility-based conditional economic voting approach. A related responsibility hypothesis based on the relative importance of the institution for which voters were casting their vote, however, did not generate any meaningful empirical support. A third hypothesis focused on the relative importance of parties within coalitions generated some degree of support, thus providing an overall mixed assessment of the general responsibility-based approach.

There is also some fairly weak evidence suggesting that perhaps economic conditions may matter less as other factors matter more. In this vein, the Incumbency hypothesis generated less empirical support in elections in which personality seemed to have an opportunity to play a larger role, although this finding is tenuous and should be interpreted as little more than encouragement to conduct further tests of this nature. Time, too, seems to have an effect on the likelihood of finding support for the Incumbency hypothesis; the clear conclusion here is that the hypothesis is not very well supported in the first wave of elections between 1990 and 1992.

The third major finding from the chapter is drawn from both the paired case studies and the country by country comparative analyses. In repeated instances, there was evidence that the Transitional Identity Model could help explain variation in the empirical support for the Incumbency hypothesis. In particular, the overlap between parties that were both incumbent and New Regime parties helped to explain the distinction between the 1992 Czech and 1992 Slovak case studies, as well as the country-by-country distinction between the Russian and Czech results, on the one hand (where there was a fair degree of support for the Incumbency hypothesis), and the Hungarian, Slovak, and Polish cases, on the other hand (where there was much less support for the hypothesis). Similar conclusions can be drawn on the basis of the paired case study focusing on the 1997 Polish and 1998 Hungarian parliamentary elections, where the Incumbency hypothesis was not at all supported in the case of the two incumbent–Old Regime parties, but was supported in the case of the one incumbent–New Regime party.

Overall, the findings presented in this chapter demonstrate that in numerous instances, after controlling for demographic variables, incumbent parties did indeed perform better in parts of the country where economic conditions were stronger. However, there are even more examples of incumbent parties for which it is not possible to find this predicted relationship with a strong degree of confidence, which raises the possibility that more than just the incumbency status of parties is necessary to understand regional economic voting patterns. In the following chapters, therefore, I turn to an assessment of the Transitional Identity Model to explore an alternative set of predictions of the relationship between regional economic conditions and regional election results.

Appendix 5.1: Coding of Primary and Other Coalition Partners

This appendix details the coding of incumbent parties in parliamentary elections as either primary or junior coalition partners (see Table 5.6). The coding rule is based on two simple criteria: the party of the coalition members that received the largest percentage of the vote in the previous election and the party from which the prime minister was selected. If both of these criteria are met by a single party, that party is coded as the primary coalition member. If either of these criteria are not applicable, the classification defaults to the other one. For example, if there is a nonparty technocratic prime minister, then the coalition partner with the highest percentage of the vote from the previous election would be the primary coalition member. Fortunately, there are no cases in the current study where these two criteria are at odds with one another, but in that situation the decision would have to be made on a case-by-case basis by the analyst, keeping in mind the theoretical perspective that the primary coalition partner should be expected to be seen as having more responsibility for government policy in the eyes of voters than the junior coalition partners.

If the election follows the dissolution of a larger party or movement and the incumbent parties did not compete individually in the previous election, then the primary coalition member ideally should be the party most closely linked to the now defunct larger party or movement and the one playing the most important role in the government in the period leading up to the election. If there are multiple coalitions before the election, then the primary member from the most recent coalition is coded as the primary coalition member,[30] unless there is a compelling reason on the basis of the theoretical logic of the argument not to do so. In a parliamentary election in a presidential system, the party closest to the president is treated as the primary coalition member. In the case of the first contested elections following the transition to a multiparty system, the primary coalition member is the one most closely linked to the largest successor party from the previous ruling regime.[31]

---

[30] An alternative rule would have been to allow one primary coalition member per coalition as opposed to one per election. However, the more parties there are coded as primary coalition members, the further the test moves from the core theoretical logic of the argument. For this reason, I elected not to use such an alternative rule.

[31] In the elections considered here, the only example of this type of election is the 1990 Hungarian parliamentary election; in this particular case, the coding decision is not difficult. The primary coalition member in that election is clearly the Hungarian Socialist Party (MSzP), the official successor to the prior ruling party from the communist era, the Hungarian Socialist Workers' Party (Swain 1993; Szajkowski 1994; Tokes 1996; Orenstein 1998). Although the Hungarian Socialist Workers' Party (MSzMP) that competed in the 1990 election shares the same name as the prior ruling party, it was actually a hard-line faction that refused to join the official successor party; Tokes (1996) refers to the MSzP and MSzMP in the 1990 Hungarian parliamentary election as the "'incumbent' and 'incumbent spin-off'" parties, respectively (p. 369).

In the 1996 Czech, 1994 and 1998 Hungarian, 1993 and 1997 Polish, and 1998 Slovak elections, both criteria for coding the primary coalition member are met by the same party: the prime minister at the time of each of these elections was a member of the party that had received the largest proportion of the vote in the previous election.[32] The coding of Russia's Choice, Our Home is Russia, and Unity as the parties most closely associated with President Yeltsin during the 1993, 1995, and 1999 Russian parliamentary elections, respectively, has already been addressed in the text of this chapter, and all are clear choices for the primary coalition partner.[33]

There are three elections in the sample in which the incumbent parties did not compete individually in the previous election but instead were part of an umbrella anticommunist coalition: the 1991 Polish and the 1992 Czech and Slovak elections. Two separate coalitions containing a total of six parties ruled between the 1989 and 1991 Polish parliamentary elections. The first government was headed by Tadeusz Mazowiecki, who went on to be the original leader of the Democratic Union (UD), while the second

[32] The circumstances leading up to the 1993 Polish parliamentary election warrant additional mention. As mentioned in note 8 earlier in this chapter, two different coalitions ruled in the first seven months after the 1991 election until Hanna Suchocka of the Democratic Union (UD) put together a multiparty coalition that ruled until the September 1993, parliamentary elections. Within that coalition, the UD meets the definition of a primary coalition member by fulfilling both criteria: the UD received the largest share of the vote in the 1991 elections of any of the coalition members and Suchocka herself was a member of the UD (Koldys 1992; Sabbat-Swidlicka 1993, 1994; Szajkowski 1994). For more on the decision to code the SLD as the primary coalition member in the 1997 election, see note 22 earlier in this chapter. Note as well that the 1998 Czech parliamentary elections are not included in this list because by the time of the election the party with the largest percentage of the vote in the 1996 election, the Civic Democratic Party (ODS), was no longer part of the government and the current prime minister was a nonparty technocrat. However, given the fact that the government was a caretaker government, the ODS, which was clearly the primary coalition member in the coalition that ruled between the May 1996 election until the installation of the caretaker government in November 1997, remains the most appropriate party to be coded as the primary coalition member.

[33] The Russian cases point out one shortcoming in the coalition responsibility hypothesis as it is currently constituted for analyzing parliamentary elections in presidential systems. Although the coding of incumbent parties in parliamentary elections allows for multiple parties to be coded as incumbents – and thus the presence of plenty of primary and other incumbent parties in a sample – the coding of parliamentary incumbents in presidential systems is more likely to have fewer incumbents. With the data employed in this book, it does not appear to be too much of a problem, as most of the elections are not from presidential systems (plus the 1993 Russian parliamentary elections did result in two parties being coded as incumbents), but it could limit the testing of the model in a study dominated by parliamentary elections in presidential systems.

was led by Jan Bielecki of the Congress of Liberal Democrats (KLD).[34] However, both governments retained Leszek Balcerowicz as their Finance Minister. And it was the Balcerowicz Plan for radical economic reform that more than anything else distinguished Polish government policy between 1989 and 1991.[35] As "the UD became the party most closely associated with the "shock therapy" of the liberal economic reforms of Finance Minister Leszek Balcerowicz," the UD seems the appropriate choice for the primary coalition member going into the 1991 Polish parliamentary elections (Szajkowski 1994, 332).

The 1992 Czech Republic election also can be coded without much difficulty based on similar logic. The three descendents of the Civic Forum anti-communist umbrella group – ODS, ODA, and OH – were all coded as incumbent parties for the election. As the parties had effectively competed under the same banner in 1990, it is impossible to identify one of them as having received the highest vote proportion in that election. Moreover, the prime minister of Czechoslovakia was actually a Slovak, and thus not a member of any of the three parties. Nevertheless, the ODS clearly stands apart as the primary coalition partner for three reasons. First, before its dissolution, Civic Forum was headed by Vaclav Klaus, who went on to become the head of ODS. Thus, the last association that voters had with Civic Forum as a movement coincided with the leadership of Klaus. Second, as Finance Minister, Klaus was as closely connected as anyone to Czechoslovakia's, and by default the Czech Republic's, economic reform program.[36] Finally, from the point when Civic Forum split into its successor parties, ODS became and remained the strongest of the three successor parties.[37]

The Slovak case is more complicated because it had not one, but two distinctly different coalitions ruling in the period between the 1990 and 1992 parliamentary elections. As noted earlier in the chapter, Vladimír Meciar had served as the country's prime minister until April 1991. At the time, he was still a member of the umbrella anticommunist organization Public Against Violence (VPN), but by the time of the 1992 election he and his supporters had left the VPN and formed the Movement for a Democratic Slovakia (HZDS). The rump membership of VPN entered the election as the Civic Democratic Union (ODU). However, the prime minister that

---

[34] See, for example, Jasiewicz 1992b, 1992a; Szajkowski 1994.
[35] See, for example, Przeworski 1993; Sachs 1993.
[36] For more, see Pehe 1991b, 1992c, 1992a; Wolchik 1994; Innes 1997, 2001.
[37] See Krejcí 1995, 286; Pehe 1991c; Wightman 1993b.

succeeded Meciar was Jan Carnogursky, the leader of the Christian Democratic Movement (KDH).[38] So there seems to be good reasons to argue that all three of these parties could be coded as the primary coalition member. HZDS was the party of the first prime minister and the largest successor of the party that won the previous election, KDH was the party of the current prime minister at the time of the election, and ODU was the remaining contingent of the party that had won the previous election and had been a constant participant in the government. However, by the criteria established earlier, the most defensible choice is the KDH. Although Meciar served as prime minister originally, Carnogursky of the KDH was prime minister for the period of time leading up to the election, and he was prime minister for a longer period of time than Meciar. Additionally, KDH became the strongest party in the parliament following the split of VPN.[39]

The 1994 Slovak parliamentary elections also followed a period of two distinctly different ruling coalitions.[40] Following the 1992 parliamentary election, Meciar again became prime minister and put together a government composed largely of members of his own party.[41] However, by March 1993, a split in the HZDS had already occurred – eight MPs left the party – and the HZDS was forced to enter into a coalition with the SNS.[42] Over the next year, support for Meciar and the HZDS continued to deteriorate, culminating in a no-confidence vote in the government on March 11, 1994.[43] Following the no-confidence vote, Meciar's government was replaced by a five-party coalition including the KDH, the Party of the Democratic Left (SDL'), and the Democratic Union of Slovakia (DU).[44]

---

[38] For details, see Obrman 1992b; Pehe 1992d; Mesežnikov 1994; Szomolanyi 1994.

[39] See Pehe 1992b. I am grateful to Anna Grzymała-Busse, Abby Innes, John Gould, and Kevin Krause, who all gave helpful written responses to my queries on this coding decision.

[40] See, for example, Fisher and Hrib 1994; Henderson 1994; Leff 1997; Szomolanyi 1999.

[41] Out of fourteen ministers in the government, twelve were from the HZDS, with one independent and one member of the Slovak National Party (SNS). The SNS was not technically part of the coalition, but it generally provided tacit support for the government (Pehe 1992d; Szomolanyi 1999).

[42] Although coalition talks began in the spring, the formal coalition was not concluded until the fall of 1993 (Szomolanyi 1999). See also Mesežnikov 1994; Leff 1997; Szomolanyi 1997.

[43] Indeed, eight of the ministers in Meciar's government were either dismissed, voted down by votes of no confidence, or resigned in the twenty months that the government was in power (Malova 1995, 72). Moreover, parliamentary defections continued even after the coalition with the SNS was formed, with MPs leaving the coalition in December 1993 and again in February 1994. For more on these events, see Fisher and Hrib 1994.

[44] See Fisher 1994. The Democratic Union of Slovakia was made up of deputies that left HZDS in the spring of 1994; it had previously been a faction within HZDS called the Alliance for Political Realism (Fisher and Hrib 1994; Szajkowski 1994).

Jozef Moravcik of the DU became the prime minister. This coalition ruled until the 1994 Slovak parliamentary election. It actually managed to pass a good deal of legislation in its seven months in office and generally pursued pro-Western policies and market-oriented reforms. Following the coding rules, the primary partner in the second coalition government is classified as the primary coalition member.[45] As Moravcik was a leader and one of the founding members of the DU, this is the party coded as the primary coalition member. Moreover, by the time of the election, the DU also had more members of parliament running on its list than the KDH and almost as many as the SDL'.[46]

---

[45] One reason not to code the party in this manner would have been if the Moravcik government functioned merely as a caretaker government. However, the government was quite active and behaved as if it expected to be in power past the 1994 election.

[46] If the SDL' had had markedly more members in parliament, then that would have been an argument for coding it as the primary coalition member despite the fact that the prime minister was a member of the DU. The fact that they were close, however, makes it an easier decision to code the DU as the primary coalition member. Additionally, the fact that the DU was made up of people who had originally been associated with the Meciar government strengthens the argument to code the DU as the primary coalition partner. Indeed, Moravcik himself had been the Foreign Minister in the Meciar government before the March 1994 crisis. Thus, while the DU can be said to have some responsibility for what went on in the Meciar government, the same cannot be said about either the KDH or the SDL'. Likewise, the HZDS and SNS cannot be said to have had any responsibility for the Moravcik government, which leaves the DU as the sole party with links to both governments.

6

The New Regime Hypothesis

As described in Chapter 2, the Transitional Identity Model is based on the premise that economic conditions affect parties' electoral fortunes based on their Transitional Identity, as opposed to their position in or out of the current government. The model yields two hypotheses. In Chapter 7, I assess the empirical support for the Old Regime hypothesis, which predicts that Old Regime parties should do better where economic conditions are worse. In this chapter, I examine the degree of empirical support for the New Regime hypothesis, which predicts that New Regime parties should enjoy more electoral support in regions of the country where economic conditions are better.

Overall, there is significantly more empirical support for the New Regime hypothesis than there is for the Incumbency hypothesis. Of the forty New Regime parties in the study – see Table 6.1 for coding – there is strong empirical support for the New Regime hypothesis in twenty-five of these cases, or 63% of the time. Moreover, there is only one case in the entire study in which we are at least 90% confident that the candidate performed better when the economy was worse. There is support for the hypothesis across a wide variety of contexts, including presidential and parliamentary elections, elections in Russia and East-Central Europe, and elections that occurred throughout the decade. Interestingly, the hypothesis generates the least support in Slovakia, a point that will be discussed in greater detail later in this chapter. And although support can be found in many contexts, the model performs especially well later in the decade, in the Czech Republic, and, to a somewhat lesser extent, in cases in which there are reasons to think that parties might be more responsible for the state of the economy.

Table 6.1. *Coding of New Regime Parties*

Country	Date*	New Regime Parties
Czech Republic	June 5–6, 1992 (L)	ODS, ODA, OH
Czech Republic	May 31–June 1, 1996 (L)	ODS, ODA
Czech Republic	June 19–20, 1998 (L)	ODS, US
Hungary	April 8, 1990 (L)	MDF, SzDSz, FIDESZ
Hungary	May 8, 1994 (L)	MDF, SzDSz, FIDESZ
Hungary	May 10, 1998 (L)	MDF, SzDSz, Fidesz-MPP
Poland	November 25, 1990 (P)	Mazowiecki, Wałęsa
Poland	October 27, 1991 (L)	UD, KLD
Poland	September 19, 1993 (L)	UD, KLD
Poland	November 5, 1995 (P)	Wałęsa, Kuroń, Gronkiewicz-Waltz
Poland	September 21, 1997 (L)	AWS, UW
Russia	June 12, 1991 (P)	Yeltsin
Russia	December 12, 1993 (L)	VR, PRES
Russia	December 17, 1995 (L)	NDR, DVR
Russia	June 16, 1996 (P)	Yeltsin
Russia	December 19, 1999 (L)	Unity, SPS
Slovakia	June 5–6, 1992 (L)	ODU
Slovakia	Sept. 30–Oct. 1, 1994 (L)	DU, DS
Slovakia	September 25–26, 1998 (L)	SDK
Slovakia	May 15, 1999 (P)	Schuster

* L = Legislative, P = Presidential. For two-round elections, date refers to first round.

This chapter is organized in a manner similar to the previous one and addresses in turn issues related to coding, findings for the paired case studies, overall results, and then an assessment of the conditional economic voting hypotheses.

Coding New Regime Parties

The primary goal of coding New Regime parties is to arrive at a set of parties that are most likely to appeal to voters primarily through their connection to, association with, and general support for the transition itself. As described in Chapter 2, this involves a two-step process. The first step is to trace out the descendents of the people or movements that initiated the transition away from communism in each of the countries. The second step is to then eliminate any parties that attempt to appeal to voters on grounds that are separate and distinct from the transition. More specifically, I exclude parties that appeal to voters on the basis of their identity or profession, which excludes religious,[1] ethnic, nationalist, agrarian, or trade union parties from the New Regime category. The remaining parties – those clearly identified with the transition away from communism and not attempting to appeal to voters on the basis of a particular identity – are those for whom the arguments underlying the New Regime hypothesis laid out in Chapter 2 most clearly apply.

How do these coding decisions play out in practice? In three of the five countries, Poland, the Czech Republic, and Slovakia, there are clear umbrella movements that contested, and came to power following, the initial elections against the communist regime: the famous Solidarity movement in Poland in 1989;[2] the Civic Forum in the Czech Republic in 1990;[3] and the Public against Violence Movement in Slovakia in 1990.[4] In each case, these umbrella movements failed to remain intact until the following election (1991 in Poland, 1992 in the Czech Republic and Slovakia), but successor parties to these movements did survive to compete in elections throughout the decade.

In Hungary, a slightly different situation emerged, as there was no umbrella movement that competed in the first (1990) parliamentary election; indeed, all of the parties that received seats in the parliament as a result of the first election would contest both the 1994 and 1998 elections. The rules for this election were, however, negotiated at a roundtable between the communist regime and a unified opposition force known as

---

[1] In order to avoid going too far down the subjective road in determining how "Christian" a party might be, I simply eliminate parties that include the phrase "Christian Democrat" in their party name. Although this is clearly a crude coding rule, it actually does get to the basis of the distinction if we assume that parties that adopted the "Christian Democratic" label in their party name clearly wanted to identify themselves as a Christian Democratic party.

[2] For more on Solidarity and its descendants, see Vinton 1990a; Heyns and Bialecki 1991; Jasiewicz 1992a; Vinton 1993b; Millard 1994a; Sabbat-Swidlicka 1994; Wenzel 1998; for an excellent account of Solidarity's role in earlier political developments in Poland, see Ash 1999. As was mentioned earlier, the 1989 Polish election was not fully free; for more on this election, see Barany and Vinton 1990; Kaminski 1991; Zubek 1991a; and Jasiewicz 1992a.

[3] For more on Civic Forum and its descendants, see Martin 1990; Pehe 1992b; Wightman 1993a; Krejcí 1995; Innes 1997; Leff 1997; and Rose and Munro 2003.

[4] For more on Public Against Violence and its descendants, see Pehe 1992d; Olson 1993; Fisher and Hrib 1994; Henderson 1994; Mesežnikov 1994; and Leff 1997.

the EKA (short for Ellenzeki Kerekasztal, or Opposition Roundtable).[5] The EKA was made up of representatives from different political organizations that became the separate political parties that contested the 1990 election. So in Hungary, the EKA plays the role of the original umbrella movement for the purpose of coding New Regime parties. Two of the parties that were part of the EKA are excluded from being coded as New Regime parties on the grounds of being a religious party (the Christian Democratic People's Party [KDNP]), and an agrarian party (the Independent Smallholder's Party [FKgP]).[6] But the three remaining opposition parties at the negotiating table, the Hungarian Democratic Forum (MDF), the Alliance of Free Democrats (SzDSz) and the Federation of Young Democrats (FIDESZ) are all coded as New Regime parties. And unlike any of the other countries, the coding of the New Regime parties in Hungary is the same for all three parliamentary elections, as the MDF, SzDSz, and FIDESZ survived to contest all of the parliamentary elections in the 1990s.[7]

Russia, a country with a presidential system in which the signature event of the transition was the election of Boris Yeltsin to the presidency of the Russian Federation in June 1991 followed by the dissolution of the Soviet Union a year and a half later, requires a slightly modified approach to coding New Regime parties. When Yeltsin first assumed control of the presidency, he brought with him a team of young reformers that would go on to institute most of Russia's major reforms over the next few years. The most well-known figures from this group were Yegor Gaidar, who was Yeltsin's first prime minister and remained in that post through December 1992, and Anatolii Chubais, who would go on to be the architect of Russia's privatization program. The reformers would find themselves in and out of power throughout the Yeltsin era, but their identity was always fairly clear. In later years, and especially as Gaidar fell from power, other faces would come to represent these young reformers in government, including Boris Nemtsov, Sergei Kirienko, and Sergei Stepashin, but their connections back

---

[5] For more on the Hungarian roundtable negotiations, see Sajo 1996; Benoit and Schiemann 2001.

[6] In addition to the FKgP, a right-wing agrarian party, there was also a left-wing Agrarian Alliance that competed in the 1990 election (Racz 1993).

[7] This pattern did not last into the next decade, as FIDESZ and MDF ran a joint list in the 2002 parliamentary election. For more on these parties, see Barany 1990; Racz 1991; Bigler 1992; Körösényi 1993; Gabel 1995; Tóka 1995; Kitschelt, Manfeldova et al. 1999; Körösényi 1999; and Schmidt and Tóth 2000.

to the original reformers from the immediate transition period was always clear.[8]

Thus, in the absence of an umbrella party contesting a first free election, Russian parties are coded as New Regime parties if they have a strong association with either Yeltsin himself or the original young reformers that engineered the drastic early moves of the transition. So on the basis of association with Yeltsin, the parties of power described in Chapter 5 (Russia's Choice and the Party of Russian Unity and Concord in 1993, Our Home is Russia in 1995, and Unity in 1999) are coded as New Regime parties; on the basis of their identity with the original young reformers, Russia's Choice in 1993, Russia's Democratic Choice in 1995, and the Union of Right Forces in 1999 are also coded as New Regime parties.[9] Yeltsin himself is of course also coded as a New Regime candidate in the 1991 and 1995 presidential elections.

In recognition of the fact that the coding of New Regime parties is the least objective of the three standard economic voting hypothesis categories, the appendix to this chapter provides additional information regarding what I have identified as ten "borderline" New Regime parties, or parties that were not coded as New Regime parties but which at first glance might have been. In the appendix, I identify these borderline cases and explain why the decision was made ultimately not to code them as New Regime parties. I also take the additional step of presenting empirical results for these borderline parties and showing the effect they would have had on the study's overall conclusions regarding the empirical support for the New Regime hypothesis had they been coded as New Regime parties as well. Thus, any reader that disagrees with my coding decisions in any of these borderline cases can fairly easily assess what the overall conclusion would have looked like had I coded the parties in the way they preferred. As it turns out, including all of the borderline cases has practically no effect on our assessment of the support for the New Regime hypothesis, as there is essentially the same degree of empirical support for the New Regime hypothesis across the ten borderline cases as there is in the forty cases included in the study (see Table 6A.1 in the appendix to this chapter).

---

[8] For more on the evolution of Russia's reformist forces, see Urban 1992; Fish 1995a; McAllister 1995; Orttung 1995; Tsygankov 1995; Hahn 1996; McFaul 1997a; Gaidar 1999; Kullberg and Zimmerman 1999; McFaul 2000; and Rose and Munro 2002.

[9] Russia's Democratic Choice was one of the parties that made up the Union of Right Forces electoral bloc. For more on the Union of Right Forces and the 1999 campaign, see McFaul, Petrov et al. 1999; Hale 2000; Oates 2000; Myagkov 2001; and Colton and McFaul 2003.

Coding the Paired Case Studies

Case Study #1: 1992 Czech and Slovak Parliamentary Elections

As mentioned above, the key to coding New Regime parties in the Czech and Slovak Republics is to identify the descendants of the umbrella movements that contested the 1990 elections, the Civic Forum (Czech Republic) and Public Against Violence (Slovakia). Turning first to the Czech Republic, recall that in Chapter 5 three parties were identified as successors to the Civic Forum: the Civic Democratic Party (ODS), the Civic Movement (OH), and the Civic Democratic Alliance (ODA). As none of these parties fall into the restricted categories of attempting to appeal to voters for reasons distinct from the transition and related to identity, they are all also classified as New Regime Parties.[10]

In Slovakia, Public Against Violence (VPN) originally ruled in a coalition with the Christian Democratic Movement (KDH). KDH is not coded as a New Regime party because of its classification as a religious party, nor was it actually ever part of the Public Against Violence movement. As was noted in Chapter 5, Public Against Violence began to split in the spring of 1991 when Vladimír Meciar led his followers out of the party to form the political party Movement for a Democratic Slovakia (HZDS). As was also described earlier, in the ensuing election HZDS ran to a large extent as a Slovak nationalist party dedicated to protecting Slovak interests from the Czechs. Both because it consciously broke with VPN and the initial direction of reform in Czechoslovakia and because it positioned itself in subsequent elections as a nationalist party, HZDS is not coded as a New Regime party in any of the elections in this study.[11] The remaining members of VPN formed the Civic Democratic Union (ODU) party to contest the 1992 election. ODU is therefore the only

---

[10] ODS would go on to contest both the 1996 and 1998 parliamentary elections, and is coded as a New Regime party in both elections. ODA would only survive to contest the 1996 election, effectively disbanding before the 1998 contest. In December of 1997, in response to disillusionment with ODS leader Vaclav Klaus and a series of financial scandals, a number of ODS deputies broke from the party to form the Freedom Union, which went on to contest the 1998 election and is coded as a New Regime party. For more on the 1998 Czech Elections, see Pehe 1998; Kopecký and Mudde 1999.

[11] As HZDS is included in the borderline New Regime parties category, additional information regarding the coding decision can be found in the appendix to this chapter along with empirical analyses of the vote for HZDS in all three Slovak parliamentary elections.

party coded as a New Regime party in the 1992 Slovak parliamentary election.[12]

Case Study #2: 1995 Polish and 1996 Russian Presidential Elections

For the 1995 Polish presidential elections, three candidates are coded as New Regime parties.[13] The first is the incumbent Lech Wałęsa, whose ties to the Solidarity movement need no explanation.[14]

The second is Jacek Kuroń, who was the official nominee of the Freedom Union (UW). The UW is one of Poland's two New Regime parties in the 1997 parliamentary election, and the two parties that merged to form it in 1994, the Democratic Union (UD) and the Congress of Liberal Democrats (KLD) are both coded as New Regime parties in the 1991 and 1993 parliamentary elections. Thus as the official nominee of a New Regime party in a presidential election, Kuroń is coded as a New Regime candidate. But even without the official nomination of the UW, Kuroń would likely have warranted coding as a New Regime candidate on his own because of his long history of association with the Solidarity movement dating back to his work in the 1970s as a member of the Workers' Defense Committee and his participation in one of the original postcommunist governments as labor minister.[15]

The final New Regime candidate is Hanna Gronkiewicz-Waltz, who at the time was the president of the Polish National Bank. Although not nominated by a political party, she had served as President of the National Bank since March 1992 and had come in to office on a pledge to "restrain the government's plans 'to abandon monetary orthodoxy.'"[16] When running for office, she positioned herself as a pro-reform candidate and sought

---

[12] For more on the ODU, see Obrman 1992a; Rose and Munro 2003. Although the ODU did not survive until the 1994 Slovak parliamentary elections, its successor party united with several other democratic parties to form the Democratic Party of Slovakia (DS), which contested the 1994 Slovak parliamentary elections and is coded as a New Regime party. In 1997, the DS, in turn, joined the Slovak Democratic Coalition (SDK), which contested the 1998 Slovak parliamentary election and is also coded as a New Regime party (see Bugajski 2002, 301–2 for details).

[13] For a discussion of why Jan Olszewski is not coded as a New Regime candidate, see the appendix to this chapter.

[14] For more on Wałęsa and his ties to both the Solidarity movement and the Polish transition, see Ash 1999; Biskupski 2000; and Lukowski and Zawadzki 2001.

[15] For more on Kuroń, see Karpinski 1995a; Ash 1999; and Biskupski 2000.

[16] Radio Free Europe/Radio Liberty (RFE/RL) Daily Report, 3/6/92.

the support of groups that were in favor of continuing Poland's economic reform, earning her accusations of trying to split the solidarity vote (Krupa 1997, 193).[17] She, too, had a background in the Solidarity movement, albeit not nearly as prominent as either Kuroń or Wałęsa, as she had been one of the founding members of the local Solidarity branch of the Warsaw University Faculty of Law and Administration in 1980 and had served as its branch chairperson from 1989 to 1992.[18]

As the rule for coding New Regime parties in Russia is to look for association with Boris Yeltsin, his government, and his early policies to transform Russia's economy, coding the New Regime candidate in the 1995 Russian election is a simple matter: only Yeltsin himself meets that definition. None of the young reformers who had been a part of the initial Yeltsin government chose to contest the election, and the other primary candidates were either communists (Gennadii Zyuganov) or nationalists (Aleksandr Lebed, Vladimir Zhirinovskii).[19]

Case Study #3: 1993, 1995, and 1999 Russian Parliamentary Elections

As explained earlier in the chapter, parties in Russian parliamentary elections are coded as New Regime parties either because they are a party of power or because they are closely associated with the young reformists that originally surrounded Yeltsin early in the transition. The appropriate party/parties of power in each election were discussed in detail in the previous chapter. To reiterate, this is Russia's Choice and the Party of Russian Unity and Concord in 1993; Our Home is Russia in 1995, and Unity in 1999. All four parties are therefore coded as New Regime parties.

The second criterion for being coded as a New Regime party is a close association with the original reformists that surrounded Yeltsin as the transition began. For the 1993 and 1995 elections, this was clearly Russia's Choice (which renamed itself Russia's Democratic Choice before the 1995 elections), the party headed by Yegor Gaidar, Yeltsin's first prime minister and the architect of Russian shock therapy. Following a dismal showing in 1995 in which it failed to even clear the 5% threshold needed to secure any

---

[17] See as well RFE/RL Daily Reports, 6/6/95, 6/14/95, 7/20/95, 8/1/95.

[18] Source: Polish Economic and Business Association, http://www.peba.org.uk/Gronkiewicz. html.

[19] Grigorii Yavlinksii's candidacy for Russian president in 1996 is included as one of the borderline New Regime cases and is thus discussed in more detail in the appendix to this chapter.

of the seats distributed by proportional representation in the parliament, Russia's Democratic Choice entered into an electoral bloc for the 1999 elections with a number of other pro-market and pro-democracy forces called the Union of Right Forces (SPS). Any concerns about whether Russia's Democratic Choice represented enough of the coalition to justify labeling it a New Regime party are greatly mitigated by the fact that the other major figures in the bloc were drawn from the same group of young reformers, including Anatolii Chubais, Sergei Kirienko, Irina Khakamada and Boris Nemtsov. So even without the presence of Russia's Democratic Choice within the bloc, SPS would have been coded as a New Regime party.[20]

Case Study #4: 1997 Polish and 1998 Hungarian Parliamentary Elections

Two parties are coded as New Regime parties for the 1997 Polish parliamentary elections. The first of these, the Freedom Union (UW), has been discussed previously. The party was formed in 1994 when the two New Regime parties from the 1991 and 1993 parliamentary elections, the Democratic Union (UD) and the Congress of Liberal Democrats (KLD), merged, and thus clearly should be coded as a New Regime party as well.

The second party coded as a New Regime party in this election has a slightly more interesting story that in many ways reflects the evolution of Poland's electoral history. Throughout the decade, all of the seats in the Polish parliament were allocated by proportional representation, but the exact mechanism of seat distribution varied a great deal. In the 1991 Polish parliamentary election, the threshold for admission to the parliament was so low that twenty-nine parties were elected to the parliament, the top party received only 62 out of 460 seats, and a total of nine parties received between 27 and 62 seats in the parliament.[21] In response, a series of changes were made to the electoral rules to favor large parties at the expense of small parties.[22] The changes had their desired impact in terms

---

[20] For more on SPS, see sources cited in note 8 of this chapter. Readers interested in why Yabloko is not coded as a New Regime party in any of these elections should see the appendix to this chapter, where Yabloko is included as one of the borderline cases.

[21] Source: Polish Election Commission: Wyniki Wyborow do Sejmu Rzeczypospolitej Polskiej, 27 pazdziernika 1991 r.

[22] Among other changes, the number of districts were changed, the D'Honte formula was instituted for allocating seats, and minimum national vote thresholds for the distribution

of reducing the size of the parliament, as only six parties entered the parliament in 1993. However, these parties accounted for only 65% of the popular vote, which meant that over a third of the electorate had voted for parties that received no representation in the parliament.[23] In particular, numerous parties that could loosely be described as hailing from the right or right-of-center of Polish politics had failed to clear the threshold.[24] In an effort to avoid such a scenario for the 1997 parliamentary election, the Solidarity Trade Union took the lead in gathering as many right-wing parties and descendents of the original Solidarity movement as possible under a single electoral banner, which contested the election as the Solidarity Electoral Action bloc (AWS).[25] In a sense, the goal was to recreate the original anticommunist Solidarity movement that had toppled communism in Poland but had subsequently splintered into so many different parties. As described in Chapter 4, the strategy proved successful, with AWS winning the election and taking control of the government.[26] Because of the clear association between AWS and the original umbrella movement that contested the 1989 parliamentary elections, AWS is coded as a New Regime party.[27]

of all seats were added. For a detailed description of the allocation rules, see Tomz, Tucker, and Wittenberg 2002, note 12. For a thorough examination of the evolution of Poland's electoral rules, see Benoit and Hayden 2004.

[23] Source: Polish Election Commission: Wyniki Wyborow do Sejmu Rzeczypospolitej Polskiej, 19 wrzesnia 1993 r.

[24] Indeed, there were three parties that received between 3.9% and 4.9% of the vote (the threshold for parties was 5%) and one coalition that received 6.4% of the vote (the threshold for coalitions was 8% for regional list seats and 7% for national list seats). See Appendix I for detailed election results from 1993, as well as Vinton 1993a, 21; Millard 1994b, 306; Chan 1995, 138–9; and Karpinski 1997a, 63–4 for more details in this regard.

[25] Indeed, AWS actively played up this imagery during the campaign; see Wenzel 1998, 152. For more on AWS and the 1997 election, see as well Karpinski 1997b; Chan 1998; and Szczerbiak 1999.

[26] Beyond the 1997 election, the emergence of AWS was supposed to usher in an era of stability in Polish politics along classic European lines with one large left-wing party (SLD), one large right-wing party (AWS), and a smaller centrist/liberal party (UW). However, the colossal failures of the AWS government led to a dismal showing in the 2001 election, as the bloc failed to even achieve representation in the 2001–2005 parliament. For more, see Maksymiuk 2001; Benoit and Hayden 2004.

[27] Readers familiar with the 1991 and 1993 Polish elections will note that the Solidarity Trade Union party that contested both of these elections is not coded as a New Regime party. This is because in contesting these elections as a trade union *per se*, the party violates the New Regime coding rule of not attempting to appeal to a specific subsection of the population on the basis of identity or profession. AWS is coded as a New Regime party

The 1998 Hungarian elections present an even simpler coding decision. As was noted earlier, the same Hungarian New Regime parties contested all three parliamentary elections in the 1990s. So as in both 1990 and 1994, the Hungarian Democratic Forum (MDF), the Alliance of Free Democrats (SzDSz), and the now renamed FIDESZ-Hungarian Civic Party (formerly just FIDESZ) are all coded as New Regime parties in 1998 based on their legacy as participants in the original round table negotiations.[28]

These two cases raise the issue of the relationship between the passing of time and a coding rule based on parties' association with the original/early moments of the transition. As noted in Chapter 2, one can explicitly theorize about how well the empirical data might support the New Regime hypothesis as time passes, but this is a different – and in a sense prior – point: testing the New Regime hypothesis requires New Regime parties. But as the brief discussion of coding decisions in the 1997 Polish, 1998 Hungarian, and 1999 Russian elections demonstrates, coding New Regime parties in the latter part of the decade is not necessarily a difficult task, and one that is facilitated by stability in party systems (e.g., the Hungarian case) or clearly demarcated lines of succession between parties (e.g., the Polish and Russian cases). At the same time, however, it is worth noting that coding New Regime parties could prove to be an increasingly complex task as time passes; I return to this point in Chapter 9.[29]

---

because it ran as a broad coalition of right-wing parties, and not specifically as a trade union. This brings up the complex distinction in Poland between the Solidarity movement that led to the collapse of the communist regime and the actual Solidarity trade union that originally spearheaded that movement, but it is sufficient for these purposes to note that the New Regime connection in Poland is intended to be to the movement and not the trade union.

[28] For more on the 1998 Hungarian election, see Benoit, Csalotzky et al. 1998; Fowler 1998; Körösényi 1999; Agh 2000; and Schmidt and Tóth 2000.

[29] In particular, the decision to code Rudolf Schuster as a New Regime candidate in the 1999 Slovak presidential election illustrates this kind of complexity, as Schuster's own party (the Party of Civic Understanding, formed prior to the 1998 Slovak election) is not coded as a New Regime party. However, as discussed in note 7 in Chapter 5, Schuster was the official nominee of the new coalition government that was dominated by the Slovak Democratic Coalition, which is coded as a New Regime party, and thus Schuster, as its representative, is also coded as a New Regime candidate. As it turns out, far from providing empirical support for the New Regime hypothesis, the vote for Schuster is the one case in the entire study in which we find strong evidence to support the opposite from what the New Regime hypothesis predicts; in other words, we are actually confident that Schuster performed better where economic conditions were worse. But in light of the discussion in the text, this is a good example of how these types of coding decisions can become more and more difficult as time passes in less stable party systems.

Table 6.2. *Empirical Support for Paired Case Studies: New Regime Hypothesis*

Party			Confidence in Predicted Effect
Czech Republic / Slovakia 1992			
Czech Rep.	1992	Civic Movement (OH)	100.0
		Civic Democratic Party (ODS)	100.0
		Civic Democratic Alliance (ODA)	99.7
Slovakia	1992	Civic Democratic Union (ODU)	81.8
Mid-Decade Presidential Elections			
Poland	1995	Lech Wałęsa	95.1
		Jacek Kuroń	71.6
		Hanna Gronkiewicz-Waltz	92.6
Russia	1996	Boris Yeltsin	98.0
Russian Parliamentary Elections			
Russia	1993	Russia's Choice (VR)	96.8
		Party of Russian Unity and Concord (PRES)	30.9
Russia	1995	Our Home is Russia (NDR)	92.6
		Russia's Democratic Choice (DVR)	69.9
Russia	1999	Inter-Regional Movement Unity (Unity)	100.0
		Union of Right Forces (SPS)	94.4
Late Decade Incumbent – Old Regime Elections			
Poland	1997	Electoral Action Solidarity (AWS)	96.2
		Union of Freedom (UW)	93.0
Hungary	1998	FIDESZ-Hungarian Civic Party (FIDESZ-MPP)	100.0
		Alliance of Free Democrats (SzDSz)	100.0
		Hungarian Democratic Forum (MDF)	99.4

Empirical Results: Paired Case Studies

Table 6.2 illustrates that there is substantial empirical support for the New Regime hypothesis among the paired case studies. Turning first to the Czech and Slovak elections of 1992, there is a similar pattern to the one found in Chapter 5, with more empirical support for the hypothesis in the former election than the latter. As the three incumbent parties in the Czech Republic in 1992 are all coded as New Regime parties, we find the same result as we did when assessing the Incumbency hypothesis: the hypothesis is very well supported by the empirical data. Indeed, we are extremely confident that ODS, ODA, and OH all performed better where the economy was stronger during this election. In the Slovak case, the effect of the economy on the one New Regime party is in the correct direction (the percentage of positive simulations is greater than 50 percent), but it does not reach the cutoff for strong confidence (at least 90 percent) that is employed in the book.

The mid-decade presidential election case studies also illustrate strong empirical support for the New Regime hypothesis. All three of the New Regime candidates in the 1995 Polish presidential election reflect effects for economic conditions in the correctly predicted direction, although there is only strong empirical support in two of the cases: Wałęsa and Gronkiewicz-Waltz. The stronger support for Wałęsa is consistent with the prediction of the responsibility based size of vote hypothesis, as he received by far the largest electoral support of the three (33% vs. 9% for Kuroń and just under 3% for Gronkiewicz-Waltz). Why there is stronger support for the New Regime hypothesis in the vote for Gronkiewicz-Waltz than for Kuroń is less clear, and there does not appear to be any particular conditional economic voting hypothesis associated with this finding.[30] In the Russian case, the empirical evidence strongly suggests that the economy affected the vote for Yeltsin in the manner predicted by the New Regime hypothesis.

Similarly, the three Russian parliamentary elections also provide empirical support for the New Regime hypothesis. Of the six new regime parties that contested these three elections, there is strong empirical evidence that four of them performed better where economic conditions were stronger. This conclusion always holds for the primary party of power: Russia's Choice (1993); Our Home is Russia (1995), and Unity (1999). The least empirical support for the hypothesis is provided by the secondary party of power in 1993, the Party of Russian Unity and Concord; indeed, in this case our best guess is that the party actually performed better where economic conditions were worse. This lack of support for the New Regime hypothesis in this case is also in line with the general responsibility based approach, as Russia's Choice was clearly the more responsible party – as

---

[30] If we examine the policy positions of the two, Gronkiewicz-Waltz would probably be classified as having a more orthodox view on economic reform than Kuroń, who is described as hailing from the left wing of UW. And as the UW had been out of power since 1993 and Gronkiewicz-Waltz had been president of the National Bank since the beginning of 1992, it is possible that by the time of the 1995 election she had a closer association in the minds of the voters with the transition as it had developed in Poland than he did. At the same time, Kuroń as a figure was certainly much more personally connected to the overall transition away from communism and to the original Solidarity movement than Gronkiewicz-Waltz, and this is the general basis for how New Regime parties are classified.

defined in Chapter 2 – in the 1993 election. The other case in which we do not have much confidence in the empirical support for the hypothesis is for Russia's Democratic Choice in 1995. Again, this is in line with the spirit of the conditional responsibility hypotheses, as Russia's Democratic Choice had ceded its position as the party of power to Our Home is Russia by the time of the 1995 election and received only 3.9% of the vote in that election. Interestingly, the one election in which there is strong empirical support for both New Regime parties is the 1999 parliamentary election, which is the latest of the three elections.

The final paired case study reveals that despite the fact that four out of the five New Regime parties that contested the 1997 Polish and 1998 Hungarian elections were out of office at the time of the election (SzDSz in Hungary was the lone incumbent of the group), all five received stronger electoral support in areas of the country where the economy was doing better. In the Hungarian case in particular, we are very confident in these effects – three parties had at least 99 percent of the simulated shocks producing the predicted electoral effect – but all five parties pass the 90% threshold for strong empirical support. Notably, this is further evidence of the trend mentioned in the discussion of the Russian parliamentary elections of the New Regime hypothesis finding strong empirical support later in the decade.

Overall, therefore, the case studies provide strong empirical support for the New Regime hypothesis. Indeed, of the nineteen New Regime parties that competed in these nine elections, there is strong empirical support for the hypothesis in fifteen cases; moreover, there is only even a majority of simulations to be in the wrong direction in a single case (PRES in the 1993 Russian parliamentary election). Thus, the case studies reveal preliminary evidence in support of the hypothesis in a wide range of contexts, including Russian and East-Central European elections, presidential and parliamentary elections, and elections that took place throughout the decade.

Comparative Analysis

Moving from the individual case studies to the overall results, a clear pattern of strong empirical support for the New Regime hypothesis continues to be evident. Of the forty New Regime parties that contested these twenty elections, we are at least 90% confident that the party enjoyed more electoral success where economic conditions were better in almost two-thirds of the cases (25 out of 40, or 63% of the cases). Moreover, in only one case in the entire data set are we at least 90% confident that the party performed worse where economic conditions were better. Furthermore, this conclusion appears to be quite robust to the different specifications of the model discussed in Chapter 3, with all of the robustness tests producing between 22 (55%) and 25 (63%) cases with at least 90% confidence that the data supported the New Regime hypothesis.[31] With this overall level of support in mind, the remainder of this chapter assesses the different conditional economic voting hypotheses in an effort to learn more about the variation in support for the New Regime hypothesis across different elections and parties.

Intuitive Explanations

Table 6.3 presents an assessment of the three intuitive conditional hypothesis focusing on the distinction between parliamentary and presidential elections, Russia and East-Central Europe, and each country individually.

Panel 1 of Table 6.3 reveals a slight distinction in the degree of empirical support for the New Regime hypothesis across presidential and parliamentary elections. Like the Incumbency hypothesis, the New Regime hypothesis enjoys more support in parliamentary elections than in presidential elections. However, it is again necessary to make the important caveat that this conclusion is based on a much smaller sample of presidential elections than parliamentary elections. Nevertheless, we can make two important observations on the basis of this panel. First, there is no evidence that the degree of empirical support for the New Regime hypothesis was artificially inflated by adding the five presidential elections to the study; indeed, had the study only included the fifteen parliamentary elections, we would have concluded that there was even stronger support for the New Regime hypothesis than we can now conclude. At the same time, there is no reason to conclude that the hypothesis is somehow inappropriate for presidential elections. Although the number of New Regime presidential candidates in the study is admittedly small, we do find strong support for the hypothesis in half of these cases.

Panel 2 presents one of the most aesthetically eye-catching results of the entire study: there is the exact same degree of support for the New Regime hypothesis generated across the thirty-two New Regime parties

---

[31] The results of these tests are discussed in greater detail in Chapter 8; see especially Table 8.3.

Table 6.3. *Intuitive Explanations of Variation in Support for New Regime Hypothesis*

Panel 1: Parliamentary vs. Presidential Elections

	All	Parliamentary	Presidential
90% Confident in Predicted Direction	25	21	4
90% Confident in Wrong Direction	1	0	1
Total Cases	40	32	8
Percentage with 90% Confidence in	**63%**	**66%**	**50%**
Predicted (Wrong) **Direction**	(3%)	(0%)	(13%)

Panel 2: East-Central Europe vs. Russia

	All	East-Central Europe	Russia
90% Confident in Predicted Direction	25	20	5
90% Confident in Wrong Direction	1	1	0
Total Cases	40	32	8
Percentage with 90% Confidence in	**63%**	**63%**	**63%**
Predicted (Wrong) **Direction**	(3%)	(3%)	(0%)

Panel 3: Country-by-Country Variation

	All	Czech R.	Hungary	Poland	Slovakia	Russia
90% Confident in Predicted Direction	25	7	6	6	1	5
90% Confident in Wrong Direction	1	0	0	0	1	0
Total Cases	40	7	9	11	5	8
Percentage with 90% Confidence in Predicted (Wrong) **Direction**	**63%** (3%)	**100%** (0%)	**67%** (0%)	**55%** (0%)	**20%** (20%)	**63%** (0%)

contesting elections in the four East-Central European countries as there is from the eight New Regime parties that competed in Russian elections. Although the fact that this proportion is exactly the same is undoubtedly a happy coincidence, it does drive home the larger point – made in the previous chapter as well – that there is nothing in the results of this study that suggests that it is an *a priori* mistake to comparatively analyze election results from Russia and its former Warsaw Bloc partners in East-Central Europe.

However, there is one country that looks quite different from the other four, which is Slovakia. As Panel 3 of Table 6.3 illustrates, all of the countries except Slovakia generate strong empirical support for the New

Table 6.4. *Variation in Support for New Regime Hypothesis among Slovak New Regime Parties*

Year	Party	Confidence in Predicted Effect
1992	Civic Democratic Union (ODU)	81.8
1994	Democratic Union of Slovakia (DU)	77.3
1994	Democratic Party (DS)	54.5
1998	Slovak Democratic Coalition (SDK)	99.7
1999	Rudolf Schuster	8.3

Regime hypothesis for more than half of their New Regime parties. In Slovakia, by contrast, there is only one New Regime party, the Slovak Democratic Coalition in the 1998 parliamentary election, with strong empirical support for the hypothesis (see Table 6.4).

What could explain why the hypothesis performs particularly badly in Slovakia? One possibility is that it is the result of a number of somewhat coincidental factors. First, there are only a small number of New Regime parties that contest the Slovak elections, which does not provide that many opportunities for testing the hypothesis. Second, one of these elections (1992 parliament) is coded as a regime future election, which means there is an *a priori* reason to expect a lack of support for any standard economic voting hypothesis. Additionally, the 1999 Slovak presidential election presented a particularly challenging coding decision (see note 29 earlier in this chapter). Furthermore, for all of the parties except one, at least a majority of the simulations are in the correctly predicted direction.

But it also may be that there is something more fundamental about Slovak political developments in the 1990s that makes the country particularly hostile to generating support for the predictions of the New Regime hypothesis. In the other four countries, New Regime parties were major political players throughout the decade, winning numerous elections and serving in important government positions. Although the Public Against Violence movement was the victor in the 1990 Slovak Republic parliamentary election, a New Regime party would not take control of the government following a Slovak election again until the 1998 parliamentary election.[32]

---

[32] This claim is of course dependent on not coding the Movement for a Democratic Slovakia (HZDS) as a New Regime party, which is discussed in detail in the appendix of this chapter. But note as well that had HZDS been coded as a New Regime party, then there would have been more support for the New Regime hypothesis in Slovakia.

New Regime parties (ODU in 1992, DU in 1994) would play important roles in the government, but only after internal power struggles that ousted Vladimír Meciar and his Movement for a Democratic Slovakia (HZDS) from power. However, in both cases when the New Regime party went to the polls following the internal power struggle, it was defeated and Meciar and the HZDS returned to power. Thus, unlike the other four countries, the major player in Slovak politics, at least through 1998, is a nationalist party. It is interesting to note that when a New Regime party finally wins an election, the Slovak Democratic Coalition (SDK) in 1998, we find strong support for the New Regime hypothesis, with over 99% confidence that the party performed better where economic conditions were better.[33]

So perhaps the failure of the New Regime hypothesis to generate empirical support in the Slovak case can teach us something about the limitations of the Transitional Identity Model. It may be the case that the New Regime hypothesis is less likely to have strong predictive power when New Regime parties do not emerge as important political actors in the years following the transition. This would suggest that the hypothesis might be more relevant as New Regime parties themselves become more relevant. And although this conclusion springs from an analysis of one of the intuitive conditional hypotheses, it does dovetail fairly well with the logic underlying the responsibility-based hypotheses, in so far as it suggests that a standard hypothesis – here the New Regime hypothesis – should generate more support as the political party contesting the election is more likely to be viewed as important by the electorate. With this in mind, I turn now to the responsibility-based conditional hypotheses.

Responsibility Hypotheses

As Panel 1 of Table 6.5 illustrates, there is some very lukewarm support for the institutional responsibility hypothesis when assessing variation in empirical support for the New Regime hypothesis. About the strongest comment to make in support of the institutional responsibility hypothesis is that we do see more empirical support for the New Regime hypothesis in dominant institutional elections (presidential elections in a presidential

---

[33] SDK is considered the winner of the election because it led the coalition that took power after the election. However, HZDS actually received the most votes in the election (27% vs. 26.3% for SDK), but it could not form a government because of the refusal of other parties to enter into a coalition with it.

Table 6.5. *Responsibility Explanations of Variation in Support for New Regime Hypothesis*

Panel 1: Institutional Responsibility

	All	Dominant Institution	Mixed Systems	Dominated Institution
90% Confident in Predicted Direction	25	15	6	4
90% Confident in Wrong Direction	1	0	0	1
Total Cases	40	22	11	7
Percentage with 90% Confidence in Predicted (Wrong) **Direction**	**63%** (3%)	**68%** (0%)	**55%** (0%)	**57%** (0%)

Panel 2: Size of National Vote

	All	<5%	≥5%	≥10%	≥20%
90% Confident in Predicted Direction	25	3	22	16	10
90% Confident in Wrong Direction	1	0	1	1	1
Total Cases	40	7	33	22	14
Percentage with 90% Confidence in Predicted (Wrong) **Direction**	**63%** (3%)	**43%** (0%)	**67%** (3%)	**73%** (5%)	**71%** (7%)

system or parliamentary elections in a parliamentary system) than we do in the other categories, which is what is predicted by the Institutional Responsibility hypothesis. That being said, the distinction is slight – 68% of the cases (15 out of 22) for the main elections versus 56% (10 out of 18) of the other elections – and there is no evidence that the New Regime hypothesis enjoys greater support in mixed elections than dominated elections, as the hypothesis also predicts.

As in the previous chapter, there is also more support for the New Regime hypothesis among parties receiving a higher proportion of the overall vote. We find the most support for this claim by examining the distinction between parties that received less than 5% of the vote, where we only find support for the New Regime hypothesis in three out of seven cases, and the parties that received more than 5% of the vote, where we find empirical support for the hypothesis in two-thirds (twenty-two out of thirty-three) of the cases (see Panel 2, Table 6.5). The usefulness of this finding, however, is tempered both by the small number of cases of parties receiving less than 5% of the overall vote – only seven New Regime parties performed that poorly – and the fact that the proportion of cases that demonstrate empirical support for the New Regime hypothesis does not really change much as we move to higher thresholds of electoral success. In contrast to the Incumbency hypothesis, which performed significantly better with parties receiving at least 20% of the vote than it did with parties receiving at least 10% of the vote, there is practically no difference in the level of support for the New Regime hypothesis across these two categories. Moreover, the difference between the support for the hypothesis among parties receiving at least 5% of the vote is actually very close to the higher thresholds as well (67% of the cases as opposed to 73% and 71%). Thus, the support for the size of vote hypothesis is really confined to the distinction between parties receiving more and less than 5% of the vote. And although this is in the direction predicted by the hypothesis, it is based on at least one category with a small number of observations.

Taken individually, neither of these tests of New Regime parties offers much support for the overall concept that economic conditions should have more of an effect on election results for New Regime parties when the party is likely to be seen as more important in the eyes of voters. However, taken in conjunction with the evidence presented in the paired case studies and the failure of the Slovak cases to generate much support for the New Regime hypothesis, we can begin to see the outlines of support for the concept that importance might matter. Even though the empirical evidence is far from dramatic, the results of breaking down New Regime parties into the categories identified by both the institutional responsibility and size of vote hypotheses do produce results that are at least in the direction proposed by these hypotheses. The New Regime hypothesis does generate more empirical support in presidential elections in presidential systems and parliamentary elections in parliamentary systems than in other combinations. And there is less empirical support for the New Regime hypothesis among parties that fared particularly poorly in their respective elections. In the paired case studies, both the 1992 Czech and Slovak parliamentary elections and the Russian parliamentary elections produced findings consistent with a responsibility-based conditional approach. Moreover, the Slovak exceptionalism in terms of the New Regime hypothesis also suggests that importance in the minds of voters may matter in predicting where we are likely to find more empirical support for the New Regime hypothesis. So although it is important not to overstate any of these findings individually, taken together they are suggestive that there may be some underlying

Table 6.6. *Supply-Side Explanations of Variation in Support for New Regime Hypothesis: Personality Hypothesis*

	All	Presidential Elections	Open-List PR Elections	Closed-List PR Elections
90% Confident in Predicted Direction	25	4	11	10
90% Confident in Wrong Direction	1	1	0	0
Total Cases	40	8	17	15
Percentage with 90% Confidence in Predicted (Wrong) Direction	**63%** (3%)	**50%** (13%)	**65%** (0%)	**67%** (0%)

validity to the responsibility based approach in allowing us to understand variation in empirical support for the New Regime hypothesis.

Supply-Side Hypotheses

Table 6.6 reveals only lukewarm support for the personality hypothesis. The cases in which we would expect personality to play the largest role – presidential elections – have the smallest proportion of cases providing strong empirical support for the New Regime hypothesis (50%). Additionally, the cases in which we expect the smallest role for personality – closed-list PR elections – have the largest proportion of parties that produce strong empirical support for the New Regime hypothesis (67% of the cases). However, a closer look at the table reveals that there is practically no difference between the empirical support for the New Regime hypothesis between parties competing in the two different types of parliamentary elections (65% of the cases for open-list elections vs. 67% of the cases for closed-list elections). As a result, all of the evidence in support of the personality hypothesis is essentially a result of the distinction between the degree of support for the New Regime hypothesis generated by presidential and parliamentary elections. As noted earlier in this chapter, a comparison of this nature is based on a fairly small number of cases of New Regime candidates competing in presidential elections. At the same time, the finding offers a theoretically based explanation for the intuitively based observation of a small distinction between the support for the New Regime hypothesis in presidential and parliamentary elections.

Table 6.7. *Breakdown of New Regime Parties by Party Orientation*

Country	Date	New Regime: Consistent Liberalizing	New Regime: Populist Leaning
Czech Republic	1990	ODS, ODA, OH	
Czech Republic	1996	ODS, ODA	
Czech Republic	1998	ODS, US	
Hungary	1990	SzDSz, FIDESZ	MDF
Hungary	1994	SzDSz, FIDESZ	MDF
Hungary	1998	SzDSz	MDF, Fidesz-MPP
Poland	1990	Mazowiecki	Wałęsa
Poland	1991	UD, KLD	
Poland	1993	UD, KLD	
Poland	1995	Kuroń, Gronkiewicz-Waltz	Wałęsa
Poland	1997	UW	AWS
Russia	1991	Yeltsin	
Russia	1993	VR	PRES
Russia	1995	DVR	NDR
Russia	1996		Yeltsin
Russia	1999	SPS	Unity
Slovakia	1992	ODU	
Slovakia	1994	DU, DS	
Slovakia	1998	SDK	
Slovakia	1999		Schuster

New Regime Orientation Hypothesis

The New Regime orientation hypothesis predicts that there should be more empirical support for the New Regime hypothesis among New Regime parties more closely identified with pro-democratic and pro-economic reform programs than among New Regime parties that strayed from these core identities in either a more conservative/nationalist or populist direction. Admittedly, the question of where to draw this line is a fairly subjective matter, and thus I urge readers to keep this caveat in mind in considering the results presented here. Nevertheless, the breakdown of New Regime parties into these two categories presented in Table 6.7 should not be too controversial.[34]

---

[34] In Russia, the distinction is perhaps most clear, with the "liberal" New Regime parties (Russia's Choice and SPS) remaining in the liberal category and the government sponsored parties of power (NDR and Unity) falling in the populist leaning category. Parties with a more conservative outlook (MDF in Hungary, PRES in Russia) and those adopting more explicitly populist campaign messages (Wałęsa and AWS in Poland) are also placed in this

Table 6.8. *New Regime Party Orientation Hypothesis*

	All	Consistent Liberalizing	Populist Leaning
90% Confident in Predicted Direction	25	18	7
90% Confident in Wrong Direction	1	0	1
Total Cases	40	28	12
Percentage with 90% Confidence in	**63%**	**64%**	**58%**
Predicted (Wrong) **Direction**	(3%)	(0%)	(8%)

The results presented in Table 6.8 show little support for the New Regime orientation hypothesis. Although there is a slightly higher proportion of cases providing strong empirical support for the New Regime hypothesis among the more liberal New Regime parties (64%) than among the populist-leaning New Regime parties (58%), the difference is practically negligible. Perhaps even more important, the proportion of cases providing strong empirical support for the New Regime hypothesis among the more liberal parties is practically identical to the proportion of all New Regime parties (63%) providing strong support for the hypothesis. Put another way, if the coding rule for New Regime parties had been crafted in a more exclusive manner to the point where it included only the more liberal parties, then conclusions regarding the general level of the empirical support for the New Regime hypothesis would be almost exactly the same as those generated using the definition employed in the study. Moreover, as will be demonstrated in the appendix to this chapter, had the definition of New Regime parties been expanded to include the ten borderline cases analyzed in the appendix, there still would be practically the same level of overall support for the hypothesis as is reported in this chapter for the cases currently included in the study. Taken together,

category. Of particular interest are Fidesz and Boris Yeltsin, both of which are placed in the liberalizing category in the first half of the decade but are switched to the populist leaning category in the second half of the decade. In Yeltsin's case, this is because of his decision to replace the liberal reformist Gaidar with the more conservative Chernomyrdin as the head of his government from 1992 on, whereas in the case of Fidesz it reflects the decision of what was essentially a liberal reformist party to recast itself as a right-wing conservative party with nationalist overtones for the 1998 Hungarian parliamentary elections (see the discussion of this topic in Chapter 4). Finally, the decision of how to code Schuster in the 1999 Slovak parliamentary elections remains problematic, but to code him as a consistent liberalizer when his own party was not coded as a New Regime party seemed inappropriate, so he rounds out the populist-leaning category.

these observations demonstrate that despite the fact that the coding rule for New Regime parties is the most subjective of the three standard economic voting hypotheses tested in the study, the overall empirical support reported in the study for the hypothesis would be practically the same had the definition been either more restrictive or more permissive than the one employed.

Moreover, the results demonstrate that in the first test of a party orientation hypothesis, there is very little evidence to suggest that deviating in a programmatic manner from the "core" of the New Regime identity dented the regional economic voting effect for these more populist New Regime parties. Despite their more conservative, nationalist, or populist rhetoric or policies, about the same proportion of these parties continued to perform better in areas of the country where economic conditions were better, as predicted by the New Regime hypothesis. Thus, we have our first evidence of the potential "stickiness" of the New Regime identity, here in terms of stickiness across different party orientations.

Time-Based Hypotheses

As was the case for the Incumbency hypothesis, variation in support for the New Regime hypothesis can be analyzed to test the contradictory predictions of the two time-based hypotheses that support should either increase or decrease as the decade progresses. However, we can now also test the interaction of time and party orientation. As laid out in Chapter 2, our expectation is that there should be approximately the same degree of empirical support for the New Regime hypothesis throughout the decade among the more liberal New Regime parties but decreasing empirical support for the New Regime hypothesis among the more populist New Regime parties as the decade progresses.

As Panel 1 of Table 6.9 clearly demonstrates, there is much stronger empirical support for the New Regime hypothesis as the decade progresses. Indeed, of all the conditional hypotheses considered in this chapter to explain variation in support for the New Regime hypothesis, the over-time hypothesis appears to have the most significant empirical support. There are quite substantial differences in support for the New Regime hypothesis across the three waves of elections. There is the least support for the New Regime hypothesis in the first wave of elections (strong empirical support for the hypothesis in 5 out of 12 cases); more support for the New Regime hypothesis in the second wave of elections (10 out of 17 cases); and an

Table 6.9. *Time-Based Explanations of Variation in Support for New Regime Hypothesis*

	All	90–92	93–96	97–99
Panel 1: All New Regime Parties				
90% Confident in Predicted Direction	25	5	10	10
90% Confident in Wrong Direction	1	0	0	1
Total Cases	40	12	17	11
Percentage with 90% Confidence in	**63%**	**42%**	**59%**	**91%**
Predicted (Wrong) **Direction**	(3%)	(0%)	(0%)	(9%)
Panel 2: Consistent Liberalizing New Regime Parties				
90% Confident in Predicted Direction	18	5	7	6
90% Confident in Wrong Direction	0	0	0	0
Total Cases	28	10	12	6
Percentage with 90% Confidence in	**64%**	**50%**	**58%**	**100%**
Predicted (Wrong) **Direction**	(0%)	(0%)	(0%)	(0%)
Panel 3: Populist Leaning New Regime Parties				
90% Confident in Predicted Direction	7	0	3	4
90% Confident in Wrong Direction	1	0	0	1
Total Cases	12	2	5	5
Percentage with 90% Confidence in	**58%**	**0%**	**60%**	**80%**
Predicted (Wrong) **Direction**	(8%)	(0%)	(0%)	(20%)

extremely high level of support during the third wave of elections, with strong empirical support in 10 out of 11 cases.

In contrast, Panels 2 and 3 of Table 6.9 reveal little support for the combined time and orientation hypothesis. Support for the New Regime hypothesis among liberal New Regime parties (see Panel 2) increases slightly across the first two waves of elections (moving from 50% of the cases in the first wave to 58% of the cases in the second wave), before increasing dramatically in the final wave of elections (100% of the cases). The results concerning the populist New Regime parties (see Panel 3) are even more troublesome for the interactive time and orientation hypothesis. Far from revealing decreasing support for the New Regime hypothesis as the decade progresses, there is actually increasing support for the New Regime hypothesis among the more populist New Regime parties during successive waves of elections. Although this is admittedly based on a small number of cases (especially in the first wave), the evidence remains far from the prediction of the hypothesis.

Thus, we arrive at a second type of conclusion regarding the stickiness of the New Regime identity, here across time. Not only is there no evidence of a decline in the empirical support for the New Regime hypothesis as the decade progresses, there is actually strong evidence of the opposite effect: increasing empirical support for the New Regime hypothesis over time. Moreover, this effect is consistent across both liberal and populist New Regime parties, again demonstrating the resiliency of the New Regime category during the 1990s .

Conclusions

Overall, there is strong empirical evidence for just under two-thirds of the New Regime parties included in the study to support the proposition that New Regime parties ought to perform better, after controlling for demographic effects, in regions of the country where the economy is stronger. Moreover, this level of empirical support would change little if the definition of New Regime parties was either more permissive (including the borderline cases discussed in the appendix to this chapter) or more restrictive (excluding the more populist New Regime parties). Support for the New Regime hypothesis is found across many contexts, including parliamentary and presidential elections, elections in East-Central Europe and Russia, and elections that took place throughout the decade. The most consistent support for the New Regime hypothesis can be found in Czech elections and in elections held in the last third of the decade. There is also preliminary evidence that suggests somewhat greater support for the New Regime hypothesis when parties may be perceived as more important in the eyes of voters and when other factors may be less important. Although there is strong support for the New Regime hypothesis overall, the empirical evidence in support of the hypothesis is particularly weak in Slovak elections. There is also less support for the hypothesis earlier as compared to later in the decade. Finally, the assessment of the time and orientation hypotheses suggests a degree of stickiness in the New Regime identity, both across time and across the different types of partisan orientations of New Regime parties.

Thus, we can confidently claim that there is more empirical support for the New Regime hypothesis than there is for the Incumbency hypothesis, and, therefore, to this point, more empirical support for the Transitional Identity Model than the Referendum Model. Of course, the New Regime hypothesis is only one of the two hypotheses produced from the Transitional

Identity Model. It is to the second hypothesis, the Old Regime hypothesis, that I turn in the next chapter.

Appendix 6.1: Borderline New Regime Parties

As noted in Chapter 2, the New Regime hypothesis presents the most difficult coding challenges of the three standard hypotheses. For this reason, I consider here the effect of economic conditions on ten "borderline" parties that I chose not to code as New Regime parties but that presented particularly difficult coding decisions. Ultimately, it was my conclusion that a better argument could be made against coding these parties as New Regime parties than for coding them as New Regime parties. In the remainder of this appendix, I briefly describe the rational for including these particular parties as borderline New Regime parties, the degree of empirical support provided for the New Regime hypothesis by these cases on a country-by-country basis, and an assessment of the overall level of support for the hypothesis across the ten borderline cases as compared to the New Regime parties included in the study. The general conclusion of this exercise is extremely clear: there is roughly the same degree of support for the New Regime hypothesis among the borderline New Regime parties as there is among the New Regime parties included in the study. Therefore, including all of these borderline parties in the study as well would have had practically no effect on any assessment of the overall empirical support for the New Regime hypothesis.

Perhaps the most difficult of all the borderline cases involved Russia's Grigorii Yavlinskii, who contested the 1995 presidential election, and his Yabloko party, which contested all three parliamentary elections.[35] Yavlinskii has long been known as a democrat with strong ties to the West, and he was active on the political scene throughout the 1990s. These factors point toward including Yavlinskii and Yabloko as New Regime parties, especially because of their clear pro-democracy outlook. At the same time, however, neither Yavlinskii nor Yabloko ever joined a Yeltsin government at any point during the 1990s, choosing instead to remain as a liberal opposition party. Given the fact that parties are coded as New Regime parties in

---

[35] For more on Yavlinskii and Yabloko, see the background information on the mid-decade presidential and Russian parliamentary election case studies in Chapter 4, as well as Brovkin 1997; Brudny 1997; Rutland 1999; Brader and Tucker 2001; Rose and Munro 2002; and Colton and McFaul 2003.

Table 6A.1. *Borderline New Regime Parties*

Panel 1: Alternative New Regime Parties by Country

	All	Poland*	Slovakia**	Russia***
90% Confident in Predicted Direction	6	2	2	2
90% Confident in Wrong Direction	1	0	0	1
Total Cases	10	3	3	4
Percentage with 90% Confidence in	**60%**	**67%**	**67%**	**50%**
Predicted (Wrong) **Direction**	(10%)	(0%)	(0%)	(25%)

Panel 2: Potential New Regime Parties by Inclusion/Exclusion from Study

	All	New Regime Parties Included in Study[#]	Borderline New Regime Parties Not Included in Study
90% Confident in Predicted Direction	30	24	6
90% Confident in Wrong Direction	2	1	1
Total Cases	50	40	10
Percentage with 90% Confidence in	**60%**	**60%**	**60%**
Predicted (Wrong) **Direction**	(4%)	(3%)	(10%)

* Poland: Non-Partisan Bloc in Support of Reform (1993) Jan Olszewski (1995); Movement for Defense of Poland (1997).

** Slovakia: Movement for a Democratic Slovakia (1992, 1994, 1998).

*** Russia: Yabloko (1993, 1995, 1999); Grigorii Yavlinskii (1996).

\# See note 40 for details on difference between results in this column and those presented in text of chapter.

Russia through their association with Yeltsin and his government, it did not seem legitimate to code a party that had consciously remained in opposition to that government as a New Regime party.[36] As Panel 1 of Table 6A.1 demonstrates, had Yavlinskii and Yabloko been coded as New Regime parties, then the empirical evidence would have supported the New Regime hypothesis in two out of the four cases (the 1995 parliamentary election for Yabloko and the 1996 presidential election for Yavlinskii).

---

[36] Note that this should not be confused with the case of FIDESZ in Hungary, which was not a member of a governing coalition until its victory in the 1998 parliamentary election but is coded as a New Regime party because of its clear role as a pro-transition anticommunist member of the Opposition Round Table (EKA). Had such a round table existed in Russia, then Yabloko would surely have participated and also would have been coded as a New Regime party. Of course, had there been a round table negotiation, Yabloko's role in the 1990s also might have been very different.

Another complicated case concerns the Movement for a Democratic Slovakia (HZDS), which, as described in Chapter 4, emerged out of the Slovak anticommunist umbrella movement Public Against Violence in March 1991. At the time, the head of HZDS, Vladimír Meciar, was the prime minister of Slovakia. Moreover, HZDS would go on to be the primary coalition member in the governing coalition with Meciar as prime minister again following the June 1992 elections through March 1994, and then again following the October 1994 elections until the September 1998 elections.[37] With its background in the Public Against Violence movement and all the time it spent in government, it might seem appropriate to code HZDS as a New Regime party. However, as opposed to other New Regime parties that emerged out of anticommunist umbrella movement, HZDS was not in any way a "successor" to that movement. Indeed, HZDS was formed in opposition to Public Against Violence and the pro-reform policies it was attempting to espouse (and especially in opposition to the pro-reform Czech Civic Forum). Once established as a separate party, HZDS consistently targeted voters with nationalist appeals and continued to pursue policies that were far from consistent with the original transitional course that Czechoslovakia had embarked on when Slovakia was still part of the country. Moreover, when Meciar was replaced as prime minister and HZDS was forced out of the government in both March 1991 and March 1994, he was replaced by more pro-reform and pro-democracy forces. Given its nationalist and almost antitransition identity, it seemed too much of a stretch to code HZDS as a New Regime party. That being said, adding HZDS to the category of New Regime parties would actually have improved the empirical support for the New Regime hypothesis as the empirical evidence supports the claim that HZDS enjoyed more electoral success in parts of the country where the economy was better in two out of the three parliamentary elections (1994, 1998) in which it competed (see Table 6A.1, Panel 1).

The next borderline case is from Poland and involves Jan Olszewski and the political party that he led in the 1997 Polish parliamentary election, the Movement for the Reconstruction of Poland (ROP). Although Olszewski himself had strong links to the Solidarity movement, having also served as a member of the Committee for the Defense of Workers and having joined

---

[37] For more details on these different governments, see Mesežnikov 1994; Szomolanyi and Mesežnikov 1994; Leff 1996, 1997; Mesežnikov 1997; and Szomolanyi 1999.

Solidarity in 1980 (see Krupa 1997, 68–9), both his presidential campaign and ROP took on a decidedly nationalist orientation.[38] Moreover, during the brief time that Olszewski served as Polish prime minister (December 1991–June 1992), he repeatedly clashed with President Wałęsa. Nevertheless, his personal pedigree and connection with the Solidarity movement at least suggests the potential for coding both his candidacy and party as a New Regime party, and for this reason both are included in the borderline category.

A final borderline case comes from the 1993 Polish parliamentary election. The Non-Partisan Bloc to Support Reforms (BBWR) was formed before the 1993 Polish parliamentary election to support Lech Wałęsa, and as such was similar to the "parties of power" found in Russia.[39] As noted earlier in this chapter, these Russian parties were coded as New Regime parties because of their association with Yeltsin. As Poland is not considered a presidential system for the purpose of this study, parties are not coded based on their association with the president. Admittedly, however, a good claim could be made that if Wałęsa is coded as a New Regime candidate and BBWR existed solely to support him, then it, too, should be coded as a New Regime party. For this reason, I include it as the last of the borderline New Regime parties.

Table 6A.1 presents the degree of empirical support for these borderline New Regime parties on a country-by-country basis (Panel 1) and in comparison to the parties that were coded as New Regime parties in the study (Panel 2).[40] For both the Polish and Slovak parties, strong empirical support for the New Regime hypothesis can be found in two out of three cases; strong support is also found in two of the four Russian cases. The overall result is strikingly clear: there is practically the same degree of

---

[38] See, for example, Bugajski 2002, 196, who classifies ROP as a nationalist party.

[39] BBWR was led by Andrzej Olechowski, an economic advisor to Wałęsa. For more, see Chan 1995, 134.

[40] The analyses presented in Table 6A.1 are taken from the extra parties robustness test described in Chapter 3 and presented in Chapter 8. For the sake of consistency, the results presented for the New Regime parties included in the study in Panel 2 of Table 6A.1 are also from the extra parties robustness test, which, as will be described in detail in Chapter 8, returned very similar but not identical results to those found in the text of this chapter. This is the reason why Table 6A.1 reports strong empirical support for twenty-four out of the forty New Regime parties, whereas the text reports strong support for twenty-five out of the forty New Regime parties. See Tables 8.1 and 8.3 in Chapter 8 for another illustration of this point.

empirical support for the New Regime hypothesis among the borderline New Regime parties as there is among the New Regime parties included in the study. Put another way, if the ten borderline New Regime parties had been included in the study from the start, the overall conclusions regarding the degree of empirical support for the New Regime hypothesis would have been almost exactly the same.

7

The Old Regime Hypothesis

Unlike both the Incumbency and the New Regime hypotheses, which predict the types of parties likely to benefit from better economic conditions, the Old Regime hypothesis predicts the type of parties – Old Regime parties – that are likely to receive more electoral support in parts of the country where economic conditions are worse. As will be demonstrated in this chapter, the Old Regime hypothesis has the most consistent empirical support of the three standard economic voting hypotheses examined in this book. Of the twenty-nine parties coded as Old Regime parties across the entire study, there is strong empirical support for the prediction that Old Regime parties should perform better where economic conditions are worse in twenty-one (or 72%) of these cases; by contrast, there is only one case of an Old Regime party that generates strong empirical evidence that the economy had the opposite effect from what was predicted by the Old Regime hypothesis. Moreover, there is support for the Old Regime hypothesis in a wide variety of contexts, including presidential and parliamentary elections, high and low responsibility elections, and elections that take place throughout the decade. Indeed, about the only context in which there is not consistently strong support for the Old Regime hypothesis is in Russian elections, a point that is addressed throughout this chapter.

The chapter is organized in largely the same manner as the first two empirical chapters, examining coding decisions, the paired case studies, overall results, and then analyses of the support provided for the different conditional economic voting hypotheses by Old Regime parties. Because of the relative consistency of Old Regime parties across elections, however, the coding of Old Regime parties is discussed for all parties on a country-by-country basis instead of only for the paired case studies.

Table 7.1. *Coding of Old Regime Parties*

Country	Date*	Party
Czech Republic	June 5–6, 1992 (L)	LB
Czech Republic	May 31–June 1, 1996 (L)	KSČM
Czech Republic	June 19–20, 1998 (L)	KSČM
Hungary	April 8, 1990 (L)	MSzP, MSzMP
Hungary	May 8, 1994 (L)	MSzP, MP
Hungary	May 10, 1998 (L)	MSzP, MP
Poland	November 25, 1990 (P)	Cimoszewicz
Poland	October 27, 1991 (L)	SLD
Poland	September 19, 1993 (L)	SLD
Poland	November 5, 1995 (P)	Kwaśniewski
Poland	September 21, 1997 (L)	SLD
Russia	June 12, 1991 (P)	Ryzhkov, Bakatin
Russia	December 12, 1993 (L)	KPRF
Russia	December 17, 1995 (L)	KPRF, KTR-SS
Russia	June 16, 1996 (P)	Zyuganov
Russia	December 19, 1999 (L)	KPRF, KTR-SS
Slovakia	June 5–6, 1992 (L)	SDL'
Slovakia	Sept. 30–Oct. 1, 1994 (L)	KSS, ZRS, SV
Slovakia	September 25–26, 1998 (L)	KSS, ZRS, SDL'
Slovakia	May 15, 1999 (P)	None

* L = Legislative, P = Presidential. For two-round elections, date refers to first round.

Coding Old Regime Parties

The specific coding rules for Old Regime parties were presented in Chapter 2. To reiterate, two categories of parties are coded as Old Regime parties: the official successor parties of the prior ruling communist party and splinter movements from that party that were established during the postcommunist period in an effort to remain closer to the old communist ideology than the official successor party. The coding of Old Regime parties from all twenty elections is listed in Table 7.1.

As Table 7.1 illustrates, in Poland and the Czech Republic there is only one Old Regime party in each election. For Poland, this is the Democratic Left Alliance (SLD). Until 1999, the SLD was actually an electoral alliance of a number of parties, associations, and trade unions, although it was dominated by the Social Democracy of the Republic Poland party (SdRP), the reformed legal successor of the Polish communist party, the

Polish United Worker's Party (PZPR).[1] The SLD is therefore coded as the only Polish Old Regime Party in the 1991, 1993 and the 1997 parliamentary elections, and its candidate, Aleksander Kwaśniewski, is coded as the Old Regime candidate in the 1995 presidential election.[2] As the SLD did not come into existence until mid-1991, the candidate of the SdRP, Woldzimierz Cimoszewicz, is coded as the Old Regime candidate in 1990.[3]

In the Czech Republic the single Old Regime party is the unreformed Communist Party of Bohemia and Moravia (KSČM), the successor to the Czechoslovak Communist Party (KSČ) in the Czech Republic (the successor in Slovakia is discussed later).[4] In 1996 and 1998, the KSČM competed on its own in the parliamentary election. In 1992, however, it competed as the dominant member of an electoral coalition called the Left Bloc (LB), so for this election the LB is coded as the Old Regime party.[5]

In Hungary, there are two parties coded as Old Regime parties in each election. When the ruling party from the communist era, the Hungarian Socialist Workers Party (MSzMP), disbanded on October 7, 1989, it invited members to join the official successor to that party, the reformist Hungarian

---

[1] In April 1999, the SLD was registered as an actual party, thus ending the independent existence of the SdRP. See Markowski 2002, 54–59 and note 1, and Grzymała-Busse 2002, 99–107, for more on the evolution of the PZPR into SdRP and the SLD.

[2] There were actually two splinter movements that emerged from the SdRP. The first, the Polish Social Democratic Union (PUS) left because they felt that the movement of the SdRP away from the old communist PZPR was not serious enough, and as such would not have been coded as an Old Regime party. As it turned out, the party disbanded before the 1991 parliamentary election, and did not even compete in any of the elections included in this study. A second spin-off of orthodox communists, the Union of Polish Communists "Proletariat" (ZKP "P"), would have qualified as an Old Regime party had it ever received the required 2% of the vote in an election, but it never did (Grzymała-Busse 2002, 106 and notes 170–2).

[3] See Sabbat-Swidlicka 1990, 10 as well as Weydenthal 1990; Zubek 1991b. For more on the SdRP and SLD, see Curry 1995; Mahr and Nagle 1995; Zubek 1995; Ishiyama 1997; Wiatr 1999; Bunce 2002; and Markowski 2002.

[4] In one of those too good to be true coincidences, the office of the KSČM in Prague at the time of the 1998 parliamentary election was located on Politických vězňů, which translates into English as Political Prisoners Street. For more on the evolution of the KSČM specifically, see Ishiyama 1997; Grzymała-Busse 1998, 2002; Hanley 2002. For more on the evolution of the KSČM in conjunction with other Czech parties, see Obrman 1992a; Pehe 1992a; Wolchik 1993; Bugge 1994; Leff 1997; Blahoz, Brokly, and Mansfeldova 1999; Kitschelt, Manfeldova et al. 1999; and Innes 2001.

[5] The only other party in the coalition was the Democratic Left party, a small regional party; there were also a number of small organizations in the coalition as well. See Grzymała-Busse 2002, 191–192 and Hanley 2002, 146 and note 4.

Socialist Party (MSzP), which was to be a reborn as a modern social-democratic party.[6] A small number of hard-line communists refused to join this party, and instead formed a "new" Hungarian Socialist Workers Party (MSzMP), which competed in the 1990 parliamentary election. By January 1991, its name had been shortened simply to the Workers Party (MP).[7] Both parties clearly fit the criteria for being coded as Old Regime parties: the MSzP because of its status as the legal successor of the old ruling communist party, and the MSzMP/MP because of its standing as a splinter group from that legal successor that formed an alternative party designed to be more faithful to communist principles than the official successor. Both parties survived to contest all three elections in the 1990s.

In Slovakia, a similar pattern developed, although two splinter parties eventually arose. The legal successor to the Czechoslovak Communist Party in Slovakia was the Communist Party of Slovakia (KSS), which officially changed its name to the Party of the Democratic Left (SDL') in February 1991 as part of an effort to pursue a reformist outlook.[8] Some of the more orthodox members of the KSS refused to join the SDL', and instead formed an alternative hard-line communist party called Communist Party of Slovakia '91 (KSS '91); the party would drop the '91 before the 1994 elections and compete as the Communist Party of Slovakia (KSS).[9] In March 1994, another faction of SDL' party members – upset over the fact that the SDL' was not doing enough to promote left-wing goals – established a new party, the Association of Workers of Slovakia (ZRS) under the leadership of the former communist "worker-hero" Jan Luptak.[10] As both the KSS and ZRS were splinter movements from the legal successor that were formed to be more adherent to communist principles than the legal successor, both are coded as Old Regime parties. As KSS '91 received only 0.75% of the

---

[6] See Racz 1993; Swain 1993; Oltay 1994. For more on the evolution of the MSzP, see Agh 1995; Tokes 1996; Ishiyama 1997; Markus 1999; Agh 2000; Bozoki 2002; Bunce 2002; and Grzymała-Busse 2002.

[7] See Pittaway and Swain 1994, 243. To make matters more complicated, in 1993 a hard-line faction of the Workers Party split off and formed a third Hungarian Socialist Workers Party (MSzMP) under the leadership of Laszlo Fazekas. This incarnation of the party, however, failed to play any role in the ensuing election (Pittaway and Swain 1994, 225).

[8] For more on the evolution of the KSS into the SDL', see Mesežnikov 1994; Mahr and Nagle 1995; Grzymała-Busse 1998; Fisher 2002, and Grzymała-Busse 2002, 92–99.

[9] See Grzymała-Busse 1998, 468. Thus, the KSS formed in 1991 was not the legal successor to original KSS; the actual legal successor was the SDL'.

[10] See Bugajski 2002, 310. Luptak was also referred to as a "crypto-Bolshevik" (Fisher 2002, 125). For more on the ZRS, see Henderson 1994; Mesežnikov 1997.

vote in 1992 and ZRS was not formed until 1994, the SDL' is the only Old Regime party in 1992.[11] SDL' participated in the 1994 election as the dominant member of the Common Choice (SV) electoral coalition, and then in 1998 on its own.[12]

In Russia, a number of parties initially laid claim to the mantle of the true successor to the Communist Party of the Soviet Union (CPSU), but the one party that unambiguously emerged to play this role was Communist Party of the Russian Federation (KPRF).[13] Led by Genadii Zyuganov throughout the 1990s, the KPRF placed third in the 1993 parliamentary election and then won the largest number of seats in the 1995 and 1999 elections, thus cementing itself as the primary opposition party throughout the Yeltsin years. As Zyuganov was the official candidate of the party in the 1995 presidential election, he is coded as the Old Regime candidate in that election. The coding of Old Regime candidates in the 1991 Russian presidential elections parallels the logic for the coding of incumbents that was discussed in Chapter 5, so both Vadim Bakatin and Nikolai Ryzhkov are coded as Old Regime candidates in 1991.

Of the other communist-oriented movements that emerged in Russia in the early 1990s, the only one that ever enjoyed even minor electoral success in parliamentary elections was the Communist Workers of Russia for the Soviet Union electoral bloc (KTR-SS), winning 4.5% of the popular vote in 1995 and then 2.2% of the vote in 1999.[14] Clearly located to the left of the KPRF, the KTR-SS "united the KPRF's radical challengers" (Urban 1996, 182) and its constituent parties and leaders have been described as "left radicals" (McFaul, Petrov et al. 1999, 83), "hardline communist" (Rose and Munro 2003), "ultra-leftist" (Urban and Solovei 1997, 149), and

---

[11] KSS did not fare that much better in the ensuing elections, but it did pass the 2% threshold for inclusion in the study with 2.7% and 2.8% of the total vote in the 1994 and 1998 elections, respectively. ZRS, after faring surprisingly well in the 1994 elections, received only 1.3% of the vote in the 1998 election. Its performance in 1998 is still included in the study, however, on the basis of its membership in the ruling coalition from 1994 to 1998; see Chapter 5 for details.

[12] Partners in the Common Choice coalition included the Social Democratic Party of Slovakia, the Green Party of Slovakia, and the Movement of Peasants of the Slovak Republic (*Volby do Narodnej Rady Slovkenskej Republiky*, 1994, 7).

[13] On the emergence of the KPRF out of the CPSU via the Communist Party of the Russian Soviet Federated Republic, see Lentini 1992; Urban 1996; Sakwa 1998; Flikke 1999; Sakwa 2002a and especially Urban and Solovei 1997, Chapters 2–3.

[14] The parties that would go on to make up this electoral bloc boycotted the 1993 Parliamentary election (Sakwa 1998, 132).

"neo-Stalinist" (Ishiyama 1997, 315).[15] Thus, the KTR-SS is coded as an Old Regime party as well.

Finally, testing the Old Regime party orientation hypothesis requires coding all of the Old Regime parties as either reformed or unreformed (see Tables 7.5 and 7A.1). The coding scheme for doing so is fairly simple. The three official successor Old Regime parties that attempted to reinvent themselves as social democratic parties and their presidential candidates are coded as reformed Old Regime parties; this includes the SLD in Poland, the MSzP in Hungary, and the SDL' in Slovakia.[16] The two official successor parties that eschewed recasting themselves as social-democratic parties, the KSČM in the Czech Republic and the KPRF in Russia, are coded as unreformed Old Regime parties, as are all of the alternative and spin-off movements that were included as Old Regime parties because of their more orthodox orientation than the official successor parties.[17] The only other coding decision that bears mentioning is the 1991 Russian presidential election, which took place before the emergence of the KPRF. As noted in Chapter 5, two Old Regime candidates contested this election, one who had the support of the hard-line communists, Nikolai Ryzhkov, and one who had the support of Gorbachev and other reformists in the CPSU, Vadim Bakatin. It therefore follows nicely that Ryzhkov is coded as an unreformed

---

[15] The bloc include the Communist Workers' Party, the Russian Party of Communists, and the Union of Communists, and such notable orthodox communists as Viktor Tyulkin, Viktor Anpilov, and Anatoli Kryuchkov; see Sakwa 2002a, 248; McFaul, Petrov et al. 1999, 77; Urban and Solovei 1997, 149, 165; Urban 1996, 182; and *Vybory Deputatov Gosudarstvenoy Dumi*, 1996, 73.

[16] At the most basic level, these parties can be identified by the fact that all were renamed in a manner that involved dropping the Communist or Socialist Workers label and instead including "socialist" "social democratic" or "democratic left" in their new name. But there also exists almost complete consensus in the literature that these three parties should be considered reformed successor parties; see, for example, Mahr and Nagle 1995; Orenstein 1998; Markus 1999; Bauer 2002; Bunce 2002. Ziblatt and Biziouras 2002 actually go so far as to create a "reform index", with the MSzP, SLD, and SDL' occupying the top three spots; the Czech KSČM has the lowest score (p. 293–4).

[17] Much has been made of the efforts of the KPRF to present different faces to the world depending on the audience. In particular, Genadii Zyuganov's trip to the World Economic Forum in Davos, Switzerland, in the run up to the 1996 presidential election is often mentioned as evidence of a moderate streak in the KPRF (McFaul 1997b, 41). That being said, it would be a much larger claim to lump the KPRF in the same general reformed camp as the SLD, MSzP, or SDL'. Although the KPRF is clearly not the same thing as the Communist Party of the Soviet Union – as is evidenced in part by the presence of parties to its left such as the aforementioned KTR-SS – it seems clear that for the purpose of this distinction between reformed and unreformed Old Regime parties it belongs in the latter category.

Old Regime candidate, whereas Bakatin is a reformed Old Regime candidate. The classification of all Old Regime parties as either reformed or unreformed can be found in Table 7A.1.

Empirical Results: Paired Case Studies

Starting with the 1992 Czech and Slovak Republic elections, we observe a familiar pattern. As with the previous hypotheses, there is strong empirical support for the prediction of the Old Regime hypothesis in the Czech case, but very weak support for the Old Regime hypothesis in the Slovak case. What could be causing this distinction? After having observed a similar pattern across all three hypotheses, one logical conclusion would be that there is something important distinguishing voting behavior across these two elections. As both are parliamentary elections in countries with parliamentary systems, employ closed-list PR voting rules, and take place at the same time early in the decade, most of the conditional hypotheses do not provide much leverage over the difference in results between these two elections.[18] The one exception is the regime future hypothesis, which does predict a reduced role for the economy in the 1992 Slovak election; I return to this point in the following chapter.

In the preceding chapters, however, I also suggested more party-based explanations for the disparity in results between the 1992 Czech and Slovak elections, including the degree of overlap between incumbency and New Regime status (Chapter 5) and the relative weakness of New Regime parties in Slovakia generally (Chapter 6). Although such party-based explanations become increasingly difficult to sustain as the pattern continues across multiple standard hypotheses, there is another potential party based explanation for the variation in the empirical support for the Old Regime hypothesis across these two elections. The Old Regime orientation hypothesis predicts that there should be more empirical support for the Old Regime hypothesis in the case of unreformed Old Regime parties than reformed Old Regime parties. As noted earlier, the Czech KSČM is coded as an unreformed Old Regime party, whereas the Slovak SDL' is coded as a reformed Old Regime party. This case study, therefore, is consistent with the prediction of the Old Regime orientation hypothesis: there is support for the Old Regime hypothesis in the case of the unreformed KSČM but not for the reformed

---

[18] And the Slovak SDL' actually received a slightly higher proportion of the overall vote (14.7%) than the Czech LB (14.1%).

SDL'. That being said, this pattern does not hold up at all when support for the hypothesis is explored systematically across all of the elections in the study (see the discussion surrounding Table 7.5 later in this chapter).

Turning to the mid-decade presidential elections case study, there is one Old Regime candidate in each election, Aleksander Kwaśniewski in Poland, the official candidate of the SLD in Poland, and Genadii Zyuganov, the official candidate of the KPRF in Russia. In both cases, there is strong empirical support for the proposition that these candidates received more support in areas of the country where the economy was worse. We have more confidence in this effect in the vote for Kwaśniewski than for Zyuganov, but both cross the 90% threshold of strong certainty. So this case study demonstrates that empirical support can be found for the Old Regime hypothesis in the context of presidential elections; it also offers another example of empirical support provided to a standard economic voting hypothesis by a Russian candidate.

The three Russian parliamentary elections, however, reveal a quite different pattern from the previous chapters. Of the five Old Regime parties that contested these three elections, there is strong support for the Old Regime hypothesis in only one case: the vote for the KPRF in the 1995 parliamentary election. In the other two elections, the majority of the simulations for the KPRF are still in the correctly predicted direction, but we do not have a high level of confidence in this effect; indeed, in the 1999 parliamentary election, it appears almost equally likely that the KPRF benefited from better economic conditions than from worse economic conditions, and our best guess is that there was practically no effect. The empirical support in the case of the hard-line KTR-SS is even worse. In neither election is there strong empirical support for the claim that the party benefited where the economy was worse, and in 1995 there is actually strong evidence that the party performed better in areas of the country where the economy was better, which directly contradicts the prediction of the Old Regime hypothesis.

In the next section of this chapter, I address in great detail the question of why the empirical support for the Old Regime hypothesis is generally so weak in the Russian context. For now, I focus on the question of the disparity in empirical support for the Old Regime hypothesis in the case of the KPRF and the KTR-SS. Given that the empirical support for the hypothesis in both cases is poor, it is certainly worse for the KTR-SS than for the KPRF. As was noted in the discussion of the mid-decade presidential elections case study, there is strong empirical support for the claim that Genadii Zyuganov, the official candidate of the KPRF in the 1996 Russian presidential election, enjoyed more electoral success in areas of the country where the economy was worse, as predicted by the Old Regime hypothesis. Thus, across the four elections in which the KPRF either ran as a party (the 1993, 1995, and 1999 parliamentary elections) or had a candidate run for president (the 1996 presidential election), in two of the cases there is strong empirical support for the Old Regime hypothesis; in the other two cases at least a majority of the simulations are in the correct direction. The analysis of the vote for the KTR-SS, by contrast, did not generate strong support for the Old Regime hypothesis in either election it contested.

As both the KPRF and the KTR-SS are unreformed Old Regime parties, this distinction is not helpful in trying to explain the variation in empirical support for the Old Regime hypothesis across the two parties. Instead, the conditional hypotheses that would appear to be most relevant in these cases are the responsibility-based hypotheses. The KPRF was the primary opposition party throughout the 1990s, its candidate for president in 1995 came in second place in the election, and the party received the largest number of seats in the parliament following the 1995 and 1999 elections. The KTR-SS, by contrast, failed to cross the minimum threshold necessary to receive delegates from the proportional representation lists in either election. So whereas the existence of the KTR-SS may have been relevant to the KPRF in terms of costing it votes,[19] the KPRF was clearly the more important Russian Old Regime party in the eyes of most Russian citizens. And as the responsibility approach suggests that the standard Old Regime hypothesis ought to generate more empirical support when parties are more important to voters, the distinction between the empirical support for the Old Regime hypothesis in the case of the KPRF and the KTR-SS is in line with this approach.

One other distinction concerning the KTR-SS is worth noting. Among all the Old Regime parties in the study, the KTR-SS is the only one that exists as a more orthodox alternative to an unreformed Old Regime party. The spin-off Old Regime parties in Hungary and Slovakia positioned themselves as alternatives to reformed Old Regime parties, and there are no relevant alternative Old Regime parties to the unreformed KSČM in the Czech Republic. Thus, the KTR-SS was in the unique position of trying to position itself as a more orthodox communist party than an official successor party that did not renounce its communist identity in an effort to follow a more social democratic path. Perhaps there is something about

---

[19] See, for example, McFaul, Petrov et al. 1999, 77.

this set of circumstances that makes it particularly unlikely that the party would in fact be affected by the economy in the manner suggested by the Old Regime hypothesis. Although with just one case, we can do little more for now than speculate in this regard, the finding may warrant examination in other countries.

The final case study, the old regime-incumbent elections, provides perhaps the most interesting set of results. In all three cases, the SLD in the 1997 Polish parliamentary election and the MSzP and MP in the 1998 Hungarian parliamentary elections, there is very strong empirical evidence that these parties performed better in areas of the country where economic conditions were worse. Indeed, both Hungarian parties have over 99% of the simulations in the predicted direction; the SLD in Poland has 98.8% of the simulations in the correct direction.

That there is empirical support for the Old Regime hypothesis in the case of the MP is not that surprising. As explained earlier in the chapter, the MP was a far left unreformed communist party that was not a part of the current government. The SLD (Poland) and MSzP (Hungary), however, were the lead parties in their countries' respective governments for the four years preceding the election, and both had presided over a period of improved economic conditions. And yet both were voted out of office, replaced by coalitions headed by New Regime parties, and, as in previous elections (see Appendix IV), continued to enjoy greater electoral success in areas of the country where the economy was performing worse than in parts of the country where the economy was performing better.

As noted previously, this final paired case study provides a stark example of an election in which the two models predict the exact opposite effect. As incumbents, the Incumbency hypothesis predicts that the SLD and MSzP should draw more support when economic conditions are better; as Old Regime parties, the Old Regime hypothesis predicts that the SLD and MSzP should draw more support where economic conditions are poorer. The results in Table 7.2 clearly demonstrate that even after controlling for traditional sociodemographic determinants of party support, the economy affected the vote for both the SLD and the MSzP in the manner predicted by the Old Regime hypothesis. Despite their incumbency status, both parties polled better where macroeconomic conditions were worse.

Overall, the case studies provide a number of interesting observations about the empirical support for the Old Regime hypothesis. As with both the New Regime and Incumbency hypotheses, there is strong support for the Old Regime hypothesis in the 1992 Czech parliamentary election but not

Table 7.2. *Empirical Support for Paired Case Studies: Old Regime Hypothesis*

Party			Confidence in Predicted Effect
Czech Republic / Slovakia 1992			
Czech Rep.	1992	Left Bloc (LB)	99.5
Slovakia	1992	Party of the Democratic Left (SDL')	31.4
Mid Decade Presidential Elections			
Poland	1995	Aleksander Kwaśniewski	97.6
Russia	1996	Genadii Zyuganov	91.4
Russian Parliamentary Elections			
Russia	1993	Communist Party of the Russian Federation (KPRF)	77.6
Russia	1995	Communist Party of the Russian Federation (KPRF)	100.0
		Communist Workers of Russia (KTR-SS)	0.8
Russia	1999	Communist Party of the Russian Federation (KPRF)	54.5
		Communist Workers of Russia (KTR-SS)	64.3
Late Decade Incumbent – Old Regime Elections			
Poland	1997	Democratic Left Alliance (SLD)	98.8
Hungary	1998	Hungarian Socialist Party (MSzP)	99.6
		Workers Party (MP)	100.0

the 1992 Slovak parliamentary election. Unlike the previous hypotheses, there is not particularly strong support for the Old Regime hypothesis in the case of the Russian parliamentary elections. There is, however, support for the Old Regime hypothesis in the two mid-decade presidential elections, and there is also very strong support for the hypothesis in the 1997 Polish and 1998 Hungarian parliamentary elections.

Comparative Analysis

Moving away from the focused case studies, there is even more empirical support for the Old Regime hypothesis in the overall comparative analysis than the case studies suggest. Although seven of the twelve Old Regime parties analyzed in the paired case studies provide strong support for the hypothesis, fourteen of the remaining seventeen Old Regime parties that are not included in the paired case studies also provide strong empirical support for the hypothesis, for a total of twenty-one out of twenty-nine cases (72%). And as was the case with the other hypotheses, this finding is quite robust to respecification of the original economic voting models in the manner described in Chapter 3, with the total number of cases surpassing the 90% threshold only varying from nineteen out of twenty-nine (65%) to twenty-two out of twenty-nine (76%).[20] Across all of the alternative specifications, therefore, the Old Regime hypothesis always has the most empirical support of the three standard hypotheses considered in the study.

Despite the high overall level of empirical support for the Old Regime hypothesis, it is still possible to examine the variation in support for the hypothesis across different Old Regime parties using the conditional hypotheses. As in the previous two chapters, I turn first to the intuitive conditional explanations before moving on to the more theoretically oriented approaches.

Intuitive Explanations

Panel 1 of Table 7.3 reveals a very similar pattern to what was observed in the previous two chapters: the Old Regime hypothesis appears to have slightly more empirical support in parliamentary than presidential elections, although this conclusion continues to be based on a small number of cases in the presidential election category. And although it is interesting to have found the same pattern across all three standard hypotheses, the caveats regarding the number of cases from presidential elections are even more important in this instance. What can be said more definitively, however, is that there is certainly evidence to support the Old Regime hypothesis in both presidential and parliamentary elections.

In contrast, Panel 2 of Table 7.3 reveals a stark distinction between the degree of empirical support for the Old Regime hypothesis in the East-Central European cases as opposed to the Russian cases. Among the East-Central European cases, however, there is practically no meaningful variation; in all four countries, the Old Regime hypothesis is almost always strongly supported by the empirical evidence (see Panel 3 of Table 7.3). This continues the trend from the two previous chapters of having one country that stands out from the others based on substantially different results. Although in Chapter 5 this was Czech Republic and in Chapter 6

---

[20] The results of these tests are discussed in greater detail in Chapter 8; see especially Tables 8.1 and 8.3.

Table 7.3. *Intuitive Explanations of Variation in Support for Old Regime Hypothesis*

Panel 1: Parliamentary vs. Presidential Elections

	All	Parliamentary	Presidential
90% Confident in Predicted Direction	21	18	3
90% Confident in Wrong Direction	1	1	0
Total Cases	29	24	5
Percentage with 90% Confidence in	**72%**	**75%**	**60%**
Predicted (Wrong) **Direction**	(3%)	(4%)	(3%)

Panel 2: East-Central Europe vs. Russia

	All	East-Central Europe	Russia
90% Confident in Predicted Direction	21	19	2
90% Confident in Wrong Direction	1	0	1
Total Cases	29	21	8
Percentage with 90% Confidence in	**72%**	**90%**	**25%**
Predicted (Wrong) **Direction**	(3%)	(0%)	(13%)

Panel 3: Country by Country Variation

	All	Czech R.	Hungary	Poland	Slovakia	Russia
90% Confident in Predicted Direction	21	3	5	5	6	2
90% Confident in Wrong Direction	1	0	0	0	0	1
Total Cases	29	3	6	5	7	8
Percentage with 90% Confidence in Predicted (Wrong) **Direction**	**72%** (3%)	**100%** (0%)	**83%** (0%)	**100%** (0%)	**86%** (20%)	**25%** (13%)

Slovakia, here it is clearly Russia, where only two of the eight Russian Old Regime parties provide strong support for the Old Regime hypothesis.

Table 7.4 presents the results for all eight of the Russian parties individually, and demonstrates that although there are only two parties that we are strongly confident provide support for the Old Regime hypothesis, it is not the case that we have strong confidence that most of these parties are performing better in areas of the country where economic conditions are better, which would be in direct contrast to the predictions of the Old Regime hypothesis. In fact, with the exception of the aforementioned KTR-SS in 1995, in all of the cases a majority of the simulations are in the

Table 7.4. *Empirical Support for Old Regime Hypothesis by Russian Old Regime Parties*

Year	Party/Candidate	Confidence in Predicted Effect
1991	Nikolai Ryzhkov	70.3
1991	Vadim Bakatin	84.9
1993	Communist Party of the Russian Federation (KPRF)	77.6
1995	Communist Party of the Russian Federation (KPRF)	100
1995	Communist Workers of Russia – For the Soviet Union (KTR-SS)	0.8
1996	Gennadii Zyuganov	91.4
1999	Communist Party of the Russian Federation (KPRF)	54.5
1999	Communist Workers of Russia – For the Soviet Union (KTR-SS)	64.3

correctly predicted direction, which means that our best guess (the mean or median of the simulations) at the effect of the economic shock is in the correctly predicted direction.[21]

That being said, we are still much less confident in these effects than in East-Central European cases, and by the criteria of this study, six of the eight Russian cases fail to provide adequate empirical support for the Old Regime hypothesis. This begs the question of what, therefore, could account for the lack of empirical support for the Old Regime hypothesis in the Russian cases? It is possible to approach this question in two ways. The first option is to explore systematic explanations for why the electoral experiences of Russia's Old Regime parties may have differed from those of their East-Central European counterparts. As was demonstrated in the previous chapters, there is strong empirical support generated by the Russian cases for the Incumbency and New Regime hypotheses, so any such systematic explanation would need to be particularly focused on the experiences of Russian Old Regime parties, as opposed to Russian political developments

---

[21] This finding again illustrates the value of using statistical simulation to estimate our uncertainty in our estimates of the the effects of the economic shocks. If one simply calculated a first difference for the eight Russian cases without any measure of uncertainty and then examined whether that first difference was positive or negative, an assessment of the eight Russian cases would have revealed exactly what the Old Regime hypothesis predicts – a negative first difference – in seven out of the eight cases. By focusing instead on our level of uncertainty in these predicted first differences, we are able to see that although roughly the same proportion of Russian cases have a "best guess" at the first difference in the correctly predicted direction as the East-Central European cases, our confidence in these effects is much lower in the Russian cases than the East-Central European cases.

The Old Regime Hypothesis

Table 7.5. *Old Regime Party Orientation Hypothesis*

	All	Reformed	Unreformed
90% Confident in Predicted Direction	21	8	13
90% Confident in Wrong Direction	1	0	1
Total Cases	29	11	18
Percentage with 90% Confidence in	**72%**	**73%**	**72%**
Predicted (Wrong) **Direction**	(3%)	(0%)	(6%)

generally or problems with the Russian data.[22] A second option is look for idiosyncratic explanations on an election-by-election base that taken together might help to explain the overall Russian pattern.

Beginning with systematic explanations, the conditional Old Regime orientation hypothesis predicts a difference in the effects for the economy on reformed and unreformed Old Regime parties. Russia is distinguished from Poland, Hungary, and Slovakia by the fact that for all of its elections except one (the 1991 presidential election), all of the Old Regime parties are of the unreformed variety. *A priori*, there are two reasons why we might not expect this distinction to explain the lack of support for the Old Regime hypothesis in Russia. First, Russia was not the only country that held elections without reformed Old Regime parties; the Czech Republic also falls into this category. But even more seriously, the Old Regime orientation hypothesis actually predicts that the economy should have a more consistent effect on the vote for unreformed Old Regime parties, and thus could only explain the lack of support for the Old Regime hypothesis in Russia if Russia was distinguished be a preponderance of more *reformed* Old Regime parties. Nevertheless, it is possible that the logic underlying the Old Regime orientation hypothesis is wrong, and perhaps empirically it is the more reformed Old Regime parties for which the Old Regime hypothesis generates the most empirical support. Either way, as a systematic explanation for the Russian exceptionalism in this case, it is worth examining.

As Table 7.5 illustrates, there is almost no difference across the entire study in the degree of empirical support for the Old Regime hypothesis

[22] Had all of three of the standard economic voting hypotheses underperformed in the Russian case, then it might have called into question the kind of concerns raised in the discussion of measurement error in the final section of Chapter 3. But as there is strong support for both the Incumbency and New Regime hypotheses in the Russian cases, it is difficult if not impossible to blame this finding on the potential for greater measurement error in Russia; see the related discussion in Chapter 3 for more on this topic.

among reformed Old Regime parties and unreformed Old Regime parties; in both categories, there is strong empirical evidence in support of the Old Regime hypothesis in slightly fewer than three-quarters of the cases (8 out of 11 for the reformed Old Regime parties, and 13 out of 18 for the unreformed Old Regime parties). There are two important implications of this finding. First, the reformed versus unreformed distinction does not provide any leverage over the question of why the Russian Old Regime results differ from the East-Central European results. Second, the finding effectively falsifies the Old Regime orientation hypothesis: the effect of the economy on the Old Regime parties included in this study does not in any way appear to be conditional on whether that party followed a more reformist path or not. Indeed, in conjunction with the findings regarding the New Regime orientation hypothesis presented in the previous chapter, the two cast strong doubt on the overall party orientation approach; like the New Regime identity, there is strong (and in fact even stronger) evidence that the Old Regime transitional identity is sticky enough to overcome different political orientations among different varieties of Old Regime parties, at least insofar as regional economic voting is concerned. In a sense, this result provides additional evidence in support of the fundamental argument underlying the Old Regime hypothesis that the identification of an Old Regime party with the prior ruling regime is the key to predicting patterns of regional economic voting for that party.

Returning to the Russian enigma, another feature of the Russian political landscape is that Russian Old Regime parties have always had significant competition from nationalist parties.[23] Although not a component of either model considered in this study, nationalist parties would seem to be a reasonable alternative option for the type of party likely to benefit from poor economic conditions. Indeed, a Weimar-like scenario whereby fascist parties would come to power in the wake of economic disarray had been posited as a possible fate for the postcommunist world.[24] So perhaps what happened in Russia was that the Old Regime parties were unable to pick up additional support in areas of the country that were worse off in economic

---

[23] See the discussion of the Russian parliamentary elections case study in Chapter 4.

[24] See, for example, Wyman, Miller et al. 1994, 254, as well as Hanson and Kopstein 1997, 1998, and Shenfield 1998 and the many citations referenced in these articles. Although for reasons why we might expect the success of nationalist parties to be more dependent on other factors not directly linked to the performance of the economy, see Marks et al. 2006 and Pop-Eleches 2001 in the post-commuunist context and Meguid 2005; Swank and Betz 2003; and Golder 2003 from the significantly larger West European literature on the topic.

The Old Regime Hypothesis

Table 7.6. *An Alternative Nationalist Hypothesis?*

Panel 1: Old Regime Vs. Nationalist Parties in Russia

	Old Regime	Nationalist
90% Confident in Predicted Direction	2	1
90% Confident in Wrong Direction	1	3
Total Cases	8	7
Percentage with 90% Confidence in Predicted (Wrong) **Direction**	**25%** (13%)	**14%** (43%)

Panel 2: Old Regime Vs. Nationalists Parties in All Five Countries

	Old Regime[#]	Nationalist
90% Confident in Predicted Direction	20	5
90% Confident in Wrong Direction	1	8
Total Cases	29	21
Percentage with 90% Confidence in Predicted (Wrong) **Direction**	**69%** (3%)	**24%** (38%)

[#] See note 26 for details on difference between results in this column and those presented in text of chapter.

terms because they were facing nationalist parties that were able to do so more successfully.

As part of the robustness tests described in Chapter 3, every model was rerun with additional parties included as part of the analysis. In choosing these parties, nationalist parties were always included when possible, resulting in a total of twenty-one nationalist parties across the twenty elections, seven of which competed in the five Russian elections.[25] Panel 1 of Table 7.6 compares the degree of support for the Old Regime hypothesis in the Russian elections with a hypothetical "Nationalist hypothesis"

[25] See Table 7A.2 for a list of the parties. To generate this list, I essentially include all parties that are commonly referred to as nationalist parties in the literature and that are not currently coded as either New Regime or Old Regime parties. Although some readers may disagree with the inclusion or exclusion of a particular party or two from the list, the starkness of the results presented in Panel 2 of Table 7.6 guarantees that adding or deleting even a few parties would have had no effect on the overall conclusion. In particular, had I included Tymiński from the 1990 Polish presidential election and the Confederation for an Independent Poland (KPN) in the 1991 and 1993 Polish parliamentary elections, none of these three parties would have increased the number of parties surpassing the 90% threshold in either direction; the table would therefore look essentially the same with the exception that the percentage of cases in the predicted direction would be 21% and the percentage in the wrong direction would be 33%.

that predicts that nationalist parties should do better in areas of the country where economic conditions are worse. The results demonstrate that, if anything, this Nationalist hypothesis receives even less empirical support in Russia than the Old Regime hypothesis, as there is strong empirical evidence that only one of the seven Russian nationalist parties performed better where economic conditions were worse. Thus, the argument that it is difficult to find empirical support for the Old Regime hypothesis in Russia because of competition from nationalist parties for the economic loser vote does not appear to be well supported by the data.

Interestingly, Panel 2 of Table 7.6 also reveals that although the lack of support for the Old Regime hypothesis in Russia does not extend to the East-Central European cases, it does for the Nationalist hypothesis.[26] In fact, of the 21 nationalist parties included in the analysis, there are more cases in which we have strong confidence that the party did better in parts of the country where economic conditions were better (8 cases) than there are cases in which we have strong confidence that the party did better where the economy was worse (5 cases). Even putting that aside, the evidence in favor of a Nationalist hypothesis is exceedingly thin, with strong empirical support for the conclusion that the nationalist party performed better where the economy was worse in only slightly less than a quarter (5 out of 21) of the cases. Although outside of the analysis of the two main models that comprise this study, it is actual a very intriguing finding; when we compare Old Regime parties to nationalist parties in terms of which performed better in areas of the country where economic conditions are worse, it is clearly the Old Regime parties that enjoy this distinction.

As neither of these more systematic explanations can explain the lack of support for the Old Regime hypothesis in Russia, I now turn to the second option, an analysis of factors that could offer an explanation on a case-by-case basis. The first Russian election, the 1991 presidential election

---

[26] As was the case with the resulted presented in Table 6A.1 in the previous chapter, the results summarized in Table 7.6 are from the extra parties robustness test described in Chapter 3 and presented in Chapter 8. For the sake of consistency, the results presented for the Old Regime parties included in the study in Panel 2 of Table 7.6 are also drawn from the extra parties robustness test that, as is described in detail in Chapter 8, returned very similar but not identical results to those described in the text of this chapter. This is the reason why Table 7.6 reports strong empirical support for 20 out of the 29 Old Regime parties, whereas the text reports strong support for 21 out of the 29 New Regime parties; see Tables 8.1 and 8.3 in the following chapter for another illustration of this point.

of Boris Yeltsin, is one of the two regime future elections in the study (see Table 2.3). As has been illustrated in the case study section of this and the previous two chapters, the other regime future election in the study, the 1992 Slovak election, has not produced strong empirical support for any of the standard economic voting hypotheses. And in fact there is no support for any of the standard hypotheses generated by any of the candidates that contested the 1991 Russian election. This may be because of the logic of the regime future hypothesis; it also may be a function of the poor quality of the data available for analyzing the results of this election, a point to which I return in the following chapter. Either way, there are reasons to suspect that the lack of support for the Old Regime hypothesis in this election may not be an indictment of the Old Regime hypothesis *per se*, but more a function of a lack of an effect for the economy (or the lack of our ability to measure this effect well) on this entire election. And with that being noted, the results for Bakatin are actually fairly close to our 90% threshold, with 85% of the simulations in the correct direction; Ryzhkov, the unreformed Old Regime candidate, has 70% of the simulations in the correct direction.[27]

As described in Chapter 4, the 1993 Russian parliamentary elections took place against a very idiosyncratic backdrop, with the elections being held slightly more than two months after street fighting had broken out in Moscow as part of a protracted struggle between Yeltsin and the communist-era parliament (see Chapter 4 for details). Moreover, this is the one election in the entire study in which there was more than passing concerns about

---

[27] For one of the robustness tests described in Chapter 3, an additional independent variable to measure poverty is added to each of the analyses. For the 1991 Russian presidential election, infant mortality rate is used as a proxy for poverty. Although including poverty measures has little effect on most results, it has a very large effect in the case of the 1991 Russian presidential election. In particular, it increases our confidence in the Old Regime hypothesis in the case of Ryzhkov from the 70% confidence level mentioned in the text to 98.9%, which would clearly provide strong support for the hypothesis. Bakatin, by contrast, goes from 85% of the simulations in the correctly predicted direction to only 42%. One reason why the poverty variable might have such a pronounced effect in this particular election is because it is the only election lacking an unemployment variable, so the poverty variable might be a way of tapping into poor economic conditions that is lacking in this case in a way that it is not lacking in the other elections. Although I do not have unemployment data for 1991, the infant mortality rates in Russia in 1991 correlate with the unemployment figures from 1992 at a .23 level. In 1999, the two correlate at a .36 level, although in 1995 they do not correlate at all (-0.003). See Chapter 8 for more details on the different robustness tests.

electoral fraud, a point that is revisited in the next chapter.[28] Despite these issues, the findings from the previous chapters illustrate that the economy did have the predicted effect on on one of the two incumbent New Regime party contesting the election (Russia's Choice), although it did not on the other (PRES). And in the case of the Old Regime party contesting this election, the KPRF, over three-quarters of the simulations are in the correctly predicted direction. So although there is not strong evidence that the KPRF was being helped by poor economic conditions in the 1993 election, there is certainly no evidence that the opposite effect occurred.

Moving on, if we consider the 1995 parliamentary and 1996 presidential election as a single electoral cycle, an interesting pattern emerges. Here there are two cases of the most relevant Russian Old Regime party contesting an election – the KPRF in the 1995 parliamentary election and its candidate, Genadii Zyuganov, in the 1996 presidential election – and one case of a much smaller extraparliamentary Old Regime party – the KTR-SS – contesting the parliamentary election. As highlighted in the previous section, the result is what any of the responsibility-based conditional hypotheses would predict: there is strong empirical support for the Old Regime hypothesis in the case of the more important party – here the KPRF and Zyuganov – and no support for the hypothesis in the case of the less important party, the KTR-SS.

With the findings from the first two waves of elections in hand, one could begin to tell a coherent story about empirical support for the Old Regime hypothesis developing over time in Russia for the primary Old Regime party but not for the less important far-left spin-off. The analysis begins in 1991 with a regime future election with weak data, leading to results that are generally in the correct direction but in which we lack much confidence. The 1993 election then take place in exceptional circumstances, and again the best guess at the effect of the economy on the Old Regime party is in the correct direction, although the empirical support in this regard is still fairly weak. By the time of the more stable atmosphere surrounding the 1995–96 election cycle, there is strong empirical support for the Old Regime hypothesis generated by two out of the three Old Regime parties. Moreover, these two parties are large and important, wherease the one Old Regime party that fails to generate empirical support for the Old Regime hypothesis is weak and marginal.

---

[28] See Filipov and Ordeshook 1997.

Unfortunately, at this point the neat over-time development story ends. In 1999 strong support is not generated for the Old Regime hypothesis by either of the Old Regime parties.[29] If the stability based explanation posited earlier is correct, then the failure of the hypothesis to generate accurate empirical predictions in the 1999 election – especially in the case of the KPRF – is puzzling, as by all accounts the Russian political scene had stabilized even more by 1999. This is not a puzzle that I can conclusively resolve at this point, but I will posit one potential explanation.

As described in Chapter 4, the previous Russian parliamentary elections had primarily featured a New Regime party competing with an Old Regime party (and the occasional nationalist party or two complicating matters). In the 1999 parliamentary election, however, the primary competition was between the Unity, the current party of power associated with the Yeltsin government and its prime minister Vladimir Putin, and Fatherland-All Russia (OVR), the alternative party of political insiders that revolved around Moscow mayor Yurii Luzhkov and former Yeltsin prime minister Yevgenii Primakov.[30] So as opposed to previous elections in which the forces around Yeltsin spent their energy attacking the KPRF, in the 1999 election this energy went into attacking OVR.[31] It is possible that with another party being raised to prominence as the clear alternative to the party of power, the KPRF lost its special position in the mind of voters. This kind of an argument is bolstered by the fact that there is strong empirical evidence that OVR performed better in areas of the country where the economy was performing worse, with 99.7% of the simulations showing a decrease in the vote for OVR following the standard positive economic shock.[32] So perhaps this is an example of the type of political competition that might tend to negate the predictive ability of the Old Regime hypothesis. That being said, there is still strong support for the Old Regime hypothesis in the Czech Republic, when the primary axis of competition is between New Regime parties and a (non–Old Regime) social democratic party, as well as in Slovakia, when the primary axis of competition has been between New

---

[29] Moreover, our confidence in the empirical support for the hypothesis is even lower for the more important KPRF than the less important KTR-SS.

[30] For more on OVR, see Colton and McFaul 2003, Chapter 4; Oates 2000, 7; Rose and Munro 2002, 112–13, and Belin 1999a.

[31] See Chapter 4, and especially note 58 in that chapter, for more information in this regard.

[32] As with the nationalist parties, OVR is one of the parties included in the robustness test that expands the number of parties in the analysis for the 1999 Russia parliamentary election; see Chapter 8 for more details.

Regime parties and nationalist parties, so this conclusion comes with the appropriate caveats.

Overall, the following observations can be made concerning the Russian cases. First, there does not appear to be any clear systematic explanation for why the Old Regime hypothesis receives so much less empirical support in Russia than in the other four countries included in the study. At the same time, on an election-by-election basis, there appear to be a number of extenuating circumstances that help to explain this pattern. Finally, it should be noted that despite the lack of strong empirical support for the Old Regime hypothesis in most of the Russian cases, there certainly is no evidence to support the conclusion that Russian Old Regime parties systematically performed better in parts of the country where economic conditions were stronger. Indeed, it is worth remembering that in seven of the eight Russian cases at least a majority of the simulations were in the correctly predicted direction.

Responsibility Hypotheses

Panel 1 of Table 7.7 reveals an interesting pattern of support for the institutional responsibility hypothesis. On the one hand, the category with the most consistent empirical support for the hypothesis, the vote for Old Regime parties in both presidential and parliamentary elections in mixed systems, is not the one predicted by the institutional responsibility hypothesis; recall that the hypothesis predicts the most support for the Old Regime hypothesis in the dominant election (presidential election in presidential systems; parliamentary elections in parliamentary systems) category. On the other hand, if the mixed category is set aside (which in practice means eliminating the Polish cases), then for the first time there is a rather dramatic difference between the dominant election category, which has almost 80% of the cases providing strong empirical support for the Old Regime hypothesis, and the dominated election category, in which only one case out of five (20 percent) provides support for the hypothesis. Obviously, there are a number of important caveats here, the most obvious being that there are only five cases in the dominated election category and they are all drawn from Russia. Nevertheless, this is clearly the strongest support for the institutional responsibility hypothesis across any of the tests considered so far in this book.

Moreover, it also may provide another tool for understanding the Russian results discussed extensively in the previous section. If the 1991 Russian

Table 7.7. *Responsibility Explanations of Variation in Support for Old Regime Hypothesis*

Panel 1: Institutional Responsibility

	All	Dominant Elections	Mixed Systems	Dominated Elections
90% Confident in Predicted Direction	21	15	5	1
90% Confident in Wrong Direction	1	0	0	1
Total Cases	29	19	5	5
Percentage with 90% Confidence in Predicted (Wrong) **Direction**	**72%** (3%)	**79%** (0%)	**100%** (0%)	**20%** (20%)

Panel 2: Size of National Vote

	All	<5%	≥5%	≥10%	≥20%
90% Confident in Predicted Direction	21	6	15	13	6
90% Confident in Wrong Direction	1	1	0	0	0
Total Cases	29	9	20	18	8
Percentage with 90% Confidence in Predicted (Wrong) **Direction**	**72%** (3%)	**67%** (11%)	**75%** (0%)	**72%** (0%)	**75%** (0%)

presidential election is set aside as exceptional, then there is one example of an Old Regime candidate competing in a dominant election in Russia – Genadii Zyuganov in the 1996 Russian presidential election – and in that case there is strong empirical support for the Old Regime hypothesis. Conversely, there are five Old Regime parties that compete in dominated elections in Russia, and among these cases there is only one party that generates strong empirical support for the Old Regime hypothesis. This is exactly the kind of variation predicted by the institutional responsibility hypothesis, thus suggesting a theoretically based explanation for the perplexing difference in results for the Russian Old Regime parties. Although in the East-Central European cases, the majority of Old Regime parties either competed in dominant elections or elections in mixed systems, in Russia a majority of Old Regime parties contested dominated elections, where the institutional responsibility hypothesis predicts that there should be less empirical support for the Old Regime hypothesis. Of course, the explanation looks slightly less compelling if the 1991 election results (where no support for the Old Regime hypothesis is provided by the two Old Regime parties competing in this dominant election) are included in the analysis, although, as mentioned previously and elaborated upon in the following chapter, there are other reasons to be suspicious of results from this particular election.

By contrast, Panel 2 of Table 7.7 reveals weaker support for the size of vote hypothesis than was presented in the previous two chapters. Although there are fairly sharp distinctions in the support for the Incumbency and New Regime hypotheses among parties receiving different sized shares of the overall vote, there is little evidence of such a pattern among Old Regime parties. Perhaps the strongest claim that can be made is that there is no overwhelming evidence that the opposite effect from what was predicted by the hypothesis is present: clearly, there is not significantly more support for the Old Regime hypothesis among parties receiving less than 5% of the overall vote than among those receiving more than 5% of the vote.

So although there is a different individual pattern of support for the responsibility-based hypotheses in explaining variation in support for the Old Regime hypothesis than for the Incumbency and New Regime hypotheses – more support for the institutional responsibility hypothesis and less for the size of vote hypothesis here and the opposite in the previous chapters – the overall pattern is actually somewhat similar. There is some potentially important support in the case of one hypothesis, and some very lukewarm support – or at least no evidence that the effect is in the opposite direction from the one predicted by the hypothesis – in the case of the other hypothesis. Additionally, there is again some suggestive evidence from the case studies – in particular, the Russian parliamentary elections – to the merits of a responsibility-based approach. Thus, an overall similar assessment of the responsibility-based conditional hypotheses can be made as in the previous chapters. Although there is far from conclusive evidence to provide irrefutable support for either of the hypotheses, everything observed is in the direction predicted by the approach. This provides at least suggestive evidence in support of the proposition that economic conditions are more likely to have an effect on the vote for Old Regime parties in the manner predicted by the Old Regime hypothesis the more important those parties are.

Supply-Side Hypotheses

Simply put, there is no evidence to support the personality hypothesis generated by the variation in empirical support for the Old Regime hypothesis. Recall that the hypothesis predicts the most empirical support for the Old Regime hypothesis among parties competing in closed-list PR elections

Table 7.8. *Supply-Side Explanations of Variation in Support for Old Regime Hypothesis: Personality Hypothesis*

	All	Presidential Elections	Open-List PR Elections	Closed-List PR Elections
90% Confident in Predicted Direction	21	3	12	6
90% Confident in Wrong Direction	1	0	0	1
Total Cases	29	5	13	11
Percentage with 90% Confidence in Predicted (Wrong) Direction	**72%** (3%)	**60%** (0%)	**92%** (0%)	**55%** (0%)

and the least support for candidates competing in presidential elections, with parties competing in open-list PR elections somewhere in between. The pattern revealed in Panel 1 of Table 7.8 bears little resemblance to the predictions of the hypothesis. The most consistent support for the Old Regime hypothesis is found among parties competing in open-list PR elections, whereas the level of support for the hypothesis generated by parties competing in closed-list PR and presidential elections is roughly the same.

Time-Based Hypotheses

In the previous chapters, more consistent empirical support for the Incumbency and New Regime voting hypotheses was found as the decade progressed. Panel 1 of Table 7.9 demonstrates that this pattern continues to be reflected in the variation in strong empirical support for the Old Regime hypothesis, although in much less dramatic fashion than for the Incumbency or New Regime hypotheses. The proportion of cases in which there is strong support for the Old Regime hypothesis does increase across successive waves of elections, with the largest change being from the first wave of elections, in which there is strong support for the Old Regime hypothesis for "only" 63% of the cases (five out of eight), and the final wave, where there is strong support for the hypothesis in 78% (seven out of nine) of the cases. That being said, the level of support for the Old Regime hypothesis obviously remained similar throughout the decade, so perhaps the safest conclusion on the basis of these results is simply that they provide yet another example of evidence that falsifies the prediction that support for the standard hypotheses would decrease as the decade progressed.

Table 7.9. *Time-Based Explanations of Variation in Support for Old Regime Hypothesis*

	All	90–92	93–96	97–99
Panel 1: All Old Regime Parties				
90% Confident in Predicted Direction	21	5	9	7
90% Confident in Wrong Direction	1	0	1	0
Total Cases	29	8	12	9
Percentage with 90% Confidence in	**72%**	**63%**	**75%**	**78%**
Predicted (Wrong) **Direction**	(3%)	(0%)	(8%)	(0%)
Panel 2: Unreformed Old Regime Parties				
90% Confident in Predicted Direction	13	3	6	4
90% Confident in Wrong Direction	1	0	1	0
Total Cases	18	4	8	6
Percentage with 90% Confidence in	**72%**	**75%**	**75%**	**67%**
Predicted (Wrong) **Direction**	(6%)	(0%)	(13%)	(0%)
Panel 3: Reformed Old Regime Parties				
90% Confident in Predicted Direction	8	2	3	3
90% Confident in Wrong Direction	0	0	0	0
Total Cases	11	4	4	3
Percentage with 90% Confidence in	**73%**	**50%**	**75%**	**100%**
Predicted (Wrong) **Direction**	(0%)	(0%)	(0%)	(0%)

Similarly, Panels 2 and 3 of Table 7.9 provide little empirical support for the combined time and partisan orientation hypothesis. Although support for the Old Regime hypothesis among unreformed Old Regime Parties does remain fairly constant throughout the decade, there is no evidence that support for the Old Regime hypothesis declines among reformed Old Regime parties over the course of the decade. Quite to the contrary, support for the Old Regime hypothesis is actually more consistent among reformed Old Regime parties later in the decade than earlier in the decade; of the three cases where there is not strong empirical evidence that a reformed Old Regime party performed better where economic conditions were worse, two occurred in the first wave of elections and the other took place in the second wave.

More important, both sets of findings provide additional evidence of the stickiness of the transitional Old Regime identity. Even as time passed, Old Regime parties continued to be affected by economic conditions in the manner predicted by the Old Regime hypothesis. Moreover, this relationship held even for reformed Old Regime parties, which further confirms the observation made earlier in the chapter regarding the stickiness of the Old Regime identity across different partisan paths of development. Even more clearly than a New Regime identity, it appears that an Old Regime identity – at least insofar as it pertained to regional economic voting – was not easily shed.

Conclusions

Overall, there is strong support for the Old Regime hypothesis across the entire data set. Indeed, there is stronger support for the Old Regime hypothesis than there is for either the New Regime or Incumbency hypotheses. This support can be found in many contexts, including parliamentary and presidential elections, elections with closed- and open-list PR voting, and elections that occurred throughout the decade. The empirical support is particularly strong in the East-Central European cases – where only two out of nineteen parties do not provide strong empirical support for the Old Regime hypothesis – in elections that took place later in the decade, and in elections for the dominant institution in a country's governing structure.

The primary exception to this overall pattern of strong empirical support for the Old Regime hypothesis is found in the Russian elections included in the study. On this subject, four general observations are warranted. First, although there is not strong evidence to support the Old Regime hypothesis generated by most of the Russian Old Regime parties, there is certainly no evidence to suggest that Old Regime parties in Russia were consistently enjoying more electoral support in areas of the country where economic conditions were stronger. Of the eight Russian Old Regime parties, seven had at least a majority of their simulations in the correctly predicted direction. Second, there are at least some compelling idiosyncratic explanations for why there may not be particularly strong support for the Old Regime hypothesis on a case-by-case basis. Third, one of the conditional hypotheses – the institutional responsibility hypothesis – offers at least a partial explanation for why there might be less support for the Old Regime hypothesis in the Russian cases, as five of the eight Russian cases were drawn from dominated elections, in this case parliamentary elections in a presidential system. Although we should be cautious about making too much of this assessment given the fact there was not as strong support for the institutional responsibility hypothesis in the previous chapters, it still offers a theoretical explanation for the variation in support for the Old Regime hypothesis across the East-Central European–Russian divide.

Finally, neither of the systematic attempts to explain the lack of support for the Old Regime hypothesis in the Russian cases proved useful in that regard. Neither in Russia alone nor across the entire dataset did there appear to be much support for the hypothesis that nationalist parties were performing better in areas of the country where the economy was worse; nor was there any evidence that the economy had a systematically different effect on reformed or unreformed Old Regime parties. Although disappointing in terms of sorting out the puzzle of the lack of support for the Old Regime hypothesis in the Russian cases, the findings are very interesting in their own right. The fact that there is roughly the same incidence of strong empirical support for the Old Regime hypothesis among reformed and unreformed Old Regime parties alike is, judging by the number of questions that I have received on the topic over the years, at least somewhat counterintuitive. And the finding that it is Old Regime parties, and not nationalist parties, that seem to have gotten the biggest bounce in regions of the country suffering from poor economic conditions, is sure to be of interest to many.

Having now thoroughly examined the empirical support for the Incumbency, New Regime, and Old Regime hypotheses individually, the next step is to analyze the Referendum and Transitional Identity Models comparatively. This task is taken up in Chapter 8.

Appendix 7.1: Supplementary Tables

Table 7A.1. *Breakdown of Old Regime Parties by Party Orientation*

Country	Year	Party/Candidate
Panel 1: Reformed Old Regime Parties		
Hungary	1990	Hungarian Socialist Party (MSzP)
Hungary	1994	Hungarian Socialist Party (MSzP)
Hungary	1998	Hungarian Socialist Party (MSzP)
Poland	1991	Democratic Left Alliance (SLD)
Poland	1993	Democratic Left Alliance (SLD)
Poland	1995	Aleksander Kwaśniewski (SLD)
Poland	1997	Democratic Left Alliance (SLD)
Russia	1991	Vadim Bakatin
Slovakia	1992	Party of the Democratic Left (SDL')
Slovakia	1994	Common Choice Coalition (SV)
Slovakia	1998	Party of the Democratic Left (SDL')
Czech Republic	1992	Left Bloc (LB)
Czech Republic	1996	Communist Party of Bohemia and Moravia (KSČM)
Czech Republic	1998	Communist Party of Bohemia and Moravia (KSČM)

Country	Year	Party/Candidate
Panel 2: Unreformed Old Regime Parties		
Hungary	1990	Hungarian Socialist Workers Party (MSzMP)
Hungary	1994	Workers Party (MP)
Hungary	1998	Workers Party (MP)
Poland	1990	Wlodzimierz Cimoszewicz
Russia	1991	Nikolai Ryzhkov
Russia	1993	Communist Party of the Russian Federation (KPRF)
Russia	1995	Communist Party of the Russian Federation (KPRF)
Russia	1995	Communist Workers of Russia for the Soviet Union (KTR-SS)
Russia	1996	Gennadii Zyuganov
Russia	1999	Communist Party of the Russian Federation (KPRF)
Russia	1999	Communist Workers of Russia for the Soviet Union (KTR-SS)
Slovakia	1994	Communist Party of Slovakia (KSS)
Slovakia	1994	Association of Workers of Slovakia (ZRS)
Slovakia	1998	Association of Workers of Slovakia (ZRS)
Slovakia	1998	Communist Party of Slovakia (KSS)

Table 7A.2. *Nationalist Parties Included in Table 7.6*

Country	Year	Party/Candidate
Czech Republic	1992	Republican Party
Czech Republic	1996	Republican Party
Czech Republic	1998	Republican Party
Hungary	1998	Hungarian Justice and Life Party
Poland	1995	Jan Olszewski
Poland	1997	Movement for the Reconstruction of Poland
Russia	1991	Vladimir Zhirinovskii
Russia	1993	Liberal Democratic Party of Russia
Russia	1995	Liberal Democratic Party of Russia
Russia	1995	Congress of Russian Communities
Russia	1996	Vladimir Zhirinovskii
Russia	1996	Aleksandr Lebed
Russia	1999	Zhirinovskii Bloc
Slovakia	1992	Slovak National Party
Slovakia	1992	Movement for a Democratic Slovakia
Slovakia	1994	Slovak National Party
Slovakia	1994	Movement for a Democratic Slovakia
Slovakia	1998	Slovak National Party
Slovakia	1998	Movement for a Democratic Slovakia
Slovakia	1999	Ján Slota
Slovakia	1999	Vladimír Meciar

8

Comparative Analysis

Having examined the degree of empirical support for each of the standard economic voting hypotheses individually in great detail in the previous three chapters, I turn now to a more synthetic comparative analysis of the findings from across the different models, approaches, and hypotheses. This analysis is structured in three parts. First and foremost, I present a comparative analysis of the empirical support for the Referendum and Transitional Identity Models. As demonstrated in the previous chapters, the cases included in the study generate more consistently strong empirical support for the Transitional Identity Model than for the Referendum Model. In this chapter, I examine how well this conclusion holds under different ways of assessing the empirical evidence. The findings from all these analyses, however, are remarkably consistent. No matter what form of analysis is applied, there is always substantially more empirical support for the Transitional Identity Model than for the Referendum Model.

The second form of comparative analysis presented is an assessment of the evidence supporting the different conditional economic voting hypotheses. In the previous chapters, I examined the degree to which the different conditional hypotheses were useful in explaining the variation in support for each standard economic voting hypothesis individually. In this chapter, I test the overall support for each conditional hypothesis generated across all of the standard hypotheses, thus allowing for a focused assessment of, for example, the support for the personality hypothesis from the different tests offered in Chapters 5, 6, and 7 at one time. Although no single conditional hypothesis returns irrefutable evidence, three of the four theoretically motivated approaches – responsibility, supply-side, and time-based – all yield interesting patterns of findings that are at least somewhat compatible with the theoretical predictions underlying the approaches.

244

In the final section of the chapter, I interact the Referendum and Transitional Identity Models. More specifically, I examine whether the Incumbency hypothesis can predict where there is more or less empirical support for the New Regime or Old Regime hypotheses and vice versa. Synthesizing the two models in this manner produces one of the more stark findings of this entire book: although incumbency status has almost no effect on whether regional economic conditions have the predicted effect on New Regime and Old Regime parties, the regional economic voting patterns of incumbent parties are largely conditional on their status as New Regime parties, Old Regime parties, or neither.

Comparing the Transitional Identity and Referendum Models

Political scientists generally evaluate the relative usefulness of models in terms of parsimony, scope, and accuracy. The question of whether the Transitional Identity Model or the Referendum Model is more parsimonious is an open one. In the universe of models, both are parsimonious, yielding very simple hypotheses about the direction of economic effects (do good economic conditions help or hurt?) on certain types of parties, or, in other words, exactly what has been defined as a standard economic voting hypothesis in this book. As the difficulty in determining the level of empirical support for both models is the same – both employ the same empirical methodology – the only way to distinguish which is more parsimonious is to focus on coding decisions. In a stable democracy, the likely conclusion would be that simply identifying incumbent parties is generally an easier and less controversial task than coding parties in most other capacities. However, as Chapter 5 demonstrates, identifying incumbent parties in new democracies can be both tricky and time-consuming. By comparison, most of the Old Regime coding decisions do not appear as difficult, although the same cannot necessarily be said for the New Regime coding decisions. Probably the safest conclusion to draw is that both models are fairly parsimonious although they do involve some coding decisions that can be difficult; as a result, there is no obvious answer to the question of which model is more parsimonious than the other.

Scope, by contrast, provides a much clearer distinction. The Transitional Identity Model has a significantly wider scope than the Referendum Model, as the former predicts the effect of economic conditions on cross-regional variation in the vote for sixty-nine parties across these twenty elections, as opposed to forty-nine for the latter. Moreover, the Transitional Identity

Table 8.1. *Comparative Assessment of Transitional Identity and Referendum Models*

| | Transitional Identity Model | | Referendum Model |
	New Regime	Old Regime	Incumbents
90% Confident in Predicted Direction	25	21	20
90% Confident in Wrong Direction	1	1	8
Total Cases	40	29	49
Percentage with 90% Confidence in Predicted (Wrong) Direction	**63%** (3%)	**72%** (3%)	**41%** (16%)

Model identifies types of parties that are likely to benefit both from better economic conditions (New Regime parties) and from worse economic conditions (Old Regime parties), whereas the Referendum Model only offers predictions about which parties are likely to benefit from better economic conditions (incumbent parties).[1] Taken together, one can argue that the Transitional Identity Model has both a wider theoretical and empirical scope than the Referendum Model.

But the most important question in contrasting the two models is determining which produces more accurate predictions, or, put another way, for which model the empirical evidence produces greater support. Table 8.1, therefore, presents the primary finding of this book: there is more empirical support for the Transitional Identity Model's predictions that regional economic voting patterns will be based on a political party's relationship to the transition away from communism than for the Referendum Model's prediction that regional economic voting patterns will be based on a party's

---

[1] The scope of the Referendum Model could of course be expanded to cover all parties that have competed in all elections by adding an "Opposition hypothesis" predicting that all nonincumbent parties and candidates should benefit where economic conditions are worse. Even putting aside any theoretical concerns with such a hypothesis, doing so would significantly decrease our assessment of the accuracy of the Referendum Model. Indeed, if such an Opposition hypothesis was tested using all of the non-incumbent parties analyzed as part of the extra parties robustness test (see Panel 3 of Table 8.3), the result would be almost as many cases with strong empirical support in the wrong direction (24%, or eighteen out of seventy-six cases surpassing the 90% threshold) as in the correctly predicted direction (36%, or twenty-seven out of seventy-six cases). Note as well that if we exclude Old Regime parties from this sample, the proportion of cases in the incorrect direction (30%, or seventeen out of fifty-six cases) would actually surpass the number of cases in the correctly predicted direction (23%, or thirteen out of fifty-six cases).

position in or out of government. From the set of five countries and twenty elections analyzed, we can conclude that if we had attempted to predict regional economic voting patterns knowing nothing more than whether or not a party was an incumbent party, a New Regime party, or an Old Regime party, we would have been correct with a strong level of confidence slightly over 40% of the time for the incumbent parties, slightly over 60% of the time for the New Regime parties, and slightly over 70% of the time for the Old Regime parties. Moreover, the prediction would have been seriously flawed – predicting that the party would do better where the economy was stronger (or weaker) when in fact we are confident that the opposite occurred – for 15% of the incumbent parties, but for only 3% of both the New Regime and Old Regime parties (or, put another way, for four times as many incumbent parties as New Regime and Old Regime parties combined). The rest of this section is devoted to testing the robustness of this conclusion by examining in turn what happens when (1) the threshold of certainty for claiming "strong" empirical support is changed, (2) the specifications of the original analyses of the effects of economic conditions on election results are changed and (3) specific subsections of cases identified as particularly relevant by the conditional economic voting hypotheses are examined for the relative empirical support they provide for the different standard economic voting hypotheses.

For the purpose of concisely comparing our confidence in different patterns of regional economic voting, I adopted a minimum threshold for claiming that there was strong empirical support for the prediction of the relevant standard hypothesis. In Chapter 3 the rationale for employing a 90% threshold was addressed. As part of that discussion, I noted that the overall conclusion of this book would not have changed had a different threshold been adopted, and Table 8.2 demonstrates that this is indeed the case. Each row of the table indicates the percentage of parties in that column (New Regime, Old Regime, or incumbent) that passed the particular threshold of that row (95%, 90%, 66% or 50% of the simulated first differences) in the correctly predicted direction (positive for New Regime and incumbent parties, negative for Old Regime parties). The actual number of parties was left off the table to make it easier to read but can be calculated by multiplying the percentage by the total number of cases listed in the last row of each column. Note that the top bolded row of the table (90% confidence) represents the same percentages found in the last row of Table 8.1.

Table 8.2. *Transitional Identity Model Has More Empirical Support Regardless of Threshold*

	Transitional Identity Model		Referendum Model
	New Regime	Old Regime	Incumbents
90% Confident in Predicted Direction	63%	72%	41%
95% Confident in Predicted Direction	50%	59%	35%
66% Confident in Predicted Direction	73%	83%	49%
Best Guess in Correct Direction (>50%)	80%	90%	63%
Total Cases	20	29	49

The evidence from the table is clear. No matter what the threshold, the conclusion remains the same: there is more empirical support for the Transitional Identity Model than for the Referendum Model. At each threshold, there is always less empirical support for the Incumbency hypothesis than there is for either the New Regime or Old Regime hypothesis. Thus, the overall conclusion of more empirical support for the Transitional Identity Model than the Referendum Model is in no way a function of the fact that I chose to summarize "strong" empirical support for any standard hypothesis using the particular threshold (90%) that I did. In addition, the ordering of the relative support for the two Transitional Identity Model hypotheses also would have remained the same, as at each threshold there is more empirical support for Old Regime hypothesis than the New Regime hypothesis.

The final row of the table – noting the number of cases in which at least a majority of the simulations were in the correct direction – is worth noting because this is essentially what the results of the study would have been had I just calculated first differences without assessing the level of uncertainty in these estimates. Two observations can be drawn in this regard. First, had I eschewed any use of statistical simulation to measure uncertainty in these estimates by simply calculating first differences and identifying the cases in which the effect of an economic shock was in the direction predicted by the relevant hypothesis (e.g., positive for the Incumbency and New Regime hypothesis or negative for the Old Regime hypothesis), the study would have yielded the same conclusion of greater empirical support for the Transitional Identity Model than for the Referendum Model. Thus, the overall conclusion of this book is not dependent on the use of the statistical simulation. However, if no attempt had been made to estimate our level of uncertainty in these first differences, the resulting conclusions would have greatly overstated our confidence in the predictions of all three hypotheses by reporting empirical support for the predictions of the hypotheses in some cases in which the level of uncertainty in these estimates makes such claims unwarranted.

Alternative Specifications of the Original Model

Another way to test the robustness of the findings is to examine what happens to the overall conclusions when the specifications of the original regional economic voting models are changed. I do so in the four different ways described in detail in Chapter 3. To reiterate, in the first test I add an additional independent variable (poverty) to each regression.[2] In the second test, I change the size of the economic shock from the 10th–90th percentile shock used in the standard model to a smaller 20th–80th percentile shock. The third test adds additional parties to the analysis and then examines the effect of including these additional parties in the statistical analysis on the results for the original parties.[3]

The final respecification involves eliminating all of the independent variables that were not available for use in all of the analyses. The result is as close as it is possible to come to using these data to run all of the models with the exact same variables, leaving three independent variables per equation: unemployment, growth, and change in income.[4] One concern in

---

[2] See note 42 in Chapter 3 for details on the coding of the poverty variables across different elections.

[3] Thus, the test is not to see if the results hold up if the definitions of the relevant categories are expanded to include more parties (see the appendix of Chapter 5 for an analysis of this type), but, rather, to examine how robust the results for the current set of incumbent, New Regime, and Old Regime parties are to having other types of parties included in the statistical analysis as well. See note 43 in Chapter 3 for details on how these additional parties were selected, as well as the related section of the text for an explanation of why adding additional parties to the analysis changes the results for the original parties. Readers also should note that it is this set of analyses that provides the basis for the analyses of the borderline New Regime parties in the appendix to Chapter 6 (see Table 6A.1) and the comparison of the Old Regime and Nationalist hypotheses in Chapter 7 (see Table 7.6).

[4] The caveats concerning growth discussed in Chapter 3 remain, as growth is measured with change in GDP when available and change in industrial output when GDP is not available. As was also noted in Chapter 3, there is no unemployment data for the 1991 Russian parliamentary election.

doing so is that this eliminates the consideration of wage arrears, which, as noted in Chapter 3, was an important economic issue in Russia but largely irrelevant in the other four countries. For this reason, I run the reduced independent variable version of the Russian regressions twice, once including only unemployment, growth, and change in income, and then a second time including these three variables plus wage arrears.[5] Thus, in Table 8.3, there are two sets of results reported for the reduced independent variable versions of the analysis: Panel 4, which includes the Russian results with just the base independent variables of growth, wage change, and unemployment but without wage arrears; and Panel 5, which includes the Russian results with the three base independent variables plus wage arrears. The results for the other four countries are the same for both tables, using only the three base independent variables in both panels.

Table 8.3 contains a great deal of information, but the overall conclusion is clear. No matter how the original regional economic voting analyses are changed, the same basic conclusions hold. Across all of the panels of the table, there is stronger empirical support for the Transitional Identity Model than the Referendum Model. Moreover, we always have the most confidence in the predictions of the Old Regime hypothesis, followed by the New Regime hypothesis and the Incumbency hypothesis in that order (although the support for the New Regime and Old Regime hypotheses is very close in Panel 2). If anything, the distinction between the support for the Transitional Identity Model and the Referendum Model gets slightly larger whereas the distinction within the Transitional Identity Model (the comparison of the support for the Old Regime as opposed to the New Regime hypothesis) gets slightly smaller. What is perhaps even more interesting is the fact that there appears to be so little variation in the degree of empirical support for the three hypotheses. The number of cases for which there is strong empirical support for the Incumbency hypothesis varies only from 18 (Panels 1 and 4) to 20 (Panels 2, 3, and 5), as compared to 20 in the standard model (see Table 8.1). Similarly, the number of cases for which there is strong empirical support for the Old Regime hypothesis varies only from 19 (Panel 2) to 22 (Panel 1), as compared to 21 in the standard model, and support for the New Regime hypothesis varies only from 22 (Panel 4) to 25 cases (Panel 2), as compared to 25 in the standard model. It is also comforting to note that the strongest support for each hypothesis comes from a different specification, as the strongest support is found for the Old

---

[5] Wage arrears data was available only for the 1993–99 elections.

Table 8.3. *Number of Cases with 90% Certainty of Predicted Effect by Model by Different Specifications of Original Analyses*

	Transitional Identity Model		Referendum Model
	New Regime	Old Regime	Incumbents
Panel 1. Including an Extra Independent Variables (Poverty)			
90% Confident in Predicted Direction	23	22	18
90% Confident in Wrong Direction	2	0	10
Total Cases	40	29	49
Percentage with 90% Confidence in Predicted (Wrong) **Direction**	**58%** (5%)	**76%** (0%)	**37%** (20%)
Panel 2. Alternative Economic Shock (20th to 80th Percentile)			
90% Confident in Predicted Direction	25	19	20
90% Confident in Wrong Direction	1	1	7
Total Cases	40	29	49
Percentage with 90% Confidence in Predicted (Wrong) **Direction**	**63%** (3%)	**66%** (3%)	**41%** (14%)
Panel 3. Including Additional Dependent Variables*			
90% Confident in Predicted Direction	24	20	20
90% Confident in Wrong Direction	1	1	7
Total Cases	40	29	49
Percentage with 90% Confidence in Predicted (Wrong) **Direction**	**60%** (3%)	**69%** (3%)	**41%** (14%)
Panel 4: Reduced Independent Variables (Unemployment, Growth, and Wage Change)			
90% Confident in Predicted Direction	22	21	18
90% Confident in Wrong Direction	2	1	7
Total Cases	40	29	49
Percentage with 90% Confidence in Predicted (Wrong) **Direction**	**55%** (5%)	**72%** (3%)	**37%** (14%)
Panel 5: Reduced Independent Variables Plus Arrears in Russia			
90% Confident in Predicted Direction	24	20	20
90% Confident in Wrong Direction	1	0	7
Total Cases	40	29	49
Percentage with 90% Confidence in Predicted (Wrong) **Direction**	**60%** (3%)	**69%** (0%)	**41%** (14%)

* See Table 8A.1 for additional parties

Regime hypothesis when we include an extra independent variable (Panel 1), for the New Regime hypothesis when we apply a smaller economic shock (Panel 2), and for the Incumbency hypothesis we reduce the number of independent variables plus arrears (Panel 5), include additional dependent variables (Panel 3) and or apply a smaller economic shock (Panel 2). Thus, there does not appear to be anything about any particular set of specifications that artificially inflates or deflates the degree of empirical support for the different hypotheses across the board.[6]

Another important conclusion that can be drawn from Panels 4 and 5 of Table 8.3 is that the decision to include extra independent variables in the regression analysis when available did not affect the overall conclusions of the study. In Chapter 3, an argument in favor of using all the available independent variables – guided by a set of *a priori* rules for which variables to include – was presented, but it was noted that doing so would not change the overall conclusion of the study regarding the superiority of the empirical support for the Transitional Identity Model as opposed to the Referendum Model. Panels 4 and 5 of Table 8.3 demonstrate that this is in fact the case. Both panels reveal stronger empirical support for the Transitional Identity Model than the Referendum Model when a reduced and more consistent set of independent variables is employed, and indeed the pattern of support across the two models is very similar to the one displayed in Table 8.1 that reflects the standard method of analysis employed in the study.

Examining Subsections of the Data

The conditional economic voting hypotheses introduced in Chapter 2 were presented with two goals in mind. One goal was to carry out some initial tests of these hypotheses, which I address in detail in the following section. But the primary goal was to use the conditional hypotheses to examine whether or not the conclusions that were drawn regarding the degree of empirical support for the different standard hypotheses would change if only specific subsections of the cases were included in the analysis. In the preceding chapters, the degree of empirical support for each of the standard hypotheses was assessed across the different categories highlighted by the various conditional hypotheses. I now turn to assessing the robustness of the overall conclusions concerning the relative support for the Transitional

---

[6] Although the discussion in the text refers to the robustness of the overall findings, similar conclusions can be drawn from examining the results on a party-by-party basis.

Table 8.4. *Comparing the Transitional Identity and Referendum Models across Selected Categories*

	Transitional Identity Model		Referendum Model
	New Regime	Old Regime	Incumbents
Panel 1. Parliamentary Elections			
90% Confident in Predicted Direction	21	18	18
90% Confident in Wrong Direction	0	1	7
Total Cases	32	24	43
Percentage with 90% Confidence	**66%**	**75%**	**42%**
in Predicted (Wrong) **Direction**	(0%)	(4%)	(16%)
Panel 2. East-Central European Elections			
90% Confident in Predicted Direction	20	19	16
90% Confident in Wrong Direction	1	0	8
Total Cases	32	21	42
Percentage with 90% Confidence	**63%**	**90%**	**38%**
in Predicted (Wrong) **Direction**	(3%)	(0%)	(19%)
Panel 3. Parties with at Least 10% of the National Vote			
90% Confident in Predicted Direction	16	13	11
90% Confident in Wrong Direction	1	0	4
Total Cases	22	18	21
Percentage with 90% Confidence	**73%**	**72%**	**52%**
in Predicted (Wrong) **Direction**	(5%)	(0%)	(19%)
Panel 4. Elections for Dominant Institutions*			
90% Confident in Predicted Direction	15	15	14
90% Confident in Wrong Direction	0	0	5
Total Cases	22	19	30
Percentage with 90% Confidence	**68%**	**79%**	**47%**
in Predicted (Wrong) **Direction**	(0%)	(0%)	(17%)
Panel 5. Elections that are not Regime Future Elections**			
90% Confident in Predicted Direction	25	21	20
90% Confident in Wrong Direction	1	1	8
Total Cases	38	26	44
Percentage with 90% Confidence	**66%**	**81%**	**45%**
in Predicted (Wrong) **Direction**	(3%)	(4%)	(18%)

* Presidential elections in presidential systems (Russia) and parliamentary elections in parliamentary systems (Hungary, Slovakia, Czech Republic).
** All elections except 1991 Russian president and 1992 Slovak parliament.

Identity and Referendum Models when examining five specific subsections of the dataset suggested by the conditional hypotheses: only parliamentary elections; only East-Central European elections; only parties receiving greater than 10% of the vote; only elections for the dominant electoral institution (e.g., presidential elections in a presidential system, parliamentary elections in a parliamentary system); and only elections that are not regime future elections. To reiterate, the goal in doing so is to see if the overall conclusion of the study that there is more empirical support for the Transitional Identity Model than the Referendum Model still holds when the explanatory power of these models is tested using a hypothetically more "appropriate" (as suggested by the conditional hypotheses) subsection of cases. Another way to conceptualize this test is as an attempt to ascertain if the overall study is somehow contaminated by "inappropriate" cases, and, if so, whether the results would change when we strip out these inappropriate cases. Readers should note that since the number of cases differs across the tests, the results can be assessed in terms of both scope and accuracy.[7]

The most important conclusion to draw from Table 8.4 is that had any of these subsets been used instead of the full dataset, the exact same overall conclusion regarding the superiority of the Transitional Identity Model to the Referendum Model – in terms of both scope and accuracy – would still have been reached. In not a single panel of the table does the number of incumbent cases exceed the combined total of the number of New Regime and Old Regime cases, nor is there stronger empirical support for the Incumbency hypothesis than for either the Old Regime or New Regime hypotheses. Indeed, the level of empirical of support for all three hypotheses – and especially the Incumbency and New Regime hypotheses – remains quite consistent across the different panels. The only conclusion that one might change from any of these panels occurs in the comparison of the support for the two hypotheses of the Transitional Identity Model. Four of the panels reflect the same result as found in the full study: stronger empirical support for the Old Regime hypothesis than for the New Regime hypothesis. However, in one panel (only parties that received at least 10% of the overall vote) there is roughly the same degree of support for the two hypotheses.

Of course, the categories suggested by the conditional economic voting hypotheses are not the only ways to test the robustness of the findings by

---

[7] This is in contrast to the previous robustness tests that changed the specification of the quantitative analysis, but not the number of cases included in the comparison.

examining subsections of the cases. For example, there are three elections included in the study for which there is more reason to question the quality of the raw data than the other elections: the 1991 Russian presidential election; the 1993 Russian parliamentary election; and the 1991 Polish parliamentary election.[8] The analysis of the 1991 Russian presidential election does not contain a measure of unemployment, and thus is the only election in the study to rely solely on growth and change in income as independent variables. The 1993 Russian parliamentary election is the one election in the study about which serious accusations of fraud have been made, although most scholars agree that it is doubtful that the overall outcome of the election was affected greatly.[9] The 1991 Polish parliamentary election is the only election in the study for which the national statistical office and national election committee did not report regional statistics using the same regions. Consequently, the analysis in this study relies on a recalculation by a Polish scholar of the election results to match the relevant economic units.[10] In addition to these three cases, the exceptional coding challenge posed by the 1999 Slovak presidential elections has been mentioned earlier, so I include this election as a potential fourth "questionable" case.

Table 8.5 therefore presents the results of eliminating these four elections from the comparative analysis in an effort to eliminate any concern that the findings have in some way been "contaminated" by the elections mentioned in the previous paragraph. The results are similar to the standard analysis, although it is interesting to note that there is almost uniformly more consistent empirical support for each of the three hypotheses, as each now has strong empirical support in roughly 10% more of the cases. On this basis, two conclusions can be drawn. First, including these four elections in the study has had no effect on the primary findings of the book: there remains more empirical support for the Transitional Identity Model than the Referendum Model; the former still has a wider scope than the latter; and there is still the strongest empirical support for the Old Regime hypothesis and

---

[8] Although it should be noted that in all three cases my concerns over the quality of the data were not serious enough for me to consider removing the election from the study altogether. The labeling of these elections as more questionable from a data perspective is purely in relation to the other elections in the study.

[9] For more, see McFaul 1996; White, Rose, and McAllister 1997 and especially Myagkov, Ordeshook, and Sobyanin 1997.

[10] Gebethner 1995. Although there is no reason to doubt the accuracy of this recalculation, by default it seems less reliable than results that do not depend on recalculating official results.

Table 8.5. *Eliminating Questionable Elections**

	Transitional Identity Model		Referendum Model
	New Regime	Old Regime	Incumbents
90% Confident in Predicted Direction	24	20	19
90% Confident in Wrong Direction	0	1	8
Total Cases	34	25	38
Percentage with 90% Confidence in Predicted (Wrong) Direction	**71%** (0%)	**80%** (4%)	**50%** (21%)

* 1991 Russian and 1999 Slovak presidential elections, 1991 Polish and 1993 Russian Parliamentary Elections.

the least empirical support for the Incumbency hypothesis. At the same time, eliminating these four elections does increase our confidence in the explanatory power for all three of the standard hypotheses.

How to interpret this second point, however, remains an open question. In terms of the coding difficulties posed by the 1999 Slovak presidential election, it seems reasonable that models should lose their predictive power as coding decisions become more arbitrary. Nevertheless, there are other theoretical arguments, such as the institutional responsibility hypothesis, that also predict less support for standard economic voting hypotheses in the 1999 Slovak presidential election. Similarly, there may be other compelling reasons besides the quality of the data to explain why there is not as much empirical support for the three standard hypotheses in the 1991 and 1993 Russian elections and the 1991 Polish election. For example, the 1991 Russian parliamentary election is coded as a regime future election, and there is another case of a regime future election (the 1992 Slovak parliamentary election) that also produces no support for any of the standard hypotheses without similar concerns over the quality of the data. Likewise, all three of these elections take place early in the decade, and, as will be discussed shortly, there is more empirical support for all of the hypotheses later in the decade. So although concerns about the quality of the data may be part of the explanation for why eliminating these three elections improves the empirical support for all of the hypotheses, there is certainly no proof that it is the primary cause of the results, especially as there are parties in both the 1991 Polish and 1993 Russian parliamentary elections that do provide support for some of the standard hypotheses. Thus, perhaps the safest observation is just to note that including these elections in no way changed the overall conclusions of the study.

Another useful way to split the cases is to use some of them as an "out of sample" test. The basic idea behind such a test is to use a second set of cases to test observations learned from the analysis of an original and different set of cases.[11] Although the research strategy is primarily designed to be used as a manner of testing hypotheses derived inductively through data analysis – and as such is not necessary here – I can take advantage of the fact that I originally only analyzed the first fourteen elections in the data set that took place from 1990 to 1996 and presented these results publicly before I had the data necessary to analyze the remaining six elections that took place between 1997 and 1999.[12] Thus, one way to conceptualize the final six elections is as an "out of sample" test for results from the 1990–96 period.

In line with all of the previous comparisons, an assessment of the results from only the original fourteen elections (1990–96) or the final six elections (1997–99) would not in any way change the overall conclusion of more consistently strong empirical support for the Transitional Identity Model than for the Referendum Model (see Table 8.6). The most noticeable difference between the two periods is within the Transitional Identity Model. Although there is roughly the same incidence of strong empirical support for the Old Regime hypothesis across the two periods, there is a strikingly higher prevalence of strong empirical support for the New Regime hypothesis in the post-1996 period, a point discussed earlier in Chapter 6. In fact, the the empirical support for the New Regime hypothesis improves to a large enough degree that it actually surpasses the support for the Old Regime hypothesis in the post-1996 period. The other interesting conclusion to make on the basis of this table is the fact that there is stronger support for all three hypotheses in the post-1996 period, a point to which I will return later in this chapter during the discussion of the time-based conditional hypotheses.

Comparative Analysis: Conclusions

Across a wide range of tests, including changing the threshold used to claim strong empirical support for hypotheses, changing the original specification

---

[11] See, for example, Ross 2003.
[12] Indeed, the first of these presentations took place in April 1998, before all but one of the last six elections had even taken place. See, for example, Tucker 1998, 1999, 2000a.

Table 8.6. *Out of Sample Test*

	Transitional Identity Model		Referendum Model
	New Regime	Old Regime	Incumbents
Panel 1. Original 14 Elections (through 1996)			
90% Confident in Predicted Direction	15	14	14
90% Confident in Wrong Direction	0	1	5
Total Cases	29	20	37
Percentage with 90% Confidence in Predicted (Wrong) Direction	**52%** (0%)	**70%** (5%)	**38%** (14%)
Panel 2. Post-1996 Elections			
90% Confident in Predicted Direction	10	7	6
90% Confident in Wrong Direction	1	0	3
Total Cases	11	9	12
Percentage with 90% Confidence in Predicted (Wrong) Direction	**91%** (9%)	**78%** (0%)	**50%** (25%)

of the regional economic voting models in a variety of ways, examining theoretically relevant subsections of the dataset, excluding questionable elections from the analysis, and performing a modified out of sample test, the same basic conclusion regarding the comparability of the Referendum and Transitional Identity Models continues to be valid: in terms of both scope and accuracy, the Transitional Identity Model remains superior to the Referendum Model. In not a single one of these tests is evidence found to suggest that there is more empirical support for the Incumbency hypothesis than for either the New Regime or Old Regime hypotheses. Moreover, in the vast majority of tests we find the exact same ordering of the degree of empirical support for the two hypotheses that make up the Transitional Identity Model, with stronger empirical support being found for the Old Regime hypothesis than the New Regime hypothesis.

Before moving on to the comparative assessment of the conditional economic voting hypotheses, it is important to emphasize a final point made earlier in the book about both the Transitional Identity and Referendum Models. Both are aggregate level models; they test hypotheses about the relationship between aggregate level economic conditions and election results. As was explained in detail in Chapter 2, both models are based on underlying assumptions about individual level behavior, but the empirical tests contained in this chapter and the previous chapters test only the aggregate level implications of these assumptions, and not the assumptions themselves. Thus, although we can conclude that New Regime parties are more likely to consistently enjoy better electoral success in areas of the country where the economy is performing well than incumbent parties, we cannot say that this demonstrates that individuals who are pleased with the state of the economy are more likely to vote for New Regime parties than incumbent parties (although it certainly would be consistent with the aggregate-level findings). Similarly, the fact that the Incumbency hypothesis is not particularly well supported by the empirical data in a study of regional economic voting should not be interpreted as contradicting evidence from either national or microlevel studies of the same phenomenon. This is especially so in comparison to studies of economic voting in established democracies, as the hypotheses tested in this book were specifically crafted to take account of political and economic conditions in transition countries.

Comparative Assessment of Conditional Economic Voting Hypotheses

As mentioned at the start of the previous section, the second reason for highlighting the conditional economic voting hypotheses in this book was to provide preliminary assessments of the degree of support for these hypotheses across the cases included in the study. In the previous three chapters, I assessed the degree to which the different classes of conditional hypotheses could explain variation in the empirical support found for each of the three standard hypotheses individually. In this section, I expand the scope of this analysis by assessing the degree to which the conditional hypotheses can explain variation in the empirical support for all three standard hypotheses in an effort to present a more general test of the conditional hypotheses.

Readers should note that the tables in this section of the chapter take a different format from those presented previously. Instead of reporting the number of cases surpassing a 90% confidence in the correct and incorrect directions as well as the total number of cases, the tables will only report the percentage of cases surpassing the 90% threshold in the correct direction,

Table 8.7. *Comparative Assessment of Intuitive Conditional Economic Voting Hypotheses*

	Transitional Identity Model		Referendum Model
	New Regime	Old Regime	Incumbents
Panel 1: % Cases with at least 90% Support for Hypothesis: Parliamentary vs. Presidential Elections			
Parliamentary Elections	66%	75%	42%
Presidential Elections	50%	60%	33%
Panel 2: % Cases with at least 90% Support for Hypothesis: East-Central Europe vs. Russia			
East-Central European Elections	63%	90%	38%
Russian Elections	63%	25%	57%

or what was previously reported in bold in the final row of each table. This is done both to save space and to facilitate easier comparisons, as all of the tables in this section summarize information presented in greater detail in the previous three chapters. However, readers interested in the number of cases for each category can find this information in the relevant tables in the previous chapters.

Intuitive Conditional Economic Voting Approaches

Table 8.7 presents comparative assessments of the two intuitive conditional hypotheses, displaying the relative support for the three standard economic voting hypotheses across parliamentary and presidential elections in Panel 1 and across East-Central European and Russian elections in Panel 2. Panel 1 reveals that there is slightly more empirical support for all three of the hypotheses in parliamentary elections than in presidential elections. The difference in the degree of support is not dramatic, with strong empirical support in approximately 10%–15% more of the cases in parliamentary elections than in presidential elections, but is noticeable for its consistency across the three standard hypotheses. As a result, the ordering of support for the three hypotheses (strong support for the Old Regime hypothesis is found in about 10% more cases than for the New Regime hypothesis, which in turn generates strong support in about 20% more cases than the Incumbency hypothesis) is almost identical across both presidential and parliamentary elections. Thus, despite the fact that there is slightly greater empirical support for all of the hypotheses in parliamentary elections, the overall conclusions of the relative empirical support for the Transition and

Referendum Models would have been the same had I included only presidential elections, only parliamentary elections, or, as I have done, both presidential and parliamentary elections in the study.

The same cannot be said of the East-Central European versus Russian distinction. Here there is a markedly different pattern: the degree of support for the New Regime hypothesis is the same in both East-Central Europe and Russia; there is more support for the Incumbency Model in Russia; and there is significantly more support for the Old Regime hypothesis in East-Central Europe. In the previous chapter, I went into great detail on the potential explanations for the different Russian results for the Old Regime hypothesis, so I will not revisit that topic here. Instead, the key point to be taken from Panel 2 of Table 8.7 is that there is no systematic pattern of differences between the Russian case and the East-Central European cases. It is certainly not the case that there are predicable regional economic voting patterns in East-Central European elections but not in Russian elections, and thus I have somehow muddied the waters by including an inappropriate set of cases for comparison. Nor is the opposite true; the models do not perform significantly better across the board in the Russian cases than the East-Central European cases. Instead, there is variation in patterns of support, with more support in the Russian context for one hypothesis, more in the East-Central European context for another, and practically the same level of support across both categories for the remaining hypothesis. Perhaps equally importantly, we would reach a similar conclusion if we created a table that singled out Slovakia (which generated much less empirical support than the other four countries for the New Regime hypothesis) or the Czech Republic (which generated much more empirical support for the Incumbency hypothesis than the other four countries). Thus, there is no empirical reason to exclude Russia from the analysis any more than there would be to exclude Slovakia or the Czech Republic. The fact that there are some country level patterns in empirical support for the individual standard hypothesis pointed us in interesting directions in the previous chapters, but the fact that there are no country level patterns across all three of the standard hypotheses serves to confirm the usefulness of including all of them in a comparative study.

This leads to two additional points. First, it is important to avoid labeling any one particular country as qualitatively different from the others on the basis of testing any one particular hypothesis. A study that examined only the Old Regime hypothesis might well have concluded that including Russian and East-Central European cases in the same analysis was a mistake, given the existing prejudices against doing so in the discipline. A similar recommendation to exclude the Czech Republic on the basis of an analysis of only the Incumbency hypothesis would not have had a similar discipline-wide bias on which to draw, but both would have missed the point that the country-by-country distinctions do not hold up across the analysis of multiple standard economic voting hypothesis. Second, no matter what country-by-country patterns can be identified, it is ultimately more satisfying to have theoretical explanations for these differences than to fall back on arguments of countries just being different from one another and inappropriate for comparison. Thus, the discussion of the greater than average support for the Incumbency hypothesis in the Czech Republic highlighted the importance of the overlap between New Regime and Incumbency status – what was labeled in Chapter 2 as the interactive conditional hypothesis – a point to which I will return later in this chapter. Similarly, the lack of empirical support for the New Regime hypothesis in Slovakia and the Old Regime hypothesis in Russia both suggested the importance of responsibility-based conditional approaches, to which I now turn.

Responsibility-Based Conditional Economic Voting Approaches

Table 8.8 displays the results of applying two of the three responsibility-based conditional hypotheses to all three standard economic voting hypotheses. Panel 1 breaks down the empirical support for these hypotheses in terms of institutional responsibility. The prediction of this hypothesis is that there should be the strongest support for the standard economic voting hypotheses in dominant elections, the weakest in dominated elections, and an intermediary level of support in mixed system elections. Although it is possible to find some results in line with the institutional responsibility hypothesis by collapsing categories (e.g., there is more support for the New Regime hypothesis in dominant elections than in dominated and mixed system elections combined), the overall results do not reveal a clear pattern in line with the predictions of the hypothesis. Indeed, the strongest support for the Old Regime hypothesis is found in mixed elections, whereas both the Incumbency and New Regime hypotheses have the least support in this category. And in complete contrast to the prediction of the institutional responsibility hypothesis, the strongest support for the Incumbency hypothesis is in dominated elections (although as noted in Chapter 5 this is based on a small number of cases).

Table 8.8. *Comparative Assessment of Responsibility Hypotheses*

	Transitional Identity Model		Referendum Model
	New Regime	Old Regime	Incumbents
Panel 1. % Cases with at least 90% Support for Hypothesis by Institutional Responsibility			
Dominant Institution Elections*	68%	79%	47%
Mixed System Elections**	55%	100%	21%
Dominated Institution Elections***	57%	20%	60%
Panel 2. % Cases with at least 90% Support for Hypothesis by National Vote			
< 5% of total vote	43%	67%	14%
≥ 5% of total vote	67%	75%	45%
≥ 10% of total vote	73%	72%	52%
≥ 20% of total vote	71%	75%	67%

* Presidential elections in presidential systems (Russia) and parliamentary elections in parliamentary systems (Hungary, Slovakia, Czech Republic).
** Presidential and parliamentary elections in mixed systems (Poland).
*** Presidential elections in parliamentary systems (Slovakia) and parliamentary elections in presidential systems (Russia).

Panel 2 of Table 8.8, however, presents evidence that is more supportive of the responsibility approach. The predicted pattern is most obvious in the case of incumbent parties, where there is a sharp increase in the percentage of cases in which there is strong empirical support for the Incumbency hypothesis among parties that received a larger percentage of the total vote. The increases are not as dramatic for either the New Regime or Old Regime parties, but they remain almost entirely in the correctly predicted direction and the distinction for New Regime parties between those receiving less than 5% of the overall vote (strong empirical support in only 43% of the cases) as opposed to greater than 10% of the vote (strong empirical support in 73% of the cases) is noteworthy. So although the evidence in support of the size of vote hypothesis may not be overwhelming, it is largely consistent with the prediction of the hypothesis and certainly does not in any way falsify the hypothesis.

Recall as well the comparison between primary and other incumbent coalition members in parliamentary elections displayed in Panel 2 of Table 5.5. Consistent with the responsibility-based approach, strong empirical support for the Incumbency hypothesis was found more often for the primary party in each coalition (53% of the cases) than for the other members of the coalitions (36% of the cases). Although this is another example of less than dramatic evidence, it is again consistent with the predictions of the responsibility-based approach.

There is also additional evidence from the paired case studies to suggest that the standard economic voting hypotheses might be more likely to generate empirical support when parties are more important in the eyes of the electorate. One example comes from the assessment in the previous chapter of the pattern of support for the Old Regime hypothesis across the five Russian elections, which revealed greater support for the hypothesis in the case of the primary communist successor party (the KPRF in the parliamentary elections and Zyuganov in the 1996 presidential election) than for the minor communist opposition (the KTR-SS). Similarly, the discussion of the discrepancy in the findings of empirical support for the New Regime hypothesis for the two New Regime parties contesting the 1993 Russian parliamentary election highlighted the fact that there was better empirical support for the New Regime hypothesis in the vote for the party that was most closely tied to the economic reform package of the previous years (Russia's Choice) than for the other, less closely linked, New Regime party competing in the election (the Party of Russian Unity and Concord). A similar pattern can be found in a presidential election by recalling the results of analyzing the 1995 Polish presidential election, where the vote for the incumbent Lech Wałesa generated support for the New Regime hypothesis, whereas the vote for Jacek Kuroń, who received a much smaller share of the vote and whose party had been out of power since 1993, did not provide support for the hypothesis. Another example is the fate of New Regime parties in Slovakia. These parties did not generate much empirical support for the New Regime hypothesis until the 1998 parliamentary election, when a Slovak New Regime party finally played a pivotal role in an election and its leader became the new prime minister following the election. All of these cases provide examples where the overall importance of candidates or parties to voters can help explain variation in the support for standard hypotheses on a party-by-party basis, and as such provide additional support for the responsibility-based conditional approach.

Overall, there is reason to cautiously suggest support in the postcommunist context for the argument that there should be more consistent signs of regional economic voting patterns when parties are likely to be seen as having more responsibility for the state of the economy. Although one comparative test – the institutional responsibility hypothesis – fails to generate any real support for the responsibility-based approach, the two other comparative tests produce some, albeit lukewarm, support. Moreover, patterns of support from individual case studies also suggest that the standard hypotheses might generate more empirical support as parties becomes more important in the eyes of voters. Thus, although it is important not to overstate the degree of empirical support for responsibility-based conditional approaches, the evidence certainly is suggestive that they are useful for understanding the kind of contexts in which economic conditions are likely to have a more consistent effect on election results.

Supply-Side Conditional Economic Voting Approaches

The supply-side conditional economic voting approach proposes that there should be less empirical support for standard economic voting hypotheses as other factors become more important. In the previous chapters, I have systematically assessed the degree of support provided for the personality hypothesis, which predicts less impact for economic conditions in institutional arrangements that highlight the personality of individual candidates. In Chapter 2, I introduced a second supply-side hypothesis, the regime future hypothesis, which predicts that the economy should matter less when fundamental regime changes are under consideration during the election. Because of the paucity of elections fitting this description (two out of twenty), I did not address the regime future hypothesis systematically in the preceding chapters, but I now return to it in the following discussion.

Panel 1 of Table 8.9 presents fairly weak support for the personality hypothesis. Similar to previous examples, the evidence clearly does not falsify the hypothesis by showing patterns that are the opposite from what the hypothesis would predict, but nor does the table reveal particularly strong support for the hypothesis. In particular, there is no evidence to support the predicted distinction between open-list and closed-list parliamentary elections. In one case, the effect is actually in the opposite direction predicted by the hypothesis – there is more support for the Old Regime hypothesis in open-list parliamentary elections than closed-list parliamentary elections – although for the other two categories the degree of support is practically the same. So there really is no evidence that the personality hypothesis can help distinguish the degree of empirical support for any of the standard hypotheses within the different types of proportional representation list elections.

Table 8.9. *Comparative Assessment of Supply-Side Hypotheses*

	Transitional Identity Model		Referendum Model
	New Regime	Old Regime	Incumbents
Panel 1.% Cases with at least 90% Support for Hypothesis by Personality			
Presidential Elections	50%	60%	33%
Open-List Parliamentary Elections	65%	92%	41%
Closed-List Parliamentary Elections	67%	55%	45%
Panel 2.% Cases with at least 90% Support for Hypothesis by Regime Future Elections			
Regime Future Elections	0%	0%	0%
All Other Elections	66%	81%	45%

However, if the two parliamentary election categories are collapsed, then the result is Panel 1 of Table 8.4, as the two remaining categories become presidential and parliamentary elections. As was illustrated earlier in the discussion of the intuitive hypotheses, there is a consistent – albeit fairly minor – pattern of greater empirical support for the standard economic voting hypotheses in parliamentary elections than in presidential elections. Thus, on a simpler level, the personality hypothesis does provide a justification for the slightly different pattern of results found in presidential and parliamentary elections.

With the appropriate caveat that it is based on a very small number of observations, Panel 2 of Table 8.9 presents the clearest evidence in support of any of the conditional economic voting hypotheses in the study. Simply put, parties competing in the two regime future elections fail to generate any empirical support for any of the standard economic voting hypotheses, exactly as the conditional regime future hypothesis predicts. Now there may certainly be other reasons for this finding than the fact that both countries were preoccupied with the future of their current regime at the time of the election, as is suggested by the hypothesis. As noted earlier, the data used to analyze the 1991 Russian presidential election is distinguished from the other cases in the database by the lack of unemployment data, although there is no reason to suspect that the 1992 Slovak data were somehow unsuited to provide results that would support any of these hypotheses. Additionally, analyses of elections that took place later in the decade in both countries do indeed provide support for the different standard hypotheses. It is also correct to note that if the regime future category was expanded to include the 1990 Hungarian and 1992 Czech parliamentary elections – see Chapter 2 for a discussion of this point and why the decision was not made to expand the category in this way – the distinction between the two categories would disappear. Nevertheless, this would not change the fact that the results from the 1991 Russian presidential and 1992 Slovak parliamentary elections are a serious anomaly when compared to the rest of the study, and that the regime future argument provides a theoretical argument that helps to explain this anomaly.[13]

Considering these two tests in tandem, there is limited support for a supply-side argument from a test with large samples in each category (the personality hypothesis) and strong support for a supply-side hypothesis from a test with a very small sample in one category (the regime future hypothesis). Additionally, the supply-side conditional approach provides a theoretical explanation for the distinction in results between parliamentary and presidential elections. Although it was not possible to expand this argument to explain distinctions within parliamentary elections, it at least takes us a step forward from merely claiming *a priori* that presidential and parliamentary elections are different. So, similar to the responsibility-based hypotheses, there is far from conclusive empirical evidence to support the general supply-side claim that there should be more consistent effects for economic conditions on election results when other factors matter less. But at the same time, the limited evidence presented above is at least consistent with this claim and certainly does nothing to falsify it, suggesting that this, too, remains a useful direction for future analysis.

Partisan Orientation and Time-Based Conditional Economic Voting Approaches

The time-based conditional economic voting approach is the only one of the approaches that generates two mutually exclusive hypotheses, with one hypothesis predicting greater support for the standard hypotheses as the decade progresses and the other predicting decreasing support for the standard hypotheses as the decade progresses.

---

[13] The 1999 Slovak presidential election also failed to generate support for any of the standard economic voting hypotheses, although it should be noted that no Old Regime candidates contested this election.

Table 8.10. *Comparative Assessment of Party Orientation and Time-Based Hypotheses*

Panel 1. % Cases with at least 90% Support for Hypothesis by Election Wave

	Transitional Identity Model		Referendum Model
	New Regime	Old Regime	Incumbents
1990–1992	42%	63%	18%
1993–1996	59%	75%	55%
1997–1999	91%	78%	50%

Panel 2. % Cases with at least 90% Support for Hypothesis by Election Wave and Party Orientation

	New Regime		Old Regime	
	Consistent Liberalizing	Populist Leaning	Reformed	Unreformed
1990–1992	50%	0%	50%	75%
1993–1996	58%	60%	75%	75%
1997–1999	100%	80%	100%	67%
Full Period	**64%**	**58%**	**73%**	**72%**

Panel 1 of Table 8.10 demonstrates that there is no support across this particular collection of cases for the prediction that support for the standard economic voting hypotheses should decrease over the course of the 1990s. Not a single one of the standard hypotheses has a declining rate of strong empirical support as the decade progresses. On the contrary, the incidence of strong empirical support for all three standard hypotheses is larger by the end of the decade than at the beginning. This pattern is clearly strongest in the variation in empirical support for the New Regime and Incumbency hypotheses, but even the minor variation in support for the Old Regime hypothesis is still in the same direction.[14]

---

[14] As noted in Chapter 3, an alternative explanation for the improving accuracy of the results over time could be that random measurement error in the work of all five statistical agencies was decreasing as the decade progressed. However, the variation across the three standard hypotheses in Panel 1 of Table 8.10 cautions against making too much of this explanation, as the support for the Old Regime hypothesis does not change much over the course of the decade, nor does the support for the Incumbency hypothesis over the last two waves of the election. A measurement error-based explanation would be more convincing if all

But perhaps even more interesting are the findings contained in Panel 2 of Table 8.10. First and foremost – as identified in the bottom row of the table – there is practically no support for the party orientation hypotheses. In the case of the New Regime version of this hypothesis, there is marginally more support for the New Regime hypothesis among the more liberal New Regime parties than the more populist New Regime parties, but this difference is so slight that it would disappear entirely if the results for a single populist party changed. Even more dramatically, there is practically the exact same incidence of support for the Old Regime hypothesis among reformed and unreformed Old Regime parties. Given the extent to which the literature on postcommunist politics has tended to highlight the distinction between reformed and unreformed Old Regime parties, this is a truly interesting – and perhaps somewhat surprising – result.

Further evidence in this regard is found by looking at the over-time variation in support for the party orientation hypotheses. These hypotheses were predicated on the idea that it might take voters more time to become aware of the subtle distinctions between the different types of New Regime and Old Regime parties. As it turns out, the first three rows of Panel 2 of Table 8.10 demonstrate absolutely no support for this hypothesis. Far from showing decreasing support as the decade progresses for the New Regime hypothesis among the more populist New Regime parties or decreasing support for the Old Regime hypothesis among more reformed Old Regime Parties, the panel reveals the opposite pattern. Although based on a small number of cases in each cell (see Tables 6.9 and 7.9), the proportion of cases providing strong empirical support for their respective standard economic voting hypothesis from both of these categories of parties actually increases as time passes.

Thus, across a variety of tests, there continues to be strong evidence in support of the stickiness of regional economic voting patterns for both New Regime and Old Regime parties. This stickiness is found across different variations of partisan orientation, over the passage of time, and even when these two factors are considered interactively. Moreover, evidence is found in this regard across both New Regime and Old Regime parties, thus making the patterns identified for each of these types of parties individually in the previous two chapters that much more convincing.

three sets of results looked like the findings for the New Regime hypothesis; as they do not, it is more difficult to pin this variation on data-related explanations.

Interacting the Transitional Identity and Referendum Models

There remains, however, one other important type of conditional hypothesis to consider, which is the effect of interacting the two standard economic voting models with one another. This interactive conditional approach was the only approach not systematically analyzed in the preceding chapters, although it was mentioned in the discussion of the paired case studies. The approach is based on the idea that the Incumbency hypothesis also can serve as a conditional hypothesis for predicting where there ought to be more or less empirical support for the New Regime and Old Regime hypotheses; similarly, the New Regime and Old Regime hypotheses can play such a role for the Incumbency hypothesis. To accomplish the latter, incumbents are divided into three categories: New Regime incumbents, Old Regime incumbents, and other incumbents.[15] As the predictions of the New Regime hypothesis and Incumbency hypothesis are in the same direction – both predict that parties should receive more support where economic conditions are stronger – the expectation is to find the most consistent empirical support for the Incumbency hypothesis among incumbent parties that are also New Regime parties. Conversely, the Old Regime and Incumbency hypotheses predict effects that are in the opposite direction from one another, suggesting that the weakest support for the Incumbency hypothesis should be found when analyzing the effect of economic conditions on the vote for incumbent parties that are also Old Regime parties. Support for the Incumbency hypothesis among other (non–New Regime and non–Old Regime) incumbent parties is predicted to be somewhere between the first two categories.

Similar predictions using the Incumbency hypothesis can be made to explain the variation in support for the New Regime and Old Regime hypotheses. More support for the New Regime hypothesis is expected among New Regime parties that are also incumbents than those that are in the opposition. Likewise, there is predicted to be more support for the Old Regime hypothesis among Old Regime parties that are in the opposition than among Old Regime parties that are also incumbents (see Table 2.6).

It is also worth noting that although these are tests of conditional economic voting hypotheses insofar as they attempt to explain variation in patterns of support for standard economic voting hypotheses, in a sense

---

[15] These three categories are mutually exclusive and exhaustive, so the "other incumbent" category covers all incumbent parties that are neither a New Regime nor an Old Regime incumbent.

Comparative Analysis

Table 8.11. *Interactive Hypotheses*

Panel 1. Transitional Identity Model: Breakdown of Certainty by Incumbency

	New Regime		Old Regime	
	Incumbent	Opposition	Incumbent	Opposition
90% Confident in Predicted Direction	14	11	7	14
90% Confident in Wrong Direction	0	1	0	1
Total Cases	21	19	9	20
Percentage with 90%	**67%**	**58%**	**78%**	**70%**
Confidence in Predicted (Wrong) **Direction**	(0%)	(5%)	(0%)	(5%)

Panel 2. Referendum Model: Breakdown of Certainty by Transitional Identity

	Incumbents			
	New Regime	Other	Old Regime	Total
90% Confident in Predicted Direction	14	6	0	20
90% Confident in Wrong Direction	0	1	7	8
Total Cases	21	19	9	49
Percentage with 90% Confidence in	**67%**	**32%**	**0%**	**41%**
Predicted (Wrong) **Direction**	(0%)	(5%)	(78%)	(16%)

they also provide additional tests of the explanatory power of the standard hypotheses themselves. If the primary means by which economic conditions affect regional variation in election results in postcommunist countries is based on the Transitional Identity of a party, then the Transitional Identity of incumbent parties should be able to explain at least some of the variation in support for the Incumbency hypothesis.

Panel 1 of Table 8.11 demonstrates that little leverage over the variation in empirical support for the New Regime and Old Regime hypotheses is gained by considering the incumbency status of these parties. As predicted, there is more support for the New Regime hypothesis generated by the analysis of New Regime incumbent parties than by New Regime opposition parties, but this distinction is fairly slight. The New Regime hypothesis still generates strong empirical support in 58% of the cases when New Regime parties are in the opposition, which is not that different from the 67% of the cases for which there is strong empirical support for the New Regime hypothesis among New Regime parties that are also incumbent parties.

The distinction between the two subcategories of Old Regime parties is similarly small, but here it is actually in the opposite direction from what the Incumbency hypothesis predicts. There is certainly strong empirical support for the Old Regime hypothesis in a large proportion of the cases (70%) in which Old Regime parties are in the opposition, but there is even more consistent empirical support for the Old Regime hypothesis (78% of the cases) when Old Regime parties are also coded as incumbent parties.

Panel 2 of Table 8.11 reveals almost the opposite finding from Panel 1: the predictions of the Transitional Identity Model can account for a great deal of the variation in the empirical support for the Incumbency hypothesis. There is strong support for the Incumbency hypothesis among incumbent parties that are also New Regime Parties, but absolutely no support for the Incumbency hypothesis among incumbent parties that are also Old Regime parties. Indeed, as discussed earlier, there is actually strong empirical evidence in support of an economic effect in the opposite direction from what the Incumbency hypothesis predicts (in other words, in the direction predicted by the Old Regime hypothesis) for 78% of the incumbent Old Regime parties. Moreover, the other incumbent category reveals empirical support for the Incumbency hypothesis in a proportion of cases (32%) that is at almost the midpoint between the proportion of cases providing empirical support for the Incumbency hypothesis among New Regime incumbents (67%) and Old Regime incumbents (0%).

Thus, we arrive at the undeniable conclusion that support for the Incumbency hypothesis is to a large extent conditional on the transitional status of different incumbent parties. New Regime incumbent parties provide strong support for the Incumbency hypothesis, Old Regime incumbent parties provide almost no support, and other incumbent parties fall somewhere between the other two categories.

Conclusions

Based on the evidence presented in the first third of the chapter, the findings regarding the superiority of the empirical evidence in support of the predictions made by the Transitional Identity Model as compared to the Referendum Model appear to be quite robust. Even when the specifications of the original regional economic voting models are changed in a variety of ways, the threshold for claiming strong support for a hypothesis is adjusted, or the hypotheses are tested using only theoretically relevant subsections of the data, there is always more empirical support for the Old Regime and

New Regime hypotheses than there is for the Incumbency hypothesis, and the number of parties for which the first two hypotheses can make predictions is always greater than the number of incumbent parties. Moreover, of the two Transitional Identity Model hypotheses there is almost always more consistent empirical support for the Old Regime hypothesis than the New Regime hypothesis (although there are a few exceptions, with the analysis of the third wave of elections being the most notable).

The second part of the chapter yields a number of observations concerning the ability of the different conditional economic voting approaches to predict the conditions under which there ought to be more or less empirical support for the standard hypotheses. The intuitive approaches reveal mixed findings. Although there is consistent evidence that all three of the standard hypotheses have slightly stronger empirical support in parliamentary elections than in presidential elections, there is no evidence for a consistently different effect for economic conditions across the East-Central European and Russian divide. And although each standard economic voting hypothesis does produce one country that has a markedly different pattern of support from the other four, this country varies by hypothesis.

Although differing in specifics, the overall assessment of the responsibility and supply-side based approaches is fairly similar. Both approaches are supported by what can best be called weak empirical evidence. Although there is no test in either case that would offer conclusive proof in support of its hypothesis, the findings clearly do not falsify the approaches either. Indeed, across the multiple tests in both cases, a pattern of weak evidence that points in the correct direction does in fact emerge. Although this should not be interpreted as a definitive finding in favor of either approach, both do show enough promise to warrant further consideration as the literature moves forward.

Perhaps the most interesting conditional observations, however, come from assessing the interaction of the two models, the passage of time, and the predictions of the party orientation hypotheses. First, from the earliest days of the transition, Old Regime parties enjoyed more electoral success in parts of the country where economic conditions were worse irrespective of incumbency status and neither the passage of time nor the decisions by these parties to pursue a more or less reformist path seems to have altered this pattern. Second, although some New Regime parties enjoyed better electoral performances in areas of the country where economic conditions were better early in the decade, this pattern increased significantly as time passed. Similarly to the Old Regime parties, the development of this regional economic voting pattern was largely independent of whether or not the party was currently in the government and did not seem to vary across the more populist-oriented New Regime parties and those that stuck more closely to a liberal reformist identity. Finally, regional economic voting patterns for incumbent parties were largely conditional on the Transitional Identity of these parties. Incumbent parties that also were Old Regime parties never performed better in areas of the country where economic conditions were stronger, whereas New Regime incumbent parties often enjoyed more support in areas of the country where economic condition were better.

Having now thoroughly examined the empirical support for these different conclusions, the task for the final chapter is to assess the implications of these findings.

Appendix 8.1: Supplementary Table

Table 8A.1. *Extra Parties Included in Panel 2 of Table 8.3*

Country	Year	Party
Czech Republic	1992	Czechoslovak Social Democratic Party
Czech Republic	1992	Movement for Self Government of Moravia and Silesia
Czech Republic	1992	Republican Party
Czech Republic	1996	Czech Social Democratic Party
Czech Republic	1996	Republican Party
Czech Republic	1998	Czech Social Democratic Party
Czech Republic	1998	Republican Party
Hungary	1990	Independent Smallholders Party
Hungary	1994	Agrarian Association
Hungary	1998	Hungarian Justice and Life Party
Poland	1990	Stanislaw Tymiński
Poland	1991	Confederation for an Independent Poland
Poland	1993	Confederation for an Independent Poland
Poland	1995	Jan Olszewski
Poland	1995	Waldemar Pawlak
Poland	1997	Movement for the Reconstruction of Poland
Poland	1997	Union of Labor
Russia	1991	Vladimir Zhirinovskii
Russia	1993	Yabloko
Russia	1993	Liberal Democratic Party of Russia
Russia	1993	Agrarian Party
Russia	1995	Liberal Democratic Party of Russia
Russia	1995	Congress of Russian Communities

Comparative Analysis

Country	Year	Party
Russia	1995	Yabloko
Russia	1996	Grigori Yavlinskii
Russia	1996	Vladimir Zhirinovskii
Russia	1996	Aleksandr Lebed
Russia	1999	Zhirinovskii Bloc
Russia	1999	Fatherland – All Russia
Russia	1999	Yabloko
Slovakia	1992	Slovak National Party
Slovakia	1992	Hungarian Christian Democrats
Slovakia	1994	Hungarian Coalition
Slovakia	1998	Hungarian Coalition
Slovakia	1999	Ján Slota

9

Economic Voting and Postcommunist Politics

In this final chapter, I return to the original motivations for the study by assessing the degree to which the findings from the previous chapters can contribute both to our understanding of postcommunist politics and the more general economic voting literature. To do so, I focus in the first half of this chapter on the implications of three of the most significant findings from the study: the consistently stronger empirical support for the Transitional Identity Model than for the Referendum Model; the numerous insights added by theorizing about the conditions in which economic conditions are likely to have more or less of an effect on election results (or what I have labeled conditional economic voting hypotheses); and the apparent "stickiness" of the Transitional Identities of both New Regime and Old Regime parties, at least insofar as they pertain to regional economic voting. In the second half of the chapter, I address three related questions raised by the overall findings: the appropriate duration for testing hypotheses based on transitional circumstances; the contributions of the study to specific debates in the postcommunist politics literature; and the potential implications of regional-level findings for understanding variation in national-level election results. I conclude with some brief final observations.

Economic Voting and Empirical Support for the Transitional Identity Model

As illustrated throughout the previous chapters, the most important empirical conclusion of this book is that there is consistently stronger evidence supporting the predictions of the Transitional Identity Model than the predictions of the Referendum Model. The fact that such consistent empirical support for the Transitional Identity Model exists demonstrates that across ten years, five countries, and twenty different elections, there is indeed a coherent pattern of regional economic voting that links postcommunist economic conditions to postcommunist political outcomes.

What can we learn from this observation? The very fact that there is a stable pattern of mass political behavior in the turbulent first decade of postcommunist political development is in itself an important finding that I return to in more detail later in the chapter. But beyond stability, the results also reveal the possibility of a degree of political sophistication on the part of postcommunist voters insofar as how economic interest affects electoral outcomes. Recall the classic view of how citizens might approach elections in transitional environments described in this book by the Incumbency hypothesis. When faced with the prospect of going to the polls in the context of economic transitions, it is often assumed that voters think first and foremost about the parties currently in the government. Economic losers are expected to gravitate away from these parties and economic winners toward them, resulting in the aggregate distribution of regional election results predicted by the Incumbency hypothesis. Such a view requires little assumption of political sophistication, especially in regard to the consequence of which opposition party (or even which incumbent party) is selected to receive one's vote, and little understanding on the part of voters of the differences between what parties might be expected to do if elected to office.

But as the previous chapters demonstrate, this type of model is not well supported at the aggregate level by patterns of regional economic voting. Instead, there is widespread evidence of Old Regime parties performing better in areas of the country where economic conditions were worse – even from the earliest days of the transition – and even when these Old Regime parties were currently in power. Similarly, better economic conditions at the regional level improved the vote not just for whichever party happened to be in power at the time, but, rather, the vote for parties whose identities were most closely tied to the transition away from communism itself, or what I have labeled New Regime parties. With the important caveat that I did not test individual level data in the study and thus cannot make claims concerning individual behavior for that reason, it does seem that collections of economic winners and losers in the aggregate were not merely trying to punish or reward the parties in the government. So even in the context of a period of time during which most incumbent parties in postcommunist countries (and especially in Eastern Europe) had trouble holding on to power, it appears evident in these five countries that certain types of parties consistently remained more popular in areas of the country with more economic losers (Old Regime parties) and other types of parties did so in areas of the country with more economic winners (New Regime parties). Again with the appropriate caveats, this finding suggests that claims that elections held during economic transitions will simply give ignorant and angry citizens an opportunity to vent their wrath on whomever is currently in power may be overstated, at the very least missing more subtle distinctions about the types of voters that may be more or less likely to do this and the types of parties to which they may be more likely to gravitate.

Although the concept of more sophisticated voters has a positive feel to it, one can also propose an interpretation of these findings that looks troubling from the standpoint of the development of accountable, representative governments. If the primary means by which voters hold the government accountable for economic performance is to withhold their votes from incumbent parties when the economy is performing poorly, then perhaps we ought to be concerned about the level of political accountability in these societies if the presence of more economic losers does not systematically lead to fewer votes for incumbent political parties. In the absence of any links between concentrations of economic losers and the vote for and against particular parties, then the answer to this question might very well be yes.[1] But here, recent theoretical work by Manin, Przeworski, and Stokes is particularly illuminative.[2] The authors argue representative government can be enforced not only by throwing the bums out, or by what they call "accountability representation," but also by citizens choosing to cast their votes based on what they believe the parties will do in office, which the authors label "mandate representation." In this framework, the Transitional Identity Model presents evidence that is at least consistent with the idea that political accountability may be developing in postcommunist politics, but only that it takes more of a mandate than sanctioning form,

---

[1] Moreover, the fact that so many incumbent parties in Eastern Europe lost reelection bids obviously mitigates against this concern to a significant degree (although here the post-Soviet experience was quite different). However, the fact that parties still seemed to get kicked out of office even if economic conditions were improving (e.g., the 1997 Polish and 1998 Hungarian parliamentary elections) somewhat complicates the picture.

[2] For more, see Manin, Przeworski, and Stokes 1999a, b. Note as well how this parallels the discussion of the distinction between the assumptions underlying the Referendum and Transitional Identity Models in Chapter 2, as well as the discussion of rethinking prospective voting later in this chapter.

at least as it pertains to regional economic voting. The evidence presented in support of the responsibility-based conditional hypotheses in the previous chapters is also quite consistent with this view; mandate representation ought to be more appealing if parties are likely to be more important after the election.

There is, however, another way to think about rectifying the belief that economic losers would want to punish those responsible for the economic pain accompanying the transition and the central finding of this study that there is greater empirical support for the Transitional Identity Model than for the Referendum Model. To do so, however, involves recasting the way the concept of retrospective voting has largely come to be applied in the current economic voting literature and returning it to its more original form found in Fiorina's classic work, *Retrospective Voting*. As discussed earlier in this book, most of the economic voting literature uses the term retrospective voting to apply to the question of whether voters are more likely to vote for (or against) the incumbent party if economic conditions are perceived to be good (or bad) for some period of time preceding the election; this is contrasted to prospective voting, whereby voters choose to support the incumbent based on their perception of what economic conditions will look like over some period of time following the election. However, Fiorina's conception of retrospective voting is broader than this, involving a running tally of voters' opinions about parties based on not just the period preceding the current election, but instead encompassing what voters remember about parties from previous time periods as well.[3]

In this spirit, it is possible to cast an alternative, classical retrospective framework on the Transitional Identity Model. Suppose that voters assign complete responsibility for the transition period to the New Regime parties most closely associated with its initiation. Concurrently, suppose that voters also use developments in the transition period as a way to assess the pretransition period: the better the economy performs in the transition period, then the worse a job the Old Regime was obviously doing managing the economy; but the worse the economy performs in the transition, then the better the pretransition period looks by comparison, and the more it looks like the Old Regime did an effective job managing the economy.

If we accept these assumptions, then it holds that more voters should seek to "reward" New Regime parties (and only New Regime parties) where economic conditions are better than where economic conditions are

[3] See Fiorina 1981.

worse, and therefore New Regime parties should perform better in areas of the country where economic conditions are better. Conversely, wherever economic conditions are worse, citizens should be more likely to punish New Regime parties and reward Old Regime parties (as the Old Regime now looks better by comparison). In this manner, an analysis of regional economic voting can function as an effective way to assess the degree to which classical retrospective voting is taking place. However, this is not a retrospective judgment of actual incumbent parties at the time of the election, but, rather, the overall "Transitional incumbent" parties (New Regime parties) and the "Old Regime incumbent" parties (Old Regime parties).[4] Moreover, if one accepts this recast view of retrospective voting, then a form of political accountability is clearly developing in the postcommunist context, although it is much stickier – in the sense that the same parties are repeatedly punished (rewarded) across multiple election cycles for disappointment (satisfaction) with the postcommunist economic environment – than the kind generally assumed to be present in more established democracies.

The idea that there could be essentially two different types of "incumbent" parties to be blamed or rewarded for the state of the economy following a dramatic change in a country's economic circumstances – the incumbent parties of the pretransition period (here the Old Regime parties) and the incumbent parties of the transition era (here the New Regime parties) – neither of which need to actually be in power at the time of a given election to be considered an incumbent, can also speak to the the vexing question of why citizens should ever reward parties for the state of the economy in an increasingly globalized world. Although it might be legitimate to question how different the unemployment rate in Austria would really look had a left of-center-government been in power over a short-term period of time as opposed to a right-of-center government, Poland's economy would have clearly looked very different in 1995 had communism not collapsed and

---

[4] If we also assume that most of the economic variables used in the study were essentially flat before the transition, then it is possible to think of all the variables included in the cross-regional models analyzed in this book as representing the change in that economic condition since the transition began. Unemployment works the best in this regard; if there really was no unemployment in the communist period, then the unemployment rate at the time of the transition is a measure of how much unemployment has increased since the transition has begun. And in a world where everyone had a salary but goods were scarce, then increases in salary – now a much more meaningful concept – really does measure a change from salaries not varying much from year to year.

been replaced with capitalism via shock therapy.[5] Thus, the idea that voters could seek to reward or punish the parties most responsible for this change – or conversely reward or punish the parties most responsible for the type of economy that preceded the change – does not seem nearly as far-fetched. At the same time, it casts some doubt on the picture of voters as having a more sophisticated forward-looking outlook in making their vote choices, instead replacing it with a kind of stubborn, repeated attempt on the part of economic winners and losers to continue to pronounce judgment on the transition away from communism itself.[6] Nevertheless, this conception of a dual "Transitional Incumbency" leading to a form of retrospective voting still requires a more sophisticated voter with an understanding of differences between parties than does the straight incumbency-based approach of the Referendum Model.

The question of whether voters were more intent on punishing and rewarding parties based on their relationship to the transition or were ultimately motivated more by their economic circumstances to vote in the manner suggested by the Transitional Identity Model is one that clearly cannot be resolved using aggregate-level data, and would likely even prove fairly difficult to sort out using individual-level data. A reasonable guess would be that some combination of both effects was at work. And, in a sense, the theoretical rational for the Transitional Identity Model put forth in Chapter 2 recognizes this point. Economic losers are predicted to shy away from New Regime parties precisely because they associate these parties with the changes since the transition; although not exactly the same, the concept is fairly similar to the idea of withholding a vote because these same parties are "blamed" for the disappointing state of the economy that

---

[5] For more on Poland's experience with shock therapy, see, for example, Murrell 1993; Sachs 1993; Orenstein 2001. Of course, Polish liberals would argue that had shock therapy not been instituted in Poland, then by 1995 the economy of a still communist Poland would have been a complete and utter disaster. But getting voters to judge Old Regime parties on the basis of a hypothetical continued deterioration of a planned economy is another matter entirely (for more on the "nostalgia" that Poles began to attach to the communist period, see Chan 1995, 127). So perhaps a better way to phrase this point is that Poland's economy in 1995 clearly looked very different from Poland's economy in 1985. This type of argument is complemented by the findings of two scholars that at the time of one of the elections included in this study (the 1993 Polish parliamentary election) individual attitudes toward the pretransition past helped to structure attitudes toward economic reform in the present; see Powers and Cox 1997.

[6] However, it should be noted that blame over the Civil War in the United States is hypothesized to have had an effect on voting behavior in the South for more than one hundred years after the war's conclusion.

emerged for economic losers after the collapse of communism. A similar argument can be made concerning economic winners and Old Regime parties.

In a related sense, the empirical support for the Transitional Identity Model also provides an impetus to rethink what it means to be a prospective, or forward-looking, voter. In the mainstream economic voting literature, a voter is assumed to be prospective if she bases her decision of whether or not to support the incumbent party not on the current state of the economy, but instead on the expected state of the economy at some point in the future. Another way, however, to conceive of a forward-looking voter in the context of economic voting is a voter who uses the current state of the economy to think about what type of party she would prefer to see in office following the election. In this conception of prospective voting, the voter would be forward-looking to the extent that she is thinking about the best type of party to have in office in the future, as opposed to judging the current incumbent parties based on her evaluation of the future performance of the economy. In an established democracy, this "type" would likely be based on partisanship, but in a transition country, as this study demonstrates, it can be based on a party's Transitional Identity. Indeed, recasting what it means to be a prospective voter in this manner is very consistent with the partisan approaches to economic voting (e.g., left-wing parties should be entrusted to deal with high unemployment) discussed in Chapter 2 that were used to motivate the Transitional Identity Model in the first place. It also, perhaps somewhat confusingly, brings the definition of a prospective voter much closer to the ideal of Fiorina's classical view of retrospective voting. In future research, such a conception of prospective economic voting might prove particularly useful for studying economic voting in multiparty systems.

Conditional Economic Voting

Another important implication of the study for the economic voting literature is the extent to which the use of what I have labeled conditional economic voting hypotheses helped inform both the theoretical and empirical analyses. In many ways, the now famous Bill Clinton 1992 campaign headquarters sign, "It's the Economy, Stupid!" still concisely summarizes the major finding of the literature on the relationship between the economy and elections in the United States, the many debates about exactly how this relationship is structured notwithstanding. Replicating this finding outside of the United States, however, has proven surprisingly more difficult than anticipated. Paldam's attempt to do just this begins with the unusual disclaimer that "it is hard to accept such negative conclusions as most of the ones reached in the chapter," and goes on to warn readers that "those who want to keep the illusions that [these models] are strong, robust tools should stop reading now!"[7] In Chapter 3, I noted a number of more recent studies, including one that extended the examination of economic voting in the American context back to the nineteenth century, that all came to the conclusion that the relationship between economic conditions and election results varied in different times and contexts.[8]

With these concerns in mind, this study offers two important insights. First, it is further evidence of a systematic relationship between economic conditions and election results across multiple countries outside of the United States, albeit of a different nature and at a different level of analysis than is common in most previous work. Nevertheless, it joins a small body of literature in demonstrating that systematic effects for economic conditions on election results can be found in a comparative context, and an even smaller body of literature in demonstrating that these types of effects can in fact be found in new democracies.

But even more important, the findings regarding the conditional economic voting hypotheses throughout this book suggest that it may be a mistake in the first place to expect the economy to always have the same effect on election results in different contexts. Moreover, a "failure" to find the exact same relationship between the state of the economy and election results across a series of different elections is not so much a cause for disappointment as it is an opportunity for theorizing about explanations for why the models work well in some cases as opposed to others. The small literature that has grown up around the clarity of responsibility hypothesis in studies of advanced industrialized democracies is one example of how to do this; my study will hopefully provide a number of new examples in this regard as well. In demonstrating generally more consistent effects for economic conditions on the vote for larger parties and for the lead members of coalitions – as well as the case-specific examples mentioned earlier in the text – this study demonstrates that there is reason for testing a responsibility based approach to economic voting in new democracies as well. But the study also shows that there may be other viable theoretical frameworks for thinking about the context in which the economy is more or less likely

---

[7] See Paldam 1991, 9–10.
[8] See, for example, Lin 1999; Whitten and Palmer 1999; Alvarez, Nagler, and Willette 2000.

to have an effect on the vote for political parties, including the presence of other pressing concerns, the degree to which electoral institutions permit a candidate's individual identity to come to the fore, or the passage of time away from a particularly dramatic event in a country's history. Such findings highlight the importance of building the context in which elections take place into our understanding of how economic conditions affect election results.

But to study these types of contextual questions thoroughly requires that the appropriate attention be paid to the methodological demands of doing so. Although it is possible to test such contextual hypotheses with cross-national data – Powell and Whitten tested their original insight by splitting their sample in two and rerunning their models on each subset separately – more nuanced studies will benefit from a methodology that allows analysts to assess support for hypotheses on an election-by-election and party-by-party basis (as was done here in the paired case studies) as well as comparatively across a larger sample of cases. Unfortunately, understanding the degree to which individual elections and parties provide support for economic voting hypotheses is more complicated with cross-national analysis where each election represents only one observation. In contrast, survey data can be used to generate estimates of the effect of the economy on the vote for numerous different parties within a given election, but it is much more difficult to compare these findings across different surveys, especially if the surveys have not been constructed for comparison and span different time periods and different countries.

This study therefore offers one methodological approach that can be used to study these types of contextual economic voting questions, which is comparative cross-regional analysis. As illustrated in Chapter 3, cross-regional analysis generates party-by-party estimates of the effect of economic conditions on the regional distribution of votes for each individual party, and in doing so facilitates case study analyses of individual elections and parties. At same time, I also have provided a method of analysis in this book for comparing these party-by-party findings across multiple cases that facilitates the more broadly based comparative assessments of support for hypotheses that form the bulk of the empirical evidence presented in the preceding chapters.

Beyond comparative cross-regional analysis, another means for producing both party-by-party estimates and more broadly based comparative studies is to rely on survey data that were explicitly designed to be used in a comparative framework. One source for such data is the increasingly popular "Barometer" surveys (e.g., the Eurobarometer, the Latinobarometer, and the Central and Eastern European Barometer) that have the advantage of asking the same questions in numerous countries. Another more costly and time-consuming option will be for researchers to design their own explicitly comparative surveys; the appropriate way in which to do so has become an important topic of late in research on political methodology.[9] But perhaps the best option for researchers without the time or resources to conduct their own surveys will be to draw on the Comparative Study of Electoral Systems (CSES) data collection, which not only contains survey data from numerous countries that are specifically designed for the analysis of voting behavior and to be compared across cases, but also comes with a common set of aggregate-level variables describing features of the election and the country in which it was held. As mentioned earlier in the text, the CSES project began too late to be incorporated into this study, but it should prove to be a very useful resource for exploring support for economic voting hypotheses (and in particular conditional economic voting hypotheses) in a comparative context in the future.[10]

In a more general sense, the conditional economic voting approaches also can suggest a theoretically based direction for future research in the field of economic voting writ large. To return to the very first table in this book (see Table 1.1), the vast majority of work on the relationship between economic conditions and elections and voting has focused almost exclusively on hammering out the most precise answer to the question found in the upper-left-hand corner of the table regarding the effect of the economy on the vote for incumbent parties. In this book, I have demonstrated that it is possible to carry out a study that explores this admittedly very important question, but that also addresses questions posed by the other three boxes in Table 1.1. For example, the primary empirical result of this study is based on an explicit comparison of the degree of empirical support for questions posed in the upper-left-hand corner of the table (the effect of the economy on incumbent parties) and the upper-right-hand corner (the effect of the economy on parties based on their "type") in Table 1.1. At the same time, the study also explored the degree of support for numerous conditional economic voting hypotheses of the type identified by the second row of the table.

---

[9] See, for example, King, Murray et al. 2004.
[10] See http://www.umich.edu/~cses/ for more details on the project, as well as access to the data.

Although it is too early to say for sure, the recent flurry of attention paid to analyzing support for the clarity of responsibility hypothesis suggests that the future development of the field will involve taking these types of conditional hypotheses seriously. Indeed, continuing to find support for economic voting hypotheses in a comparative framework may very well depend on correctly identifying the most relevant contextual factors for understanding the types of conditions under which economic conditions have a more or less systematic effect on election results. This study can play an important role in this regard by its expansion of the very concept of the conditional hypothesis, the specific conditional approaches and hypotheses introduced in the book, and the provision of at least one method for testing these types of hypotheses at both a party-by-party and more general comparative level.

Postcommunist Politics and the Stickiness of Transitional Identities

The final major substantive finding of the study identified in the opening paragraph of this chapter concerns the consistently strong empirical support for the New Regime and Old Regime hypotheses across a wide variety of contexts, or what I have referred to throughout this book as the stickiness of Transitional Identities. Of particular interest is the fact that support for both hypotheses did not diminish as the decade progressed, was apparently unaffected by the political orientation of the New Regime (populist vs. liberal) or Old Regime (reformed vs. unreformed) parties, and that even over time no distinction between the effect of the economy on these different subcategories of parties appeared.

This observation offers an important window into how people may have made sense of politics in the postcommunist era. As noted in Chapter 2, voters often faced large numbers of parties about which little was known competing for their votes in postcommunist elections, and especially in elections held earlier in the decade. The classical conception of a democratic citizen carefully weighing the pros and cons of each candidate or party was clearly not going to be appropriate in such a context, and the idea that the process could take an almost random pattern because of pervasive levels of uncertainty did not seem beyond the realm of possibility. Nevertheless, the Transitional Identity of parties does seem to have provided some guidance to economic winners and losers in casting their votes. New Regime parties and Old Regime parties systematically enjoyed greater support in areas of the country where economic conditions were better and worse, respectively, than did other types of parties.[11] This holds open the possibility that voters were motivated to seek out these types of parties and to do so in a fairly rational manner. The fact that this pattern continued throughout the decade – and in the case of New Regime parties even strengthened as the decade passed – suggests that the ability of voters to identify the Transitional Identity of parties and their willingness to rely on these identities in guiding vote choices may have provided a source of stability to politics. Thus, voters may have been able to filter the inherent uncertainty in the electoral arena through the prism of Transitional Identities in a manner that helped them to identify their preferred party in a given election. Without such a tool at their disposal, there might have been even more volatility across postcommunist elections than actually occurred.[12]

And in a larger sense, the existence of a type of party that systematically provided an outlet for economic losers' votes within the democratic system also may have contributed to the overall stability of postcommunist political society in a Huntingtonian fashion. Who knows what would have happened in Russia had the Communist Party of the Russian Federation (KPRF) not provided a democratic (or at least quasi-democratic) outlet for discontent with the economic transformation of society? This is even more apparent in the case of the reformed Old Regime parties of East-Central Europe, which continued to enjoy greater support in areas of the country

---

[11] Of the original eighty-eight parties included in the study, there were nineteen that were coded as neither a New Regime nor an Old Regime party. In addition, all of the thirty-seven parties added to the analyses for the extra parties robustness test were by definition neither Old Regime nor New Regime parties, yielding a total of fifty-six non-New Regime and non-Old Regime parties across the twenty elections for which a regional economic voting effect was estimated as part of the study. Of these fifty-six, thirteen had at least 90% of the simulations in a positive direction and thirteen had at least 90% of the simulations in a negative direction (leaving a majority of cases in which there was not strong confidence in a regional economic voting effect in either direction). Put another way, this sample of cases would provide absolutely no empirical support for a hypothesis that predicted that these "other" (non-New Regime and non-Old Regime) parties would perform better in parts of the country where the economy was better, nor would it provide any support for a hypothesis predicting that these "other" parties would perform better in parts of the country where economic conditions were worse. With equal numbers of parties surpassing the threshold in both directions, there is simply no consistent regional economic voting pattern across these cases. By contrast, twenty-five New Regime parties surpassed the 90% threshold in the positive direction as compared to only one in the negative direction. Similarly, twenty-one Old Regime parties surpassed the 90% threshold in the negative direction as compared to only one in the positive direction (see Table 8.1).

[12] For studies of electoral volatility in postcommunist countries, see Powell 2004 and Tavits 2005.

with larger concentrations of economic losers even as they remained com-mitted to democratization, European integration, and, in many cases, eco-nomic reform. By simultaneously providing an outlet for those dissatisfied with the state of the economy without acting to dismantle the changes implemented in the postcommunist era when in power, these types of par-ties may have helped provide valuable time for democratic consolidation to take hold, especially in East-Central Europe. At the same time, the funda-mental paradox inherent in such a task may help explain the recent collapse in support for the Democratic Left Alliance in Poland and the surprising resurgence of the unreformed Communist Party of Bohemia and Moravia in the Czech Republic.

The stickiness of Transitional Identities also highlights the role that dra-matic events in history can play in shaping the politics that follow them. In Chapter 3, the role of the American Civil War in structuring regional support for political parties in the United States for nearly a century after the war's conclusion was noted. Although it is far too early to claim effects of a similar duration for the transition away from communism, the fact that the effect of economic conditions on the vote for New Regime par-ties became even more consistent as the decade progressed, even in the face of parties collapsing, merging, and being reinvented anew, and that the empirical support for the Old Regime hypothesis was so consistently strong throughout the decade – even among reformed and incumbent Old Regime parties – certainly suggests that the relationship between parties and the transition continued to play an important role throughout at least the first decade of postcommunist elections. How long this pattern is likely to continue, however, remains an open question to which I turn in the following section.

Long-Term Future of the Transitional Identity Model

One of most the vexing questions facing the larger field of "transition studies" is how one will know that the transition has been completed.[13] Similarly, when are models designed for a "transitional context" no longer appropriate? Recognizing the difficulty in providing an *a priori* answer to

---

[13] Again, this statement is made with all of the caveats listed when the term was introduced in the first chapter. Readers particularly interested in the topic of when the transition will be over should see the provocative essay by John Mueller entitled "Democracy, Capitalism, and the End of Transition" (Mueller 1996).

either of these questions, I consciously built this question into the study in the guise of the time-based conditional economic voting hypotheses. To the extent that the standard hypotheses were transition specific, this provided an opportunity for testing the degree to which empirical support for these hypotheses decreased as time passed. Had there been strong empirical support for such hypotheses early in the decade but declining support as the decade progressed, then one could have put this forward as evidence of the declining usefulness of a transition-inspired theory.[14] However, as was repeatedly illustrated in the preceding chapters, there was no support for the prediction that empirical support for either model would diminish over the course of the decade. Nevertheless, how long we might expect to see political behavior continue to revolve around the transitional identities of parties remains an important and interesting question. On the one hand, political behavior in the southern United States continued to be influenced by the Civil War for at least a century after the conclusion of that event. And this study demonstrates that insofar as regional economic voting is concerned, transitional identities were clearly important throughout the first decade of postcommunist elections in the five countries examined.

On the other hand, however, it may be the case that the overall instability of party systems in postcommunist countries renders this question moot as both New Regime and Old Regime parties start to fade from the political scene in increasing numbers of countries. The case in which this is most apparent is in Poland. Following the 1997 Polish parliamentary elections, the government was formed by a coalition of two New Regime parties, the Solidarity Electoral Action (AWS) and the Freedom Union (UW). After a difficult four years in office, neither one of these parties was even returned to the parliament, let alone the government, following the 2001 Polish parliamentary election. Instead, the Old Regime Democratic Left Alliance (SLD) again returned to power. However, during its time in office the SLD has essentially self-destructed as well, including defections from its own members of parliament to set up a new rival social democratic party; polling data as of the summer of 2005 suggest that the party may not even make it into the next parliament. However, it is not the UW and AWS that are poised to benefit most from this collapse, but, rather, a set of new parties that appeared for the first time to contest the 2001 parliamentary elections. This of course raises serious challenges for continuing to code parties according

---

[14] Although it is far from clear what the end of specific patterns of regional economic voting would actually symbolize about a country's path away from transitional status.

to the categories of the Transitional Identity Model. Although some of these new parties clearly have roots in the original New Regime parties, it is obviously a stretch to claim that a party founded ten years after the transition could have its primary identity rooted in the transition itself. One possibility would be to theorize about regional economic voting and "second generation" New Regime parties, but this is only going to stretch the theoretical arguments further and further.

Russia in the twenty-first century also presents an interesting challenge for the Transitional Identity Model. In Chapter 6, I noted that New Regime parties in Russia were identified either based on links to the original young reformers surrounding President Yeltsin, or the "party of power" that was associated with the president. However, to the extent that Putin in recent years has taken steps to return elements of Soviet rule, it will become harder and harder to justify whether the "party of power" really stands for the world that emerged after the transition. Clearly this was the case with Russia's Choice and Our Home is Russia, but is it still the case with Unified Russia, the successor party to both Unity and Fatherland-All Russia? Although Putin's scaling back of transitional changes have to date been more political than economic, it may become harder to justify a hypothesis that economic winners would turn to Putin or Putin's party following the Yukos affair.[15] Additionally, Russia also has seen a recent collapse of its primary Old Regime party, the Communist Party of the Russian Federation (KPRF), which received less than 13% of the vote in the 2003 Russian parliamentary election. Like the Polish SLD, some have even predicted that the KPRF could fail to return to the parliament following the next round of parliamentary elections. Thus, Russia, too, may no longer have important New Regime or Old Regime parties by the latter part of the second decade of postcommunist elections.

At the other end of the spectrum, however, is Hungary. Here, the primary political players are still the same New Regime and Old Regime parties as in the 1990s. Following the 2002 Hungarian parliamentary election, the Old Regime Hungarian Socialist Party (MSzP) and the New Regime Alliance for Free Democrats (SzDSz) returned to power, with the New Regime Fidesz-MPP becoming the largest opposition party. And despite various ups and

---

[15] I refer here to the events surrounding the levying of a massive back tax bill on the Yukos company (currently over $25 billion), the imprisonment of its principal shareholder Mikhail Khodorkovsky, and the December 2004 forced sale of its core asset, the oil-producing Yugaskneftegaz.

downs in their popularity and the mid-term replacement of Prime Minister Peter Medgessy by Ferenc Gyurcsany, neither the MSzP nor Fidesz-MPP show any sign of yielding their leadership positions on either the left or right side of the Hungarian political spectrum anytime soon. This suggests there will be opportunities to continue testing the Transitional Identity Model in Hungary for at least the near future. As an aside, the question of why the Hungarian party system has remained so stable relative to some of the other countries included in this study, and in particular relative to Poland, is an excellent subject for future research.

The Czech Republic is similar to Hungary insofar as its primary New Regime party, the Civic Democratic Party (ODS), and its primary Old Regime party, the Communist Party of Bohemia and Moravia (KSČM), both continue to play important roles in the Czech political process. Unlike in Hungary, however, both are currently in the opposition, as a party that is neither a New Regime nor an Old Regime party, the Czech Social Democratic Party (CSSD) has led the governing coalition for the past six years. However, the KSČM, which has never served in government, is currently enjoying some of its highest levels of popularity of the postcommunist period after receiving over 18% of the vote in the 2002 parliamentary elections. In fact, as of July 2005, the ODS was the most popular party in the country and the KSČM was only percentage points behind the ruling CSSD for second place.[16] This suggests that the next election, currently scheduled for 2006, might actually feature a New Regime and an Old Regime party as the two most popular parties for the first time since 1992. So like Hungary, the Czech Republic may offer continued opportunities for testing the Transitional Identity Model in the future.

Somewhere in between the Hungarian and Polish examples lies the case of Slovakia. The 1998 Slovak parliamentary election resulted in a four-party coalition coming to power. The lead member of this coalition, the Slovak Democratic Coalition (SDK), the party of Prime Minister Mikuláš Dzurinda, was itself a coalition of a number of different parties aimed at keeping Vladimír Meciar and his Movement for Democratic Slovakia political party out of power. The SDK was coded as a New Regime party because

---

[16] According to a July 2005 public opinion poll conducted by the STEM Polling Agency, the ODS was supported by 32% of voters, the CSSD by 21%, and the KSČM by 17%. Moreover, this was the first time that the CSSD had been ahead of the KSČM since October, 2004. The junior members of the coalition, the Christian Democratic Union and the Freedom Union, were supported by just 7% and 1% of voters, respectively. See http://www.ceskenoviny.cz/vyhledavani/index_view.php?id=139716 for more details.

it contained the two New Regime parties (the Democratic Union and the Democratic Party) that contested the 1994 Slovak election. However, by the time of the 2002 parliamentary election, the coalition had dissolved into its constituent parts, with the primary successor being the Slovak Democratic and Christian Union (SDKU), which was headed by Prime Minister Dzurinda. As many of the members of the SDK (including prominent government minister) joined the SDKU, a case could certainly be made for coding the SDKU as a New Regime party. However, doing so would require rethinking the requirement that Christian democratic parties not be coded as a New Regime parties, a point complicated by the fact that Slovakia already had a traditional Christian democratic party called the Christian Democratic Movement (KDH). Moreover, the 2002 parliamentary election also featured the emergence of two new political parties that finished third and fifth in the election. The smaller of these, the Alliance of the New Citizen (ANO, which is "yes" in Slovak), joined the new government and was arguably the most neoliberal of any of the parties in the Slovak parliament. Thus, Slovakia again raises the possibility of thinking about second-generation New Regime parties along the lines of the Polish example. So it is conceivable that both ANO and SDKU could be coded as some sort of second-generation New Regime parties, or one could decide that Slovakia no longer had any New Regime parties.[17] So although Slovakia could still possibly provide opportunities for testing the New Regime hypothesis, the political evolution of the party system significantly complicates matters.

Similarly to Poland, it seemed that Old Regime parties could also disappear from the political scene in Slovakia. Following the 2002 parliamentary election, the Slovak reformed Old Regime party, the Party of the Democratic Left (SDL'), which had been a member of the 1998–2002 coalition government, failed to make it into the parliament for the first time since Slovakia's independence, receiving less than 2% of the popular vote. The SDL' never recovered from this setback, and at the end of 2004 the remnants of the party merged with the now-dominant center-left party Smer.[18]

---

[17] In some ways, this would be ironic given the substantial recent progress on economic reform in Slovakia; the World Bank even recognized Slovakia as "the country that had made the most progress in reforming its business environment in 2003" (Katzman 2004, 8).

[18] For a rather depressing visualization of what happens when a once vibrant party collapses, see the SDL' Web site (http://www.sdl.sk), which as of the summer of 2005 is still up but has all of its links deactivated. Moreover, if you click on the party name, it takes you to the Smer Web site. Had the SDL' and Smer merged on more equal grounds, it could raise the possibility of a second-generation Old Regime party, but at the time of the merger Smer

However, the unreformed Communist Party of Slovakia (KSS) secured parliamentary representation for the first time "with support mainly from the impoverished regions of eastern Slovakia, where the unemployment rate often tops 30%" (Katzman 2002, 8). So the next Slovak election will still likely present an opportunity for testing the Old Regime hypothesis, but on an unreformed Old Regime party as opposed to a reformed one.

So it may be that in certain postcommunist countries, labels such as New Regime and Old Regime are largely ready to yield to more traditional designations such as left and right. Still, it should be noted that many of the same problems discussed in Chapter 2 in coding parties in these terms that existed in the first decade of postcommunist elections will persist well into the second, especially for the new parties that have emerged during this decade. But even setting aside the degree to which country-by-country political developments affect opportunities for continued testing of the Transitional Identity Model, there also may be good theoretical reasons for abandoning the New Regime and Old Regime categories if another dramatic event occurs that leads to a reorientation of the parties that economic winners and losers perceive to be acting in their interest. The most likely event to play this role in the case of the four East-Central European countries included in this study is the recent accession of these countries to the European Union. Recall that the rationale underlying the Old Regime hypothesis was that Old Regime parties were distinguished from other parties because they were the only type of party with which voters could concretely associate a different set of economic circumstances. Although it is difficult to imagine that the accession of these countries to the European Union will have as profound an effect on economic life as did the transition away from communism, it seems quite reasonable to assume both that some citizens will find their personal economic situation deteriorating in the aftermath of accession to the European Union and that economic losers could blame membership in the European Union for their personal economic situation (even if they would have been doing poorly had their country not joined the European Union). Post–European Union accession elections might then feature a different type of party appealing to economic losers, namely, those parties that opposed membership from the outset. And although voters might not have the same ability to identify these parties with a concrete set of economic

was the most popular party at the country with the support of approximately 25% of the population, whereas the SDL', in contrast, barely moved above the 2% level of support throughout 2003 and 2004 (Butorova, Gyarfasova, and Velšic 2005, Table 8).

circumstances in the manner of the Old Regime parties, the parties could similarly be distinguished by their perceived credibility in their willingness to fight against the new supposedly European Union–inflicted economic pain.[19]

Had the debate over European Union membership in these countries simply been another manifestation of the split between New Regime and Old Regime parties, then these types of developments would not unto themselves suggest the possibility of any fundamental change in regional economic voting patterns. But because of the fairly widespread consensus across most mainstream political elites on the advantages of European Union membership, most overt opposition to membership came from the fringes of the political spectrum.[20] To take Poland as an example, the primary opposition to European Union membership came from the League of Polish Families, a far-right Catholic party, and Self-Defense of the Republic of Poland, a sort of radical populist party.[21] Therefore, if the scenario unfolds of anti–European Union parties replacing Old Regime parties as the preferred choice among the more economically worse off – and note that as discussed in Chapter 6 nationalist parties clearly did not play this role in the 1990s – then the consequences for East-Central European politics in the coming years may be significant. And indeed, in the June 2004 European Union parliamentary elections, the first election held following Poland's accession to the European Union, the League of Polish Families and Self-Defense of the Republic of Poland, practically nonexistent on the Polish political scene in 1990s, finished second and fourth, respectively, winning over a quarter of the total vote combined.[22] In contrast, the unreformed Czech Old Regime party, the KSČM, untainted by support for European

---

[19] And there has been strong cross-national evidence found on the individual level of a link between disenchantment with one's own personal economic situation and opposition to European Union membership; see Tucker, Pacek, and Berinsky 2002.

[20] Perhaps anticipating the possibility of the effects that I am describing, as the actual referenda on membership approached, some right-of-center parties – most specifically the Civic Democratic Party in the Czech Republic and Fidesz-MPP in Hungary – began offering some qualified opposition to the manner in which their countries were entering the European Union, but this remains far from outright opposition. Moreover, while in power, both parties had clearly participated in moving their countries along the accession process.

[21] For more details, see Markowski and Tucker 2005.

[22] The League of Polish Families received 15.92% of the vote and Self-Defense of the Republic of Poland received 10.78% (Obwieszczenie Państwowej Komisji Wyborczej z dnia 15 czerwca 2004 r. o wynikach wyborów posłów do Parlamentu Europejskiego przeprowadzonych w dniu 13 czerwca 2004 r., Państwowej Komisji Wyborczej).

Union membership, continues to enjoy the aforementioned resurgence in popularity.

As a final note, all of these developments highlight the fact that the presence (or absence) of patterns of regional economic voting in postcommunist countries has little to reveal about the prospect of a successful democratic consolidation in a country over time. As this study demonstrates, patterns of regional economic voting can in fact be found in Russia in the 1990s, and this certainly has not prevented the Putin administration from taking anti-democratic steps in Russia. Conversely, the fact that there was little support for the New Regime or Incumbency hypotheses in Slovakia did not prevent the resurgence of pro-democratic forces in that country following the 1998 parliamentary elections. Nor did the presence of strong empirical support for both the New Regime and Old Regime hypotheses in Poland prevent the emergence of corruption scandal after corruption scandal in that country. The fate of the overall democratization process in postcommunist countries clearly rests on much larger foundations than whether or not citizens vote in a manner consistent with the predictions of either the Referendum or Transitional Identity Models. Nevertheless, the study is still able to contribute to many of the outstanding debates in the general literature on postcommunist politics, and it is to this topic that I turn in the following section.

The Postcommunist Politics Literature

In this section, I address four of the primary areas in which my study contributes to general debates in the literature on postcommunist politics: the extent to which mass political behavior has developed stable patterns that are linked to theories from other subfields of political science; the ways in which the communist experience has influenced developments in the postcommunist era; the manner in which communist successor parties have affected political behavior; and finally the role of uncertainty in affecting both political outcomes and theory building in the postcommunist world.

One of the overriding questions in postcommunist politics has been the degree to which stable patterns of political behavior can be identified. Many factors obviously complicate any claims of stability in postcommunist political life, especially the short life spans of many political parties. It is easy to lay blame for these patterns on the citizens who choose to vote a party into office in one election and then to not even provide that party with enough votes to make it back into the parliament in the following election. My study, however, suggests that despite a layer of instability and rapid flux at the highest levels of postcommunist politics, there may be a good deal of underlying stability at the mass political level. Namely, certain types of parties are overwhelmingly more likely than other types of parties to benefit in parts of the country where economic conditions are either stronger or weaker. The difference between Old Regime parties and New Regime parties is striking in this regard. Across ten years and five countries, twenty-five out of forty New Regime parties performed better in areas of the country where economic conditions were stronger, whereas only one out of twenty-nine Old Regime parties followed this pattern. Similarly, twenty-one out of twenty-nine Old Regime parties performed better in areas of the country where economic conditions were worse, whereas only one out of the forty New Regime parties did so. Regardless of what microlevel logic ultimately underlies this pattern – I have suggested a logic here based on economic rationality, but there may be others at work as well[23] – the fact remains that for countries undergoing such dramatic simultaneous political and economic transitions, this is a somewhat remarkable degree of aggregate-level stability. In identifying such patterns, this book joins such important previous books as Colton's *Transitional Citizens* (Russia) and Tworzecki's *Learning to Choose* (Poland, Hungary, Czech Republic) in pointing to the existence of theoretically based patterns of at least somewhat stable electoral behavior in the first decade of postcommunist elections and voting.

My study also joins these works and others in highlighting the value of directly linking theoretical work in the postcommunist arena to work from other areas of political science.[24] For many years, the study of the communist world was in part defined in opposition to the study of politics in

---

[23] For example, it is possible that Old Regime and New Regime parties, recognizing their early advantage in more economically disadvantaged/advantaged areas of the country, also chose to concentrate more political resources in those parts of the country. Were this the case, we also would have a political explanation for the voting patterns in addition to the economic-based explanations put forward in this book – although by no means would this necessarily exclude the fact that the economic mechanisms I have posited also were at work – but it would not change the fact that the relationships identified at the aggregate level by my analyses are still present. No matter what the microlevel mechanism at work, the aggregate level consistency of the regional economic voting patterns predicted by the Transitional Identity Model is an empirical fact. And to the extent that such consistency is counterintuitive, this fact remains interesting in itself.

[24] For examples from other substantive areas, see Fish's *Democracy from Scratch* and his adaptation of the civil society theoretical framework to Russia, which he labels not a "civil society" but a "movement society" (Fish 1995b, especially Chapter 3) and Frye's *Brokers and Bureaucrats*, in which he builds off of and augments the general literature on institutions and social

established democracies. In recent years, as transitions have brought aspects of democracy and democratization to the postcommunist world, this wall has started to come down. However, this is obviously a nuanced process; merely transporting theories wholesale into new contexts is likely to cause as many problems as it solves. So similar to Colton's attempt in *Transitional Citizens* to refashion the "funnel of causality" from the *New American Voter* (Miller and Shanks 1996) to take account of differences between the United States and Russia, I modified the idea of partisan approaches to economic voting to create the Transitional Identity Model. Additionally, this study highlights the importance of taking the appropriateness of data in different contexts seriously. In the United States, there are enough observations and enough confidence in the comparability of these data that single-country time-series analyses of national election results can be conducted. In the postcommunist context, this is not the case, which has led to the growing popularity of studies of what I have labeled regional economic voting.[25] But the basic concept – that the state of the economy can affect variation in election results – is one that is clearly portable across different levels of experience with democracy. Thus, the study can be considered additional evidence of both the value that existing theory can play in structuring studies of postcommunist politics and, at the same time, the way in which studies of postcommunist politics can contribute to the mainstream political science literature.

The strong empirical support for the Transitional Identity Model also allows the study to make a contribution to the path dependence versus *tabula rasa* debate that has been a common theme in the postcommunist politics literature. On the one hand, some have argued that the transition represented an opportunity for politics to begin completely anew, with future political and economic development to be shaped by the choices of actors and the institutions they create. On the other hand, others have argued that the *tabula rasa* analogy is off mark, with politics in the postcommunist era being to a large extent a function of the legacies of the communist era. Most recent scholarship has operated on the assumption that the truth most likely lies somewhere in between these extremes – and indeed involves an interaction between past legacies and contemporary developments – but the challenge has been to identify exactly how the past matters. Numerous

order as part of his analysis of the attempts of five emerging markets to govern themselves in Russia in the early 1990s (Frye 2000, especially Chapter 2).

[25] See the work cited in Chapter 1, note 25.

important works have attempted to answer this question in different ways. In one of the most ambitious examples, Kitschelt, Mansfeldova, Markowski, and Toka in *Post-Communist Party Systems* link variation in different modes of communist rule – what they label as either bureaucratic-authoritarian communism, national accommodative communism, or patrimonial communism – to the form of emergence from communist rule, the electoral rules and government institutional design chosen following this emergence, and ultimately the nature of the postcommunist party system.[26] In *Post-Socialist Pathways*, Stark and Bruszt apply this approach to economic change, explicitly linking what they call different "paths of extrication from state socialism" in conjunction with "the preceding differences in social structure and political organization that brought them about" to variation in privatization strategies.[27] In the post-Soviet context, Jones Luong's *Institutional Change and Political Continuity in Post-Soviet Central Asia* highlights the role that the Soviet institutional legacy played in affecting elites' perceptions of their interests and relative strength in negotiating postcommunist electoral systems.[28]

Following in these traditions, one could conceptualize the Referendum Model as more in line with the *tabula rasa* approach and the Transitional Identity Model as more rooted in the argument that the communist past matters. As discussed in Chapter 2, the Referendum Model is based on the idea that the slate has been wiped so clean that the only information voters are likely to posses about parties and their relationship to economic outcomes is which parties are in the government and which parties are out

---

[26] See Kitschelt, Manfeldova et al. 1999, especially Chapter 1 and Table 1.1.

[27] Stark and Bruszt 1998. See especially Chapter 3; quotes in the text are from page 101.

[28] Tworzecki's *Learning to Choose* (discussed earlier) and Grzymała-Busse's *Redeeming the Communist Past* (discussed later) also ground their studies to a significant extent in efforts to understand how the communist past affected postcommunist political developments. Tworzecki focuses in particular on the role of the past in structuring contemporary societal cleavages (see Chapter 2, and especially the summary on pages 71–3), whereas Grzymała-Busse highlights the importance of what she calls "communist practice" – this includes patterns of elite recruitment and the extent to which communist elites negotiated with society – in the communist era in determining the fates of communist successor parties in the postcommunist era (see Chapter 1, and especially the model summary on pages 9–10). Another book sure to make an important contribution to this literature is Jason Wittenberg's forthcoming *Crucibles of Political Loyalties*, in which he argues that in Hungary, local religious institutions at a parish level played an important role in transmitting right-wing political loyalties from the precommunist period to the postcommunist era (Wittenberg 2006). For more general discussions of the topic, see Johnson 2001; Kopstein 2003; and Wittenberg 2003.

of the government. In contrast, the Transitional Identity Model assumes that voters associate parties either with the communist era (the Old Regime parties) or with the extrication from the communist era (the New Regime parties). Empirically, the study therefore demonstrates a very concrete way in which the communist past affects political behavior in the postcommunist present: regional economic voting patterns take the exact opposite forms for Old Regime and New Regime parties. Moreover, these regional economic voting patterns differ in both cases from parties that are neither Old Regime nor New Regime parties (see note 11 of this chapter). In contrast, the lack of support for the Incumbency hypothesis – and the fact that so much of the variation in support for the Incumbency hypothesis can be explained by the Transitional Identity of incumbent parties – casts renewed doubt on the *tabula rasa* approach. Taken together, I offer a specific example of exactly how the hand of the past reaches forward to have an effect on political behavior in the postcommunist era, and as such help to identify another way in which the current political environment is in part a product of both the communist era and the transition itself.[29] In this manner, the work also builds on the example put forward by Kitschelt et al. in *Post-Communist Party Systems* by demonstrating how the communist past and the postcommunist present can interact to shape an environment in which political behavior can be both consistent and rationally structured.

As mentioned earlier in this book, the fate of communist successor parties, or what I have labeled Old Regime parties, has attracted a good deal of attention in the postcommunist politics literature. The contributions of this particular subfield are too numerous to be recounted here; interested readers are especially encouraged to see Grzymała-Busse's *Redeeming the Communist Past* on the experience of communist successor parties in Poland, Hungary, Slovakia and the Czech Republic, Urban and Solovei's *Russia's Communists at the Crossroads* on Russia, Bozóki and Ishiyama's edited volume *The Communist Successor Parties of Central and Eastern Europe*, and Curry and Urban's edited volume *The Left Transformed in Post-Communist Societies*. However, one important theme of this literature has been the question of the different fates of reformed and unreformed communist successor parties, or what I have labeled reformed and unreformed Old Regime parties.

---

[29] Moreover, the role of the past can be seen on the right-hand side of the equation as well, to the extent that current variation in regional economic conditions is a function of decisions made during the communist era (although such variation is also clearly a result of decisions made since the beginning of the transition period).

More often than not, the focus of this literature has been on the differences between these two types of Old Regime parties. Grzymała-Busse, for example, demonstrates the factors that led to the emergence of reformed (or what she labels "regenerated") successor parties in Hungary, Poland, and, to a lesser extent, Slovakia, as opposed to the unreformed successor party in the Czech Republic, as well as the consequences of these paths for parties' abilities to generate broad national appeals and function effectively in parliament and in government. Similarly, Bozóki and Ishiyama largely organize their edited volume around the question of understanding "*variation* concerning how the communist successor parties have adapted to the fundamentally altered political environment of the post-cold war era" (Bozóki and Ishiyama 2002, 4, emphasis added).

In contrast, I have identified an element of similarity between the different types of communist successor parties. As documented in Chapter 7 and highlighted earlier in this chapter, regional economic voting patterns are extremely similar across both reformed and unreformed Old Regime parties. In both cases, there is strong empirical evidence in roughly the same proportion of cases that these parties enjoy greater electoral success in parts of the country where economic conditions are worse. So although the reformed parties may have generally proved more successful at attracting widespread support – at least in East-Central Europe in the 1990s – the effect of regional variation in economic conditions on the regional variation in support for these parties was quite similar. Although this observation highlights an area of similarity across two categories that are generally noted for their differences, I want to be clear that I am not presenting this as evidence that contrasts with that of earlier studies. In no way am I claiming that communist successor parties have not adapted to the postcommunist era differently, nor that these choices did not have important consequences for both the parties themselves and the political systems of which they are a part. Instead, it complements these many works by highlighting a less studied area – that of regional economic voting – in which the mass reaction to these types of parties has been more consistent across the reformed and unreformed categories.

Finally, one of the overriding concerns about understanding politics in the postcommunist era has been how to conceptualize the presence of uncertainty. Perhaps the most commonly cited piece on the topic is Bunce and Csanadi's 1993 *East European Politics and Society* article, "Uncertainty in Transition: Post Communism in Hungary." The question of how to correctly account for uncertainty in studies of transition politics is certainly a tricky one. On the one hand, everyone knows that uncertainty was a pervasive feature of the post-communist landscape. On the other hand, how exactly should this factor be incorporated into theories and arguments? One approach is to include it as a kind of an underlying null hypothesis, offering an omnipresent reason why we might not find support for logically consistent hypotheses. Another option is to leave it as a residual category: if I expect X and instead find half of X, then the missing half is due to uncertainty. Ultimately, both of these approaches are somewhat unsatisfying. Just because we can find support for a hypothesis concerning political behavior does not falsify Bunce and Csandi's fundamental claim that postcommunist politics – and especially early postcommunist politics – are likely to be greatly affected by uncertainty. Similarly, to simply chalk up the failure of hypotheses to underlying uncertainty does not prove the uncertainty argument either.

In this book, I have attempted to address the question of uncertainty more head-on, embracing as a fundamental feature of the postcommunist political landscape by building it directly into the models.[30] Uncertainty plays the strongest role in the Referendum Model, in which voters are assumed to have no useful information about parties. But it also plays an important role in the Transitional Identity Model, in which uncertainty over parties' likely behavior in office pushes voters toward assumptions based on parties' identity as New Regime or Old Regime parties. Moreover, a number of the conditional economic voting hypotheses in this book also rely at least somewhat on uncertainty. This is most clear in the case of the over-time hypotheses, but is also present in the hypotheses regarding the effects of the economy on different variants of New Regime and Old Regime parties.

The evidence from the study regarding the importance of uncertainty is mixed. The model placing the greatest emphasis on uncertainty, the Referendum Model, is not particularly well supported by the empirical data. However, the Transitional Identity Model, which is well supported by the data, also heavily relies on uncertainty to motivate its focus on partisan "type," or, more specifically, the Transitional Identity of parties. Furthermore, the fact that the empirical evidence in support of both the New Regime and Old Regime hypotheses is so consistent across time and different variants of New Regime and Old Regime parties also suggests that

---

[30] I am certainly not alone in being explicit about trying to build uncertainty into models of postcommunist political behavior; see in particular Stark and Bruszt 1998, Chapter 1; Colton 2000b, Chapter 1; and Jones Luong 2002, Chapter 2, for examples.

the issue of uncertainty was not merely a one-off feature of the first set of competitive elections in postcommunist countries.

Regional Economic Voting and Patterns of National Election Results

Finally, it is always tempting in studies of economic voting that focus their level of analysis at either the micro or regional level to attempt to extrapolate conclusions about national election results from one's findings. After all, as much as we may be interested in the various factors that either motivate individuals to vote or account for subnational distributions of aggregate-level results, much of our interest in elections stems from a desire to know why certain parties win elections and certain parties lose them. Clearly, that has not been the focal point of this study, for the myriad of reasons raised early in this book.

Nevertheless, I have often been asked what I think the implications of the study are for understanding patterns of national election results. Given the fact that different factors affect the distribution of votes at the regional level and the overall support a party receives in that election – for example, a scandal could seriously hurt the overall vote for a particular party without having any impact on the regional distribution of votes – I have consciously avoided any discussion of the findings of this study in terms of national election results for most of this book. However, in the spirit of merely raising interesting questions for future research, I turn to this topic now in this final section. I do so admittedly with trepidation, and only with the strong hope that readers will treat these observations merely as speculation and not as demonstrated results of any empirical analysis. Just as I have noted repeatedly that empirical tests of regional economic voting can neither confirm nor falsify the microlevel arguments put forth to justify the aggregate-level hypotheses, the same holds for variation in cross-national results. The fact that Old Regime parties tend to perform better in areas of the country where economic conditions are worse would be perfectly consistent with a finding that Old Regime parties enjoy more national support in elections in which national economic conditions are worse, but it does not demonstrate that this is in fact the case.[31] The same holds for the New Regime and Incumbency hypotheses.

---

[31] That being said, the only published paper of which I am aware to assess the impact of economic conditions on election results in the postcommunist context using a cross-national

With these very important caveats in mind, let me suggest a number of facets of the postcommunist electoral experience at the national level that could be illuminated if indeed some of the hypotheses put forward in this book also hold in terms of explaining variation in national election results. Perhaps most fundamentally, the consistent support for the Old Regime hypothesis provides one explanation for why, in so many countries, communist successor parties came to be the dominant opposition during the 1990s to the forces that came to power in the aftermath of the collapse of communism. Although from our current vantage point this development seems almost a foregone conclusion, in 1989 such a scenario could have seemed very unlikely; recall that in the 1989 Polish parliamentary elections, the ruling communist party (the Polish United Worker's Party) lost practically every single seat that was legitimately contested.[32] Moreover, as noted in Chapter 7, the Weimarization of the postcommunist experience was suggested as one possible future for the region. But as the 1990s progressed, in country after country Old Regime parties emerged to play an important role in postcommunist politics. Concurrently, although the patterns differed from country to country, the transition to a market economy did lead to an initial deterioration in economic conditions involving falling GDP, rising unemployment and inflation, and the emergence in many cases of widescale poverty. In this book, a clear link at the regional level between better performance for Old Regime parties and worse economic conditions was repeatedly demonstrated across a variety of different contexts. Whether or not the deterioration of economic conditions on the national level also explains why communist successor parties came to play such an import role in so many postcommunist countries in the 1990s cannot be demonstrated by the data I have analyzed, but it is certainly consistent with the regional level patterns observed.[33]

data set (seventeen parliamentary elections from seven Eastern European countries) does in fact find a more systematic effect for economic conditions on "types" of parties (in this case, what the author labels pro-reform and left wing plus nationalist) than on incumbent parties. See Fidrmuc 2000b, Table 4.

[32] The magnitude of this defeat cannot be overstated. The opposition Solidarity movement won ninety-nine of the one hundred Senate seats and all 161 contested seats in the lower house of the parliament. See Heyns and Bialecki 1991, 354, and Biskupski 2000, 171, for details, as well as Ash 1993, 25–46, for an illuminating description of the shock these results produced.

[33] This is not to deny in any way that there were other factors at work in this process as well; in particular it seems foolish to dismiss the importance of grassroots organization in the resurgence of many Old Regime parties.

Additionally, the Transitional Identity Model helps explain perhaps the most puzzling election results at the national level from the standpoint of standard models of economic voting, which are the 1997 Polish and 1998 Hungarian parliamentary elections. As described in Chapter 4, in each country an Old Regime party had come to power in the previous election promising to improve economic conditions, the economy had improved, and the party was then voted out of office.[34] Through the prism of a traditional incumbency based approach, such results appear startling. However, in light of findings supporting the Transitional Identity Model at the regional level, the proposition that an increasing number of economic winners across the entire country could benefit New Regime parties more than Old Regime parties seems quite reasonable. Indeed, approached from this perspective, the late decade election results from across all five countries included in the study seem to reflect a pattern of strong performances for New Regime parties – especially relative to the previous round of elections – at a time when overall economic conditions also were generally improving.[35]

There is another way to interpret the national level results suggested by the consistent support for the Old Regime hypothesis at the regional level. Assume that in general, by the end of the communist era, most citizens were not particularly enamored with their respective ruling communist parties. This seems to be a safe assumption, given the fact that people tend not to like outgoing authoritarian regimes; almost by definition, had the Old Regime party remained truly popular, it probably would not have lost power in the first place. Thus, all things being equal, we can assume that many citizens of postcommunist countries would prefer not to vote for Old Regime parties and not to have former communists ruling their country.

Nevertheless, suppose that there is a grudging acceptance that the communists were, at times, competent managers. They made sure everyone had a roof over his or her head, a job, health care, and education. These are

---

[34] Although, as was noted in Chapter 4, the Hungarian Old Regime party (the Hungarian Socialist Party) received practically the same proportion of the vote as in the previous election, and the Polish Old Regime party (the Democratic Left Alliance) saw its proportion of the overall vote increase. So, on closer observation, the puzzle is perhaps not as puzzling as it first appears, although by American "It's the Economy, Stupid!" standards, both parties should have been returned to office with substantial victories.

[35] I include the 1998 Czech parliamentary elections in this category because although the Civic Democratic Party (ODS) lost control of the government following the election, it still greatly exceeded expectations from even a few months earlier in light of a series of scandals and defections from the party; see note 10 in Chapter 6 for more details.

not trivial accomplishments, and they most likely grow in stature once the New Regime parties come to power and unleash a host of economic ills on a population that is expecting a capitalist paradise overnight. As those economic ills multiply, enough people may be moved to support Old Regime parties. Something has to be done to stabilize the situation, and these Old Regime parties may seem more capable of getting the job done than other unknown alternatives. The worse the state of the economy, the more likely more people are to feel this way. This effect could easily be seen at both the regional level (more people willing to tolerate Old Regime parties in power in areas of the country where economic conditions are worse than where they are better) and at the national level (more people across the country willing to tolerate Old Regime parties when it looks like the whole country is suffering than when it looks like it is prospering).

But here is the main point that follows from the preceding logic: based on the assumptions laid out earlier, some of the people supporting the Old Regime parties will do so while holding their noses. Although they may grudgingly vote for Old Regime parties out of necessity, they may not be happy about returning former communists to power. If economic conditions improve, this sense of dissatisfaction with seeing ex-communists in power should only increase as the original actions of the reformers begin to appear to have been wise. Correspondingly, the rationale for having Old Regime parties in power – that they are qualified to deal with economic ills caused by reform – begins to disappear. The better economic conditions are, the more voters can do what they wanted to do in the first place, which is to keep the Old Regime parties out of power. From this framework, it follows quite naturally that Old Regime parties are rewarded for their economic success by being voted out of office. And, paradoxically, New Regime parties continue to reap the benefits of economic prosperity long after leaving the government. Thus, we arrive at the predictions of the Transitional Identity Model: New Regime parties benefit from strong economic conditions and Old Regime parties benefit from poor economic conditions.

What is appealing about this interpretation of over time events is that it is supported at the regional level by the empirical evidence found in the preceding chapters and that it manages to take into account the quick swing from the complete and utter rejection of communist ruling parties that occurred at the time of the collapse of communist rule to their swift reentry into mainstream democratic politics as important political players. Although it is easy for Western observers to note that the Democratic

Left Alliance in Poland or the Hungarian Socialist Party in Hungary have come to espouse pro-market policies and resemble West European Social Democratic parties, to Poles and Hungarians, many of the people in these parties may very well be seen as the same people who made their lives miserable during communist rule. And here is where the consistency of support for the Old Regime hypothesis across both reformed and unreformed Old Regime parties is so illuminating, because it demonstrates – or at least insofar as regional economic voting is concerned – that an Old Regime party remained an Old Regime party to its own citizens in the first decade out from communist rule even if it presented a different face to the rest of the world.

Before concluding this section, I want again to stress that the observations made above regarding economic causes of variation in national electoral performance by New Regime and Old Regime parties remain very much at the level of speculation. Although these observations are consistent with the findings demonstrated at the regional level, they have not been tested in the manner of the regional level relationships reported on in the previous chapters.

Final Observations

The study contained in this book will clearly not be the last word on either economic voting in new democracies or the postcommunist electoral experience. But at the same time, it does fill important gaps in both literatures. In a postcommunist politics literature that has seen many excellent studies of the effects of political factors on economic outcomes, this study reverses the arrows and demonstrates systematically across time and space how economic developments have had an impact on a fundamental component of the postcommunist political process: the manner in which votes are cast as citizens select their governments through competitive multiparty elections. Moreover, in a postcommunist elections and voting literature that has been largely dominated by single election and single country studies that attempt to assess all of the many factors that make up the voting calculus or determine a particular set of election results, this study stands in marked contrast by attempting to assess one electoral phenomenon – the degree to which economic conditions affect the distribution of votes in elections – across a wide variety of contexts, namely, twenty presidential and parliamentary elections held in five countries over a ten-year period.

This study also fills a number of important gaps in the economic voting literature. Perhaps most obviously, it is the first systematic, comparative book length analysis of the phenomenon of economic voting outside of established democracies. But beyond the actual countries being analyzed, the study also explores new substantive and theoretical territory. In both its research design and its empirical conclusions, this study highlights the fact that incumbent parties are not the only types of parties whose electoral fortunes are affected by variation in economic conditions. Although I consciously eschew making predictions about left-wing and right-wing parties in this particular book because of the peculiarities of the postcommunist context, it is not difficult to see how the arguments made concerning New Regime and Old Regime parties in a transitional context could be translated into left-wing and right-wing parties in more established democracies.[36] Moreover, the study also lays out a framework for thinking broadly not just about the type of parties affected by economic conditions (standard economic voting hypotheses) but also the context in which these effects are likely to be felt more or less consistently (conditional economic voting hypotheses). Finally, the study highlights the role that cross-regional analysis can play in identifying links between the state of the economy and the distribution of votes. Scholars have long been fascinated with the relationship between the economy and election results, and yet there have been only a handful of studies that have ever explored this relationship at the sub-national level. At a time at which more and more sub-national data are available to scholars, this would seem to be both an important and now feasible avenue for further development of the field.

Finally, it is worth emphasizing again the significance of finding stable patterns of political behavior to our understanding of the postcommunist political experience. The fact that there is such strong empirical support for the Transitional Identity Model underscores the point that across different countries, elections, and time periods, citizens behaved in a remarkably consistent way in providing more support in certain parts of the country for certain types of political parties. There obviously has been a great deal of political instability in the postcommunist world. Parties and party systems

---

[36] Moreover, there is no reason that we need to stop with traditional ideological divides. The insight also could apply to distinctions between extremist and moderate parties generally, or between other context-specific salient divisions, much in the way that "Old Regime" and "New Regime" categorizations are important for the postcommunist context.

are much, much more fluid than in stable democracies. Crises and scandals have removed parties from the entire political map, not to mention the government. And yet, across this all, in perhaps one of the most turbulent periods of political and economic development in recent history anywhere, regional economic voting patterns were remarkably consistent in the cases examined in this study. To the extent that the quality of democratic governance and representation depends on stable relations between elites and masses, much in the postcommunist political experience cautions against optimism. The empirical support for the Transitional Identity Model, by contrast, suggests some evidence of consistent political behavior – at least at the mass level – that could hopefully provide a basis for more system-wide stability in the future.

The manner in which the state of the economy affects election results has been, and will undoubtedly continue to be, of great interest to scholars and policy makers alike. In part, this is because it is one of those crucial relationships that affects democracies at all their various stages of development. Although the original literature on the relationship between economic conditions and election results emerged out of the stable two-party atmosphere of one of the world's oldest democracies, it is likely that the consequences of the economy's influence on election results are even more important in the unstable atmosphere of new democracies, and especially those that are also facing economic crises or undertaking far-reaching economic reform. Although there are undoubtedly different processes at work in these disparate contexts, at the end of the day links between the state of the economy and elections and voting are likely to be present in varied forms in all democracies. This study demonstrates that not only is it possible to look for and find these links in newer democracies, but also that doing so can add in valuable ways to our overall understanding of this substantively important and theoretically rich topic of political economy.

Appendix I

National Election Results

Table AI.1. *1992 Czech Republic Parliamentary Election*

Party	Percentage of Party List Vote	Total Seats
Civic Democratic Party	29.73	76
Left Bloc	14.05	35
Czech Social Democratic Party	6.53	16
Liberal Social Union	6.52	16
Christian Democratic Union	6.28	15
Republican Party	5.98	14
Civic Democratic Alliance	5.93	14
Movement for the Self-Government of Moravia and Silesia	5.87	14
Civic Movement	4.59	0
Other	14.52	0
Total	**100**	**200**

Source: Czechoslovak Statistical Office: Vysledky Voleb do FS a CNR 5. a 6. cervna 1992.

Table AI.2. *1996 Czech Republic Parliamentary Election*

Party	Percentage of Party List Vote	Total Seats
Civic Democratic Party	29.62	68
Czech Social Democratic Party	26.44	61
Communist Party of Bohemia and Moravia	10.33	22
Christian Democratic Union	8.08	18
Republican Party	8.01	18
Civic Democratic Alliance	6.36	13
Other	11.16	0
Total	**100**	**200**

Source: Czech Statistical Office: Volby do Poslanecke Snemovny Parlamentu Ceske Republiky v Roce 1996.

Table AI.3. *1998 Czech Republic Parliamentary Election*

Party	Percentage of Party List Vote	Total Seats
Czech Social Democratic Party	32.31	74
Civic Democratic Party	27.74	63
Communist Party of Bohemia and Moravia	11.03	24
Christian Democratic Union	9.00	20
Union of Freedom	8.60	19
Republican Party	3.90	0
Movement of Pensioners for Life Securities	3.06	0
Other	4.36	0
Total	**100**	**200**

Source: Czech Statistical Office: Volby do Poslanecke Snemovny Parlamentu Ceske Republiky v Roce 1998.

Appendix I

Table AI.4. *1990 Hungarian Parliamentary Election*

Party	Percentage of Party List Vote	Total Seats
Hungarian Democratic Forum	24.73	165
Alliance of Free Democrats	21.39	92
Independent Smallholders Party	11.73	43
Hungarian Socialist Party	10.89	33
League of Young Democrats	8.95	21
Christian Democratic People's Party	6.46	21
Hungarian Socialist Workers Party	3.68	0
Hungarian Social Democratic Party	3.55	0
Others	8.62	11
Total	**100**	**386**

Source: Hungarian Central Election Commission: Szabadon Valasztott, 1990.

Table AI.5. *1994 Hungarian Parliamentary Election*

Party	Percentage of Party List Vote	Total Seats
Hungarian Socialist Party	32.99	209
Alliance of Free Democrats	19.74	69
Hungarian Democratic Forum	11.74	38
Independent Smallholders Party	8.82	26
Christian Democratic People's Party	7.03	22
League of Young Democrats	7.02	20
Workers Party	3.19	0
Others	9.47	2
Total	**100**	**386**

Source: Hungarian Central Election Commission: Az 1994. evi orszaggyulesi kepviselovalasztasok hivtalos vegeredmenye.

Table AI.6. *1998 Hungarian Parliamentary Election*

Party	Percentage of Party List Vote	Total Seats
Hungarian Socialist Party	˙32.25	134
Fidesz-Hungarian People's Party (Fidesz-MPP)	28.18	113
Independent Smallholders Party	13.78	48
Alliance of Free Democrats	7.88	24
Hungarian Justice and Life Party	5.55	14
Workers Party	4.08	0
Hungarian Democratic Forum	3.12	2
Fidesz-MPP/Hungarian Democratic Forum*	–	50
Christian Democratic People's Party	2.59	0
Others	2.57	1
Total	**100**	**386**

* Candidates jointly nominated by Fidesz-MPP and Hungarian Democratic Forum in single member districts.

Source: Hungarian Central Election Commission: http://www.election.hu/v98stata/val98ind.htm

Table AI.7. *1990 Polish Presidential Election*

Candidate	Percentage of the Vote: Round 1	Percentage of the Vote: Round 2
Lech Wałęsa	39.4	74.25
Stanislaw Tymiński	22.7	25.75
Tadeusz Mazowiecki	17.8	
Wlodzimierz Cimoszewicz	9.1	
Roman Bartoszcze	7.0	
Leszek Moczulski	2.5	
Invalid	1.5	

Source: Polish Election Commission: Wyniki Wyborow Prezidenta Rzeczpospolitej Polskiej, 1990.

Appendix I

Table AI.8. *1991 Polish Parliamentary Election*

Party	Percentage of Party List Vote	Total Seats
Democratic Union	12.31	62
Democratic Left Alliance	11.80	60
Catholic Electoral Action	8.73	49
Polish Peasant Party	8.67	48
Confederation for an Independent Poland	7.50	46
Center Alliance	8.71	44
Liberal Democratic Congress	7.48	37
Agrarian Alliance	5.46	28
Self-Governed Solidarity Trade Union	5.05	27
Polish Party of Beer Lovers	3.27	16
German Minority	1.17	7
Others	19.85	36
Total	**100**	**460**

Source: Polish Election Commission: Wyniki Wyborow do Sejmu Rzeczypospolitej Polskiej, 27 pazdziernika 1991 r.

Table AI.9. *1993 Polish Parliamentary Election*

Party	Percentage of Party List Vote	Total Seats
Democratic Left Alliance	20.41	171
Polish Peasant Party	15.40	132
Democratic Union	10.59	74
Union of Labor	7.28	41
Confederation for an Independent Poland	5.77	22
Nonparty Bloc in Support of Reforms	5.41	16
Catholic Electoral Committee "Fatherland"	6.37	0
Self-Governed Solidarity Trade Union	4.90	0
Center Alliance	4.22	0
Congress of Liberal Democrats	3.99	0
German Minority	0.61	4
Others	15.05	0
Total	**100**	**460**

Source: Polish Election Commission: Wyniki Wyborow do Sejmu Rzeczypospolitej Polskiej, 19 wrzesnia 1993r.

Table AI.10. *1995 Polish Presidential Election*

Candidate	Percentage of the Vote: Rnd 1	Percentage of the Vote: Rnd 2
Aleksander Kwaśniewski	35.11	51.72
Lech Wałęsa	33.11	48.28
Jacek Kuroń	9.22	
Jan Olszewski	6.86	
Waldemar Pawlak	4.31	
Tadeusz Zielinski	3.53	
Hanna Gronkiewicz-Waltz	2.76	
Janusz Korwin-Mikke	2.40	
Others	2.70	

Source: Polish Election Commission: Wyniki Wyborow Prezidenta Rzeczpospolitej Polskiej, 1995.

Table AI.11. *1997 Polish Parliamentary Election*

Party	Percentage of Party List Vote	Total Seats
Solidarity Electoral Action	33.83	201
Democratic Left Alliance	27.13	164
Union of Freedom	13.37	60
Polish Peasant Party	7.31	27
Movement for the Reconstruction of Poland	5.56	6
Union of Labor	4.74	0
Party of Pensioners	2.18	0
Citizens' Union of Labor of the Republic	2.03	0
Others	3.85	2
Total	**100**	**460**

Source: Polish Election Commission: Wybory do Parlamentu Rzeczypospolitej Polskiej Sejm i Senat: Warszawa 21 IX 1997.

Table AI.12. *1991 Russian Presidential Election: Round 1*

Candidate	Percentage of the Vote
Boris Yeltsin	59.7
Nikolai Ryzhkov	17.6
Vladimir Zhirinovskii	8.1
Aman-Geldy Tuleev	7.1
Albert Makashov	3.9
Vadim Bakatin	3.6

Source: Pravda, June 20, 1991, 1, as cited in White et. al., 1997.

Appendix I

Table AI.13. *1993 Russian Parliamentary Election*

Party	Percentage of Party List Vote	Total Seats
Russia's Choice	15.51	70
Liberal Democratic Party of Russia	22.92	64
Communist Party of the Russian Federation	12.40	48
Agrarian Party	7.99	33
Yabloko	7.86	23
Women of Russia	8.13	23
Party of Russian Unity and Concord	6.76	19
Democratic Party of Russia	5.52	15
Others	12.91	8
Independents	–	141
Postponed	–	6
Total	**100**	**450**

Source: Rossiskaya Gazeta, December 28, 1993, 1, Byulleten' Tsentral'noi izbiratel'noi komissii Rossiiskoi Federatsii, no.12 (1994) as cited in White et al., 1997.

Table AI.14. *1995 Russian Parliamentary Election*

Party	Percentage of Party List Vote	Total Seats
Communist Party of the Russian Federation	22.3	157
Our Home Is Russia	10.1	55
Liberal Democratic Party of Russia	11.2	51
Yabloko	6.9	45
Agrarian Party of Russia	3.8	20
Russia's Democratic Choice	3.9	9
Power to the People!	1.6	9
Congress of Russian Communities	4.3	5
Women of Russia	4.6	3
Forward Russia	1.9	3
Communist Workers of Russia for the Soviet Union	4.5	1
Party of Workers' Self Choice	4.0	1
Others	20.9	13
Independents	–	78
Total	**100**	**450**

Source: Central Election Commission of the Russian Federation: Vybory Deputatov Gosudarstvenoy Dumi 1995.

Table AI.15. *1996 Russian Presidential Election*

Candidate	Percentage of the Vote: Round 1	Percentage of the Vote: Round 2
Boris Yeltsin	35.28	53.83
Gennadii Zyuganov	32.03	40.30
Aleksandr Lebed	14.52	
Grigorii Yavlinskii	7.34	
Vladimir Zhirinovskii	5.70	
Others	2.17	
Against All / Invalid	2.96	5.87

Source: Central Election Commission of the Russian Federation: Vybory Prezidenta Rossiiskoi Federatsii 1996.

Table AI.16. *1999 Russian Parliamentary Election*

Party	Percentage of Party List Vote	Total Seats
Communist Party of the Russian Federation	24.23	113
Inter-Regional Movement "Unity"	23.26	73
Fatherland – All Russia	13.30	68
Union of Right Forces	8.49	29
Zhirinovskii Bloc	5.97	17
Yabloko	5.92	20
Communist Workers of Russia for the Soviet Union	2.22	0
Women of Russia	2.03	0
Party of Pensioners – Russia	1.94	1
Our Home is Russia	1.18	7
Against All	3.29	–
Others	8.17	8
Independents	–	114
Total	**100**	**450**

Source: Central Election Commission of the Russian Federation (via Carnegie Endowment for International Peace, Moscow Center) for vote totals; Rose and Munroe 2003 for seat totals.

Appendix I

Table AI.17. *1992 Slovak Republic Parliamentary Election*

Party	Percentage of Party List Vote	Total Seats
Movement for a Democratic Slovakia	37.26	74
Party of the Democratic Left	14.70	29
Christian Democratic Movement	8.88	18
Slovak National Party	7.93	15
Hungarian Christian Democrats	7.42	14
Civic Democratic Union	4.03	0
Social Democratic Party of Slovakia	4.00	0
Other	15.78	0
Total	**100**	**150**

Source: Czechoslovak Statistical Office: Vysledky Voleb do FS a CNR 5. a 6. cervna 1992 and Volby do Slovenskej Narodnej Rady 5.-6 Jun 1992.

Table AI.18. *1994 Slovak Republic Parliamentary Election*

Party	Percentage of Party List Vote	Total Seats
Movement for a Democratic Slovakia	34.96	61
Common Choice Coalition	10.41	18
Hungarian Coalition	10.18	17
Christian Democratic Movement	10.08	17
Democratic Union of Slovakia	8.57	15
Union of Slovak Workers	7.34	13
Slovak National Party	5.40	9
Democratic Party	3.42	0
Communist Party of Slovakia	2.72	0
Other	6.92	0
Total	**100**	**150**

Source: Slovak Republic Statistical Office: Volby do Narodnej Rady Slovenskej Republiky konane 30.9 a 1.10.1994.

Table AI.19. *1998 Slovak Republic Parliamentary Election*

Party	Percentage of Party List Vote	Total Seats
Movement for a Democratic Slovakia	27.00	43
Slovak Democratic Coalition	26.33	42
Party of the Democratic Left	14.66	23
Hungarian Coalition	9.13	15
Slovak National Party	9.07	14
Party of Civic Understanding	8.02	13
Communist Party of Slovakia	2.80	0
Union of Slovak Workers	1.30	0
Other	1.69	0
Total	**100**	**150**

Source: Slovak Republic Statistical Office: Volby v Slovenskej republike: Volby do NR SR 1998.

Table AI.20. *1999 Slovak Republic Presidential Election*

Party	Percentage of Vote: Round 1	Percentage of Vote: Round 2
Rudolf Schuster	47.38	57.18
Vladimír Meciar	37.24	42.82
Magdaléna Vásáryová	6.60	
Ivan Mjartan	3.59	
Ján Slota	2.50	
Boris Zala	1.01	
Juraj Svec	0.82	
Juraj Lazareík	0.52	
Michal Kovác	0.18	
Ján Demikát	0.15	
Total	**100**	**100**

Source: Slovak Republic Statistical Office: Volby v Slovenskej republike: Volba prezidenta SR 1999.

Appendix II

Regression Results and Documentation

Table AII.1. *Estimated Coefficients (Standard Errors) of Effect on Party Vote for the 1992 Czech Parliamentary Election**

	ODS	ODA	OH	LB
Unemployment Rate	−.084	−.170	−.144	.003
	(.016)	(.043)	(.023)	(.018)
Change in Income	.018	.031	.015	.001
	(.005)	(.014)	(.007)	(.006)
Inflation	−.001	−.008	−.009	.006
	(.006)	(.016)	(.008)	(.006)
Industrial Growth	−.003	−.010	−.003	.001
	(.003)	(.007)	(.004)	(.003)
Percent Agriculture	−.026	−.060	−.030	−.018
	(.007)	(.020)	(.010)	(.008)
Percent Industry	−.011	−.018	−.015	−.009
	(.004)	(.010)	(.005)	(.004)
Percent Elderly	.004	.024	.008	.008
	(.006)	(.016)	(.008)	(.006)
Percent Urban	−.002	−.014	−.001	−.001
	(.003)	(.007)	(.004)	(.003)
Log Population	−.111	−.214	−.217	.19209
	(.062)	(.164)	(.086)	(.067)
Constant	.352	1.737	1.704	.358
	(1.700)	(4.529)	(2.366)	(1.837)
N	76	76	76	76

* Models estimated using seemingly unrelated regression (SUR) with logistic transformation of dependent variable.

Table AII.2. *Variables used in 1992 Czech Parliamentary Election*

Variable Name	Date	Definition	Source
Unemployment Rate	5/31/1992	Unemployment Rate	1
Change in Income	7/1/1992	Income in 1992, 1991 = 100	2
Inflation	12/31/1992	Consumer Price Index. Prices in 1992 as% of price in 1989	3
Industrial Growth	12/31/1992	Industrial sales in 1992, 1991 = 100	4
Percent Agriculture	12/31/1991	Percent of workers in agriculture	4
Percent Industry	12/31/1991	Percent of workers in industry	5
Percent Elderly	7/1/1992	Percent of elderly population (men >60, women > 55)	5
Percent Urban	12/31/1993	Percent of people living in urban areas	6
Log Population	7/1/1992	Log of population	5

Sources: (1) (1992). Aktuality CSU: 1992 Prosniec – 1.cast (Latest News of the Czech Statistical Office: December 1992 – Part I). Praha, Czech Republic, Cesky Statisticky Urad., (2) (1992). Statisticke Informace: 5 – Prace a Mzdy: Evidencni pocet, mzdove prostredky a prumerne mzdy pracovniku v Ceske republice za 2 ctvrtleti 1992. Praha, Czech Republic, Cesky Statisticky Urad. (3) (1993). Okresy Ceske Republiky v roce 1992 (Regions of the Czech Republic in 1992). Praha, Czech Republic, Cesky Statisticky Urad. (4) (1993). Okresy Ceske Republiky v roce 1992 (Regions of the Czech Republic in 1992). Praha, Czech Republic, Cesky Statisticky Urad. (5) (1993). Demographicie Vekove Slozeni Obyatlestva Ceske Republiky v roce 1992. Praha, Czech Republic, Cesky Statisticky Urad. (6) (1995) Okresy Ceske Republiky v roce 1994 (Regions of the Czech Republic in 1994). Praha, Czech Republic, Cesky Statisticky Urad.

Appendix II

Table AII.3. *Estimated Coefficients (Standard Errors) of Effect on Party Vote for the 1996 Czech Parliamentary Election*

	ODS	ODA	KDU	KSČM
Unemployment Rate	−.087	−.113	−.087	.029
	(.013)	(.021)	(.033)	(.013)
Change in Income	.001	.008	.004	.000
	(.007)	(.011)	(.018)	(.007)
Industrial Growth	−.001	.002	−.006	.001
	(.001)	(.002)	(.003)	(.001)
Percent Agriculture	−.016	−.016	.082	.003
	(.006)	(.009)	(.015)	(.006)
Percent Industry	−.005	−.005	.018	−.009
	(.003)	(.005)	(.007)	(.003)
Percent Elderly	.036	.052	.000	.007
	(.013)	(.020)	(.031)	(.012)
Percent Urban	.000	−.000	−.012	−.003
	(.002)	(.002)	(.004)	(.001)
Log Population	.050	.099	.806	−.069
	(.047)	(.073)	(.115)	(.045)
Constant	−1.266	−4.675	−11.418	−.531
	(1.038)	(1.628)	(2.564)	(1.008)
N	76	76	76	76

* Models estimated using seemingly unrelated regression (SUR) with logistic transformation of dependent variable.

Table AII.4. *Variables used in 1996 Czech Parliamentary Election*

Variable Name	Date	Definition	Source
Unemployment Rate	5/31/1996	Unemployment rate	1
Change in Income	12/31/1996	Monthly wage in 96, 95 = 100	2
Industrial Growth	12/31/1996	Industrial production in 1996, 1995 = 100	2
Percent Agriculture	12/31/1995	Percent of workers in agriculture	2
Percent Industry	12/31/1995	Percent of workers in industry	2
Percent Elderly	7/1/1996	Percent of population over age 60	3
Percent Urban	12/31/1995	Percent of people living in urban areas	4
Log Population	7/1/1996	Log of population	5

Sources: (1) (1996). Aktuality CSU: 1996 Duben, Kveten – 1.cast (Latest News of the Czech Statistical Office: April, May 1996 – Part I). Praha, Czech Republic, Cesky Statisticky Urad. (2) (1997). Okresy Ceske Republiky v roce 1996 (Regions of the Czech Republic in 1996). Praha, Czech Republic, Cesky Statisticky Urad. (3) (1997). Vekove Slozeni Obyvatelstva Ceske Republiky v roce 1996. Praha, Czech Republic, Cesky Statisticky Urad. (4) (1996). Okresy Ceske Republiky v roce 1995 (Regions of the Czech Republic in 1995). Praha, Czech Republic, Cesky Statisticky Urad. (5) (1997). Vekove Slozeni Obyvatelstva Ceske Republiky v roce 1996. Praha, Czech Republic, Cesky Statisticky Urad.

Table AII.5. *Estimated Coefficients (Standard Errors) of Effect on Party Vote for the 1998 Czech Parliamentary Election**

	US	KDU	ODS	KSČM
Unemployment Rate	−.074	−.071	−.064	.030
	(.011)	(.016)	(.009)	(.008)
Change in Income	−.010	−.001	−.002	.006
	(.009)	(.014)	(.008)	(.007)
Industrial Growth	−.000	.002	−.000	−.000
	(.001)	(.002)	(.001)	(.001)
Foreign Direct Investment	.000	−.000	.000	.000
	(.000)	(.000)	(.000)	(.000)
Percent Agriculture	.002	.055	−.014	.010
	(.007)	(.011)	(.006)	(.005)
Percent Industry	−.005	.012	−.006	−.009
	(.004)	(.006)	(.003)	(.003)
Percent Elderly	.041	.006	.046	−.001
	(.015)	(.024)	(.013)	(.012)
Percent Urban	.004	−.012	.004	−.004
	(.002)	(.003)	(.002)	(.001)
Log Population	.072	.663	−.020	−.045
	(.054)	(.084)	(.046)	(.043)
Constant	−1.921	−9.217	−.500	−1.162
	(1.084)	(1.681)	(.924)	(.848)
N	77	77	77	77

* Models estimated using seemingly unrelated regression (SUR) with logistic transformation of dependent variable.

Table AII.6. *Variables used in 1998 Czech Parliamentary Election*

Variable Name	Date	Definition	Source
Unemployment Rate	5/31/1998	Unemployment rate	1
Change in Income	3/30/1998	Change in average monthly wage 1998, 1997 = 100	5
Industrial Growth	12/31/1998	Growth in industrial sales, 1998 = 100	2
Foreign Direct Investment	12/31/1998	Per capita FDI in U.S. dollars per person	3
Percent Agriculture	12/31/1997	Percent workers in agriculture	4
Percent Industry	12/31/1997	Percent workers in industry	4
Percent Elderly	12/31/1997	Percent of people >= 60 years of age	4
Percent Urban	12/31/1997	Percentage of people living in urban areas	4
Log Population	12/31/1997	Log of population	4

Sources: (1) (1998). Aktuality CSU: 1998 Duben, Kveten – 1.cast (Latest News of the Czech Statistical Office: April, May 1998 – Part I). Praha, Czech Republic, Cesky Statisticky Urad. (2) (1999). Okresy Ceske Republiky v roce 1998 (Regions of the Czech Republic in 1998). Praha, Czech Republic, Cesky Statisticky Urad. (3) (2003). 1998–1999 Foreign Direct Investment, Czech National Bank (http://www.cnb.cz/en/publikace.php). Electronic Source. (4) (1998). Okresy Ceske Republiky v roce 1997 (Regions of the Czech Republic in 1997). Praha, Czech Republic, Cesky Statisticky Urad. (5) (1998). Statisticke Informace: Evidencni pocet zamestnancu a jejich mzdy v CRza 1–2 ctvrtleti 1998 (Workers and their Wages in the Czech Republic in the 1st–2nd quarters of 1998). Praha, Czech Republic: Cesky Statisticky Urad.

Table AII.7. *Estimated Coefficients (Standard Errors) of Effect on Party Vote for the 1990 Hungarian Parliamentary Election**

	MSzP	SzDSz	FIDESZ	MDF	MSzMP
Unemployment Rate	.107	−.570	−.153	−.131	1.081
	(.203)	(.161)	(.112)	(.181)	(.227)
Change in Income	−.031	−.035	−.086	−.047	−.064
	(.046)	(.037)	(.025)	(.041)	(.052)
Industrial Growth	−.016	.015	.022	.031	−.013
	(.015)	(.012)	(.008)	(.013)	(.017)
Foreign Direct Investment	−.002	.024	.010	−.003	.036
	(.019)	(.015)	(.010)	(.017)	(.021)
Percent Agriculture	−.033	−.026	−.040	−.016	.007
	(.016)	(.012)	(.009)	(.014)	(.017)
Percent Industry	−.032	−.013	−.019	.013	.040
	(.017)	(.014)	(.009)	(.015)	(.019)
Percent Elderly	−.010	−.028	−.030	.028	.177
	(.038)	(.030)	(.021)	(.034)	(.042)
Percent Urban	.005	−.009	−.003	.006	.029
	(.008)	(.007)	(.005)	(.008)	(.009)
Log Population	.108	.052	.189	.305	−.416
	(.218)	(.173)	(.120)	(.195)	(.244)
Constant	4.700	4.286	7.456	−2.146	4.508
	(6.604)	(5.246)	(3.640)	(5.899)	(7.397)
N	19	19	19	19	19

* Models estimated using seemingly unrelated regression (SUR) with logistic transformation of dependent variable.

Table AII.8. *Variables used in 1990 Hungarian Parliamentary Election*

Variable Name	Date	Definition	Source
Unemployment Rate	1/1/1990	Unemployment rate	1
Change in Income	12/31/1990	Change in wages, 1989 = 100	1
Industrial Growth	12/31/1990	% of industrial production compared to previous year	1
Foreign Direct Investment	12/31/1990	FDI in 1990 in thousands of forints per person.	2
Percent Agriculture	12/31/1989	Percent of workers in agriculture	3
Percent Industry	12/31/1989	Percent of workers in industry	3
Percent Elderly	12/31/1990	Percent of people >= 60 years of age	4
Percent Urban	1/1/1990	Percent of people living in urban areas	5
Log Population	1/1/1990	Log of population	6

Sources: (1) (1990). Zala Megye Statisztikai Evkonyve (Zala Megye Statistical Yearbook). Zalaegenszeg, Hungary, Kozporti Statisztikai Hivatal. (2) (1991). A Kulfoldi Mukodo Toke Magyarorszagon 1990 (Foreign Direct Investment in Hungary 1990). Budapest, Hungary, Kozponti Statisztikai Hivatal. (3) (1989). Zala Megye Statisztikai Evkonyve (Zala Megye Statistical Yearbook). Zalaegenszeg, Hungary, Kozporti Statisztikai Hivatal. (4) (1991). Teruleti Statisztikai Evkonyv 1990 (Statistical Yearbook of Hungary 1990). Budapest, Hungary, Kozponti Statisztikai Hivatal. (5) (1995). Teruleti Statisztikai Evkonyv 1994 (Regional Statistical Yearbook of Hungary 1994). Budapest, Hungary, Kozponti Statisztikai Hivatal. (6) (1994). Magyar Statisztikai Evkonyv 1993 (Statistical Yearbook of Hungary 1993). Budapest, Hungary, Kozponti Statisztikai Hivatal.

Appendix II

Table AII.9. *Estimated Coefficients (Standard Errors) of Effect on Party Vote for the 1994 Hungarian Parliamentary Election**

	MSzP	SzDSz	FIDESZ	MDF	MP	KDNP	FKgP
Unemployment Rate	.050	−.005	.011	−.005	.121	−.010	−.028
	(.023)	(.014)	(.019)	(.016)	(.023)	(.021)	(.022)
Change in Income	.052	.016	.031	−.003	.008	.000	.019
	(.029)	(.018)	(.024)	(.020)	(.028)	(.026)	(.028)
Industrial Growth	.007	.008	.008	.008	.004	.012	.013
	(.006)	(.003)	(.005)	(.004)	(.006)	(.005)	(.005)
Foreign Direct	.005	.003	.003	.002	.004	.000	−.002
Investment	(.003)	(.002)	(.002)	(.002)	(.002)	(.002)	(.002)
Percent Agriculture	−.0465	−.051	−.031	−.060	−.070	−.108	−.016
	(.025)	(.015)	(.021)	(.018)	(.024)	(.023)	(.023)
Percent Industry	.006	.016	.012	.001	.029	−.003	.019
	(.015)	(.009)	(.012)	(.011)	(.015)	(.014)	(.014)
Percent Elderly	.018	.019	−.032	.032	.171	.064	.028
	(.045)	(.027)	(.037)	(.031)	(.043)	(.040)	(.042)
Percent Urban	−.010	−.004	−.006	−.006	−.008	−.017	−.001
	(.006)	(.004)	(.005)	(.004)	(.006)	(.006)	(.006)
Log Population	−.473	−.529	−.457	−.425	−.481	−.723	−.376
	(.188)	(.113)	(.154)	(.130)	(.182)	(.169)	(.178)
Constant	−.269	4.594	1.517	5.671	−.962	9.009	.565
	(5.592)	(3.359)	(4.572)	(3.880)	(5.400)	(5.012)	(5.299)
N	20	20	20	20	20	20	20

* Models estimated using seemingly unrelated regression (SUR) with logistic transformation of dependent variable.

Table AII.10. *Variables used in 1994 Hungarian Parliamentary Election*

Variable Name	Date	Definition	Source
Unemployment Rate	6/1/1994	Unemployment rate	1
Change in Income	12/31/1994	Change in monthly income, 1993 = 100.	2, 3
Industrial Growth	12/31/1994	Growth in industrial sales, 1993 = 100	4
Foreign Direct Investment	12/31/1994	Foreign direct investment in thousands of forints per person	5
Percent Agriculture	12/31/1993	Percent of workers in agriculture	2
Percent Industry	12/31/1993	Percent of workers in industry	2
Percent Elderly	12/31/1993	Percent of older people.	6
Percent Urban	12/31/1994	Percent of people living in urban areas	4
Log Population	1/1/1994	Log of population	6

Sources: (1) (1994). Teruleti Statisztikai Evkonyv 1993 (Regional Statistical Yearbook of Hungary 1993). Budapest, Hungary, Kozponti Statisztikai Hivatal. (2) (1993). Zala Megye Statisztikai Evkonyve (Zala Megye Statistical Yearbook). Zalaegenszeg, Hungary, Kozporti Statisztikai Hivatal. (3) (1994). Zala Megye Statisztikai Evkonyve (Zala Megye Statistical Yearbook). Zalaegenszeg, Hungary, Kozporti Statisztik. (4) (1995). Magyar Statisztikai Evkonyv 1994 (Statistical Yearbook of Hungary 1994). Budapest, Hungary, Kozponti Statisztikai Hivatal. (5) (1995). A Kulfoldi Mukodo Toke Magyarorszagon 1994 (Foreign Direct Investment in Hungary. Budapest, Hungary, Kozponti Statisztikai Hivatal. (6) (1994). Magyar Statisztikai Evkonyv 1993 (Statistical Yearbook of Hungary 1993). Budapest, Hungary, Kozponti Statisztikai Hivatal.

Appendix II

Table AII.11. *Estimated Coefficients (Standard Errors) of Effect on Party Vote for the 1998 Hungarian Parliamentary Election**

	MSzP	SzDSz	FIDESZ-MPP	MDF	MP
Unemployment Rate	.042	−.007	−.019	−.025	.080
	(.009)	(.010)	(.008)	(.012)	(.020)
Change in Income	−.031	.072	−.015	.047	−.121
	(.044)	(.045)	(.038)	(.056)	(.094)
GDP Growth	−.011	−.036	.013	.020	−.006
	(.009)	(.009)	(.008)	(.011)	(.019)
Foreign Direct Investment	2.430	2.417	.278	−.485	1.509
	(.466)	(.479)	(.403)	(.596)	(1.000)
Percent Agriculture	.014	.003	−.008	−.007	−.034
	(.012)	(.013)	(.011)	(.016)	(.027)
Percent Industry	.007	.005	.002	−.012	.033
	(.007)	(.007)	(.006)	(.009)	(.015)
Percent Elderly	−.054	−.049	−.034	−.028	.146
	(.023)	(.024)	(.020)	(.029)	(.049)
Percent Urban	.000	−.005	.005	.002	.007
	(.003)	(.004)	(.003)	(.004)	(.007)
Log Population	−.367	−.504	−.239	−.026	−.055
	(.118)	(.121)	(.102)	(.151)	(.253)
Constant	9.838	1.912	3.940	−8.469	8.516
	(4.612)	(4.741)	(.997)	(5.902)	(9.902)
N	20	20	20	20	20

* Models estimated using seemingly unrelated regression (SUR) with logistic transformation of dependent variable.

Table AII.12. *Variables used in 1998 Hungarian Parliamentary Election*

Variable Name	Date	Definition	Source
Unemployment Rate	4/30/1998	Unemployment rate	1
Change in Income	12/31/1998	Change in monthly income, 1997 = 100	2
GDP Growth	12/31/1998	Change in GDP, 1997 = 100	3
Foreign Direct Investment	12/31/1998	Per capita FDI in millions of HUF per person	4
Percent Agriculture	12/31/1997	Percent of workers in agriculture	5
Percent Industry	12/31/1997	Percent of workers in industry	5
Percent Elderly	1/1/1998	Percent of people over age 60	5
Percent Urban	12/31/1997	Percent of people living in urban areas	5
Log Population	12/31/1998	Log of population	2

Sources: (1) (1998). Statisztikai Havi Kozlemenyek 1998/3 (Monthly Bulletin of Statistics, 1998, Vol.3). Budapest, Hungary, Kozponti Statisztikai Hivatal. (2) (1999). Teruleti Statisztikai Evkonyv 1998 (Regional Statistical Yearbook of Hungary 1998). Budapest, Hungary, Kozponti Statisztikai Hivatal. (3) (2001). Teruleti Statisztikai Evkonyv 2000 (Regional Statistical Yearbook of Hungary 2000). Budapest, Hungary, Kozponti Statisztikai Hivatal. (4). (1998). Budapest Statisztikai Evkonyve (Budapest Statistical Yearbook). Budapest, Hungary, Kozporti Statisztikai Hivatal Budestip es Pest Megyei Igazyatosaya (Central Statistical Office Budapest and Pest County Directorate). (5) (1998). Teruleti Statisztikai Evkonyv 1997 (Regional Statistical Yearbook of Hungary 1997). Budapest, Hungary, Kozponti Statisztikai Hivatal.

Appendix II

Table AII.13. *Estimated Coefficients (Standard Errors) of Effect on Party Vote for the 1990 Polish Presidential Election**

	Mazowiecki	Wałęsa	Cimoszewicz
Unemployment Rate	−.052	−.029	.035
	(.027)	(.033)	(.027)
Change in Income	−.001	.002	−.002
	(.002)	(.002)	(.002)
Industrial Growth	−.000	−.013	.006
	(.007)	(.008)	(.006)
Percent Agriculture	−.064	−.023	−.015
	(.013)	(.016)	(.013)
Percent Industry	−.041	−.037	−.030
	(.012)	(.014)	(.011)
Percent Elderly	−.019	.091	.064
	(.031)	(.038)	(.030)
Percent Urban	−.009	−.008	.012
	(.009)	(.010)	(.008)
Log Population	.057	.325	.037
	(.141)	(.171)	(.138)
Constant	3.700	−.457	−1.148
	(1.570)	(1.899)	(1.529)
N	49	49	49

* Models estimated using seemingly unrelated regression (SUR) with logistic transformation of dependent variable.

Table AII.14. *Variables used in 1990 Polish Presidential Election*

Variable Name	Date	Definition	Source
Unemployment Rate	12/31/1990	Unemployment rate	1
Change in Income	12/31/1990	Change in wages, 1989 = 100	1
Industrial Growth	12/31/1990	Change in industrial sales, 1989 = 100	1
Percent Agriculture	12/31/1990	Percent of workers in agriculture	1
Percent Industry	12/31/1990	Percent of workers in industry	1
Percent Elderly	12/31/1990	Percent of older people.	1
Percent Urban	12/31/1990	Percent of people living in urban areas	1
Log Population	12/31/1990	Log of population	1

Sources: (1) (1991). Rocznik Statystyczny Wojewodztw 1991 (1991 Regional Statistical Yearbook). Warsaw, Poland, Glowny Urzad Statystyczny.

Table AII.15. *Estimated Coefficients (Standard Errors) of Effect on Party Vote for the 1991 Polish Parliamentary Election**

	UD	KLD	PC	WAK	PSL	PL	SLD
Unemployment Rate	−.006	.024	.020	.009	.013	.018	.045
	(.016)	(.020)	(.023)	(.026)	(.018)	(.029)	(.020)
Change in Income	−.006	.009	.011	.002	.015	−.002	.008
	(.009)	(.012)	(.013)	(.015)	(.011)	(.017)	(.011)
Industrial Growth	−.003	.001	.001	−.006	−.006	−.008	−.005
	(.005)	(.006)	(.007)	(.008)	(.005)	(.010)	(.006)
Percent Agriculture	−.055	−.037	−.027	.009	.000	.009	−.001
	(.013)	(.017)	(.019)	(.022)	(.015)	(.025)	(.016)
Percent Industry	−.027	−.028	−.017	−.013	.012	−.029	−.005
	(.014)	(.017)	(.019)	(.022)	(.016)	(.026)	(.017)
Percent Elderly	.074	.047	.101	.118	.041	.119	.122
	(.037)	(.047)	(.052)	(.060)	(.043)	(.069)	(.045)
Percent Urban	−.012	−.001	−.021	.015	−.023	−.030	.018
	(.009)	(.011)	(.012)	(.014)	(.010)	(.017)	(.011)
Log Population	−.142	.293	.327	−.069	−.405	−.039	−.233
	(.137)	(.173)	(.195)	(.223)	(.158)	(.254)	(.169)
Constant	3.296	−4.333	−4.597	−3.114	−.352	.075	−3.231
	(2.051)	(2.589)	(2.918)	(3.328)	(2.368)	(3.984)	(2.530)
N	48	48	48	48	48	43**	48

* Models estimated using seemingly unrelated regression (SUR) with logistic transformation of dependent variable

** See note 13 in Chapter 3 for details on the different N for the PL.

Appendix II

Table AII.16. *Variables used in 1991 Polish Parliamentary Election*

Variable Name	Date	Definition	Source
Unemployment Rate	10/1/1991	Unemployment rate	1
Change in Income	12/31/1991	Change in wages, 1990 = 100	2
Industrial Growth	12/31/1991	Change in industrial sales, 1990 = 100	2
Percent Agriculture	12/31/1991	Percent of workers in agriculture	2
Percent Industry	12/31/1991	Percent of workers in industry	2
Percent Elderly	12/31/1991	Percent of people aged 65 and over	2
Percent Urban	12/31/1991	Percent of people living in urban areas	2
Log Population	12/31/1991	Log of population	2

Sources: (1) (1992). Bezrobocie w Polsce: I–III Kwartal 1992 (Unemployment in Poland: 1st–3rd Quarter 1992). Warsaw, Poland, Glowny Urzad Statystyczny. (2) (1992). Rocznik Statystyczny Wojewodztw 1992 (1992 Regional Statistical Yearbook). Warsaw, Poland, Glowny Urzad Statystyczny.

Table AII.17. *Estimated Coefficients (Standard Errors) of Effect on Party Vote for the 1993 Polish Parliamentary Elections**

	UD	KLD	KKW	PL	SLD
Unemployment Rate	−.018	.011	−.031	.021	.019
	(.009)	(.011)	(.014)	(.010)	(.009)
Change in Income	−.007	−.002	−.010	−.003	−.005
	(.005)	(.006)	(.009)	(.006)	(.006)
Industrial Growth	.005	−.003	.008	−.006	−.005
	(.005)	(.006)	(.008)	(.005)	(.005)
Foreign Direct Investment	.003	.009	.007	.009	.004
	(.004)	(.005)	(.007)	(.005)	(.005)
Percent Agriculture	−.033	−.027	.025	.004	−.005
	(.009)	(.011)	(.014)	(.010)	(.009)
Percent Industry	−.014	−.037	.013	−.021	.005
	.010	(.012)	(.016)	(.011)	(.011)
Percent Elderly	−.043	−.048	−.099	.035	.032
	(.030)	(.037)	(.049)	(.035)	(.032)
Percent Urban	−.005	.005	.015	.001	.013
	(.007)	(.008)	(.011)	(.008)	(.007)
Log Population	.143	.321	−.020	.189	−.195
	(.103)	(.127)	(.168)	(.120)	(.110)
Constant	−.392	−4.888	−.902	−3.873	1.816
	(1.874)	(2.311)	(3.066)	(2.185)	(2.008)
N	49	49	49	49	49

* Models estimated using seemingly unrelated regression (SUR) with logistic transformation of dependent variable.

Table AII.18. *Variables used in 1993 Polish Parliamentary Election*

Variable Name	Date	Definition	Source
Unemployment Rate	9/1/1993	Unemployment rate	1
Change in Income	12/31/1993	Change in wages, 1991 = 100	2
Industrial Growth	12/12/1993	Value of industrial production in 1993, using 1992 = 100	2
Foreign Direct Investment	12/31/1993	Foreign direct investment in Polish companies (thousand of zlotys/person)	3
Percent Agriculture	12/12/1993	Percent of workers in agriculture	2
Percent Industry	12/12/1993	Percent of workers in industry	2
Percent Elderly	12/12/1993	Percent of older people	2
Percent Urban	12/12/1993	Percent of people living in urban areas	2
Log Population	6/30/1993	Log of population	2

Sources: (1) Bezrobocie w Polsce: I–III Kwartal 1993 (Unemployment in Poland: 1st–3rd Quarter 1993). Warsaw, Poland: Glowny Urzad Statystyczny. (2) Rocznik Statystyczny Wojewodztw 1993 (1993 Regional Statistical Yearbook). Warsaw, Poland: Glowny Urzad Statystyczny. (3) Zagrozdzinska, Izabella (1998). "Podmioty z Udzialem Kapitalu Zagranicznego w Polsce w Latach 1993–1996" in Inwestycje Zagraniczne w Polsce (Foreign Investment in Poland). Barbara Durka, Ed. Warszawa, Polska, Institut Koniunkur i Cen Handlu Zagranicznego.

Appendix II

Table AII.19. *Estimated Coefficients (Standard Errors) of Effect on Party Vote for the 1995 Polish Presidential Election**

	Wałęsa	Kwaśniewski	Kuroń	Gronkiewicz-Waltz
Unemployment Rate	−.029	.022	−.005	−.024
	(.014)	(.012)	(.008)	(.010)
Change in Income	.000	−.010	−.003	−.008
	(.011)	(.009)	(.007)	(.008)
Industrial Growth	.000	−.006	.002	−.005
	(.009)	(.007)	(.005)	(.006)
Foreign Direct Investment	−.006	.007	.004	−.002
	(.006)	(.005)	(.003)	(.004)
Per Capita Exports	−.000	−.000	−.000	−.000
	(.000)	(.000)	(.000)	(.000)
Percent Agriculture	−.027	−.016	−.044	−.030
	(.010)	(.008)	(.006)	(.007)
Percent Industry	−.008	.018	−.003	−.009
	(.012)	(.010)	(.007)	(.009)
Percent Elderly	−.089	−.035	−.081	−.142
	(.040)	(.033)	(.024)	(.029)
Percent Urban	−.016	−.001	−.008	−.011
	(.008)	(.007)	(.005)	(.006)
Log Population	.165	−.286	−.201	.035
	(.148)	(.122)	(.089)	(.105)
Constant	2.760	4.962	3.674	3.485
	(2.548)	(2.112)	(1.542)	(1.818)
N	49	49	49	49

* Models estimated using seemingly unrelated regression (SUR) with logistic transformation of dependent variable.

Table AII.20. *Variables used in 1995 Polish Presidential Election*

Variable Name	Date	Definition	Source
Unemployment Rate	11/1/1995	Unemployment rate	1
Change in Income	12/31/1995	Change in income, 1993 = 100	2
Industrial Growth	12/31/1995	Change in industrial growth, 1993 = 100	2
Foreign Direct Investment	12/31/1995	Foreign direct investment in 1995 in dollars per person	3
Per Capita Exports	12/31/1995	Exports in U.S. dollars per person	4
Percent Agriculture	12/31/1995	Percent of workers in agriculture	2
Percent Industry	12/31/1995	Percent of workers in industry	2
Percent Elderly	12/31/1995	Percent of older people	2
Percent Urban	12/31/1995	Percent of people living in urban areas	2
Log Population	12/31/1995	Log of population	2

Sources: (1) (1997). Bezrobocie w Polsce: I–IV Kwartal 1996 (Unemployment in Poland: 1st–4th Quarter 1996). Warsaw, Poland, Glowny Urzad Statystyczny. (2) (1996). Rocznik Statystyczny Wojewodztw 1996 (1996 Regional Statistical Yearbook). Warsaw, Poland, Glowny Urzad Statystyczny. (3) (1996). Wyniki Finansowe Podmiotow Gospodarczych z Udzialem Kapitalu Zagranicznego w 1995 Roku (Results of Financing of Economic Enteriprises with Foreign Capital in 1995). Warsaw, Poland, Glowny Urzad Statystyczny. (4). Komorinsku, Tomasz (2000). Potoki Towarowe Poslkiego Handlu Zagranicznego a Miedzynarodowe Powiazania Transportowe. Wroclaw, Poland, Instytut Geografii i Przestrzennego Zagospodarowania PAN.

Appendix II

Table AII.21. *Estimated Coefficients (Standard Errors) of Effect on Party Vote for the 1997 Polish Parliamentary Election**

	AWS	UW	PSL	SLD
Unemployment Rate	−.033	−.023	.003	.014
	(.015)	(.011)	(.020)	(.014)
Change in Income	.006	.004	−.001	.014
	(.016)	(.012)	(.021)	(.014)
GDP Growth	.002	.007	.002	−.004
	(.010)	(.007)	(.014)	(.009)
Foreign Direct Investment	−.004	−.001	.002	−.000
	(.001)	(.001)	(.002)	(.001)
Per Capita Exports	.000	−.000	.000	−.000
	(.000)	(.000)	(.000)	(.000)
Percent Agriculture	.004	−.031	.025	−.004
	(.011)	(.008)	(.015)	(.010)
Percent Industry	−.021	−.010	.016	.027
	(.013)	(.010)	(.017)	(.012)
Percent Elderly	−.066	−.050	−.007	.022
	(.040)	(.029)	(.054)	(.036)
Percent Urban	.002	−.001	−.014	.006
	(.009)	(.006)	(.012)	(.008)
Log Population	.228	.120	−.131	−.306
	(.134)	(.098)	(.178)	(.120)
Constant	−.492	.148	−.558	−.220
	(2.907)	(2.125)	(3.870)	(2.613)
N	49	49	49	49

* Models estimated using seemingly unrelated regression (SUR) with logistic transformation of dependent variable.

Table AII.22. *Variables used in 1997 Polish Parliamentary Election*

Variable Name	Date	Definition	Source
Unemployment Rate	9/30/1997	Unemployment rate	1
Change in Income	12/31/1997	Change in average monthly income, 1996 = 100	2
GDP Growth	12/31/1997	GDP growth: GDP in 1996 = 100	3
Foreign Direct Investment	12/31/1997	Foreign direct investment in 1997 in dollars per person	4
Per Capita Exports	12/31/1997	Exports in U.S. dollars per person	5
Percent Agriculture	12/31/1997	Percent of workers in agriculture	2
Percent Industry	12/31/1997	Percent of workers in industry	2
Percent Elderly	12/31/1997	Percent of older people	2
Percent Urban	12/31/1997	Percent of people living in urban areas	2
Log Population	12/31/1997	Log of population	2

Sources: (1) (1997). Bezrobocie w Polsce: I–III Kwartal 1997(Unemployment in Poland: 1st–3rd Quarter 1997). Warsaw, Poland, Glowny Urzad Statystyczn. (2) (1998). Rocznik Statystyczny Wojewodztw 1998 (1998 Regional Statistical Yearbook). Warsaw, Poland, Glowny Urzad Statystyczny. (3) (2000). Product Krajowy Brutto Wedlug Wojewodztw w Latach 1995–1998 (Gross Domestic Product by Region 1995–1998). Warsaw, Poland, Glowny Urzad Statystyczny and Urzad Statystyczny w Katowicach. (4) (1998). Dzialnosc Gospodarcza Spolek z Udzialem Kapitalu Zagranicznego w 1997 Roku. Warsaw, Poland, Glowny Urzad Statystyczny. (5) Komorinsku, Tomasz (2000). Potoki Towarowe Poslkiego Handlu Zagranicznego a Miedzynarodowe Powiazania Transportowe. Wroclaw, Poland, Instytut Geografii i Przestrzennego Zagospodarowania PAN.

Appendix II

Table AII.23. *Estimated Coefficients (Standard Errors) of Effect on Party Vote for the 1991 Russian Presidential Election**

	Yeltsin	Ryzhkov	Bakatin
Change in Income	−.011	−.012	−.015
	(.005)	(.004)	(.005)
Industrial Growth	.000	.001	.001
	(.011)	(.010)	(.012)
Percent Agriculture	−.026	−.043	−.034
	(.020)	(.018)	(.022)
Percent Industry	.029	−.014	.008
	(.010)	(.009)	(.011)
Percent Elderly	−.010	.021	−.011
	(.014)	(.013)	(.015)
Percent Urban	−.010	−.023	−.011
	(.010)	(.009)	(.011)
Log Population	.267	−.046	.159
	(.072)	(.065)	(.079)
Constant	1.204	4.328	.737
	(1.677)	(1.523)	(1.841)
N	76	76	76

* Models estimated using seemingly unrelated regression (SUR) with logistic transformation of dependent variable.

Table AII.24. *Variables used in 1991 Russian Presidential Election*

Variable Name	Date	Definition	Source
Change in Income	12/31/1991	Change in average monthly wage 91, 90 = 100	1
Industrial Growth	12/31/1991	Industrial production in 1991, 1990 = 100	2
Percent Agriculture	12/31/1990	Percent of workers in agriculture	2
Percent Industry	12/31/1990	Percent of workers in industry	2
Percent Elderly	12/31/1991	Percent of older people	2
Percent Urban	12/31/1991	Percent of people living in urban areas	2
Log Population	1/1/1991	Log of population	2

Sources: (1) (1997). RECEP Data I. Moscow, Russia, Russian European Center for Economic Progress. (2) (1997). Regioni Rossiya (Regions of Russia). Moscow, Russia, Goskomstat.

Table AII.25. *Estimated Coefficients (Standard Errors) of Effect on Party Vote for the 1993 Russian Parliamentary Election**

	VR	PRES	KPRF
Unemployment Rate	−.031	.056	.033
	(.020)	(.029)	(.033)
Change in Income	−.000	−.001	.000
	(.000)	(.001)	(.001)
Industrial Growth	.009	.005	−.011
	(.005)	(.007)	(.008)
Foreign Trade	−.000	−.001	−.001
	(.003)	(.004)	(.004)
Wage Arrears	−.012	−.019	−.010
	(.006)	(.009)	(.010)
Percent Agriculture	−.036	−.009	.019
	(.010)	(.015)	(.017)
Percent Industry	−.015	−.009	−.009
	(.007)	(.011)	(.012)
Percent Elderly	.001	−.045	.014
	(.011)	(015)	(.018)
Percent Urban	.007	−.007	−.008
	(.006)	(.008)	(.009)
Log Population	.047	.017	.034
	(.051)	(.073)	(.083)
Constant	−1.770	−.469	−.926
	(.832)	(1.201)	(1.368)
N	75	75	75

* Models estimated using seemingly unrelated regression (SUR) with logistic transformation of dependent variable.

Appendix II

Table AII.26. *Variables used in 1993 Russian Parliamentary Election*

Variable Name	Date	Definition	Source
Unemployment Rate	12/31/1993	Unemployment rate	1
Change in Income	12/31/1993	Monthly wage in 1993, 1992 = 100	2
Industrial Growth	12/31/1993	Industrial production in 1993, 1992 = 100	1
Foreign Trade	12/31/1993	Exports per capita in 10,000s of rubles per person.	3
Wage Arrears	12/1/1993	Per capita wage arrears, in thousands of rubles per person	4
Percent Agriculture	12/12/1994	Percent of workers in agriculture	6
Percent Industry	12/31/1994	Percent of workers in industry	6
Percent Elderly	12/31/1993	Percent men over 60 and women over 55	5
Percent Urban	12/31/1993	Percent of people living in urban areas	5
Log Population	1/1/1993	Log of population	1

Sources: (1) (1997). Regioni Rossiya (Regions of Russia). Moscow, Russia, Goskomstat. (2) (1997). RECEP Data I. Moscow, Russia, Russian European Center for Economic Progress. (3) (1996). Analiz Tendentsia Razvitia Regionov Rossii v 1992–1995. (Analysis of Developmental Tendencies of Russia's Regions). Moscow, Russia, Tacis. (4) (1993). Sotzialno-Ekonomicheskoi Polozhenue Rossii 1993 (Social Economic Situation in Russia, 1993). Moscow, Russia, Gosudarstvenii Komitet Rossiskoy Federatsii po Statistikie (State Committe of the Russian Federation for Statistics, Goskomstat). (5) (1994). Demographicheskii Ezhegodnik Rossiskoi Federatsii (Demographic Yearbook of the Russian Federation). Moscow, Russia, Gosudarstvenii Komitet Rossiskoy Federatsii po Statistikie (State Committe of the Russian Federation for Statistics, Goskomstat. (6) Lavrov, A. (1996). Predprinima-telskii Klimat Regionov Rossii: Geographia Rossii dlya Investorov i Predprinimatelej (Investment Climate of the Regions of Russia: Russian Geography for Investors and Manufacturers). Moscow, Russia, Russian Union of Industry.

Table AII.27. *Estimated Coefficients (Standard Errors) of Effect on Party Vote for the 1995 Russian Parliamentary Election**

	DVR	NDR	KPRF	KTR-SS
Unemployment Rate	.007	.047	.066	.027
	(.020)	(.021)	(.016)	(.013)
Change in Income	−.004	.008	−.010	.006
	(.004)	(.004)	(.003)	(.003)
GDP Growth	−.287	.171	.185	.275
	(.241)	(.259)	(.189)	(.154)
Wage Arrears	−.002	−.002	.003	.001
	(.001)	(.001)	(.001)	(.001)
Inflation	.003	.003	.007	−.004
	(.004)	(.004)	(.003)	(.002)
Percent Agriculture	−.028	.010	.022	.030
	(.021)	(.023)	(.017)	(.014)
Percent Industry	.005	−.023	−.005	−.005
	(.013)	(.014)	(.010)	(.008)
Percent Elderly	−.020	−.028	.089	.011
	(.023)	(.024)	(.018)	(.014)
Percent Urban	−.000	.008	−.007	−.005
	(.012)	(.013)	(.010)	(.008)
Log Population	.287	.173	.069	.021
	(.104)	(.112)	(.082)	(.067)
Constant	−3.494	−5.450	−2.923	−4.568
	(1.626)	(1.752)	(1.278)	(1.042)
N	76	76	76	76

* Models estimated using seemingly unrelated regression (SUR) with logistic transformation of dependent variable.

Table AII.28. *Variables used in 1995 Russian Parliamentary Election*

Variable Name	Date	Definition	Source
Unemployment Rate	12/31/1995	Unemployment rate	1
Change in Income	12/31/1995	Monthly wage in 1995, 1994 = 100	2
GDP Growth	12/31/1995	% Change in GDP from the previous year	3
Wage Arrears	12/1/1995	Per capita wage arrears (thousands of rubles per person)	4
Inflation	12/31/1995	Consumer price index, 1995.	2
Percent Agriculture	12/31/1995	Percent of workers in agriculture	1
Percent Industry	12/31/1995	Percent of workers in industry	1
Percent Elderly	1/1/1996	Percent of older people	1
Percent Urban	12/31/1995	Percent of people living in urban areas	2
Log Population	12/31/1995	Log of population	2

Sources: (1) (1997). Regioni Rossiya (Regions of Russia). Moscow, Russia, Goskomstat. (2) (1997). RECEP Data I. Moscow, Russia, Russian European Center for Economic Progress. (3) (1999). Regioni Rossiya (Regions of Russia). Moscow, Russia, Goskomstat. (4) (1995). Sotzialno-Ekonomicheskoi Polozhenue Rossii (Social Economic Situation in Russia). Moscow, Russia, Gosudarstvenii Komitet Rossiskoy Federatsii po Statistikie (State Committe of the Russian Federation for Statistics, Goskomstat).

Table AII.29. *Estimated Coefficients (Standard Errors) of Effect on Party Vote for the 1996 Russian Presidential Election**

	Yeltsin	Zyuganov
Unemployment Rate	.004	.010
	(.011)	(.012)
Change in Income	−.000	−.004
	(.002)	(.003)
GDP Growth	.420	.853
	(.312)	(.352)
Wage Arrears	−.001	.000
	(.000)	(.001)
Inflation	.003	.017
	(.010)	(.012)
Percent Agriculture	−.000	.057
	(.016)	(.018)
Percent Industry	−.008	.003
	(.010)	(.012)
Percent Elderly	−.061	.025
	(.019)	(.021)
Percent Urban	−.002	−.008
	(.009)	(.010)
Log Population	.161	.151
	(.072)	(.082)
Constant	.423	−2.234
	(.922)	(1.042)
N	77	77

* Models estimated using seemingly unrelated regression (SUR) with logistic transformation of dependent variable.

Appendix II

Table AII.30. *Variables used in 1996 Russian Presidential Election*

Variable Name	Date	Definition	Source
Unemployment Rate	12/31/1995	Unemployment rate	1
Change in Income	5/31/1996	Average income in May 1996, May 1995 = 100	5
GDP Growth	12/31/1996	% change in GDP from the previous year	2
Wage Arrears	5/6/1996	Per capita wage arrears in thousands of rubles per person.	3
Inflation	12/31/1996	Measure of inflation	4
Percent Agriculture	12/31/1995	Percent of workers in agriculture	1
Percent Industry	12/31/1995	Percent of workers in industry	1
Percent Elderly	1/1/1996	Percent of older people.	1
Percent Urban	12/12/1995	Percent of people living in urban areas	4
Log Population	12/12/1995	Log of population	4

Sources: (1) (1997). Regioni Rossiya (Regions of Russia). Moscow, Russia, Goskomstat. (2) (1999). Regioni Rossiya (Regions of Russia). Moscow, Russia, Goskomstat. (3) (1996). Sotzialno-Ekonomicheskoi Polozhenue Rossii (Social Economic Situation in Russia). Moscow, Russia, Gosudarstvenii Komitet Rossiskoy Federatsii po Statistikie (State Committe of the Russian Federation for Statistics, Goskomstat). (4) (1997). RECEP Data I. Moscow, Russia, Russian European Center for Economic Progress. (5) (1996). Ekonomika Rossii, January –June 1996. Moscow, Russia, Gosudarstvenii Komitet Rossiskoy Federatsii po Statistikie (State Committe of the Russian Federation for Statistics, Goskomstat).

Table AII.31. *Estimated Coefficients (Standard Errors) of Effect on Party Vote for the 1999 Russian Parliamentary Election**

	Unity	SPS	KPRF	KTR-SS
Unemployment Rate	−5.037	−7.292	−2.865	−5.092
	(1.420)	(1.081)	(1.168)	(1.291)
Change in Income	1.635	.468	1.215	.485
	(1.026)	(.782)	(.845)	(.933)
GDP Growth	−.005	−.005	−.005	−.007
	(.004)	(.003)	(.003)	(.003)
Foreign Trade	−.001	−.001	−.000	.002
	(.002)	(.001)	(.001)	(.002)
Inflation	−4.005	−1.088	−2.136	−.236
	(1.117)	(.851)	(.919)	(1.016)
Wage Arrears	.164	.066	.298	.155
	(.185)	(.141)	(.152)	(.168)
Percent Agriculture	6.155	−.730	6.956	2.306
	(1.602)	(1.220)	(1.318)	(1.456)
Percent Industry	−.160	.283	.138	.340
	(1.497)	(1.140)	(1.232)	(1.361)
Percent Elderly	−3.789	−1.639	1.392	−.903
	(2.501)	(1.905)	(2.058)	(2.273)
Percent Urban	1.910	.618	1.206	−.751
	(1.025)	(.780)	(.843)	(.931)
Log Population	−.369	−.039	−.134	−.143
	(.106)	(.081)	(.087)	(.097)
Constant	3.188	.570	−.293	.229
	(1.215)	(.925)	(1.000)	(1.104)
N	77	77	77	77

* Models estimated using seemingly unrelated regression (SUR) with logistic transformation of dependent variable.

Appendix II

Table AII.32. *Variables used in 1999 Russian Parliamentary Election*

Variable Name	Date	Definition	Source
Unemployment Rate	12/31/1999	Unemployment rate	1
Change in Income	12/31/1999	Change in average monthly wage, 1998 = 100	1
GDP Growth	12/31/1999	% change in GDP from the previous year	3
Foreign Trade	12/31/1999	Per capita foreign trade in thousands of U.S. dollars per person	3
Inflation	12/31/1999	Measure of inflation from December 1998 to December 1999	1
Wage Arrears	12/1/1999	Per capita wage arrears (thousands of rubles/person)	2
Percent Agriculture	12/31/1999	Percent of workers in agriculture	1
Percent Industry	12/31/1999	Percent of workers in industry	1
Percent Elderly	12/31/1999	Percent of older people	1
Percent Urban	12/31/1999	Percent of people living in urban areas	1
Log Population	12/31/1999	Log of population	1

Sources: (1) (1999). Regioni Rossiya (Regions of Russia). Moscow, Russia, Goskomstat. (2) (1999). Sotzialno-Ekonomicheskoi Polozhenue Rossii (Social Economic Situation in Russia). Moscow, Russia, Gosudarstvenii Komitet Rossiskoy Federatsii po Statistikie (State Committe of the Russian Federation for Statistics, Goskomstat). (3) (2000). Regioni Rossiya (Regions of Russia). Moscow, Russia, Goskomstat.

Table AII.33. *Estimated Coefficients (Standard Errors) of Effect on Party Vote for the 1992 Slovak Parliamentary Election**

	ODU	SDL'	HZDS	KDH
Unemployment Rate	−.025	.014	.003	−.010
	(.024)	(.021)	(.021)	(.021)
Change in Income	−.032	−.019	.015	−.026
	(.010)	(.009)	(.009)	(.009)
Industrial Growth	.014	.015	−.007	.009
	(.006)	(.005)	(.005)	(.005)
Percent Agriculture	−.029	−.009	−.012	−.016
	(.016)	(.013)	(.013)	(.013)
Percent Industry	−.018	−.006	.018	−.010
	(.008)	(.007)	(.007)	(.007)
Percent Elderly	−.043	.014	.089	−.125
	(.029)	(.025)	(.025)	(.025)
Percent Urban	.000	.011	−.006	−.026
	(.008)	(.007)	(.007)	(.007)
Log Population	−.142	−.671	−.261	.350
	(.186)	(.158)	(.157)	(.158)
Percent Hungarian	−.020	−.027	−.036	−.045
	(.003)	(.002)	(.002)	(.002)
Constant	4.281	7.586	.801	1.429
	(2.449)	(2.082)	(2.076)	(2.090)
N	38	38	38	38

* Models estimated using seemingly unrelated regression (SUR) with logistic transformation of dependent variable.

Appendix II

Table AII.34. *Variables used in 1992 Slovak Parliamentary Election*

Variable Name	Date	Definition	Source
Unemployment Rate	12/31/1991	Unemployment rate	1
Change in Income	12/31/1992	Change in income in 1992; 1991 = 100	2
Industrial Growth	12/31/1992	Change in industrial growth, 1991 = 100	1
Percent Agriculture	12/31/1991	Percent of workers in agriculture	3
Percent Industry	12/31/1991	Percent of workers in industry	3
Percent Elderly	12/31/1991	Percent of older people	4
Percent Urban	12/31/1992	Percent of people living in urban areas	5
Log Population	7/1/1992	Log of population	1
Percent Hungarian	1/1/1997	Hungarian percent of population	6

Sources: (1) (1993). Statisticka Rocenka Slovenskej Republiky, 1993 (Statistical Yearbook of the Slovak Republic, 1993). Bratislava. Slovakia, Statiskicky urad Slovnskej Republiky. (2) (1993). Medziokresne porovnania v SR za rok 1992 (Inter-district Comparison in the Slovak Republic in 1992). Bratislava, Slovakia, Statiskicky urad Slovnskej Republiky. (3) (1996). Statisticka Rocenka Slovenskej Republiky, 1996 (Statistical Yearbook of the Slovak Republic, 1996). Bratislava, Slovakia, Statiskicky urad Slovnskej Republiky. (4) (1997). Statistcka Rocenka Okresov Slovenskej Republiky za Roky 1990–1995 (Regional Statistical Yearbook of the Slovak Republic from 1990–1995). Bratislava, Slovakia, Statiskicky urad Slovnskej Republiky. (5) (2002). Demografika Statistika za rok 1992 (Demographic Statistics from 1992); Special Data Order from Slovak Statistical Department. Bratislava, Slovakia, Slovensky Statisticky Urad (Slovak Statistical Department). (6) Krivy, Vladimir, Viera Feglova and Daniel Balko (1996). Slovensko a jeho regio'ny: sociokultu'rne su'vislosti volebne'ho spra'vania. Bratislava, Slovakia, Nada'cia Me'dia.

Table AII.35. *Estimated Coefficients (Standard Errors) of Effect on Party Vote for the 1994 Slovak Parliamentary Election**

	ODU	DS	HZDS	KDH	SV	KSS	ZRS	SNS
Unemployment	−.016	−.008	−.031	−.021	−.004	.043	.032	−.056
Rate	(.011)	(.011)	(.013)	(.013)	(.009)	(.012)	(.012)	(.016)
Change in	−.012	.014	.030	−.004	−.031	.001	−.010	.039
Income	(.019)	(.020)	(.024)	(.023)	(.016)	(.022)	(.022)	(.029)
GDP Growth	.006	.001	−.012	.004	−.001	−.001	−.003	−.011
	(.006)	(.006)	(.007)	(.007)	(.005)	(.007)	(.007)	(.009)
Foreign Direct	.001	−.001	.000	−.001	.001	.001	.001	.002
Investment	(.001)	(.001)	(.002)	(.001)	(.001)	(.001)	(.001)	(.002)
Percent	−.014	.000	−.040	−.022	.007	.005	−.019	−.050
Agriculture	(.014)	(.014)	(.017)	(.017)	(.012)	(.016)	(.016)	(.021)
Percent	.001	.011	.017	−.013	.005	.012	.010	.030
Industry	(.007)	(.007)	(.008)	(.008)	(.006)	(.008)	(.007)	(.010)
Percent Elderly	.016	.020	.065	−.104	.016	.032	.023	.049
	(.023)	(.024)	(.029)	(.028)	(.020)	(.027)	(.026)	(.035)
Percent Urban	.006	.011	−.023	−.020	.013	(.015)	.003	−.032
	(.006)	(.006)	(.007)	(.007)	(.005)	(.007)	(.006)	(.009)
Log Population	.212	.239	−.016	.350	−.112	−.459	−.327	.520
	(.131)	(.133)	(.161)	(.156)	(.110)	(.149)	(.146)	(.197)
Percent	−.038	−.042	−.050	−.058	−.037	−.040	−.049	−.033
Hungarian	(.003)	(.003)	(.003)	(.003)	(.002)	(.003)	(.003)	(.004)
Constant	−2.169	−6.729	.180	.188	3.911	1.740	4.106	−8.714
	(2.780)	(2.829)	(3.415)	(3.304)	(2.350)	(3.165)	(3.092)	(4.178)
N	38	38	38	38	38	38	38	38

* Models estimated using seemingly unrelated regression (SUR) with logistic transformation of dependent variable.

Appendix II

Table AII.36. *Variables used in 1994 Slovak Parliamentary Election*

Variable Name	Date	Definition	Source
Unemployment Rate	9/30/1994	Unemployment rate	1
Change in Income	12/31/1994	Change in average income 1994, 1993 = 100	2
GDP Growth	6/30/1994	Change in GDP, 1993 = 100	3
Foreign Direct Investment	12/31/1994	Per capita foreign capital investment (hundreds of crowns/person)	2
Percent Agriculture	12/31/1994	Percent of workers in agriculture	3
Percent Industry	12/31/1994	Percent of workers in industry	3
Percent Elderly	12/31/1994	Percent of older people	3
Percent Urban	12/31/1994	Percent of people living in urban areas	4
Log Population	12/31/1994	Log of population	3
Percent Hungarian	1/1/1997	Hungarian percent of population	5

Sources: (1) (1995). Vybrane Udaje o Regionoch v Slovenskej republike za Rok 1994 (Selected Data on Regions in the Slovak Republic in 1994). Bratislava, Slovakia, Statiskicky urad Slovnskej Republiky. (2) (1997). Statistcka Rocenka Okresov Slovenskej Republiky za Roky 1990–1995 (Regional Statistical Yearbook of the Slovak Republic from 1990–1995). Bratislava, Slovakia, Statiskicky urad Slovnskej Republiky. (3) (1996). Statisticka Rocenka Slovenskej Republiky, 1996 (Statistical Yearbook of the Slovak Republic, 1996). Bratislava, Slovakia, Statiskicky urad Slovnskej Republiky. (4) (2002). Demografika Statistika za rok 1994 (Demographic Statistics from 1994); Special Data Order from Slovak Statistical Department. Bratislava, Slovakia, Slovensky Statisticky Urad (Slovak Statistical Department). (5) Krivy, Vladimir, Viera Feglova and Daniel Balko (1996). Slovensko a jeho regio'ny: sociokultu'rne su'vislosti volebne'ho spra'vania. Bratislava, Slovakia, Nada'cia Me'dia.

Table AII.37. *Estimated Coefficients (Standard Errors) of Effect on Party Vote for the 1998 Slovak Parliamentary Election**

	HZDS	SDL'	SDK	KSS	ZRS	SNS
Unemployment Rate	−.049	−.021	−.042	.014	.003	−.070
	(.012)	(.010)	(.009)	(.010)	(.017)	(.015)
Change in Income	−.003	−.029	−.022	−.016	−.021	−.020
	(.021)	(.017)	(.016)	(.018)	(.030)	(.026)
Industrial Growth	−.001	.000	−.001	−.000	.004	.001
	(.002)	(.002)	(.001)	(.002)	(.003)	(.002)
Foreign Direct Investment	−.016	−.011	.027	.011	−.018	−.031
	(.019)	(.015)	(.014)	(.016)	(.027)	(.024)
Percent Agriculture	−.062	−.024	−.004	−.031	−.055	−.065
	(.014)	(.012)	(.011)	(.012)	(.020)	(.018)
Percent Industry	.006	.003	.003	.004	.008	.013
	(.006)	(.005)	(.004)	(.005)	(.008)	(.007)
Percent Elderly	.041	.058	−.057	.070	−.004	.028
	(.026)	(.021)	(.019)	(.022)	(.036)	(.032)
Percent Urban	−.019	.000	−.001	−.004	−.008	−.021
	(.005)	(.004)	(.004)	(.004)	(.007)	(.006)
Log Population	−.353	−.154	−.094	−.449	−.876	−.225
	(.122)	(.099)	(.092)	(.103)	(.172)	(.154)
Percent Hungarian	−.040	−.039	−.030	−.039	−.038	−.042
	(.004)	(.003)	(.003)	(.003)	(.005)	(.005)
Constant	7.004	4.302	5.514	4.225	10.210	6.241
	(2.869)	(2.320)	(2.157)	(2.425)	(4.032)	(3.611)
N	72	72	72	72	72	72

* Models estimated using seemingly unrelated regression (SUR) with logistic transformation of dependent variable.

Appendix II

Table AII.38. *Variables used in 1998 Slovak Parliamentary Election*

Variable Name	Date	Definition	Source
Unemployment Rate	9/30/1998	Unemployment rate	1
Change in Income	9/30/1998	Change in average monthly wage 1998, 1997 = 100	1
Industrial Growth	12/31/1998	Change in gross industrial output, 1997 = 1000	2
Foreign Direct Investment	12/31/1998	Percentage of private for profit organization that are foreign owned	1
Percent Agriculture	12/31/1998	Percent of workers in agriculture	3
Percent Industry	12/31/1998	Percent of workers in industry	3
Percent Elderly	12/31/1998	Percent of older people	3
Percent Urban	12/31/1998	Percent of people living in urban areas	2
Log Population	12/31/1998	Log of population	3
Percent Hungarian	3/31/1999	Percent of ethnic Hungarians	4

Sources: (1) (1999). Vybrane Udaje o Regionoch v Slovenskej republike za 1–3. stvrtrok 1998 (Selected Data on Regions in the Slovak Republic in the first three quarters of 1998). Bratislava, Slovakia, Statiskicky urad Slovnskej Republiky. (2) (2002). Statistcka Rocenka Okresov SR 1995–2000 (Regional Statistical Yearbook of the Slovak Republic from 1995–2000). Bratislava, Slovakia, Statiskicky urad Slovnskej Republiky. (3) (1999). Statistcka Rocenka Okresov Slovenskej Republiky za Roky 1998 (Regional Statistical Yearbook of the Slovak Republic from 1998). Bratislava, Slovakia, Statiskicky urad Slovnskej Republiky. (4) (2000). Bilancia pohybu obyvatelsta podla narodnosti v SR 1999 (Population by nationality in the Slovak Republic in 1999). Bratislava, Slovakia, Statiskicky urad Slovnskej Republiky.

Table AII.39. *Estimated Coefficients (Standard Errors) of Effect on Party Vote for the 1999 Slovak Presidential Election**

	Schuster	Meciar
Unemployment Rate	.034	.013
	(.008)	(.008)
Change in Income	.003	−.027
	(.018)	(.016)
Industrial Growth	−.002	−.001
	(.002)	(.002)
Foreign Direct Investment	−.011	−.024
	(.011)	(.010)
Percent Agriculture	.026	−.048
	(.010)	(.010)
Percent Industry	−.009	−.000
	(.004)	(.004)
Percent Elderly	−.011	.053
	(.019)	(.018)
Percent Urban	.007	−.015
	(.003)	(.003)
Log Population	.378	−.056
	(.088)	(.080)
Percent Hungarian	.016	−.009
	(.003)	(.003)
Constant	−4.043	5.092
	(2.450)	(2.244)
N	70	70

* Models estimated using seemingly unrelated regression (SUR) with logistic transformation of dependent variable.

Appendix II

Table AII.40. *Variables used in 1999 Slovak Presidential Election*

Variable Name	Date	Definition	Source
Unemployment Rate	3/31/1999	Unemployment rate	1
Change in Income	6/30/1999	Change in average wage 1999; 1998 = 100	1
Industrial Growth	12/31/1999	Change in gross industrial output, 1998 = 1000	2
Foreign Direct Investment	3/31/1999	Percentage of private for profit organization that are foreign/ int'l owned	3
Percent Agriculture	12/31/1998	Percent of workers in agriculture	4
Percent Industry	12/31/1998	Percent of workers in industry	4
Percent Elderly	12/31/1998	Percent of older people	4
Percent Urban	12/31/1998	Percent of people living in urban areas	5
Log Population	6/30/1999	Log of population	5
Percent Hungarian	3/31/1999	Percent of ethnic Hungarians	6

Sources: (1) (1999). Vybrane Udaje o Regionoch v Slovenskej republike za 1 stvrtrok 1999 (Selected Data on Regions in the Slovak Republic in the first quarter of 1999). Bratislava, Slovakia, Statiskicky urad Slovnskej Republiky. (2) (2002). Statistcka Rocenka Okresov SR 1995–2000 (Regional Statistical Yearbook of the Slovak Republic from 1995–2000). Bratislava, Slovakia, Statiskicky urad Slovnskej Republiky. (3) (1999). Vybrane Udaje o Regionoch v Slovenskej republike za 1–3. stvrtrok 1998 (Selected Data on Regions in the Slovak Republic in the first three quarters of 1998). Bratislava, Slovakia, Statiskicky urad Slovnskej Republiky. (4) (1999). Statistcka Rocenka Okresov Slovenskej Republiky za Roky 1998 (Regional Statistical Yearbook of the Slovak Republic from 1998). Bratislava, Slovakia, Statiskicky urad Slovnskej Republiky. (5) (2002). Pocet obyvateľov pod'la pohlavia a území v roku 1999: Special Order Data prepared by Slovak Statistcal Office. Bratislava, Slovakia, Slovensky Statisticky Urad (Slovak Statistical Department). (6) (2000). Bilancia pohybu obyvatelsta podla narodnosti v SR 1999 (Population by nationality in the Slovak Republic in 1999). Bratislava, Slovakia, Statiskicky urad Slovnskej Republiky.

Appendix III

Estimated Distributions of First Differences

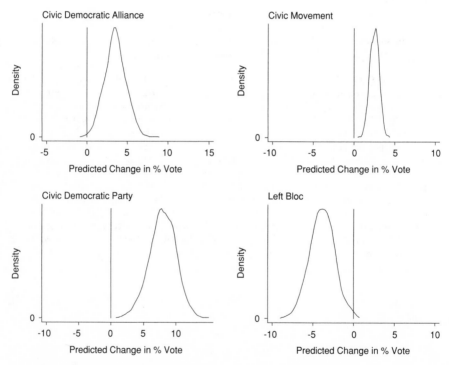

Figure AIII.1 Estimated Distribution of Predicted Change in the % Vote for Parties in 1992 Czech Parliamentary Election

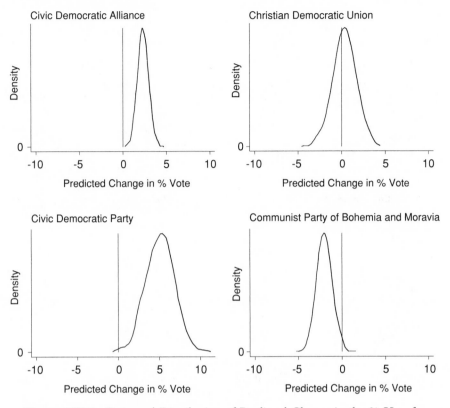

Figure AIII.2 Estimated Distribution of Predicted Change in the % Vote for Parties in 1996 Czech Parliamentary Election

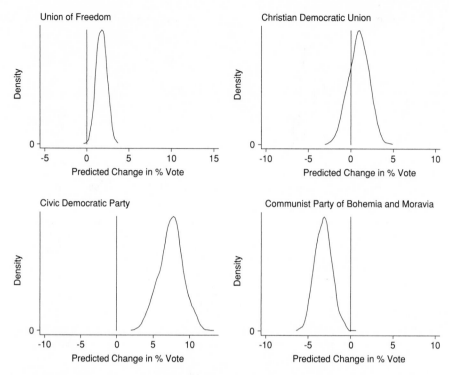

Figure AIII.3   Estimated Distribution of Predicted Change in the % Vote for Parties in 1998 Czech Parliamentary Election

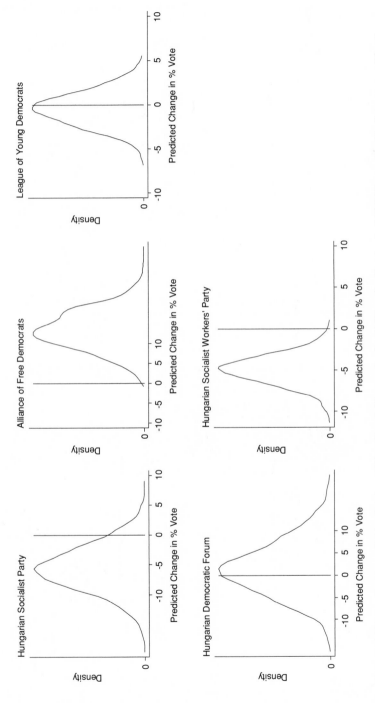

Figure AIII.4 Estimated Distribution of Predicted Change in the % Vote for Parties in 1990 Hungarian Parliamentary Election

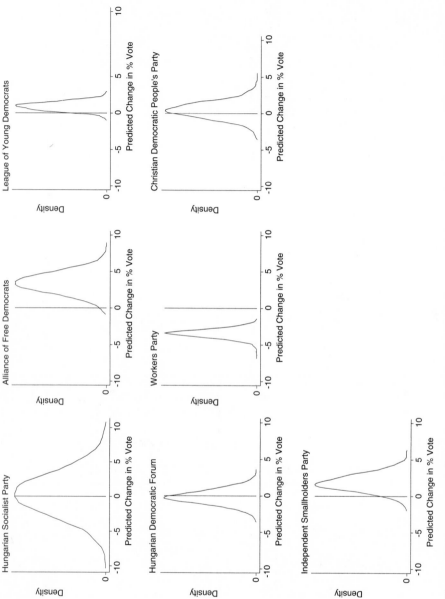

Figure AIII.5 Estimated Distribution of Predicted Change in the % Vote for Parties in 1994 Hungarian Parliamentary Election

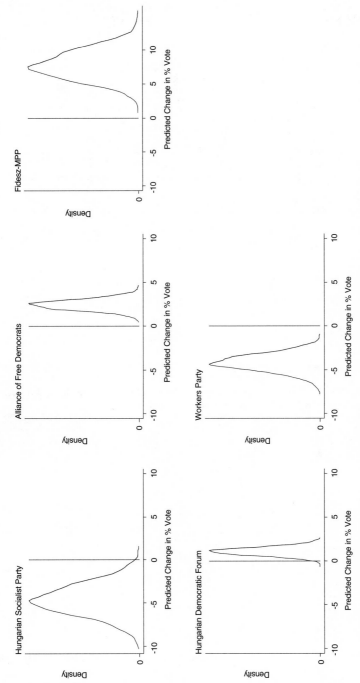

Figure AIII.6 Estimated Distribution of Predicted Change in the % Vote for Parties in 1998 Hungarian Parliamentary Election

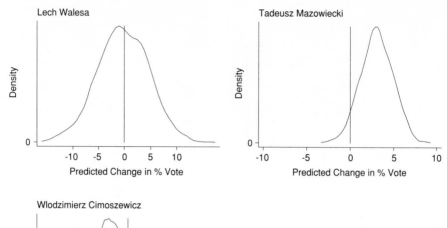

Figure AIII.7 Estimated Distribution of Predicted Change in the % Vote for Candidates in 1990 Polish Presidential Election

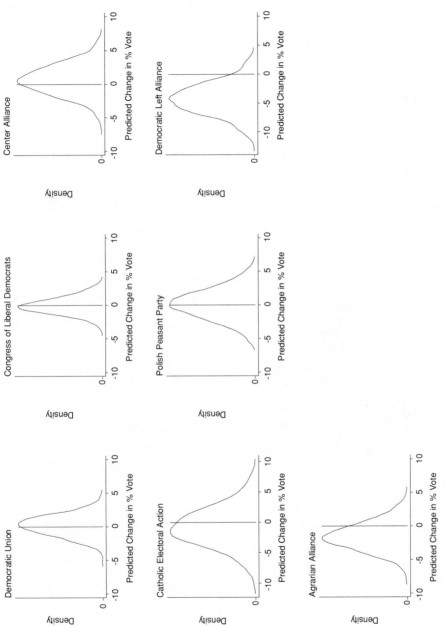

Figure AIII.8 Estimated Distribution of Predicted Change in the % Vote for Parties in 1991 Polish Parliamentary Election

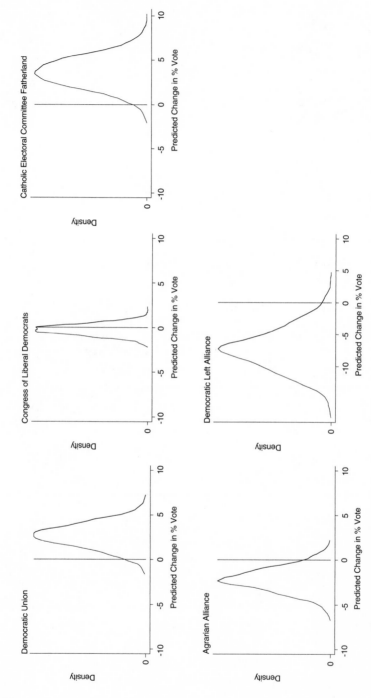

Figure AIII.9 Estimated Distribution of Predicted Change in the % Vote for Parties in 1993 Polish Parliamentary Election

Appendix III

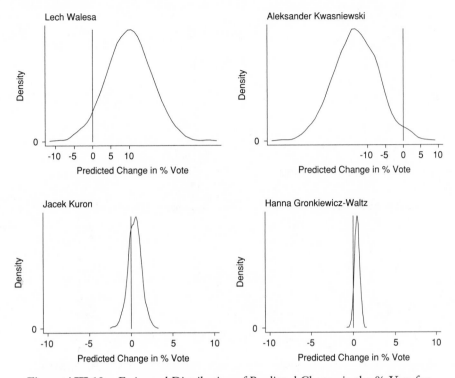

Figure AIII.10   Estimated Distribution of Predicted Change in the % Vote for Candidates in 1995 Polish Presidential Election

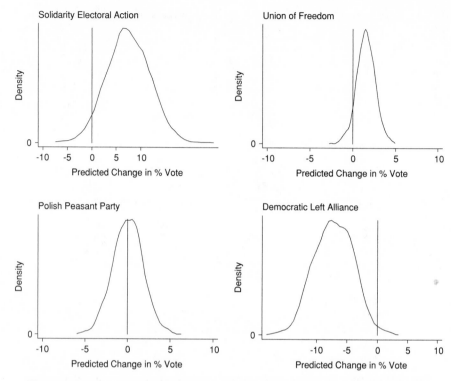

Figure AIII.11 Estimated Distribution of Predicted Change in the % Vote for Parties in 1997 Polish Parliamentary Election

Appendix III

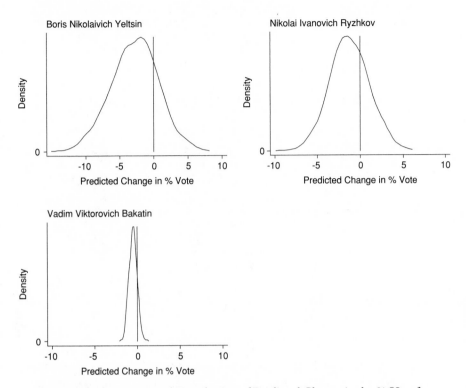

Figure AIII.12   Estimated Distribution of Predicted Change in the % Vote for Candidates in 1991 Russian Presidential Election

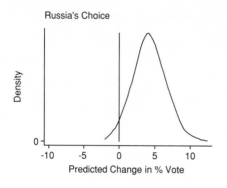

Russia's Choice

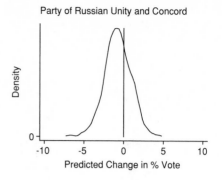

Party of Russian Unity and Concord

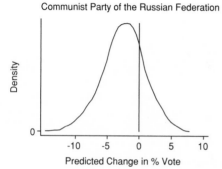

Communist Party of the Russian Federation

Figure AIII.13   Estimated Distribution of Predicted Change in the % Vote for Parties in 1993 Russian Parliamentary Election

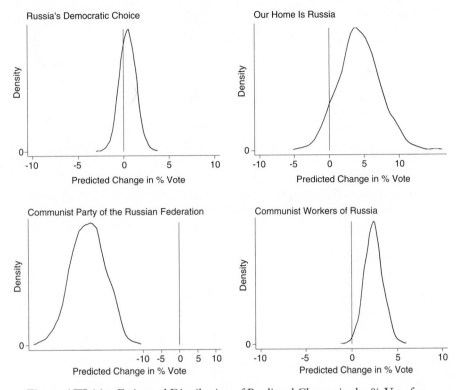

Figure AIII.14 Estimated Distribution of Predicted Change in the % Vote for Parties in 1995 Russian Parliamentary Election

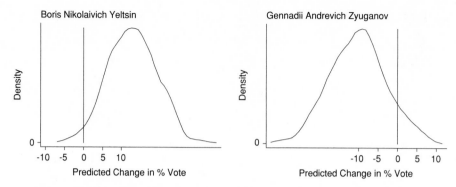

Figure AIII.15   Estimated Distribution of Predicted Change in the % Vote for Candidates in 1996 Russian Presidential Election

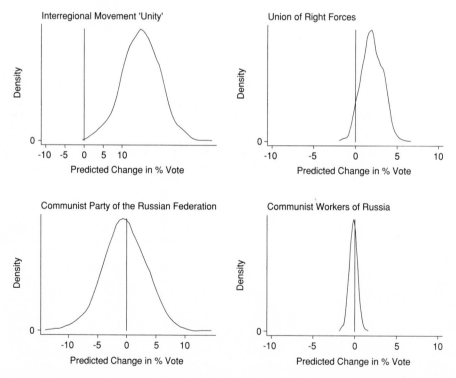

Figure AIII.16   Estimated Distribution of Predicted Change in the % Vote for Parties in 1999 Russian Parliamentary Election

Appendix III

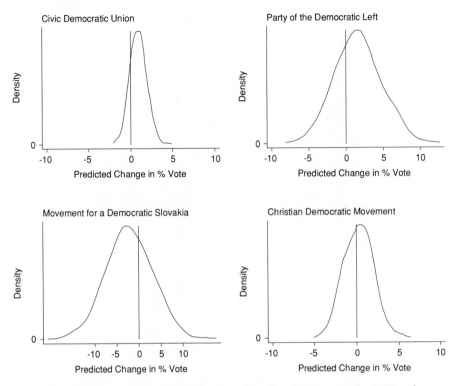

Figure AIII.17 Estimated Distribution of Predicted Change in the % Vote for Parties in 1992 Slovak Parliamentary Election

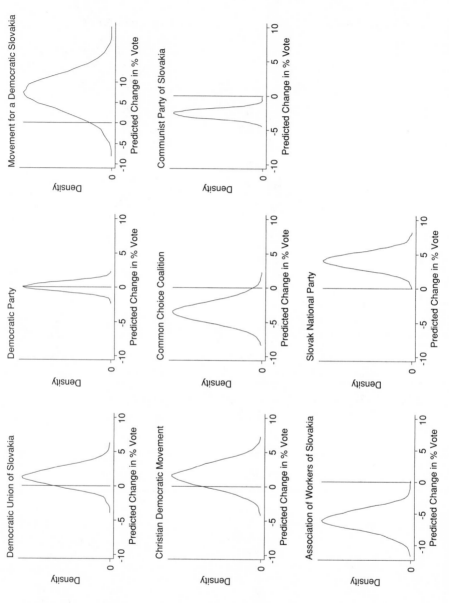

Figure AIII.18 Estimated Distribution of Predicted Change in the % Vote for Parties in 1994 Slovak Parliamentary Election

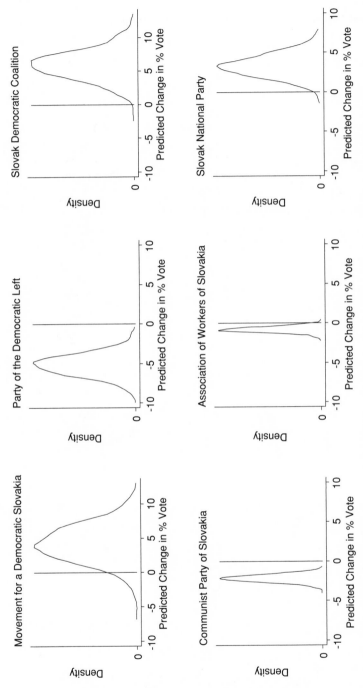

Figure AIII.19 Estimated Distribution of Predicted Change in the % Vote for Parties in 1998 Slovak Parliamentary Election

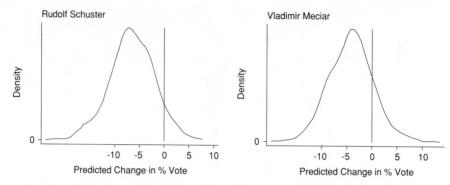

Figure AIII.20 Estimated Distribution of Predicted Change in the % Vote for Candidates in 1999 Slovak Presidential Election

Appendix IV

Percentage of Positive Simulations by Party

Country	Year	Party	Percentage Positive
Czech Republic	1992	Civic Democratic Alliance	99.7
Czech Republic	1992	Civic Democratic Party	100.0
Czech Republic	1992	Civic Movement	100.0
Czech Republic	1992	Left Bloc	0.5
Czech Republic	1996	Christian Democratic Union	60.6
Czech Republic	1996	Civic Democratic Alliance	100.0
Czech Republic	1996	Civic Democratic Party	99.7
Czech Republic	1996	Communist Party of Bohemia and Moravia	1.2
Czech Republic	1998	Christian Democratic Union	77.6
Czech Republic	1998	Civic Democratic Party	100.0
Czech Republic	1998	Communist Party of Bohemia and Moravia	0.3
Czech Republic	1998	Union of Freedom	99.9
Hungary	1990	Alliance of Free Democrats	100.0
Hungary	1990	League of Young Democrats	40.4
Hungary	1990	Hungarian Democratic Forum	59.4
Hungary	1990	Hungarian Socialist Party	7.7
Hungary	1990	Hungarian Socialist Workers Party	0.2
Hungary	1994	Alliance of Free Democrats	99.0
Hungary	1994	Christian Democratic People's Party	65.6
Hungary	1994	League of Young Democrats	93.5
Hungary	1994	Hungarian Democratic Forum	40.5
Hungary	1994	Hungarian Socialist Party	53.9
Hungary	1994	Workers Party	0.0
Hungary	1994	Independent Smallholders Party	94.9
Hungary	1998	Alliance of Free Democrats	100.0

(continued)

(continued)

Country	Year	Party	Percentage Positive
Hungary	1998	Fidesz-Hungarian People's Party	100.0
Hungary	1998	Hungarian Democratic Forum	99.4
Hungary	1998	Hungarian Socialist Party	0.4
Hungary	1998	Workers Party	0.0
Poland	1990	Lech Wałęsa	47.5
Poland	1990	Tadeusz Mazowiecki	95.1
Poland	1990	Wlodzimierz Cimoszewicz	9.8
Poland	1991	Catholic Electoral Action	39.6
Poland	1991	Center Alliance	61.5
Poland	1991	Congress of Liberal Democrats	48.0
Poland	1991	Democratic Left Alliance	5.2
Poland	1991	Democratic Union	58.1
Poland	1991	Agrarian Alliance	22.9
Poland	1991	Polish Peasant Party	52.8
Poland	1993	Catholic Electoral Committee Fatherland	98.3
Poland	1993	Congress of Liberal Democrats	36.4
Poland	1993	Democratic Left Alliance	1.9
Poland	1993	Democratic Union	97.4
Poland	1993	Agrarian Alliance	5.8
Poland	1995	Aleksander Kwaśniewski	2.4
Poland	1995	Hanna Gronkiewicz-Waltz	92.6
Poland	1995	Jacek Kuroń	71.6
Poland	1995	Lech Wałęsa	95.1
Poland	1997	Democratic Left Alliance	1.2
Poland	1997	Polish Peasant Party	50.7
Poland	1997	Solidarity Electoral Action	96.2
Poland	1997	Union of Freedom	93.0
Russia	1991	Boris Yeltsin	21.3
Russia	1991	Nikolai Ryzhkov	29.7
Russia	1991	Vadim Bakatin	15.1
Russia	1993	Communist Party of the Russian Federation	22.4
Russia	1993	Party of Russian Unity and Concord	30.9
Russia	1993	Russia's Choice	96.8
Russia	1995	Communist Party of the Russian Federation	0.0
Russia	1995	Communist Workers of Russia for the Soviet Union	99.2
Russia	1995	Our Home is Russia	92.6
Russia	1995	Russia's Democratic Choice	69.9
Russia	1996	Boris Yeltsin	98.0
Russia	1996	Gennadii Zyuganov	8.6
Russia	1999	Communist Party of the Russian Federation	45.5

Appendix IV

Country	Year	Party	Percentage Positive
Russia	1999	Communist Workers of Russia for the Soviet Union	35.7
Russia	1999	Inter-Regional Movement "Unity"	100.0
Russia	1999	Union of Right Forces	94.4
Slovakia	1992	Christian Democratic Movement	54.9
Slovakia	1992	Civic Democratic Union	81.8
Slovakia	1992	Movement for a Democratic Slovakia	34.0
Slovakia	1992	Party of the Democratic Left	68.6
Slovakia	1994	Association of Workers of Slovakia	0.0
Slovakia	1994	Christian Democratic Movement	82.8
Slovakia	1994	Common Choice Coalition	1.3
Slovakia	1994	Communist Party of Slovakia	0.0
Slovakia	1994	Democratic Party	55.2
Slovakia	1994	Democratic Union of Slovakia	84.1
Slovakia	1994	Movement for a Democratic Slovakia	95.6
Slovakia	1994	Slovak National Party	100.0
Slovakia	1998	Communist Party of Slovakia	0.0
Slovakia	1998	Movement for a Democratic Slovakia	94.9
Slovakia	1998	Party of the Democratic Left	0.0
Slovakia	1998	Slovak Democratic Coalition	99.7
Slovakia	1998	Slovak National Party	99.2
Slovakia	1998	Union of Slovak Workers	0.9
Slovakia	1999	Rudolf Schuster	7.3
Slovakia	1999	Vladimír Meciar	16.7

Works Cited

1993. "Every Man a Tsar." *New Yorker*. 69: 8.

Achen, Christopher H. 2000. *Why Lagged Dependent Variables Can Suppress the Explanatory Power of Other Independent Variables*. Ann Arbor, MI: manuscript.

Agh, Attila. 1995. "Partial Consolidation of the East Central European Parties: The Case of the Hungarian Socialist Party." *Party Politics* 1 (4): 491–514.

Agh, Attila 2000. "Party Formation Process and the 1998 Elections in Hungary: Defeat as Promoter of Change for the HSP." *East European Politics and Societies* 14 (2): 288–315.

Aguilar, Edwin and Alexander Pacek. 2000. "Macroeconomic Conditions, Voter Turnout, and the Working-class/Economically Disadvantaged Party Vote in Developing Countries." *Comparative Political Studies* 33 (8): 995–1017.

Ahdieh, Robert B. 1997. *Russia's Constitutional Revolution: Legal Consciousness and the Transition to Democracy, 1985–1995*. University Park: Pennsylvania State University Press.

Aidt, Toke. 2000. "Economic Voting and Information." *Electoral Studies* 19: 349–62.

Alesina, Alberto and Howard Rosenthal. 1995. *Partisan Politics, Divided Government, and the Economy*. Cambridge: Cambridge University Press.

Alvarez, R. Michael, Jonathan Nagler and Jennifer Willette. 2000. "Measuring the Relative Impact of Issues and the Economy in Democratic Elections." *Electoral Studies* 19: 237–53.

Anderson, Christopher J. 2000. "Economic Voting and Political Context: A Comparative Perspective." *Electoral Studies* 19 (2/3): 151–70.

Ash, Timothy Garton. 1993. *The Magic Lantern*. New York: Vintage Books.

Ash, Timothy Garton. 1999. *The Polish Revolution: Solidarity*. New York: Viking Penguin.

Aslund, Anders. 1995. "The Case for Radical Reform," in *Economic Reform and Democracy*. Larry Diamond and Marc Plattner, eds. Baltimore, MD: Johns Hopkins University Press: 74–85.

Barany, Zoltan D. 1990. "The State of the Parties as Elections Approach." *Report on Eastern Europe*, March 16: 11–13.

379

Barany, Zoltan D. and Louisa Vinton. 1990. "Breakthrough to Democracy: Elections in Poland and Hungary." *Communist and Post-Communist Studies* 23 (2): 191–212.

Barnes, Catherine. 1996. "Federal Elections in Russia: The Necessity of Systemic Reforms." *Demokratizatsiya* 4 (3): 389–408.

Bauer, Michael. 2002. "Changing Cleavage Structure and the Communist Successor Parties of the Visegrad Countries," in *The Communist Successor Parties of Central and Eastern Europe.* András Bozóki and John T. Ishiyama, eds. Armonk, NY: M.E. Sharpe: 341–66.

Belin, Laura. 1999a. "Fatherland-All Russia Urges Voters to 'Believe Only in Deeds'." *RFE/RL Russian Election Report* 1999–2000 (4): http:// www.rferl.org/ specials/russianelection/archives/04-261199.asp.

Belin, Laura. 1999b. "State TV Is Kinder Than Ever To Zhirinovsky." *Radio Free Europe/Radio Liberty Election Reports: 1999–2000 Russian Election Cycle* (5): http://www.rferl.org/specials/russianelection/archives/05-031299.asp.

Belin, Laura. 1999c. "State TV Wages Unprecedented 'Information War'." *Radio Free Europe/Radio Liberty Election Reports: 1999–2000 Russian Election Cycle* (7): http://www.rferl.org/specials/russianelection/archives/07-171299.asp.

Belin, Laura. 1999d. "Union Of Right Forces Plays Putin Card." *Radio Free Europe/Radio Liberty Election Reports: 1999–2000 Russian Election Cycle* (7): http://www.rferl.org/specials/russianelection/archives/07-171299.asp.

Belin, Laura and Robert W. Orttung. 1997. *The Russian Parliamentary Elections of 1995: The Battle for the Duma.* Armonk, NY: M.E. Sharpe.

Bell, Janice. 1997. "Unemployment Matters: Voting Patterns during the Economic Transition in Poland, 1990–1995." *Europe-Asia Studies* 49 (7): 1263–91.

Bellucci, Paolo. 1984. "The Effect of Aggregate Economic Conditions on the Political Preferences of the Italian Electorate, 1953–1979." *European Journal of Political Research* 12 (4): 387–401.

Benoit, Ken, Gyorgy Csalotzky, Ilona Cseve, Zoltan Kovacs, Attila Peteri and Zsolt Szolnoki. 1998. *Parliamentary Elections in Hungary 1998: A Guide for International Observers.* Budapest, Hungary: Hungarian Ministry of Interior: National Election Office.

Benoit, Ken and Jacqueline Hayden. 2004. "Institutional Change and Persistence: The Origins and Evolution of Poland's Electoral System 1989–2001." *Journal of Politics* 66 (2): 396–427.

Benoit, Kenneth and John W. Schiemann. 2001. "Institutional Choices in New Democracies: Bargaining over Hungary's 1989 Electoral Law." *Journal of Theoretical Politics* 13 (2): 153–82.

Berinsky, Adam J. 2004. *Silent Voices: Public Oinion and Political Participation in America.* Princeton, NJ: Princeton University Press.

Berinsky, Adam and Joshua A. Tucker. 2003. *Transitional Survey Analysis: Measuring Bias in Russian Public Opinion.* Paper presented at the Annual Meeting of the International Society of Political Psychology, Berlin, Germany.

Bernhard, Michael. 1997. "Semipresidentialism, Charisma, and Democratic Institutions in Poland," in *Presidential Institutions and Democratic Politics: Comparing*

Works Cited

Regional and National Contexts. Kurt von Mettenheim, ed. Baltimore, MD: Johns Hopkins University Press: 177–203.

Bigler, Robert M. 1992. "From Communism to Democracy: Hungary's Transition Thirty Five Years After the Revolution." *East European Quarterly* XXV (4): 437–59.

Birch, Sarah, Frances Millard, Marina Popescu and Kieran Williams. 2002. *Embodying Democracy: Electoral System Design in Post-Communist Europe*. New York: Palgrave Macmillan.

Biskupski, Mieczyslaw B. 2000. *The History of Poland*. Westport, CT: Greenwood Press.

Blahoz, Josef, Lubomir Brokly and Zdenka Mansfeldova. 1999. "Czech Political Parties and Cleavages after 1989," in *Cleavages, Parties, and Voters: Studies from Bulgaria, the Czech Republic, Hungary, Poland, and Romania*. Kay Lawson, Andrea Römmele and Georgi Karasimeonov, eds. Westport, CT: Praeger: 123–40.

Blount, Simon. 1999. "The Microeconomic Voter." *Electoral Studies* 18: 505–17.

Bozóki, Andras. 2002. "The Hungarian Socialists: Technocratic Modernization or New Social Democracy?," in *The Communist Successor Parties of Central and Eastern Europe*. András Bozóki and John T. Ishiyama, eds. Armonk, NY: M.E. Sharpe: 89–115.

Bozóki, András and John T. Ishiyama. 2002. "Introduction and Theoretical Framework," in *The Communist Successor Parties of Central and Eastern Europe*. András Bozóki and John T. Ishiyama, eds. Armonk, NY: M.E. Sharpe: 1–13.

Brader, Ted and Joshua A. Tucker. 2001. "The Emergence of Mass Partisanship in Russia, 1993–96." *American Journal of Political Science* 45 (1): 69–83.

Brandt, Patrick T., Burt L. Monroe and John T. Williams. 1999. "Time Series Models for Compositional Data." Paper presented at the 1999 Annual Meeting of the American Political Science Association, Atlanta, GA.

Brovkin, Vladimir. 1997. "Time to Pay the Bills: Presidential Elections and Political Stabilization in Russia." *Problems of Communism* 44 (6): 34–42.

Brown, Archie and Lilia Fedorovna Shevtsova. 2001. *Gorbachev, Yeltsin, and Putin: Political Leadership in Russia's Transition*. Washington, DC: Carnegie Endowment for International Peace.

Brudny, Yitzhak M. 1997. "In Pursuit of the Russian Presidency: Why and How Yeltsin Won the 1996 Presidential Election." *Communist and Post-Communist Studies* 30 (3): 255–75.

Bugajski, Janusz. 2002. *Political Parties of Eastern Europe: A Guide to Politics in the Post-Communist Era*. Armonk, NY: M.E. Sharpe.

Bugge, Peter. 1994. "The Czech Republic," in *Political Parties of Eastern Europe, Russia, and the Successor States*. Bogdan Szajkowski, ed. Harlow, Essex, UK: Longman Information and Reference: 149–73.

Bunce, Valerie. 2001. "Democratization and Economic Reform." *Annual Review of Political Science* 4: 43–65.

Bunce, Valerie. 2002. "The Return of the Left and Democratic Consolidation in Poland and Hungary," in *The Communist Successor Parties of Central and Eastern Europe*. András Bozóki and John T. Ishiyama, eds. Armonk, NY: M.E. Sharpe.

Bunce, Valerie and Maria Csanadi. 1993. "Uncertainty in Transition: Post Communism in Hungary." *East European Politics and Societies* 7 (2): 240–75.

Butorova, Martin, Grigorij Meseznikov, Zora Butorova and Sharon Fisher, Eds. 1999. *The 1998 Parliamentary Elections and Democratic Rebirth in Slovakia*. Bratislava, Slovakia: Institute for Public Affairs.

Butorova, Zora, Olga Gyarfasova and Marian Velšic. 2005. "Verejna Mienka (Public Opinion)," in *Slovensko 2004: Súhrnná správa o stave spolocnosti (Slovakia 2004: Global Report on the State of Society)*. Miroslav Kollár and Grigorij Mesežnikov, eds. Bratislava, Slovakia: Institute for Public Affairs.

Campbell, Angus, Philip E. Converse, Warren E. Miller and Donald E. Stokes. 1960. *The American Voter*. New York: Wiley.

Carothers, Thomas. 2002. "The End of the Transition Paradigm." *Journal of Democracy* 13 (1): 5–21.

Castle, Marjorie and Ray Taras. 2002. *Democracy in Poland*. Boulder, CO: Westview Press.

Cepl, Vojtech and Mark Gillis. 1994. "Czech Republic." *East European Constitutional Review* 3 (1): 64–8.

Chan, Kenneth. 1995. "Poland at the Crossroads: The 1993 General Election." *Europe-Asia Studies* 47 (1): 123–45.

Chan, Kenneth. 1998. "The Polish General Election of 1997." *Electoral Studies* 17 (4): 561–7.

Chappell, Henry W. and William R. Keech. 1985. "A New View of Political Accountability for Economic Performance." *American Political Science Review* 79 (1): 10–27.

Chappell, Henry W. and Linda Goncalves Veiga. 2000. "Economics and Elections in Western Europe: 1960–1997." *Electoral Studies* 19 (2/3): 183–97.

Clem, Ralph S. and Peter R. Craumer. 1993. "The Geography of the April 25 (1993) Russian Referendum." *Post-Soviet Geography and Economics* 34 (8): 481–96.

Clem, Ralph S. and Peter R. Craumer. 1995a. "The Geography of the Russian 1995 Parliamentary Election: Continuity, Change, and Correlates." *Post-Soviet Geography and Economics* 36 (10): 587–616.

Clem, Ralph S. and Peter R. Craumer. 1995b. "The Politics of Russia's Regions: A Geographical Analysis of the Russian Election and Constitutional Plebiscite of December 1993." *Post-Soviet Geography and Economics* 36 (2): 67–86.

Clem, Ralph S. and Peter R. Craumer. 1995c. "A Rayon-Level Analysis of the Russian Election and Constitutional Plebiscite of December 1993." *Post-Soviet Geography and Economics* 36 (8): 459–75.

Clem, Ralph S. and Peter R. Craumer. 1996. "Roadmap to Victory: Boris Yel'tsin and the Russian Presidential Elections of 1996." *Post-Soviet Geography and Economics* 37 (6): 335–54.

Clem, Ralph S. and Peter R. Craumer. 1997. "Urban-Rural Voting Differences in Russian Elections, 1995–1996: A Rayon Level Analysis." *Post-Soviet Geography and Economics* 38 (7): 379–95.

Works Cited

Clem, Ralph S. and Peter R. Craumer. 2001. "Regional Patterns of Political Preference in Russia: The December 1999 Duma Elections." *Post-Soviet Geography and Economics* 41 (1): 1–29.

Clem, Ralph S. and Peter R. Craumer. 2002. "Urban and Rural Effects on Party Preference in Russia: New Evidence from the Recent Duma Election." *Post-Soviet Geography and Economics* 43 (1): 1–12.

Colitt, Leslie. 1991. "Jobs Must Go, Says Prague Minister". *Financial Times*, Februrary 6, 1991, 4.

Colton, Timothy J. 1995. "Boris Yeltsin, Russia's All-Thumbs Democrat," in *Patterns in Post-Soviet Leadership*. Timothy J. Colton and Robert C. Tucker, eds. Boulder, CO: Westview Press: 49–74.

Colton, Timothy J. 1996a. "Economics and Voting in Russia." *Post-Soviet Affairs* 12 (4): 289–318.

Colton, Timothy J. 1996b. "From the Parliamentary to the Presidential Election: Russians Get Real about Politics." *Demokratizatsiya* 4 (3): 371–9.

Colton, Timothy J. 1998a. "Ideology and Russian Mass Politics: Uses of the Left-Right Continuum," in *Elections and Voting in Post-Communist Russia*. Matthew Wyman, Stephen White and Sarah Oates, eds. Northampton, MA: Edward Elgar: 167–89.

Colton, Timothy J. 1998b. "Introduction: The 1993 Election and the New Russian Politics," in *Growing Pains: Russian Democracy and the Election of 1993*. Timothy J. Colton and Jerry F. Hough, eds. Washington, DC: Brookings Institution Press: 1–36.

Colton, Timothy J. 1999. "Understanding Iurii Luzhkov." *Problems of Post-Communism* 46 (5): 14–26.

Colton, Timothy J. 2000a. "Parties, Citizens, and Democratic Consolidation in Russia." Paper presented at Ten Years after the Collapse of the Soviet Union: Lessons and Perspectives Conference, Oct. 13–14, Princeton, NJ.

Colton, Timothy J. 2000b. *Transitional Citizens: Voters and What Influences Them in the New Russia*. Cambridge, MA: Harvard University Press.

Colton, Timothy J. 2002. "The Leadership Factor in the Russian Presidential Election of 1996," in *Leaders' Personalities and the Outcomes of Democratic Elections*. Anthony King, ed. New York: Oxford University Press.

Colton, Timothy J. and Jerry F. Hough, eds 1998. *Growing Pains: Russian Democracy and the Election of 1993*. Washington, DC: Brookings Institution Press.

Colton, Timothy J. and Michael McFaul. 2000. "Reinventing Russia's Party of Power: "Unity" and the 1999 Duma Election." *Post Soviet Affairs* 16 (3): 201–24.

Colton, Timothy J. and Michael McFaul. 2003. *Popular Choice and Managed Democracy: The Russian Elections of 1999 and 2000*. Washington, DC: Brookings Institution Press.

Cox, Gary W. 1997. *Making Votes Count: Strategic Coordination in the World's Electoral Systems*. Cambridge: Cambridge University Press.

Curry, Jane. 1995. "Elected Communists in Poland." *Problems of Communism* 42 (1): 46–50.

Curry, Jane. 1997. "Which Way is Right?" *Transitions* 4 (5): 74–9.

Curry, Jane Leftwich and Joan Barth Urban. 2003. *The Left Transformed in Post-communist Societies: the Cases of East-Central Europe, Russia, and Ukraine*. Lanham, MD: Rowman & Littlefield.

Daniels, Robert V. 1999. "Evgenii Primakov: Contender by Chance." *Problems of Post-Communism* 46 (5): 27–36.

Downs, Anthony. 1957. *An Economic Theory of Democracy*. New York: Harper & Row.

Duch, Raymond. 2000. "Heterogeneity in Perceptions of National Economic Conditions." *American Journal of Political Science* 44 (4): 635–52.

Eagleton, Thomas. 1993. "Road to Capitalism Proves Bumpy." *St. Louis Times-Dispatch*, September 26: 3B.

Editorial. 1993. "Polish Voters Want Less Pain." *Montreal Gazette*, September 21: B2.

Erikson, Robert S. 1989. "Economic Conditions and the Presidential Vote." *American Political Science Review* 83 (2): 567–73.

Erikson, Robert S. 1990. "Economic Conditions and the Congressional Vote." *American Journal of Political Science* 34 (2): 373–99.

Erikson, Robert S., Michael B. MacKuen and James A. Stimson. 2000. "Bankers or Peasants Revisited: Economic Expectations and Presidential Approval." *Electoral Studies* 19 (2/3): 295–312.

Evans, Geoffrey and Stephen Whitefield. 1998. "The Structure of Cleavages in Post-Communist Societies: The Case of the Czech Republic and Slovakia." *Political Studies* 46 (1): 115–39.

Feld, Lars and Gebhard Kirchgassner. 2000. "Official and Hidden Unemployment and the Popularity of the Government: An Econometric Analysis for the Kohl Government." *Electoral Studies* 19: 333–47.

Fidrmuc, Jan. 2000a. "Economics of Voting in Post-Communist Countries." *Electoral Studies* 19 (2/3): 199–217.

Fidrmuc, Jan. 2000b. *Liberalization, Democracy, and Economic Performance During Transition*. Bonn, Germany, Center for European Integration Studies (ZEI) Working Paper.

Fidrmuc, Jan. 2000c. "Political Support for Reforms: Economics of Voting in Transition Countries." *European Economic Review* 44: 1491–1513.

Filipov, Mikhail and Peter C. Ordeshook. 1997. "Who Stole What in Russia's December 1993 Elections." *Demokratizatsiya* 5 (1): 36–52.

Fiorina, Morris P. 1981. *Retrospective Voting in American National Elections*. New Haven, CT: Yale University Press.

Fish, M. Steven. 1995a. "The Advent of Multipartism in Russia, 1993–95." *Post Soviet Affairs* 11 (4): 340–83.

Fish, M. Steven. 1995b. *Democracy From Scratch: Opposition and Regime in the New Russian Revolution*. Princeton, NJ: Princeton University Press.

Fish, M. Steven. 1997. "The Predicament of Russian Liberalism: Evidence from the December 1995 Parliamentary Elections." *Europe-Asia Studies* 49 (2): 191–220.

Fish, M. Steven. 1999. "The End of Meciarism." *East European Constitutional Review* 8 (1/2): 47–55.

Works Cited

Fish, M. Steven. 2000. "The Executive Deception: Superpresidentialism and the Degredation of Russian Politics," in *Building the Russian State: Institutional Crisis and the Quest for Democratic Governance*. Valerie Sperling, ed. Boulder, CO: Westview Press: 177–92.

Fisher, Sharon. 1994. "New Slovak Government Formed after Meciar's Fall." *RFE/RL Research Report* 3 (13): 7–13.

Fisher, Sharon. 1996. "Backtracking on the Road to Democratic Reform," in *Building Democracy: The OMRI Annual Survey of Eastern Europe and the Former Soviet Union*. Armonk, NY: M.E. Sharpe.

Fisher, Sharon. 2002. "The Troubled Evolution of Slovakia's Ex-Communists," in *The Communist Successor Parties of Central and Eastern Europe*. András Bozóki and John T. Ishiyama, eds. Armonk, NY: M.E. Sharpe: 116–40.

Fisher, Sharon and Stefan Hrib. 1994. "Political Crisis in Slovakia." *RFE/RL Research Report* 3 (10): 20–6.

Fitzmaurice, John. 1996. "The 1996 Czech Elections." *Electoral Studies* 15 (4): 575–80.

Fitzmaurice, John. 1999. "The Slovak Elections of 25th and 26th September 1998." *Electoral Studies*, 18: 271–300.

Fitzmaurice, John. 2001. "The Slovak Presidential Election, May 1999." *Electoral Studies* 20: 305–39.

Flikke, Geir. 1999. "Patriotic Left-Centrism: The Zigzags of the Communist Party of the Russian Federation." *Europe-Asia Studies* 51 (2): 275–98.

Fowler, B. 1998. "Notes on Recent Elections Hungarian Parliamentary Elections, May 1998." *Electoral Studies* 17 (2): 257–62.

Fricz, Tamas. 2000. "Democratisation, the Party System, and the Electorate in Hungary," in *From Totalitarian to Democratic Hungary: Evolution and Transformation 1990–2000*. Mária Schmidt and László G. Tóth, eds. New York: Columbia University Press: 106–46.

Frye, Timothy. 2000. *Brokers and Bureaucrats: Building Market Institutions in Russia*. Ann Arbor: University of Michigan Press.

Fule, Erika. 1997. "Changes on the Czech Political Scene." *Electoral Studies* 16 (3): 341–7.

Gabel, Matthew J. 1995. "The Political Consequences of Electoral Laws in the 1990 Hungarian Elections." *Comparative Politics* 27 (2): 205–14.

Gaidar, Yegor T. 1999. *Days of Defeat and Victory*. Seattle: University of Washington Press.

Gall, Carlotta and Thomas De Waal. 1998. *Chechnya: Calamity in the Caucuses*. New York: New York University Press.

Gans-Morse, Jordan. 2004. "Searching for Transitologists: Contemporary Theories of Post-Communist Transition and the Myth of a Dominant Paradigm." *Post-Soviet Affairs* 20 (4): 320–49.

Gebethner, Stanislaw. 1995. *Wybory Parlamentarne 1991 i 1993 A Polska Scena Politycyna*. Warsaw, Poland: Wydawnictwo Sejmowe.

Gershanok, Gennady. 1996. "Cats and Mice: The Presidential Campaign in the Russian Heartland." *Demokratizatsiya* 4 (3): 349–57.

Gibson, John and Anna Cielecka. 1995. "Economic Influences on the Political Support for Market Reform in Post-Communist Transitions: Some Evidence from the 1993 Polish Parliamentary Elections." *Europe-Asia Studies* 47 (5): 765–85.

Goidel, Robert and Ronald Langley. 1994. "Media Coverage of the Economy and Aggregate Economic Evaluations." *Political Research Quarterly* 48 (2): 291–312.

Golder, Matt. 2003. "Explaining Variation in the Success of Extreme Right Parties in Western Europe." *Comparative Political Studies* 36 (4): 432–66.

Goldman, Minton F. 1997. *Revolution and Change in Central and Eastern Europe: Political, Economic, and Social Challenges.* Armonk, NY: M.E. Sharpe.

Gomez, Brad, and J. Matthew Wilson. 2001. "Political Sophistication and Economic Voting in the American Electorate: A Theory of Heterogeneous Attribution." *American Journal of Political Science* 45 (4): 899–914.

Greene, William H. 1993. *Econometric Analysis.* Englewood Cliffs, NJ: Prentice Hall.

Grigoriev, Sergei and Matthew Lantz. 1996. "Lessons of the 1995 State Duma Elections." *Demokratizatsiya* 4 (2): 159–72.

Grzymala-Busse, Anna. 1998. "Reform Efforts in the Czech and Slovak Communist Parties and Their Successors, 1988–1993." *East European Politics and Societies* 12 (3): 442–71.

Grzymala-Busse, Anna. 2002. *Redeeming the Communist Past: the Regeneration of Communist Parties in East Central Europe.* Cambridge: Cambridge University Press.

Gustafson, Thane. 1999. *Capitalism Russian-Style.* Cambridge: Cambridge University Press.

Haggard, Stephan and Robert R. Kaufman. 1989. "Economic Adjustment in New Democracies," in *Fragile Coalitions: The Politics of Economic Adjustment.* Joan M. Nelson, ed. Washington, DC: Overseas Development Council: 57–78.

Haggard, Stephan and Robert R. Kaufman. 1992. "Economic Adjustment and the Prospects for Democracy," in *The Politics of Economic Adjustment: International Constraints, Distributive Conflicts, and the State.* Stephan Haggard and Robert R. Kaufman, eds. Princeton, NJ: Princeton University Press: 319–50.

Haggard, Stephan and Robert R. Kaufman. 1995a. "The Challenges of Consolidation," in *Economic Reform and Democracy.* Larry Diamond and Marc Plattner, eds. Baltimore, MD: Johns Hopkins University Press: 1–12.

Haggard, Stephan and Robert R. Kaufman. 1995b. *The Political Economy of Democratic Transitions.* Princeton, NJ: Princeton University Press.

Haggard, Stephan and Steven Webb. 1993. "What Do We Know About the Political Economy of Economic Policy Reform?" *The World Bank Research Observer* 8 (2): 143–68.

Hahn, Gordon M. 1996. "Russia's Polarized Political Spectrum." *Problems of Post-Communism* XLIII (3): 11–22.

Hale, Henry E., ed. 2000. *Russia's Electoral War of 1999–2000: The Russian Election Watch Compendium.* Cambridge, MA: Harvard University.

Hancock, M. Donald and John Logue. 2000. *Transitions to Capitalism and Democracy in Russia and Central Europe: Achievements, Problems, Prospects.* Westport, CT: Praeger.

Works Cited

Hanley, Sean. 2002. "The Communist Party of Bohemia and Moravia after 1989: "Subcultural Party" to Neocommunist Force?," in *The Communist Successor Parties of Central and Eastern Europe*. András Bozóki and John T. Ishiyama, eds. Armonk, NY: M.E. Sharpe: 141–65.

Hanson, Stephen E. and Jeffrey Kopstein. 1997. "The Weimar/Russia Comparison." *Post-Soviet Affairs* 13 (3): 252–83.

Hanson, Stephen E. and Jeffrey Kopstein. 1998. "Paths to Uncivil Societies and Anti-Liberal States: A Reply to Shenfield." *Post-Soviet Affairs* 14 (4): 369–75.

Haraszti, Miklos. 1998. "Young Bloods: Hungary's Election Results Promise a New Taste of Political Salami." *Transitions* (14): 48–53.

Harper, Marcus. 2000. "Economic Voting in Postcommunist Eastern Europe." *Comparative Political Studies* 33 (9): 1191–1227.

Hellman, Joel, Joshua A. Tucker and Timothy Frye. 1996. *An Index of Presidential and Prime Ministerial Powers in the Former Soviet Union and East Central Europe*, http://www.wws.princeton.edu/~jtucker/pcelections.html.

Henderson, Karen. 1994. "The Slovak Republic," in *Political Parties of Eastern Europe, Russia, and the Successor States*. Bogdan Szajkowski, ed. Harlow, Essex, UK: Longman Information and Reference: 525–55.

Herrera, Yoshiko. 2005. *Imagined Economies: The Sources of Russian Regionalism*. Cambridge: Cambridge University Press.

Hetherington, Marc. 1996. "The Media's Role in Forming Voter's National Economic Evaluations in 1992." *American Journal of Political Science* 40 (2): 372–95.

Heyns, Barbara and Ireneusz Bialecki. 1991. "Solidarnosc: Reluctant Vanguard or Makeshift Coalition?" *American Political Science Review* 85 (2): 351–70.

Hirshman, Albert. 1970. *Exit, Voice, and Loyalty: Response to Decline in Firms, Organizations, and States*. Cambridge, MA: Harvard University Press.

Holbrook, Thomas and James Garand. 1996. "Homo Economus? Economic Information and Economic Voting." *Political Research Quarterly* 49 (2): 351–75.

Holmes, Stephen. 1994. "A Forum on Presidential Power." *East European Constitutional Review* 3 (1): 36–9.

Honaker, James, Jonathan Katz and Gary King. 2002. "A Fast, Easy, and Efficient Estimator for Multiparty Data." *Political Analysis* 10 (1): 84–100.

Host, Viggo and Martin Paldam. 1990. "An International Element in the Vote?" *European Journal of Political Research* 18: 221–39.

Hough, Jerry F. 1998. "The Political Geography of European Russia: Republics and Oblasts." *Post-Soviet Geography and Economics* 39 (2): 63–95.

Hough, Jerry F., Evelyn Davidheiser and Susan Goodrich Lehmann. 1996. *The 1996 Russian Presidential Election*. Washington, DC: Brookings Institution Press.

Huber, John D., Georgia Kernell and Eduardo L. Leoni. 2005. "Institutional Contact, Cognitive Resources and Party Attachment Across Democracies." *Political Analysis* 13 (4): 365–86.

Huskey, Eugene. 1999. *Presidential Power in Russia*. Armonk, NY: M.E. Sharpe.

Innes, Abby. 1997. "The Breakup of Czechoslovakia: The Impact of Party Development on the Separation of the State." *East European Politics and Societies* 11 (3): 393–435.

Innes, Abby. 2001. *Czechoslovakia: The Short Goodbye*. New Haven, CT: Yale University Press.

Ishiyama, John. 1997. "The Sickle or the Rose? Previous Regime Types and the Evolution of the Ex-Communist Parties in Post-Communist Politics." *Comparative Political Studies* 30 (3): 299–330.

Ishiyama, John T., ed. 1999. *Communist Successor Parties in Post-Communist Politics*. Commack, NY: Nova Science Publishers.

Jackson, John E. 2002. "A Seemingly Unrelated Regression Model for Analyzing Multiparty Elections." *Political Analysis* 10 (1): 49–65.

Jackson, John E., Jacek Klich, and Krystyna Poznanska. 2003a. "Democratic Institutions and Economic Reform: The Polish Case." *British Journal of Political Science* 33 (1):85–108.

Jackson, John E., Jacek Klich, and Krystyna Poznańska. 2003b. "Economic Transition and Elections in Poland." *Economics of Transition* 11 (1):41–66.

Jackson, John E., Jacek Klich, and Krystyna Poznańska. 2005. *The Political Economy of Poland's Transition*. Cambridge: Cambridge University Press.

Jasiewicz, Krzystof. 1992a. "From Solidarity to Fragmentation." *Journal of Democracy* 3 (2): 55–69.

Jasiewicz, Krzystof. 1992b. "Poland." *European Journal of Political Research* 22: 489–504.

Jasiewicz, Krzystof. 1993. "Polish Politics on the Eve of the 1993 Elections: Toward Fragmentation or Pluralism?" *Communist and Post-Communist Studies* 26 (4): 387–411.

Jasiewicz, Krzystof. 1997. "Poland: Walesa's Legacy to the Presidency," in *Postcommunist Presidents*. Ray Taras, ed. Cambridge: Cambridge University Press: 130–67.

Javeline, Debra. 2003a. *Protest and the Politics of Blame: The Russian Response to Unpaid Wages*. Ann Arbor: University of Michigan Press.

Javeline, Debra. 2003b. "The Role of Blame in Collective Action: Evidence from Russia." *American Political Science Review* 97 (1): 107–21.

Johnson, Juliet. 2001. "Path Contingency in Postcommunist Trasnformations." *Comparative Politics* 33 (3): 253–74.

Johnson, Ron and Charles Pattie. 2001. "Dimensions of Retrospective Voting." *Party Politics* 7 (4): 469–90.

Jones Luong, Pauline. 2002. *Institutional Change and Political Continuity in Post-Soviet Central Asia: Power, Perceptions, and Pacts*. Cambridge: Cambridge University Press.

Jusko, Karen Long and W. Phillips Shively. 2005. "Applying a Two-Step Strategy to the Analysis of Cross-National Public Opinion Data." *Political Analysis* 13 (4): 327–44.

Kaminski, Bartlomiej. 1991. "Systemic Underpinnings of the Transition in Poland: The Shadow of the Round-Table Agreement." *Communist and Post-Communist Studies* 34 (2): 173–90.

Karpinski, Jakub. 1995a. "Kwasniewski Unseats Walesa as President." *Transitions* 1 (23): 48–50.

Works Cited

Karpinski, Jakub. 1995b. "Setting the Stage for the Presidential Election." *Transitions* 1 (20): 40–3, 71.

Karpinski, Jakub. 1996. "Former Communists Solidify Their Power, Retain Predecessors' Policies," in *Building Democracy*. Josephine Schmidt, ed. Armonk, NY: M.E. Sharpe: 44–55.

Karpinski, Jakub. 1997a. "Poland's Phoenix Rises." *Transitions* 4 (6): 62–5.

Karpinski, Jakub. 1997b. "With the Left in Charge, The Polish Right Prepares for 1997," in *Forging Ahead, Falling Behind*. Josephine Schmidt, ed. Armonk, NY: M.E. Sharpe: 42–8.

Katz, Jonathan and Gary King. 1999. "A Statistical Model for Multiparty Electoral Data." *American Political Science Review* 93 (1): 15–32.

Katzman, Mark. 2002. "Slovakia Country Report." *Economist Intelligence Unit* November: 1–34.

Katzman, Mark. 2004. "Slovakia Country Report." *Economist Intelligence Unit* November: 1–32.

Key, V. O. 1966. *The Responsible Electorate*. Cambridge, MA: Harvard University Press.

Kiewiet, D. Roderik. 1983. *Macroeconomics & Micro Politics: The Electoral Effect of Economic Issues*. Chicago: University of Chicago Press.

Kiewiet, D. Roderik and Douglas Rivers. 1985. "A Retrospective on Retrospective Voting," in *Economic Conditions and Electoral Outcomes*. Michael S. Lewis-Beck and Heinz Eulau, eds. New York: Agathon Press, Inc.: 207–29.

Kiewiet, D. Roderik and Michael Udell. 1998. "Twenty-five Years After Kramer: An Assessment of Economic Retrospective Voting Based Upon Improved Estimates of Income and Unemployment." *Economics and Politics* 10 (3): 219–48.

Kinder, Donald R. and D. Roderik Kiewiet. 1979. "Economic Discontent and Political Behavior: The Role of Personal Grievances and Collective Economic Judgments in Congressional Voting." *American Journal of Political Science* 23 (3): 495–527.

Kinder, Donald R. and D. Roderik Kiewiet. 1981. "Sociotropic Politics: The American Case." *British Journal of Political Science* 11 (1): 129–61.

King, Gary. 1997. *A Solution to the Ecological Inference Problem: Reconstructing Individual Behavior from Aggregate Data*. Princeton, NJ: Princeton University Press.

King, Gary, James Honaker, Anne Joseph and Kenneth Scheve. 2001. "Analyzing Incomplete Political Science Data: An Alternative Algorithm for Multiple Imputation." *American Political Science Review* 95 (1): 45–69.

King, Gary, Robert Keohane and Sidney Verba. 1994. *Designing Social Inquiry: Scientific Inference in Qualitative Research*. Princeton, NJ: Princeton University Press.

King, Gary, Christopher J. L. Murray, Joshua A. Salomon and Ajay Tandon. 2004. "Enhancing the Validity and Cross-cultural Comparability of Measurement in Survey Research." *American Political Science Review* 98 (1): 191–207.

King, Gary, Michael Tomz and Jason Wittenberg. 2000. "Making the Most of Statistical Analyses: Improving Interpretation and Presentation." *American Journal of Political Science* 44 (2): 347–61.

Kipp, Jacob W. 1999. "Aleksandr Lebed: The Man, His Program, and His Political Prospects." *Problems of Post-Communism* 46 (5): 55–63.

Kitschelt, Herbert. 1992. "The Formation of Party Systems in East Central Europe." *Politics and Society* 20 (1): 7–50.

Kitschelt, Herbert, Zdenka Manfeldova, Radoslaw Markowski and Gabor Toka. 1999. *Post-Communist Party Systems: Competition, Representation, and Inter-Party Cooperation.* Cambridge: Cambridge University Press.

Koldys, Gregory. 1992. *Politics and Political Development in Post-Communist Poland*, mimeo.

Kolesnikov, Sergei. 1996. "The Dilemma of "Our Home is Russia" A View from the Inside." *Demokratizatsiya* 4 (3): 358–70.

Kopecký, Petr. 2001. *Parliaments in the Czech and Slovak republics: Party Competition and Parliamentary Institutionalization.* Burlington, VT: Ashgate.

Kopecký, Petr and Cas Mudde. 1999. "The 1998 Parliamentary and Senate Elections in the Czech Republic." *Electoral Studies* 18: 411–50.

Kopstein, Jeffrey. 1992. "Communist Social Structure and Post-Communist Elections: Voting for Reunification in East Germany." *Communist and Post-Communist Studies* 25 (4): 363–80.

Kopstein, Jeffrey. 2003. "Postcommunist Democracy: Legacies and Outcomes." *Comparative Politics* 35 (2): 231–50.

Körösényi, András. 1993. "Stable or Fragile Democracy? Political Cleavages and Party System in Hungary." *Government and Opposition* 28 (1): 87–104.

Körösényi, András. 1999. *Government and Politics in Hungary.* Budapest, Hungary: Central European University Press.

Kostelecky, Tomas. 1995. "Changing Party Allegiances in a Changing System: The 1990 and 1992 Parliamentary Elections in the Czech Republic," in *Party Formation in East-Central Europe: Post-Communist Politics in Czechoslovakia, Hungary, Poland, and Bulgaria.* Gordon Wightman, ed. Aldershot, Hants, UK: Edward Elgar: 79–106.

Kramer, Gerald H. 1971. "Short-Term Fluctuations in U.S. Voting Behavior: 1896–1964." *American Political Science Review* 65: 131–43.

Kramer, Gerald H. 1983. "The Ecological Fallacy Revisited: Aggregate versus Individual-Level Findings on Economics and Elections, and Sociotropic Voting." *American Political Science Review* 77 (1): 92–111.

Krause, George. 1997. "Voters, Information Heterogeneity, and the Dynamics of Aggregate Economic Expectation." *American Journal of Political Science* 41 (4): 1170–1200.

Krause, Kevin Deegan. 2000. *Accountability and Party Competition in Slovakia and the Czech Republic.* Notre Dame, South Bend, IN (doctoral dissertation).

Krejcí, Oskar. 1995. *History of Elections in Bohemia and Moravia.* Boulder, CO: East European Monographs.

Krupa, Andrzej. 1997. *Prawie Biala Ksiega Polskiej Sceny Politycznej.* Warszawa: Ars Print.

Kullberg, Judith and William Zimmerman. 1999. "Liberal Elites, Socialist Masses, and Problems of Russian Democracy." *World Politics* 51 (3): 323–58.

Works Cited

Kurski, Jaroslaw. 1993. *Lech Walesa: Democrat or Dictator?* Boulder, CO: Westview Press.

Lanoue, David. 1994. "Retrospective and Prospective Voting." *Political Research Quarterly* 47 (1): 193–205.

Lavigne, Marie. 1994. *A Comparative View on Economic Reform in Poland, Hungary, and Czechoslovakia.* New York: United Nations.

Lavigne, Marie. 1995. *The Economics of Transition: From Socialist Economy to Market Economy.* Basingstoke, UK: Macmillan Press.

Lawson, Kay, Andrea Römmele and Georgi Karasimeonov. 1999. *Cleavages, Parties, and Voters: Studies from Bulgaria, the Czech Republic, Hungary, Poland, and Romania.* Westport, CO: Praeger.

Leff, Carol Skalnik. 1996. "Dysfunctional Democratization? Institutional Conflict in Post-Communist Slovakia." *Problems of Post-Communism* XLIII (5): 36–50.

Leff, Carol Skalnik. 1997. *The Czech and Slovak Republics.* Boulder, CO: Westview Press.

Lentini, Peter. 1992. "Post-CPSU Communist Political Formations." *Journal of Communist Studies* 8 (4): 280–92.

Lentini, Peter, ed. 1995. *Elections and Political Order in Russia: The Implications of the 1993 Elections to the Federal Assembly.* Budapest, Hungary: Central European University Press.

Levitsky, Steven and Lucan Way. 2002. "Elections Without Democracy: The Rise of Competitive Authoritarianism." *Journal of Democracy* 13 (2): 51–65.

Lewis, Paul G. 1994. "Political Institutionalization and Party Development in Post-Communist Poland." *Europe-Asia Studies* 46 (5): 779–99.

Lewis-Beck, Michael S. and Paolo Bellucci. 1982. "Economic Influences on Legislative Elections in Multi-Party Systems: France and Italy." *Political Behavior* 4 (1): 93–107.

Lewis-Beck, Michael S. and Richard Nadeau. 2000. "French Electoral Institutions and the Economic Vote." *Electoral Studies* 19 (2/3): 171–82.

Lewis-Beck, Michael S. and Mary Stegmaier. 2000. "Economic Determinants of Electoral Outcomes." *Annual Review of Political Science* 3: 183–219.

Lijphart, Arend, ed. 1992. *Parliamentary versus Presidential Government.* New York: Oxford University Press.

Lin, Tse-min. 1999. "The Historical Significance of Economic Voting 1872–1996." *Social Science History* 23 (4): 562–91.

Linz, Juan. 1994. "Introduction: Some Thoughts on Presidentialism in Postcommunist Europe," in *Postcommunist Presidents.* Ray Taras, ed. Cambridge: Cambridge University Press: 1–14.

Lipinski, Edmund Wnuk. 1993. "Left Turn in Poland: A Sociological and Political Analysis." Warsaw, Poland: Instytut Studiów Politicznych Polskiej Akademii Nauk. Working paper.

Lipset, Seymour Martin and Stein Rokkan. 1967. *Party Systems and Voter Alignments: Cross-National Perspectives.* New York: Free Press.

Lockerbie, Brad. 1991. "The Temporal Pattern of Economic Evaluations and Vote Choice in Senate Elections." *Public Choice* 69 (3): 279–94.

Lohmann, Susanne, David W. Brady and Douglas Rivers. 1997. "Party Identification, Retrospective Voting, and Moderating Elections in a Federal System: West Germany, 1961–89." *Comparative Political Studies* 26 (2): 198–229.

Lucky, Christian. 1994. "Table of Presidential Powers in Eastern Europe." *East European Constitutional Review* 3 (1): 81–94.

Lukowski, Jerzy and Hubert Zawadzki. 2001. *A Concise History of Poland.* Cambridge: New York: Cambridge University Press.

MacKuen, Michael B., Robert S. Erikson and James A. Stimson. 1992. "Peasants or Bankers? The American Electorate and the U.S. Economy." *American Political Science Review* 86 (3): 507–611.

Mahr, Alison and John Nagle. 1995. "Resurrection of the Successor Parties and Democratization in East-Central Europe." *Communist and Post-Communist Studies* 28 (4): 393–409.

Makarenko, Boris. 1999. "Fatherland-All Russia," in *Primer on Russia's 1999 Duma Elections.* Michael McFaul, Nikolai Petrov, Andrei Ryabov et al., eds. Moscow, Russia: Carnegie Endowment for International Peace: 61–75.

Maksymiuk, Jan. 2001. "Left Alliance Takes Over in Poland." *RFE/RL Newsline* 5 (184), September 27.

Malova, Darina. 1995. "Parliamentary Rules and Legislative Dominance: Slovakia." *East European Constitutional Review* 4 (2): 71–7.

Manin, Bernard, Adam Przeworski and Susan Stokes. 1999a. "Elections and Representation," in *Democracy, Accountability, and Representation.* Adam Przeworski, Susan Stokes and Bernard Manin, eds. Cambridge: Cambridge University Press: 29–54.

Manin, Bernard, Adam Przeworski and Susan Stokes. 1999b. "Introduction," in *Democracy, Accountability, and Representation.* Adam Przeworski, Susan Stokes and Bernard Manin, eds. Cambridge: Cambridge University Press: 1–26.

Maravall, Jose Maria. 1995. "The Myth of the Authoritarian Advantage," in *Economic Reform and Democracy.* Larry Diamond and Marc Plattner, eds. Baltimore, MD: Johns Hopkins University Press: 13–27.

Markowski, Radoslaw. 1999. *Wybory Parlamentarne 1997: System Partyjny, Podstawy Polityczne, Zachowania Wyborcze.* Warsaw, Poland: Fundacja im. Friedricha Eberta.

Markowski, Radoslaw. 2002. "The Polish SLD in the 1990s: From Opposition to Incumbents and Back," in *The Communist Successor Parties of Central and Eastern Europe.* András Bozóki and John T. Ishiyama, eds. Armonk, NY: M.E. Sharpe: 51–88.

Markowski, Radoslaw and Joshua A. Tucker. 2005. "Pocketbooks, Politics, and Parties: A Micro and Macro-Level Analysis of the June 2003 Polish EU Referendum." *Electoral Studies* 24 (3): 409–433.

Marks, Gary, Liesbet Hooghe, Moira Nelson, and Erica Edwards. 2006. "Party Competition and European Integration in East and West: Different Structure, Same Causality." Forthcoming in *Comparative Political Studies.*

Markus, Gregory B. 1988. "The Impact of Personal and National Economic Conditions on the Presidential Vote: A Pooled Cross-Sectional Analysis." *American Journal of Political Science* 32 (1): 137–54.

Works Cited

Márkus, György. 1999. "Cleavages and Parties in Hungary after 1989," in *Cleavages, Parties, and Voters: Studies from Bulgaria, the Czech Republic, Hungary, Poland, and Romania*. Kay Lawson, Andrea Römmele and Georgi Karasimeonov, eds. Westport, CT: Praeger: 141–58.

Marsh, Christopher. 2002. *Russia at the Polls: Voters, Elections, and Democratization*. Washington, DC: Congressional Quarterly Press.

Martin, Peter. 1990. "The New Governments." *Report on Eastern Europe*, July 27: 9–13.

Mason, David S. and Svetlana Sidorenko-Stephenson. 1997. "Public Opinion and the 1996 Elections in Russia: Nostalgic and Statist, Yet Pro-Market and Pro-Yeltsin." *Slavic Review* 56 (4): 698–717.

Mateju, Peter and Klara Vlachova. 1998. "Values and Electoral Decisions in the Czech Republic." *Communist and Post-Communist Studies* 31 (3): 249–69.

McAllister, Ian. 1995. "Communists, Democracy and Reform in Post-Communist Russia." *Demokratizatsiya* 3 (3): 262–9.

McFaul, Michael. 1996. "Russia's 1996 Presidential Elections." *Post Soviet Affairs* 12 (4): 318–50.

McFaul, Michael. 1997a. *Russia between Elections: What the December 1995 Results Really Mean*. Stanford, CA: University manuscript.

McFaul, Michael. 1997b. *Russia's 1996 Presidential Election: The End of Polarized Politics*. Stanford, CA: Hoover Institution Press Stanford University.

McFaul, Michael. 2000. "Russia's 1999 Parliamentary Elections: Party Consolidation and Fragmentation." *Demokratizatsiya* 8 (1): 5–23.

McFaul, Michael. 2001. *Russia's Unfinished Revolution: Political Change from Gorbachev to Putin*. Ithaca, NY: Cornell University Press.

McFaul, Michael and Sergei Markov. 1995. "Parties and Electoral Blocs," in *Previewing Russia's 1995 Parliamentary Elections*. Michael McFaul and Nikolai Petrov, eds. Moscow, Russia: Carnegie Moscow Center: 15–100.

McFaul, Michael and Nikolai Petrov. 1999. "The 1999 Duma Elections in Comparative Perspective," in *Primer on Russia's 1999 Duma Elections*. Michael McFaul, Nikolai Petrov, Andrei Ryabov et al., eds. Moscow, Russia: Carnegie Endowment for International Peace: 3–10.

McFaul, Michael, Nikolai Petrov, Andrei Ryabov and Elizabeth Reisch, eds 1999. *Primer on Russia's 1999 Duma Elections*. Moscow, Russia: Carnegie Endowment for International Peace.

Mebane, Walter R. Jr., and Jasjeet J. Sekhon. 2004. "Robust Estimation and Outlier Detection for Overdispersed Multinomial Models of Count Data." *American Journal of Political Science* 48 (2): 392–411.

Meguid, Bonnie. 2005. "Competition between Unequals: The Role of Mainstream Party Strategy in Niche Party Success". Forthcoming in the *American Political Science Review*.

Meirowitz, Adam and Joshua A. Tucker. 2004. *Strategic Voting and Information Transmission in Sequential Elections: Run Boris Run*. Princeton, NJ: manuscript.

Mesežnikov, Grigorij. 1994. "The Programs of Political Parties in Slovakia: In Practice and Declarations," in *The Slovak Path of Transition – To Democracy?* Sona

Szomlanyi and Grigorij Meseznikov, eds. Bratislava, Slovakia: Slovak Political Science Association: 83–110.

Mesežnikov, Grigorij. 1997. "The Open-Ended Formation of Slovakia's Political Party System," in *Slovakia: Problems of Democratic Consolidation and the Struggle for the Rules of the Game.* John Gould and Sona Szomolanyi, eds. Bratislava, Slovakia: Friedrich Ebert Stiftung/Slovak Academy of Sciences.

Mikhailov, Nikolai, Richard G. Niemi and David L. Weimer. 2002. "Application of Theil Group Logit Methods to District-Level Vote Shares: Tests of Prospective and Retrospective Voting in the 1991, 1993, and 1997 Polish Elections." *Electoral Studies* 21 (4): 631–48.

Millard, Frances. 1994a. "Poland," in *Political Parties of Eastern Europe, Russia, and the Successor States.* Bogdan Szajkowski, ed. Harlow, Essex, UK: Longman Information and Reference: 313–42.

Millard, Frances. 1994b. "The Polish Parliamentary Election of September, 1993." *Communist and Post-Communist Studies* 27 (3): 295–313.

Millard, Frances. 1994c. "The Shaping of the Polish Party System, 1989–93." *East European Politics and Societies* 8 (3): 467–94.

Miller, Arthur H. 1998. "The Russian 1996 Presidential Election: Referendum on Democracy or a Personality Contest?" *Electoral Studies* 17 (2): 175–96.

Miller, Arthur H. and Thomas F. Klobucar. 2000. "The Development of Party Identification in Post-Soviet Societies." *American Journal of Political Science* 44 (4): 667–86.

Miller, Warren E., and J. Merrill Shanks. 1996. *The New American Voter.* Cambridge, Massachusetts: Harvard University Press.

Miller, William and Stephen White. 1998. "Political Values Underlying Partisan Cleavages in Former Communist Countries." *Electoral Studies* 17 (2): 197–216.

Moraski, Bryon and Gerhard Loewenberg. 1999. "The Effect of Legal Thresholds on the Revival of Former Communist Parties in East-Central Europe." *The Journal of Politics* 61 (1): 151–70.

Moser, Robert. 1995. "The Impact of the Electoral System on Post-Communist Party Development: The Case of the 1993 Russian Parliamentary Elections." *Electoral Studies* 14 (4): 337–98.

Moser, Robert. 1999. "Independents and Party Formation: Elite Partisanship as an Intervening Variable in Russian Politics." *Comparative Politics* 37 (2): 147–66.

Moser, Robert G. 2001. "Executive-Legislative Relations in Russia, 1991–1999," in *Russian Politics: Challenges of Democratization.* Zoltan D. Barany and Robert Moser, eds. Cambridge: Cambridge University Press: 64–102.

Mueller, John. 1996. "Democracy, Capitalism, and the End of Transition," in *Postcommunism: Four Perspectives.* Michael Mandelbaum, ed. New York: Council on Foreign Relations: 102–167.

Mughan, Anthony and Dean Lacy. 2002. "Economic Performance, Job Insecurity and Electoral Choice." *British Journal of Political Science* 32: 513–33.

Murrell, Peter. 1993. "What is Shock Therapy? What Did It Do in Poland and Russia?" *Post-Soviet Affairs* 9 (2): 111–40.

Works Cited

Myagkov, Mikhail. 2001. *The 1999 Duma Elections in Russia: A Step Toward Democracy of the Elites' Game?* University of Oregon: manuscript.

Myagkov, Mikhail and Peter Ordeshook. 2001. "The Trail of Voters in Russia's 1999 Duma and 2000 Presidential Elections." *Communist and Post-Communist Studies* 34 (3): 353–70.

Myagkov, Mikhail, Peter Ordeshook and Alexander Sobyanin. 1997. "The Russian Electorate, 1991–1996." *Post Soviet Affairs* 13 (2): 134–66.

Nadeau, Richard, Richard G Niemi and Antoine Yoshinaka. 2002. "A Cross-National Analysis of Economic Voting: Taking Account of the Political Context across Time and Nations." *Electoral Studies* 21 (3): 403–23.

Naim, Moises. 1995. "Latin America: The Second Stage of Freedom," in *Economic Reform and Democracy*. Larry Diamond and Marc Plattner, eds. Baltimore, MD: Johns Hopkins University Press: 28–44.

Nelson, Joan. 1994. "Overview: How Market Reforms and Democratic Consolidation Affect Each Other," in *Intricate Links: Democratization and Market Reforms in Latin America and Eastern Europe*. Joan Nelson, ed. New Brunswick, NJ: Transaction Publishers: 1–36.

Nichols, Thomas M. 2001. *The Russian Presidency: Society and Politics in the Second Russian Republic*. New York: Palgrave.

Nickelsburg, Michael and Helmut Norpoth. 2000. "Commander in Chief or Chief Economist? The President in the Eye of the Public." *Electoral Studies* 19 (2/3): 313–32.

Oates, Sarah. 2000. "The 1999 Russian Duma Elections." *Problems of Post-Communism* 47 (3): 3–14.

Obrman, Jan. 1992a. "The Czechoslovak Elections: A Guide to the Parties." *RFE/RL Research Report* 1 (22): 10–16.

Obrman, Jan. 1992b. "Czechoslovakia's New Governments." *RFE/RL Research Report* 1 (29): 1–8.

Offe, Claus. 1991. "Capitalism by Democratic Design? Democratic Theory Facing the Triple Transition in East Central Europe." *Social Research* 58 (4): 865–92.

Ogburn, William F. and Lolagene C. Coombs. 1940. "The Economic Factor in the Roosevelt Elections." *American Political Science Review* 34 (4): 719–27.

O'Loughlin, John, Vladimir Kolossov and Olga Vendina. 1997. "The Electoral Geographies of a Polarizing City: Moscow, 1993–1996." *Post-Soviet Geography and Economics* 38 (10): 567–600.

Olson, David. 1993. "Dissolution of the State: Political Parties and the 1992 Election in Czechoslovakia." *Communist and Post-Communist Studies* 26 (3): 301–14.

Olson, Mancur. 1971. *The Logic of Collective Action; Public Goods and the Theory of Groups*. Cambridge, MA: Harvard University Press.

Oltay, Edith. 1994. "Hungarian Socialists Prepare for Comeback." *RFE/RL Research Report* 9 (4): 21–6.

Orenstein, Mitchell. 1998. "A Genealogy of Communist Successor Parties in East-Central Europe and the Determinants of Their Success." *East European Politics and Societies* 12 (3): 472–99.

Orenstein, Mitchell A. 2001. *Out of the Red: Building Capitalism and Democracy in Postcommunist Europe*. Ann Arbor: University of Michigan Press.

Orttung, Robert W. 1995. "Divided Democrats Face Uncertain Prospects." *Transitions* 1 (22): 32–4.

Osiatynski, Wiktor. 1995. "After Walesa: The Causes and Consequences of Walesa's Defeat." *East European Constitutional Review* 4 (4): 35–44.

Osiatynski, Wiktor. 1996. "The Roundtable Talks in Poland," in *The Roundtable Talks and the Breakdown of Communism*. Jon Elster, ed. Chicago: University of Chicago Press: 21–68.

Otto, Robert C. 1999. "Gennadii Zyuganov: The Reluctant Candidate." *Problems of Post-Communism* 46 (5): 37–47.

Pacek, Alexander. 1994. "Macroeconomic Conditions and Electoral Politics in East Central Europe." *American Journal of Political Science* 38 (3): 723–44.

Paldam, Martin. 1986. "The Distribution of Election Results and the Two Explanations of the Cost of Ruling." *Europaische Zeitschrift fur Politische Okonomie / European Journal of Political Economy* 2 (1): 5–24.

Paldam, Martin. 1991. "How Robust is the Vote Function? A Study of Seventeen Nations over Four Decades," in *Economics and Politics: The Calculus of Support*. Helmut Norpoth, Michael S. Lewis-Beck and Jean-Dominique Lafay, eds. Ann Arbor: University of Michigan Press: 9–31.

Paldam, Martin and Peter Nannestad. 2000. "What do Voters Know about the Economy? A Study of Danish Data, 1990–93." *Electoral Studies* 19 (2/3): 363–91.

Palmer, Harvey D. and Guy D. Whitten. 1999. "The Electoral Impact of Unexpected Inflation and Economic Growth." *British Journal of Political Science* 29 (4): 623–39.

Palmer, Harvey D. and Guy D. Whitten. 2000. "Government Competence, Economic Performance, and Endogenous Election Dates." *Electoral Studies* 19 (2/3): 413–26.

Pehe, Jiri. 1991a. "The Civic Forum Becomes a Political Party." *Report on Eastern Europe*, February 1: 1–4.

Pehe, Jiri. 1991b. "Czech and Slovak Leaders Deadlocked over Country's Future." *Report on Eastern Europe*, November 28: 7–11.

Pehe, Jiri. 1991c. "The Realignment of Political Forces." *Report on Eastern Europe*, May 24: 1–5.

Pehe, Jiri. 1992a. "Czechoslovakia: Parties Register for Elections." *RFE/RL Research Report* 1 (18): 20–5.

Pehe, Jiri. 1992b. "Czechoslovakia's Changing Political Spectrum." *RFE/RL Research Report* January 31: 1–7.

Pehe, Jiri. 1992c. "Czech-Slovak Conflict Threatens State Unity." *RFE/RL Research Report* January 3: 83–87.

Pehe, Jiri. 1992d. "The New Slovak Government and Parliament." *RFE/RL Research Report* 1 (28): 32–36.

Pehe, Jiri. 1998. "The Disappointments of Democracy." *Transitions* 5 (5): 38–42.

Pereira, Luiz Carlos Bresser, Jose Maria Maravall and Adam Przeworski. 1993. *Economic Reforms in New Democracies*. Cambridge: Cambridge University Press.

Petrov, Nikolai and Alexey Makarkin. 1999. "Fatherland-All Russia," in *Primer on Russia's 1999 Duma Elections*. Michael McFaul, Nikolai Petrov, Andrei Ryabov et al., eds. Moscow, Russia: Carnegie Endowment for International Peace: 121–5.

Pettai, Vello and Marcus Kreuzer. 1999. "Party Politics in the Baltic States: Social Bases and Institutional Contest." *East European Politics and Societies* 13 (1): 148–89.

Pittaway, Mark and Nigel Swain. 1994. "Hungary," in *Political Parties of Eastern Europe, Russia, and the Successor States*. Bogdan Szajkowski, ed. Harlow, Essex, UK: Longman Information and Reference: 185–245.

Plattner, Marc and Larry Diamond. 1995. "Introduction," in *Economic Reform and Democracy*. Larry Diamond and Marc Plattner, eds. Baltimore, MD: Johns Hopkins University Press: ix–xxii.

Pop-Eleches, Grigore. 2001. "Romania's Politics of Dejection." *Journal of Democracy* 12 (3): 156–169.

Pop-Eleches, Grigore. 2004. *Radicalization or Protest Vote? Explaining the Electoral Success of Unorthodox Parties in Eastern Europe*. Princeton, NJ: manuscript.

Posner, Daniel N. and David J. Simon. 2002. "Economic Conditions and Incumbent Support in Africa's New Democracies: Evidence From Zambia." *Comparative Political Studies* 35 (3): 313–36.

Powell, Eleanor N. 2004. *Volatility and Party Systems*. Princeton, NJ: manuscript.

Powell, G. Bingham and Guy D. Whitten. 1993. "A Cross-National Analysis of Economic Voting: Taking Account of the Political Context." *American Journal of Political Science* 37 (2): 391–414.

Powers, Denise V. and James H. Cox. 1997. "Echoes from the Past: The Relationship between Satisfaction with Economic Reforms and Voting Behavior in Poland." *American Political Science Review* 91 (3): 617–33.

Przeworski, Adam. 1991. *Democracy and the Market*. Cambridge: Cambridge University Press.

Przeworski, Adam. 1992. "The Neoliberal Fallacy." *Journal of Democracy* 3 (3): 45–59.

Przeworski, Adam. 1993. "Economic Reforms, Public Opinion, and Political Institutions: Poland in the Eastern European Perspective," in *Economic Reforms in New Democracies*. Luiz Carlos Bresser Pereira, Jose Maria Maravall and Adam Przeworski, eds. Cambridge: Cambridge University Press: 132–98.

Racz, Barnabas. 1991. "Political Pluralism in Hungary: The 1990 Elections." *Soviet Studies* 43 (1): 107–36.

Racz, Barnabas. 1993. "The Socialist-Left Opposition in Post-Communist Hungary." *Europe-Asia Studies* 45 (4): 647–70.

Rahr, Alexander. 1991. "The Presidential Race in the RSFSR." *Reports on the Soviet Union* 3 (23): 27–9.

Rattinger, Hans. 1991. "Unemployment and Elections in West Germany," in *Economics and Politics: The Calculus of Support*. Helmut Norpoth, Michael S. Lewis-Beck and Jean-Dominique Lafay, eds. Ann Arbor: University of Michigan Press: 49–62.

Reddaway, Peter and Dmitri Glinski. 2001. *The Tragedy of Russia's Reforms: Market Bolshevism Against Democracy*. Washington, DC: United States Institute of Peace Press.

Remington, Thomas F., ed. 1994. *Parliaments in Transition: The New Legislative Politics in the Former USSR and Eastern Europe*. Boulder, CO: Westview Press.

Remmer, Karen L. 1991. "The Political Impact of Economic Crisis in Latin America in the 1980s." *American Political Science Review* 85 (3): 777–800.

Remmer, Karen L. 1993. "The Political Economy of Elections in Latin America, 1980–1991." *The American Political Science Review* 87 (2): 393–407.

Rice, Stuart Arthur. 1928. *Quantitative Methods in Politics*. New York: A.A. Knopf.

Roberts, Andrew. 2004. "The State of Socialism: A Note on Terminology." *Slavic Review* 63 (2): 349–66.

Roberts, Kenneth and Erik Wibbels. 1999. "Party Systems and Electoral Volatility in Latin America: A Test of Economic, Institutional, and Structural Explanations." *The American Political Science Review* 93 (3): 575–90.

Roland, Gerard. 1994. "The Role of Political Constraints in Transition Strategies." *Economics of Transition* 2 (1): 27–41.

Rosa, Jean-Jacques and Daniel Amson. 1976. "Conditions Economiques et Elections." *Revue Francaise de Science Politique* 26 (6): 1101–19.

Rose, Richard. 1998. "Negative and Positive Party Identification in Post-Communist Countries." *Electoral Studies* 17 (2): 217–34.

Rose, Richard and Neil Munro. 2002. *Elections without Order: Russia's Challenge to Vladimir Putin*. Cambridge: Cambridge University Press.

Rose, Richard and Neil Munro. 2003. *Elections and Parties in New European Democracies*. Washington, DC: Congressional Quarterly Press.

Rose, Richard, Neil Munro and Stephen White. 2001. "Voting in a Floating Party System: the 1999 Duma Election." *Europe-Asia Studies* 53 (3): 419–43.

Rose, Richard and Evgeny Tikhomirov. 1996. "Russia's Forced-Choice Presidential Election." *Post-Soviet Affairs* 12 (4): 351–79.

Rose, Richard, Evgeny Tikhomirov and William Mishler. 1997. "Understanding Multi-Party Choice: The 1995 Duma Election." *Europe-Asia Studies* 49 (5): 799–823.

Ross, Michael. 2003. "Testing Inductively Generated Hypotheses with Independent Data Sets." *Comparative Politics Newsletter (APSA-CP)* 14 (1): 14–17.

Royed, Terry, Kevin Leyden and Stephen Borrelli. 2000. "Is 'Clarity of Responsibility' Important for Economic Voting? Revisiting Powell and Whitten's Hypothesis." *British Journal of Political Science* 30 (4): 669–698.

Rutland, Peter. 1999. "Grigorii Yavlinskii: The Man Who Would Be King." *Problems of Post-Communism* 46 (5): 48–54.

Sabbat-Swidlicka, Anna. 1990. "The Electoral Platform of Presidential Candidates." *Radio Free Europe/Radio Liberty Reports on Eastern Europe, Reports on Eastern Europe* 1 (49): 10–15.

Sabbat-Swidlicka, Anna. 1993. "Poland: A Year of Three Governments." *RFE/RL Research Report* 2 (1): 102–7.

Works Cited

Sabbat-Swidlicka, Anna. 1994. "Poland: The End of the Solidarity Era?" *RFE/RL Research Report* 3 (1): 81–6.

Sachs, Jeffrey. 1993. *Poland's Jump to the Market Economy*. Cambridge, MA: MIT Press.

Sajo, Andras. 1996. "The Roundtable Talks in Hungary," in *The Roundtable Talks and the Breakdown of Communism*. Jon Elster, ed. Chicago: University of Chicago Press: 69–98.

Sakwa, Richard. 1995. "The Russian Elections of December 1993." *Europe-Asia Studies* 47 (2): 195–227.

Sakwa, Richard. 1998. "Left or Right? CRPF and Democratic Consolidation," in *Party Politics in Post-Communist Russia*. John Lowenhardt, ed. London: Frank Cass: 128–58.

Sakwa, Richard. 2002a. "The Russian KPRF: The Powerlessness of the Powerful," in *The Communist Successor Parties of Central and Eastern Europe*. András Bozóki and John T. Ishiyama, eds. Armonk, NY: M.E. Sharpe: 240–67.

Sakwa, Richard. 2002b. *Russian Politics and Society*. New York: Routledge.

Sanders, David. 2000. "The Real Economy and the Perceived Economy in Popularity Functions: How Much Do Voters Need to Know? A Study of British Data, 1974–97." *Electoral Studies* 19 (2/3): 275–94.

Sanders, David. 2003. "Party Identification, Economic Perceptions, and Voting in British General Elections, 1974–97." *Electoral Studies* 22 (2): 239–63.

Sartori, Giovanni. 1994. *Comparative Constitutional Engineering*. London: Macmillan Press.

Schmidt, Mária and László G. Tóth. 2000. *From Totalitarian to Democratic Hungary: Evolution and Transformation 1990–2000*. New York: Columbia University Press.

Schopflin, George. 1991. "Conservatism and Hungary's Transition." *Problems of Communism* 40 (1/2): 60–8.

Shabad, Goldie and Kazimierz Slomczynski. 1999. "Political Identities in the Initial Phase of Systemic Transformation in Poland: A Test of the Tabula Rasa Hypothesis." *Comparative Political Studies* 32 (6): 690–723.

Shenfield, Stephen D. 1998. "The Weimar/Russia Comparison: Reflections on Hanson and Kopstein." *Post-Soviet Affairs* 14 (4): 355–68.

Shevtsova, Lilia. 1999. *Yeltsin's Russia: Myths and Reality*. Washington, DC: Brookings Institution Press.

Shugart, Matthew Soberg. 1993. "Of Presidents and Parliaments." *East European Constitutional Review* 2 (1): 30–2.

Shugart, Matthew Soberg and John M. Carey. 1992. *Presidents and Assemblies: Constitutional Design and Electoral Dynamics*. Cambridge: Cambridge University Press.

Slider, Darrel, Vladimir Gimpelson and Sergei Chugrov. 1994. "Political Tendencies in Russia's Regions: Evidence from the 1993 Parliamentary Elections." *Slavic Review* 53 (3): 711–32.

Stark, David Charles and László Bruszt. 1998. *Postsocialist Pathways: Transforming Politics and Property in East Central Europe*. Cambridge: Cambridge University Press.

Stokes, Susan C. 1996. "Public Opinion and Market Reform: The Limits of Economic Voting." *Comparative Political Studies* 29 (5): 499–519.

Swain, Nigel. 1993. "Hungary," in *Developments in East European Politics*. Stephen White, Judy Batt and Paul G. Lewis, eds. Durham, NC: Duke University Press: 66–82.

Swank, Duane, and Hans-Georg Betz. 2003. "Globalization, the Welfare State, and Right-Wing Populism in Western Europe."*Socio-Economic Review* 1 (2): 215–45.

Szajkowski, Bogdan, ed. 1994. *Political Parties of Eastern Europe, Russia, and the Successor States*. Harlow, Essex, UK: Longman Information and Reference.

Szczerbiak, Aleks. 1999. "Interests and Values: Polish Parties and their Electorates." *Europe-Asia Studies* 51 (8): 1401–32.

Szelenyi, Ivan, Eva Fodor and Eric Hanley. 1997. "Left Turn in Postcommunist Politics: Bringing Class Back In?" *East European Politics and Societies* 11 (1): 190–224.

Szomolanyi, Sona. 1994. "Old Elites in the New Slovak State and their Current Transformations," in *The Slovak Path of Transition – To Democracy?* Sona Szomolanyi and Grigorij Mesežnikov, eds. Bratislava, Slovakia: Slovak Political Science Association: 63–82.

Szomolanyi, Sona. 1997. "Identifying Slovakia's Emerging Regime," in *Slovakia: Problems of Democratic Consolidation and the Struggle for the Rules of the Game*. John Gould and Sona Szomolanyi, eds. Bratislava, Slovakia: Friedrich Ebert Stiftung/Slovak Academy of Sciences.

Szomolanyi, Sona. 1999. "Slovakia's Transition Path and the 1998 Elections," in *The 1998 Parliamentary Elections and Democratic Rebirth in Slovakia*. Martin Butorova, Grigorij Mesežnikov, Zora Butorova et al., eds. Bratislava, Slovakia: Institute for Public Affairs: 25–47.

Szomolanyi, Sona and Grigorij Mesežnikov, eds 1994. *The Slovak Path of Transition – To Democracy?* Bratislava, Slovakia: Slovak Political Science Association.

Taras, Ray. 1995. *Consolidating Democracy in Poland*. Boulder, CO: Westview Press.

Taras, Ray, ed. 1997. *Postcommunist Presidents*. Cambridge: Cambridge University Press.

Tavits, Margit. 2005. "The Development of Stable Party Support Dynamics in Post-Communist Europe." *American Journal of Political Science* 49 (2): 283–298.

Tóka, Gábor, ed. 1995. *The 1990 Election to the Hungarian National Assembly: Analyses, Documents and Data*. Berlin: Edition Sigma.

Tokes, Rudolf L. 1996. *Hungary's Negotiated Revolution: Economic Reform, Social Change and Political Succession*. Cambridge: Cambridge University Press.

Tomz, Michael, Joshua A. Tucker and Jason Wittenberg. 2002. "An Easy and Accurate Regression Model for Multiparty Electoral Data." *Political Analysis* 10 (1): 66–83.

Tomz, Michael, Jason Wittenberg and Gary King. 2003. *CLARIFY: Software for Interpreting and Presenting Statistical Results. Version 2.1*. Stanford University, University of Wisconsin, and Harvard University. January 5. Available at: http://gking.harvard.edu/.

Treisman, Daniel. 1998. "Dollars and Democratization: The Role and Power of Money in Russia's Transitional Elections." *Comparative Politics* 31 (1): 1–19.

Tsipko, Alexander. 1996. "Why Gennady Zyuganov's Communist Party Finished First." *Demokratizatsiya* 4 (2): 185–200.

Tsygankov, Andrei. 1995. "Russia: Strategic Choices Facing Democrats." *Problems of Communism* 42 (2): 49–53.

Tucker, Joshua A. 1998. "It's the Economy, Comrade! Economic Conditions and Election Results in Russia, Poland, Hungary, the Czech Republic and Slovakia." Paper presented at the Annual Meeting of the Midwest Political Science Association, Chicago, IL.

Tucker, Joshua A. 1999. "Reconsidering Economic Voting: Party Type vs. Incumbency in Transition Countries." Paper presented at the 1999 Annual Meeting of the American Political Science Association, Atlanta, GA.

Tucker, Joshua A. 2000a. *It's the Economy, Comrade! Economic Conditions and Election Results in Post-Communist Russia, Poland, Hungary, Slovakia, and the Czech Republic from 1990–96.* Harvard University, Cambridge, MA (doctoral dissertation).

Tucker, Joshua A. 2000b. "Taking Account of the Institutional Effect: How Institutions Mediate the Effect of Economic Conditions on Election Results in Five Post-Communist Countries." Paper presented at the Annual Meeting of the American Political Science Association, Washington, DC.

Tucker, Joshua A. 2001. "Economic Conditions and the Vote for Incumbent Parties in Russia, Poland, Hungary, Slovakia, and the Czech Republic from 1990–1996." *Post-Soviet Affairs* 17 (4): 309–31.

Tucker, Joshua A. 2002. "The First Decade of Post-Communist Elections and Voting: What Have We Studied, and How Have We Studied It?" *Annual Review of Political Science* 5: 271–304.

Tucker, Joshua A. 2004. *Red, Brown, and Regional Economic Voting: Evidence from Russia, Poland, Hungary, Slovakia and the Czech Republic from 1990–99.* Princeton, NJ: manuscript.

Tucker, Joshua A., Alexander Pacek and Adam Berinsky. 2002. "Transitional Winners and Losers: Attitudes Toward EU Membership in Post-Communist Countries." *American Journal of Political Science* 46 (3): 557–71.

Tufte, Edward R. 1975. "Determinants of the Outcomes of Midterm Congressional Elections." *American Political Science Review* 69 (3): 812–26.

Tufte, Edward R. 1978. *Political Control of the Economy.* Princeton, NJ: Princeton University Press.

Turnovec, Frantisek. 1997. "Votes, Seats and Power: 1996 Parliamentary Election in the Czech Republic." *Communist and Post-Communist Studies* 30 (3): 289–305.

Tworzecki, Hubert. 1996. "The Polish Presidential Election of 1995." *Electoral Studies* 15 (3): 403–9.

Tworzecki, Hubert. 2003. *Learning to Choose: Electoral Politics in East-Central Europe.* Stanford, CA: Stanford University Press.

Urban, Joan. 1996. "The Communist Movement in Post-Soviet Russia." *Demokratizatsiya* 4 (2): 173–84.

Urban, Joan Barth and Valery D. Solovei. 1997. *Russia's Communists at the Crossroads.* Boulder, CO: Westview Press.

Urban, Michael E. 1992. "Boris El'tsin, Democratic Russia, and the Campaign for the Russian Presidency." *Soviet Studies* 44 (2): 187–207.

Vinton, Louisa. 1990a. "Solidarity's Rival Offspring: Center Alliance and Democratic Action." *Report on Eastern Europe*, September 21: 15–25.

Vinton, Louisa. 1990b. "Walesa and Tyminski into the Second Round." *Report on Eastern Europe*, December 21: 14–18.

Vinton, Louisa. 1993a. "Poland Goes Left." *RFE/RL Research Report* 2 (40): 21–23.

Vinton, Louisa. 1993b. "Poland's Political Spectrum on the Eve of the Elections." *RFE/RL Research Report* 2 (36): 1–16.

Wade, Larry, Alexander Groth and Peter Lavelle. 1994. "Estimating Participation and Party Voting in Poland: The 1991 Parliamentary Elections." *East European Politics and Societies* 8 (1): 94–121.

Waterbury, John. 1989. "The Political Management of Economic Adjustment and Reform," in *Fragile Coalitions: The Politics of Economic Adjustment.* Joan M. Nelson, ed. Washington, DC: Overseas Development Council: 39–56.

Way, Lucan. 2004. *Pluralism by Default and the Sources of Political Competition in Weak States.* Philadelphia, PA: manuscript.

Wenzel, Michal. 1998. "Solidarity and Akcja Wyborcza Solidarnosc: An Attempt at Reviving the Legend." *Communist and Post-Communist Studies* 31 (2): 139–56.

Weydenthal, Jan B. de. 1990. "The Start of the Presidential Campaign?" *Radio Free Europe/Radio Liberty Reports on Eastern Europe* 1 (37): 26–8.

White, Stephen. 1997. "Russia: Presidential Leadership under Yeltsin," in *Postcommunist Presidents.* Ray Taras, ed. Cambridge: Cambridge University Press: 38–66.

White, Stephen, Richard Rose and Ian McAllister. 1997. *How Russia Votes.* Chatham, NJ: Chatham House Publishers.

White, Stephen, Matthew Wyman and Sarah Oates. 1997. "Parties and Voters in the 1995 Russian Duma Election." *Europe-Asia Studies* 49 (5): 767–98.

Whitefield, Stephen. 2002. "Political Cleavages and Post-Communist Politics." *Annual Review of Political Science* 5: 181–200.

Whitefield, Stephen and Geoffrey Evans. 1999. "Class, Markets, and Partisanship in Post-Soviet Russia: 1993–96." *Electoral Studies* 18 (2): 155–78.

Whiteley, Paul. 1980. "Politico-Econometric Estimation in Britain: An Alternative Explanation," in *Models of Political Economy.* Paul Whiteley, ed. London: Sage Publications: 85–100.

Whitten, Guy D. and Harvey D. Palmer. 1999. "Cross-National Analyses of Economic Voting." *Electoral Studies* 18: 49–67.

Wiatr, Jerzy J. 1999. "Political Parties and Cleavage Crystallization in Poland, 1989–93," in *Cleavages, Parties, and Voters: Studies from Bulgaria, the Czech Republic, Hungary, Poland, and Romania.* Kay Lawson, Andrea Römmele and Georgi Karasimeonov, eds. Westport, CT: Praeger: 159–68.

Wightman, Gordon. 1993a. "The Czech and Slovak Republics," in *Developments in East European Politics.* Stephen White, Judy Batt, and Paul G. Lewis, eds. Durham, NC: Duke University Press: 51–65.

Works Cited

Wightman, Gordon. 1993b. "The Czechoslovak Parliamentary Elections of 1992." *Electoral Studies* 12 (1): 83–6.

Wilkin, Sam, Brandon Haller and Helmut Norpoth. 1997. "From Argentina to Zambia: a World-Wide Test of Economic Voting." *Electoral Studies* 16 (3): 301–16.

Williamson, Oliver E. 1987. *The Economic Institutions of Capitalism: Firms, Markets, Relational Contracting.* New York: Collier Macmillan Publishers.

Wittenberg, Jason. 2003. "Historical Legacies and Post-Communism." Paper presented at the Annual Meeting of the American Political Science Association, Philadelphia, PA.

Wittenberg, Jason. 2006. *Crucibles of Political Loyalties: Church Institutions and Electoral Continuity in Hungary.* Cambridge: Cambridge University Press.

Wlezien, Christopher, Mark Franklin and Daniel Twiggs. 1997. "Economic Perceptions and Vote Choice: Disentangling the Endogeneity." *Political Behavior* 19 (1): 7–17.

Wolchik, Sharon. 1992. "Czechoslovakia," in *The Columbia History of Eastern Europe in the Twentieth Century.* Joseph Held, ed. New York: Columbia University Press: 119–63.

Wolchik, Sharon. 1993. "The Repluralization of Politics in Czechoslvakia." *Communist and Post-Communist Studies* 26 (4): 412–31.

Wolchik, Sharon. 1994. "The Czech Republic: Havel and the Evolution of the Presidency since 1989," in *Postcommunist Presidents.* Ray Taras, ed. Cambridge: Cambridge University Press: 168–94.

Woodruff, David. 1999. *Money Unmade: Barter and the Fate of Russian Capitalism.* Ithaca, NY: Cornell University Press.

Wyman, Matthew. 1997. "The Russian Elections of 1995 and 1996." *Electoral Studies* 16 (1): 79–85.

Wyman, Matthew, Bill Miller, Stephen White and Paul Heywood. 1994. "The Russian Elections of December 1993." *Electoral Studies* 13 (3): 254–71.

Wyman, Matthew, Stephen White, Bill Miller and Paul Heywood. 1995. "Public Opinion, Parties and Voters in the December 1993 Russian Elections." *Europe-Asia Studies* 47 (4): 591–614.

Yeltsin, Boris Nikolayevich. 1990. *Against the Grain.* New York: Summit Books.

Yeltsin, Boris Nikolayevich. 1994. *The Struggle for Russia.* New York: Belka Publications Corp.

Yeltsin, Boris Nikolayevich. 2000. *Midnight Diaries.* New York: Public Affairs.

Ziblatt, Daniel and Nick Biziouras. 2002. "Doomed to be Radicals? Organization, Ideology, and the Communist Successor Parties in East Central Europe," in *The Communist Successor Parties of Central and Eastern Europe.* András Bozóki and John T. Ishiyama, eds. Armonk, NY: M.E. Sharpe: 287–302.

Zielinski, Jakub, Kazimierz Slomczynski and Goldie Shabad. 2004. *Electoral Control in New Democracies: The Peverse Incentives of Fluid Party Systems.* Columbus, OH: manuscript.

Zlobin, Nikolai. 1994. "Finita la Comedia?" *Demokratizatsiya* 2 (2): 173–6.

Zubek, Voytek. 1991a. "The Threshold of Poland's Transition: 1989 Electoral Campaign as the Last Act of a United Solidarity." *Studies in Comparative Communism* 24 (4): 355–76.

Zubek, Voytek. 1991b. "Walesa's Leadership and Poland's Transition." *Problems of Communism* XL (1/2): 69–83.

Zubek, Voytek. 1993. "The Fragmentation of Poland's Political Party System." *Communist and Post-Communist Studies* 26 (1): 47–71.

Zubek, Voytek. 1995. "The Phoenix Out of the Ashes: The Rise to Power of Poland's Post-Communist SdRP." *Communist and Post-Communist Studies* 28 (3): 275–306.

Index

Note: Page numbers in *italics* indicate tables.

Index

Index

Index

411

Index

Index